TOMORROW-LAND

THE 1964–65 WORLD'S FAIR AND THE
TRANSFORMATION OF AMERICA

JOSEPH TIRELLA

LYONS PRESS
Guilford, Connecticut

An imprint of Globe Pequot Press

For Kelly, Leo & Zoë

To buy books in quantity for corporate use
or incentives, call **(800) 962-0973**
or e-mail **premiums@GlobePequot.com.**

Lyons Press is an imprint of Globe Pequot Press.

Project editors: Meredith Dias and Lauren Brancato
Layout artist: Sue Murray

Library of Congress Cataloging-in-Publication Data is available on file.

ISBN 978-0-7627-8035-8

Printed in the United States of America

10 9 8 7 6 5 4 3 2 1

CONTENTS

Part One

The Greatest Single Event in History

The basic purpose of the Fair is to help achieve "Peace Through Understanding," that is, to assist in educating the peoples of the world as to the interdependence of nations and the need for universal and lasting peace.
> —New York World's Fair 1964–65 Progress Report from
> Robert Moses, January 16, 1961

It is insane that two men, sitting on opposite sides of the world, should be able to decide to bring an end to civilization.
> —President John F. Kennedy, October 1962

Standing outside the World's Fair Administration Building in Flushing Meadow Park in the late morning cold of December 14, 1962, Robert Moses knew that nearly three years of work were about to pay off. Since May 1960, when he assumed the presidency of the World's Fair Corporation in a sleight-of-hand coup d'état, he had taken charge of every aspect of the upcoming 1964–65 World's Fair; no detail was too insignificant for his attention. Now, after much political intrigue and maneuvering, the most powerful man in the free world, President John F. Kennedy, was coming to Queens to bestow his personal blessing on Moses' Fair by participating in the ground-breaking ceremony for the $17 million United States Federal Pavilion.

New York City's Master Builder had worked tirelessly to enact his grand schemes for what he called "the Olympics of Progress." Moses knew that World's Fairs were historic opportunities for cities and nations to enhance their images on a global stage. London's Great Exhibition of 1851 showcased the famed Crystal Palace—an immense structure of metal and glass that illustrated Victorian England's industrial might—and was opened by the Queen herself; Paris's Exposition Universelle of 1889 gave the world the Eiffel Tower; and in 1893 the United States hosted its second World's Fair in Chicago (Philadelphia had hosted a smaller fair in 1876), one that demonstrated America's maturity as a nation. The Fair's planners transformed part of Chicago into the neoclassical White City (and introduced a ride that would become a staple of fairs the world over: the Ferris wheel). In 1904 St. Louis hosted a World's Fair that marked the debut of a new form of communication, the first wireless telegraph machine, and more prosaically, introduced a new way of eating ice cream—the ice-cream cone.

However, it was New York's 1939–40 World's Fair, which a younger Moses had worked on, with its dramatic, geometric-shaped sculptures—the Trylon and the Perisphere—that offered Depression-era America a glimpse of "the World of Tomorrow," a futuristic fantasy world of skyscrapers, superhighways, and televisions that, like economic prosperity, was just around the corner.

Now, in the beginning of the 1960s, Moses and his team had spent years negotiating with Washington, DC, politicos for federal funding (often arousing more ill will than good) while playing diplomatic chess matches with foreign bureaucrats. He also initiated colossal plans for the reconstruction of major New York City thoroughfares such as the Van Wyck Expressway and the Grand Central Parkway, both of which would lead millions of Fairgoers to his exhibition. As usual, Moses, the holder of a dozen unelected positions, including New York City Parks Commissioner, chairman of the City Planning Commission, and chairman of the Triborough Bridge and Tunnel Authority, disrupted the streets of New York as he saw fit, with little regard for the impact his plans had on the lives of its citizens. "You have to break eggs to make an omelet" was his standard reply to his increasingly vocal critics. As was his style, when either obstacles or opponents got in his way, he outmaneuvered or, if necessary, ran roughshod over them.

Moses had spent much of the previous forty years molding and transforming New York to fit his own personal vision of a modern metropolis. He built a vast network of highways, bridges, parkways, public pools, playgrounds, beaches, and state power projects while clearing huge tracts of land with federal funds—sometimes destroying neighborhoods in the process. Casting a shadow over his beloved New York at least as large as the Manhattan skyline, Moses served as an unelected government employee under seven governors and six mayors, and for nearly half a century was an inevitable fact of life in Gotham, as much as death, taxes, and rush hour traffic.

After Kennedy's motorcade pulled up to the building, the president stepped out of his limousine and greeted Moses, with whom he had maintained a cordial connection since his days as a Massachusetts senator. The youthful Kennedy, who had removed his heavy overcoat despite the frosty chill, was a striking contrast to the graying bureaucrats who had gathered to meet him, like the Fair's US commissioner, Norman K. Winston, a real estate developer and close ally of Moses, or the dour mayor of New York, Robert F. Wagner Jr. described by Norman Mailer as "plump, groomed, blank" in the pages of *Esquire*.

Regardless of his host's combative and autocratic style, Kennedy knew that Moses got things done. Certainly Kennedy, ever the political pragmatist, admired Moses' ability to survive—and dominate—New York's cutthroat political system. Side by side on the stage set up for the ground-breaking, surrounded by the four-and-a-half-acre construction site of the US Federal Pavilion, they now sat: On the left was Kennedy, the only man on the stage not wearing a fedora or an overcoat, or apparently under the age of fifty; his youthful image and forward-looking New Frontier policies seemed to embody the hopeful idealism that was still at the heart of American life. Beside him, the elderly Moses personified bare-knuckled power as New York's Machiavellian Master Builder.

When it was Kennedy's turn to speak, he rose to a podium bearing the presidential seal and delivered a short speech that was a peaceful call to arms. As his words turned to frosty breaths in the cold December air, the president reminded the crowd that the upcoming World's Fair represented "a chance for us in 1964 to show seventy-five million people . . . from all over the world, what kind of a people we are and what kind of a country we are . . . and what is coming in the future. That is what a World's Fair should be about and the theme of this World's Fair— Peace Through Understanding—is most appropriate in these years of the Sixties. I want the people of the world to visit this Fair and all the various exhibits of our American industrial companies and the foreign companies, who are most welcome, and to come to the American exhibit—the exhibit of the United States—and see what we have accomplished through a system of freedom."

Kennedy's trip to the Fairgrounds was a welcome respite. The Fair's "Peace Through Understanding" theme was more than just an idealistic slogan to the young president. Two months earlier, the Cold War had almost exploded into an atomic showdown after the Soviet Union installed nuclear missiles in Cuba, only ninety miles off American shores. It was a terrible gamble for Nikita Khrushchev, the unpredictable Soviet premier, who had the missiles sent to Cuba after asking his advisors, "Why not throw a hedgehog into the United States pants?"

For nearly two weeks in October, President Kennedy secretly met with a group of senior advisors and top military brass, poring over the photographic evidence courtesy of U-2 spy planes. The president and his men explored every option, including a preemptive military strike against Fidel Castro's Communist regime. Ultimately, Kennedy dismissed the war cry of his trigger-happy generals and Southern Democrats like senators Richard B. Russell of Georgia and J. William Fulbright of Arkansas. Instead, he opted for a naval blockade of Cuban waters—preferring to call it a "quarantine" to strike a less confrontational tone—to prevent more nuclear warheads from arriving on the island. At the same time, he amassed more than a hundred thousand troops in Florida—the largest invasion force since the Second World War. Just in case.

When the crisis ended in late October, the world drew a collective sigh of relief. Kennedy had steered the country away from nuclear war by heeding his most pragmatic and least militant advisors, and in the process gave Khrushchev what he needed most: time. Time to rethink his gamble of putting missiles so close to the United States, time to silence the hardliners of the Kremlin—just as Kennedy needed to silence his own Washington warmongers—and more importantly, time to save face. As leader of the world's other superpower, Kennedy understood Khrushchev's position only too well. "If we had invaded Cuba . . . I am sure the Soviets would have acted," he said afterward. "They would have to, just as we would have to. I think there are certain compulsions on any major power."

Further emboldened by his administration's performance in the 1962 midterm elections the month before these ground-breaking ceremonies—the Democrats picked up four seats in the Senate (including Massachusetts's new junior senator, Edward M. Kennedy) and lost only two seats in the House—the president began exploring other, more subtle ways to exhibit American power. The New York World's Fair—especially with its universal peaceful themes—would provide the perfect forum. Kennedy knew such an exhibition could be an important front in the Cold War, one that the United States could win without firing a single bullet.

Despite those peaceful ideas, the World's Fair had started a major fight in Washington, DC. Kennedy's predecessor, President Dwight D. Eisenhower, had picked New York over the nation's capital to host an American exhibition. But to secure the approval of Congress—and to soothe the bruised ego of DC insiders who were lobbying against New York—the Empire State's congressional delegation, led by liberal Republican senator Jacob K. Javitz, and Moses had to promise that the New York Fair wouldn't cost the federal government anything.

By September 1961, however, they had changed their minds. Javitz and Moses now sought $300,000 in funding for a study on the feasibility of building a US Federal Pavilion. This request outraged Ohio's Democratic senator Frank J. Lausche, who along with Senator Fulbright, blocked the appropriations bill from being voted on by the full Senate, essentially killing the funding days before Congress's session ended. As was the case with much of Kennedy's political agenda—whether it was diplomacy with the Soviets, civil rights, or the World's Fair—it was often his own party who fought him the hardest.

Moses was livid. He told the *New York Times* that the failure of Congress to invest in his exhibition would cause "irreparable damage" to the Fair's prestige. He chided the senators for not allowing the bill to reach the chamber floor (it had already passed the House of Representatives), where there was "no question" the bill would pass. He also reminded them "that under identical circumstances the Federal Government has made a large appropriation" to the upcoming 1962 Seattle Century 21 Exposition.

Frustrated with Congress, Moses appealed to Kennedy directly, and after talking with the commander in chief for a half hour, secured his support. The Master Builder probably didn't need to make a hard sell: Kennedy had backed the Fair from the early days of his presidency. He recognized that such an exhibition could be a two-year advertisement for the American way of life. The Senate, however, would still need some convincing.

In March 1962, Moses made his move. Speaking at a luncheon at Manhattan's University Club, he played the Cold War trump card, warning that "time was running out" for Congress to act. The Soviet Union, he noted, had announced its intentions, along with the entire Eastern Bloc, to build a pavilion—and at 78,000 square feet, it was the largest of the entire Fair to date. Moses didn't need to ask the obvious question: Were the two Democratic senators, both members of the Foreign Relations Committee and avowed Cold Warriors, really going to allow America's Communist nemesis to exhibit its cultural, industrial, and scientific wares for the world to see—on American soil, no less—without a world-class US Federal Pavilion at a World's Fair in New York?

Aides to Kennedy had been asking the same question. A November 1961 memo warned the president that the United States risked being embarrassed by the Soviets on their own turf. "Delay at this stage could result in a second class exhibit . . . the Soviets and others are already much further along on their exhibit preliminaries than is the US." Only five years earlier, the Soviet Union had launched *Sputnik,* kick-starting the Space War in the process. President Kennedy had a vested interest in making sure the 1964–65 World's Fair was a success.

A few days after Moses' University Club speech, Kennedy asked Congress for $25 million to fully fund a Federal Pavilion, declaring that it was in American interests to "present to the world not a boastful picture of our unparalleled progress but a picture of democracy—its opportunities, its problems, its inspirations, and its freedoms." A *New*

York Times editorial urged Congress to fund the "construction of a show-case that will document before the world our way of life."

In April 1962, Congress begrudgingly handed over $17 million for a US Federal Pavilion to be administered by the Commerce Department. Moses had won—but not before adding a few more names to his enemies list. Senator Paul Douglas, Democrat of Illinois, a brainy, bowtie-wearing ex-Marine and former economics professor at the University of Chicago, called Moses "one of the most competent and irritating men in the history of the United States . . . an amazingly efficient man, the most egotistical, the most intolerant, the most hot-tempered public servant I have ever known."

Douglas wasn't alone in his feelings. Less than two weeks before the December ground-breaking ceremony, Attorney General Robert F. Kennedy passed to his older brother an internal report about a recent meeting between Fair executives and Commerce Department officials, along with a handwritten note: "Thought you might want to see this . . . it's a rather unsatisfactory situation." At the meeting, Moses had complained that Herb Klotz, the coordinator for the US Federal Pavilion, was "arrogant, unimaginative and very difficult to work with." (He also grumbled that Klotz was "Prussian and unapproachable" and that his ideas for the pavilion were "hogwash.") Nor did Moses care for Los Angeles–based Charles Luckman, the pavilion's architect, or its Phoenix-based construction firm, Dell Webb; at least one, if not both, he noted, should be New Yorkers.

Whatever the president thought of Moses' management style, he didn't show it that day in Flushing Meadow Park. Kennedy was in full campaign mode, working the crowd of VIPs, Fair officials, and hard-hat construction workers alike. While Moses' handlers had arranged the de rigueur "shovel shot" for the photographers covering the ground-breaking ceremony, the president decided to improvise. Spotting a construction worker behind the wheel of a large bulldozer, Kennedy bounded off the stage and shook the driver's hand.

"You want to try it?" the blue-collar worker asked the wealthy president, motioning toward the truck's controls.

To the delight of those present, Kennedy climbed into the driver's seat and began moving the snow-covered soil of Flushing Meadow with the bulldozer's large blade. The president flashed "a boyish smile full of glee," said one onlooker. "He waved a hand and his eyes seemed to say, 'Damn, but this is fun!'"

The president launched the World's Fair's final phase in another ceremony on April 22, 1963—exactly one year before the Fair's opening day. Kennedy, this time from his desk in the Oval Office, dialed 1-9-6-4 into a new RCA Touch-Tone phone (which would be on display at the Fair). That day, the president promised to attend the opening festivities in New York and gave his assurance to the millions of future Fairgoers that it would "compare with the greatest shows on earth . . . and [people would] come away with the true impression of what can be accomplished when the people of the world are given the chance to work in an era of peace and understanding."

The future and the Fair, however, would arrive without Kennedy. Just seven months later, while on a campaign trip to Dallas, accompanied by his beautiful and elegant wife, First Lady Jacqueline Kennedy, America's young, charismatic president was assassinated. In the span of a few seconds, shots rang out and the nation's history was irrevocably altered. As the country meandered through the coming months of shock and gloom, it seemed the Fair's promised era of "Peace Through Understanding" would never arrive.

Moses is a man you have to take as he is . . .
　　　　—*New York Times* editorial on December 18, 1963,
　　　　　　　　　　Moses' seventy-fifth birthday

The seeds of the 1964–65 New York World's Fair were first planted by a poetry-loving, idealistic, and well-connected real estate lawyer named Robert Kopple. One night in May 1958, while dining at his Roslyn, Long Island, home with his wife and young daughters, Kopple turned the conversation toward current events. He was shocked to hear what his children had to say. "We were discussing the world," he later explained, "and I found that my daughters, who were then nine and twelve, had very little contact with what was going on in it. Everything was in terms of black and white; everything was hate. And it occurred to me that I would like to bring home to them that people around the world were basically the same. And I thought it would be nice to bring the nations of the world together again."

Kopple's notion of uniting people, breaking down racial and national barriers, was still considered forward thinking in 1958 America, but such ideas had slowly been invading mainstream thought from the nation's political margins. The dinnertime conversation got him thinking. Kopple belonged to a monthly lunch club, which he organized, the Mutual Admiration Society, comprised of politically connected New Yorkers. At their next meeting at the New York University Club, he recalled his conversation with his daughters. He suggested to his associates that what was needed to educate children was another World's Fair. All the men at the table fondly recalled New York's previous World's Fair in 1939–40 and its fabled "World of Tomorrow."

Kopple had even worked at that Fair, running a voice-recording booth located opposite famed entertainment impresario Billy Rose's Aquacade exhibit. Despite two years of work, the booth hadn't turn a profit, but it left Kopple a self-professed "Fair buff." It also left him a true believer in the potential of such international exhibitions to foster understanding and mutual respect among the nations of the world—attitudes that were in short supply in the anxious years of the Cold War.

Kopple's insistence impressed his friends, and he immediately got to work: He read the complete minutes of the planning and assessment meetings from the earlier Fair and interviewed its president, the fast-talking, mustachioed showman Grover Whalen. He recruited important New York politicians he knew, like Joseph Carlino and Anthony Travia, the majority and minority leaders, respectively, of the New York State Assembly (both were members of the Mutual Admiration Society). Soon Kopple was traveling to Washington, DC, on his own dime and with New York's Republican senators Jacob K. Javitz and Kenneth Keating. He also arranged introductions to officials at both the Commerce and State Departments.

One of his lunch partners, Charles F. Preusse, a New York City administrator, got him his most important meeting: a sit-down with Mayor Robert F. Wagner Jr. If Kopple was going to organize the kind of world-class fair that he envisioned, he knew he needed City Hall's support. Sitting in the anteroom at Gracie Mansion, waiting for the mayor, Kopple noticed the seal of the city of New York hanging on the wall; it featured a picture of a Pilgrim and Native American standing side by side with the date 1664 at the bottom.

The Duke of York had conquered the Dutch colony of New Amsterdam in 1664, and renamed the bustling port city after his own dominion. New York, as it was henceforth known, became an English-speaking colony of the British Empire; 1964 would mark the 300th anniversary of this historical event and, as Kopple soon found out, Wagner had been looking for a way to celebrate the city's tercentennial. By the end of the meeting, Kopple was the city's official representative to organize the forthcoming celebrations.

In the meantime, Kopple sent feelers out to the Paris-based Bureau of International Expositions, or BIE, the ruling body that sanctioned World's Fairs. Seattle had already petitioned the BIE for its Century 21 Exposition in 1962, and several other cities—Toronto, Vienna, Moscow,

Los Angeles, and Washington, DC—were already angling to host exhibitions in the mid-1960s. According to BIE bylaws, a country could only host a Fair once every ten years, and the exhibitions themselves had to be spaced apart. New York was a contender but a dark horse.

Kopple pressed ahead. He put together a group of power brokers to jumpstart New York's bid. He enlisted public relations executive Thomas J. Deegan to be the Fair Corporation's acting president, offered Whalen the position of honorary chairman (emphasizing the link to the earlier Fair), and would serve as executive vice president himself.

In May 1959 Kopple invited thirty-five prominent businessmen for drinks at New York's famed "21" restaurant. He asked them to sit on the Mayor's Committee for a proposed World's Fair—and to fork over $1,000 apiece for seed money. Deegan soon got another fifty high rollers to do the same. Now all the pieces were coming together: Kopple's non-profit World's Fair Corporation had cash in hand (up until now, he had been paying expenses out of his own pocket) and had secured the services of advertising firm Doyle Dane Bernbach, whose groundbreaking work for Volkswagen and Polaroid was upending Madison Avenue. The corporation had also acquired rent-free office space in the Empire State Building for one year thanks to Kopple's connections. They even found a site for the Fair itself. Robert Moses, as City Parks Commissioner, offered Flushing Meadow Park in Queens—site of the 1939–40 World's Fair—for an unbeatable rental fee of $1 a year.

The next step for the New York organizers was to secure the support of President Eisenhower. Of the other American cities in contention—Los Angeles and Washington, DC—the nation's capital was the clear frontrunner. Without the consent of the federal government, city and state officials could not invite foreign nations to participate in an exhibition on American soil. As it happened, Senator Fulbright, the powerful head of the Foreign Relations Committee, and others were lobbying hard for a DC fair. The deck seemed stacked against New York. However, in early October 1959, Eisenhower appointed a three-man commission to consider the various bids. New York's delegation, headed by Governor Nelson A. Rockefeller, Mayor Wagner, and Moses—who had no official connection to the Fair at this point (but without whom, nothing in New York got built)—traveled to Washington to make their case.

Moses, in his usual heavy-handed style, laid out the reasons why the Fair should be held in "the World Capital" of New York: The city already had an abundance of hotel rooms, cultural offerings, a vast transportation system, and, of course, the ready-made fairgrounds of Flushing Meadow Park—1,257 acres of green space that he reminded the committee he had created from a "dump" into New York City's second-largest park. He also noted that a state-of-the-art major-league baseball stadium— soon to be the home of New York's new National League team, the Mets—was going to be built in the park, an enterprise, Moses argued, that would "supplement" the World's Fair.

Moses' case was convincing. By the end of the month, Eisenhower gave New York the green light for its World's Fair. Kopple's dream would now become a reality. With the blessing of the White House and the full support of New York's political and business classes, the only obstacle left was to address the "slight diplomatic problem" of the BIE in Paris. There were specific bylaws of the organization that conflicted with Kopple's plans: For starters, there was the 1962 Seattle exposition. Second, the New York planners insisted foreign governments pay rent for their pavilions, whereas American state governments would pay nothing (the BIE insisted that all land be provided for free). And finally, the New York Fair would be held for two six-month seasons in both 1964 and 1965 (World's Fairs were supposed to be held for only one six-month period).

The European bureaucrats in the BIE were quick to point out that the United States had never joined the organization, which counted among its thirty member-nations almost all of Europe, the Soviet Union, Israel, and several countries in South America and Asia. Back in 1939, Whalen had promised the BIE that he would lobby Congress to ratify the organization's treaty, but as Europe fell to Hitler's *Wehrmacht*, the deal was promptly forgotten. In fact, a deal was completely unlikely in 1939 or '40 given the strong isolationist bent of American policy at the time. Many in America wanted the United States to steer clear of any international treaty that would bind the country to the war-prone nations of Europe.

Despite these seemingly insurmountable roadblocks facing the New York organizers in 1959, pragmatic solutions were rather simple: Seattle's exposition was, technically, a "second-category" affair; its very size, no more than 74 acres, was completely dwarfed by the 646 acres that New York's exhibition would occupy. The rents that the city would charge could be shifted around to different columns on the official accountant spreadsheets (the 1939–40 Fair had also charged rent). And finally, if need be, the BIE could sanction only the first year of the Fair, while informal arrangements could be made with BIE members for the second season in 1965.

Before any deals could be struck, however, the World's Fair Corporation had two internal problems to solve. One was to secure the services of a president, someone with a name that resonated with the public but who was not a politician (or who would be running for office in the future). They wanted someone with impeccable credentials, the toughness to maneuver through New York's bureaucracy, and yet the diplomacy to work with foreign governments.

While the search proceeded, Kopple and Deegan had to secure funding for their Fair. Like the 1939–40 World's Fair, they planned on issuing bonds and would pay the bondholders back with some of the Fair's estimated $100 million profit. But as Kopple knew, the earlier Fair, albeit a cherished memory for a generation of Americans who grew up during the Great Depression and the war years, was a bust business-wise. In fact, Whalen had sold more than $26.8 million in bonds, while only paying back $8.2 million to his investors: a whopping thirty-two cents to the dollar. And to make things worse, many of the bankers who were stiffed twenty-five years earlier occupied the same seats on the current boards of New York banks. "We found that the same people who had been policy-makers at the banks in those days were still the policy-makers twenty-five years later," complained Deegan. "There hadn't been much turnover."

Initially, Deegan hoped to offer $500 million in bonds, but the Fair's economic forecast made him hedge his bets. By early 1960 he downgraded the figure to $150 million. It wasn't nearly enough money, but the banking community still balked. Enter David Rockefeller, the powerful vice chairman of Chase Manhattan Bank and brother to New York's Republican governor—and soon-to-be presidential candidate—Nelson Rockefeller. The younger Rockefeller put up $3 million to settle the Fair's finances, for the moment.

Rockefeller became a consultant to the Executive Committee, which continued to seek a new president. Names were tossed around, among them General Lucius D. Clay, the architect of the Berlin Airlift and Eisenhower's deputy during WWII, as well as John J. McCloy, the former US High Commissioner of West Germany and World Bank president (his insider status would later land him on the Warren Commission). Both were serious men with international reputations and impeccable credentials. Neither was interested.

In March the group met at Rockefeller's Manhattan office to go over a list of eight names. As they deliberated over their choices, one member, William E. Robinson, the chairman of the board at Coca-Cola, suggested that there was a very powerful New Yorker whose name hadn't been mentioned yet: Robert Moses. Kopple immediately voiced his opposition. Moses, he said, lacked style and grace. He reminded his colleagues that the Master Builder wasn't a showman but a dictator who steamrolled over people like they were asphalt. Moses' authoritarian techniques might work in New York but would hardly win the Fair any friends among foreign governments or American corporations. But Kopple's concerns were the exact reasons why Robinson nominated the Master Builder. "I suspect that his arbitrary and dictatorial method may be necessary in the organization and operation of a World's Fair of this kind," Robinson would later say.

Kopple tried a different tactic: He suggested that given Moses' advanced age—he was already seventy—he was too old for the job. That comment irritated Bernard Gimbel, the seventy-five-year-old department store tycoon and Moses' confidant, who argued that he was in the prime of his life. Some members of the committee backed Moses; others, like Rockefeller, sat silently.

The real estate lawyer hadn't seen this coming. The tide of the room soon turned against him. Trying to defuse the situation, Kopple mentioned that the whole conversation might be premature. He suggested to the room that Moses, who already held more than a dozen positions in New York, might not even be interested in the job. That's when Deegan spoke up. Actually, the public relations executive nonchalantly informed the committee, "I took the liberty of calling Bob just before we met."

If suddenly Kopple felt that he had been set up, no one who knew Moses would have been surprised.

3.

In the twentieth century, the influence of Robert Moses on the cities of America was greater than that of any other person.

—Lewis Mumford

For Robert Moses, it all came down to parks. More than the bridges he built (the Whitestone, the Verrazano, the Throg's Neck, the Triborough, to name a few); or the vast interlocking network of expressways he erected above and below its streets (the Van Wyck, the Clearview, the Whitestone, the Cross-Bronx, the Brooklyn-Queens, among others); or the 416 miles of scenic parkways that course in and out of metropolitan New York and its outer environs; or even the hundreds of playgrounds, dozen or so public pools, amenities, tennis courts, or skating rinks that he created, what mattered most to Moses were parks. Fighting for parks, he said, was always a winning proposition for a public figure, even an unelected one such as himself. "As long as you're on the side of parks," he would often tell his underlings, "you're on the side of the angels. You can't lose."

More than all his other monuments of concrete and steel and feats of ingenuity and engineering, parks would be Moses' pathway to history. And history is what Moses intended to make. In 1960 he got the chance to build the park of his dreams, one that he had been envisioning for almost forty years. This would be his crowning achievement; and if his vision was carried out—and he would use all the power at his disposal to see that it was—this park would reshape the very geography of New York, improving upon Nature itself.

Considering his privileged background, it's a wonder that Moses was interested in parks at all. Born in 1888 in New Haven, Connecticut, Robert Moses was the son of an industrious German immigrant father, Emmanuel Moses, and a demanding mother, Isabella Silverman Cohen, known as Bella. Both families had fled the pastoral beauty of Bavaria, due to its systemic anti-Semitism, for America. Emmanuel Moses became a successful businessman, owning and operating his own local depart-ment store. Bella, who doted on her youngest son, Robert, hailed from a well-connected and prosperous New Haven clan. By 1897 the family had moved to Manhattan and lived in a five-story brownstone inherited from Bella's father on East 46th Street, just off Fifth Avenue.

Young Moses wanted for nothing. He lived in a household with cooks and maids who prepared his meals, served his food on the finest china, and made his custom-built bed daily. He and his older brother shared a private library with more than two thousand books. Rembrandt prints hung from the home's oak-paneled walls. The family vacationed in upstate New York's Adirondack Mountains, imbuing Moses with a love of nature, and they summered on the Continent, fueling his intellectual and cultural appetites. As a Manhattanite, Moses never had to endure the subway or any other aspect of the public transportation system; he was driven everywhere he went by the family chauffeur. In his long life, he would never learn to drive.

Educated at prep schools and an excellent athlete—Moses dis-dained team sports, preferring swimming, a lifelong passion, and track—he began his studies at Yale while only sixteen. Unable to penetrate the top social clubs at the university as a Jew, he settled for less prestigious student organizations. Throwing himself into his studies, Moses read voraciously and developed a passion for Samuel Johnson, the learned eighteenth-century man of letters. He spoke Latin and recited lengthy poems from memory. He even wrote his own Victorian-style poetry, which got published in a Yale literary magazine.

The ambitious Moses had a gift for words, especially when moti-vated to defend a position or attack an opponent. He penned pointed editorials for the *Yale Daily News* and ran for student government. He graduated Phi Beta Kappa in 1909. It was said by his fellow students that he could have graduated at the very top of his class if he had spent less time reading books that interested him but had nothing to do with his coursework.

After Yale, Moses earned his master's degree in political science at Wadham College at Oxford University. There he wrote his master's thesis on reforming government, creating a new paradigm based on meritocracy instead of the crooked system of patronage and kickbacks that ruled big-city political machines like New York's infamous Tammany Hall. Back in New York, he earned his PhD in political science at Columbia. Thus armed with degrees from some of the best colleges in the world, Moses dedicated himself to public service.

Quickly aligning himself with the progressive movement, then a national force in politics, Moses worked for no pay—since he could afford to—at the Municipal Research Bureau in New York. When a young prosecuting attorney named John Purroy Mitchel swept into City Hall on an anticorruption, anti–Tammany Hall platform in 1914, Moses joined his administration. Only thirty-four years old, Mitchel was dubbed "the Boy Mayor" and was exactly the kind of university-bred man that Moses thought should hold the highest positions in government.

After proposing the government operating system that he had detailed in his master's thesis, Moses quickly became a target of Tammany Hall. At raucous Board of Estimate meetings in 1917, dressed in a white suit and tie, he publicly defended his plan, citing facts and figures, while the rough-and-tumble Tammany faithful crowded the back of the hall, hurling insults and curses at the PhD Ivy Leaguer. Unfortunately, 1917 was an election year, and Mayor Mitchel buckled under pressure from the political bosses and failed to support Moses' plan. When Mitchel lost his reelection bid, Moses lost his job.

The following year, Moses got the break he was looking for. Belle Moskowitz, a trusted aide to New York's Democratic governor Alfred E. Smith, offered him a job, but Moses had his doubts. He didn't think much of the bighearted and affable Smith, a former Brooklyn street kid with gold-filled teeth who spoke in classic New Yorkese. The governor had an incomplete formal education; when asked what kind of degree he possessed, Smith famously quipped "F.F.M."—as in the Fulton Fish Market, where he had labored after he quit the twelfth grade to help support his family. The governor, it was well known, was a product of Tammany Hall. "What can you expect from a man who wears a brown derby on the side of his head and always has a big cigar in the corner of his mouth?" Moses complained to a friend. But he soon learned that Moskowitz shared his passion for reform, and she had the governor's ear.

Moses got to work in impressive fashion. He wrote up a 419-page report on the restructuring and streamlining of 175 state agencies into 16 departments. The government, Moses firmly believed, needed to be efficient in order to effect lasting and significant change. Although Smith was voted out of office in 1920 before he could implement Moses' plan, the pair became close. Together the unlikely duo—the Ivy League-bred, Latin-quoting Jewish Moses and the cigar-chomping, whiskey-swigging Irish Catholic Smith—would go for long walks, forming a bond that would last decades.

Smith lauded Moses' skills and worth ethic. "Bob Moses is the most efficient administrator I have ever met in public life," he said. "He was the best bill drafter in Albany . . . he didn't get that keen mind of his from any college. He was a hard worker. He worked on trains anywhere and any time. When everyone else was ready for bed he would go back to work."

Although Moses would go on to work for seven governors, Smith was the only man that he could ever bring himself to actually call "Governor"; to Moses, all of Smith's successors were unworthy in comparison. His loyalty to his friend knew few bounds. In 1936, when New York's hopelessly corrupt mayor Jimmy Walker—a smirking songwriting dandy whom Moses deplored—publicly embarrassed Smith, the Master Builder exacted revenge. Walker enjoyed carousing with his cronies at the Central Park Casino, a structure with a unique architectural style: On the outside it was a nineteenth-century cottage; inside it was a decadent modernist playground with black mirrors and huge glass chandeliers for the city's moneyed elite. As City Parks Commissioner, Moses would later have the place razed and the vacant lot turned into a playground (Smith had a soft spot for children). Moses was nothing, if not loyal.

In 1922 Smith was voted back into office. Moses was now his aide-de-camp; his job was to do whatever the governor needed, whether it was writing legislation or speaking on his behalf with Albany insiders.

While Moses was happy to be an important player in New York government, there was one job he truly wanted: the position of Parks Commissioner, which would enable him to reshape the landscape of New York and lead to his involvement in both New York World's Fairs in the twentieth century.

He got the idea while vacationing in Babylon, Long Island, with his wife and young daughters. It was there that he encountered the beaches, bays, and untamed wetlands of Long Island's South Shore, thousands of acres of gorgeous coastline with mesmerizing views of the Atlantic Ocean and the Great Southern Bay. Miles of it belonged to New York City and State, and yet there was no systematic way for New Yorkers to access these natural surroundings as well as no system in place for local government to develop the property. But Moses had a way to fix that. "He was always burning up with ideas, just burning up with them!" a colleague said. "Everything he saw walking around the city made him think of some way that it could be better."

He proposed a new department—which he would head, naturally—that would create and build a vast system of parks, not only on eastern Long Island, but also in the Adirondacks and the Catskills, making the most of the state's geological wonders. Devoting so much time, energy, and resources to the creation of a statewide park system was visionary; at the time, twenty-nine US states had no state parks at all.

When Moses presented his plan to Smith, the Irishman was suspicious. "You want to give the people a fur coat when what they need is red flannel underwear," he complained. The cost wouldn't be cheap: A parks system would require $15 million worth of bonds; land would have to be purchased, roadways built. But Moses highlighted the upside for the governor: The public loved parks, working families needed places to go on the weekend or for vacation. It would be a public relations boon for the governor, who would ultimately receive the credit and acclaim for giving the people the fur coat that they wanted (even if they really needed flannel underwear).

As long as you're on the side of parks, you're on the side of the angels. You can't lose.

Moses got his appointment. In 1924 Smith made him the president of the New York State Council of Parks and chairman of the Long Island State Park Commission. (For a political reformer hell-bent on reducing state agencies, Moses had a knack for creating new ones when it fit his plans.) He went to work converting Jones Beach into a state park. For the first time, Moses came into direct contact with the public he so longed to serve; only this time he wasn't a reformer, but a builder. His plans for Jones Beach called for the appropriation of private land, invoking the wrath of many Long Islanders, from the moneyed estate owners to small family farmers. "If we want your land," he told one farmer, "we can take it."

The opposition hardened. Rich Long Islanders complained that "rabble" from the city would flood the pristine oceanfront, creating "a second Coney Island." But this ploy backfired after the *New York Times* ran a story with the headline A FEW RICH GOLFERS ACCUSED OF BLOCKING PLAN FOR STATE PARK. When Jones Beach finally opened in 1930, it was hailed as a masterpiece of public planning, and millions flocked to its sun-kissed shores. "It is one of the finest beaches in the United States, and almost the only one designed with forethought and good taste," wrote British novelist H. G. Wells after surveying Moses' handiwork.

By 1928 when Smith launched his presidential campaign—marking the first time a Roman Catholic was nominated by a leading party for the nation's highest office—Moses was New York's Secretary of State, yet another position he could use to achieve his goals. As Smith toured the country by train, he listed his administration's achievements—parks, hospitals, roads, and amenities for the public, many of which were built by Moses.

It was there, traveling through the country with the governor, that Moses witnessed the hatred and bigotry that Smith faced, particularly in states where the Ku Klux Klan held sway. Moses never forgot those experiences or the affect it had on his friend. Decades later, he would recall those memories in a letter to a Smith biographer. "I don't think you have stressed enough the cross burning and bigotry Smith ran into during the 1928 campaign," he wrote, "an experience from which he never really recovered." It was anti-Catholic fervor that ensured Smith, the quintessential "Happy Warrior," would lose to the Republican free-market fundamentalist Herbert H. Hoover. Smith's lieutenant governor, Franklin Delano Roosevelt, won the former's gubernatorial seat and became Moses' boss.

It must have been gut-wrenching for Moses to see his beloved Smith in political exile while Roosevelt, whom he utterly detested, moved into the Governor's Mansion in Albany. Moses was the only member of Smith's cabinet that Roosevelt did not retain (the animosity was mutual). When Moses learned of his imminent dismissal as Secretary of State, he quit before Roosevelt could fire him. Still, Moses continued on as Parks Commissioner. His parks were popular with the public, who had just handed Roosevelt the governorship of New York, a well-established launching pad to the White House at the time. Roosevelt, happily or not, was politically savvy enough to leave the Parks Commissioner where he was.

Whatever their personal differences, the two worked together when required. When Roosevelt swept into the White House in 1932, he launched the New Deal, a massive spending stimulus package meant to jumpstart an American economy ravaged by the Great Depression. Moses made the most of the situation and lured millions in New Deal funds to New York for his projects. He quickly dusted off plans for what would consolidate his reputation as America's premier builder: the Triborough Bridge.*

To help finance this massive project, which would unite three of the five boroughs—Manhattan, the Bronx, and Queens—Moses dreamed up the Triborough Bridge Authority,** or TBA, a public entity that was entirely outside the boundaries of government. The TBA could borrow money, issue bonds, and fund itself through the tolls it would collect; it had its own fleet of cars and boats, even a small police force; and it didn't have to answer to the public it was supposedly serving. Its Randall Island office space underneath the bridge was now Moses' headquarters, his own private island lair from which he could extend the boundaries of his growing influence.

---

* Renamed the Robert F. Kennedy Bridge in 2008.
** Later renamed the Triborough Bridge and Tunnel Authority.

Moses' influence grew again in 1933 when Fiorello H. La Guardia became the mayor of New York. Although a Republican, La Guardia was a progressive who aligned himself with Democratic causes such as Roosevelt's New Deal. The "Little Flower," as he was known, turned to Moses to improve the city's infrastructure, and in return the mayor consolidated the Master Builder's power by making him New York City Parks Commissioner. Now all five boroughs were under Moses' aegis. La Guardia also made Moses the CEO and chairman of the TBA, giving him near total control of his own public authority.

The following year Moses switched his party affiliation to Republican and ran for governor against Herbert H. Lehman, who had replaced Roosevelt as New York's chief executive. The onetime reformer ran a nasty campaign, lambasting Lehman, a gentlemanly New Deal liberal (and close ally of the hated Roosevelt), in the press, calling him "stupid," a "puppet" of Tammany Hall, and "a miserable, sniveling type of man . . . contemptible." He was equally dismissive of the reporters who followed him around as a gubernatorial candidate. Attacking the press would prove to be a favorite pastime for the rest of Moses' life.

When he lost in a landslide to Lehman, Moses expected to get fired. But Lehman was in many ways the anti-Moses. Despite intense pressure from the White House—President Roosevelt got word to both Governor Lehman and Mayor La Guardia that unless Moses was dismissed, New Deal funds for New York would dry up—Moses was left in place. After the Master Builder discovered the president's plot to have him fired, he quickly informed reporters, who ran stories about the president's personal vendetta against him. Smith rallied to his friend's defense, calling the plot "narrow, political, vindictive," and Roosevelt eventually backed off. Even the President of the United States couldn't touch Moses. *That* was power.

Throughout the 1930s, Moses continued to mold and reshape New York. He often had hundreds of projects, sometimes thousands, going at the same time; there was always more to do. Then in 1935, when a few local businessmen wanted to hold a World's Fair in New York, a major international exhibition, something to rouse the city out of the Great Depression, he got his first opportunity to achieve a long-cherished dream.

The Flushing Meadow, a three-mile stretch of natural marshlands in the middle of Queens, had beguiled developers for decades. By the 1920s it had become a vermin-infested, mountainous heap of refuse and trash, brought daily from Brooklyn via private train, thanks to a shady Tammany Hall figure named Fishhooks McCarthy. The 1,346 acres of defiled marshlands had been described by F. Scott Fitzgerald in *The Great Gatsby* as "the valley of ashes a . . . fantastic farm where ashes grow like wheat into ridges and hills and grotesque gardens, where ashes take the forms of houses and chimneys and rising smoke."

Moses wanted to change that. Just as he saw the untamed wilds of Jones Beach and envisioned a world-class park that would serve millions, he saw Flushing Meadow and dreamed of a park that would surpass the grandeur of Central Park. In fact, as the city's population continued its steady migration eastward—partly due to the network of highways and bridges that Moses himself had built—this new park would be a truer "central park," closer as it was to both the geographic and population centers of the city. In a bustling metropolis like New York City, the Flushing Meadow was the largest—one-and-a-half times the size of Central Park—blank canvas that nature would provide for him. When Moses heard about the World's Fair plan, he slammed his fist on a table and exclaimed, "By God, that's a wonderful idea!'"

He rallied behind the flamboyant Grover Whalen, the Fair's president, and quickly suggested Flushing Meadow could be developed—with some of the public funds that the Fair would be receiving—into a wonderful, elegant fairground. A lease was drawn up, and Moses, as City Parks Commissioner, became the Fair's landlord. In return he requested a piece of the profits to design and sculpt Flushing Meadow Park as he wished.

But it never happened. Although Moses was able to bury "the valley of ashes"—ingeniously using the miles of refuse as landfill for what would become the Van Wyck Expressway—the 1939–40 World's Fair, the grandest and largest exposition of its time, was a financial disaster.

When it was over, the Fair that had offered forty-six million visitors a glimpse of "the World of Tomorrow"—a world of futuristic wonders like television and skyscrapers—only paid investors thirty-three cents on the dollar.

Thanks to Moses' protean efforts, there was now a Flushing Meadow Park, meticulously landscaped with two man-made lakes, an elaborate new drainage system, a new art deco–style civic building (the former New York City Pavilion), and the wide asphalt roads and pathways that serviced park-goers. However, it wasn't the grandiose public space he originally envisioned, which would have included everything from a boat basin, bike paths, and a nature preserve to both a Japanese garden and another modeled on the Garden of Versailles. His dream would have to wait.

Although World War II slowed down the pace of his building, Moses continued to plan for the postwar surge he anticipated. In 1943 New York City initiated its own plans to stem the tide of citizens who had already begun to eschew cities for the suburbs. The catchphrase for this process would come to be known as "urban renewal," the systematic clearance of decayed and blighted slum areas—"cancerous areas in the heart of the city," according to Moses—that could be redeveloped and turned into affordable housing for middle-class families.

By 1943 Moses, then the chairman of the Mayor's Committee on Slum Clearance, had "induced" the Metropolitan Life Insurance Company to build Stuyvesant Town, a series of large, concrete-slab apartment buildings that would stretch along Manhattan's East Side from 14th Street to 20th Street between Avenue A and Avenue C. The complex would ultimately create nearly nine thousand affordable and comfortable apartments for twenty-five thousand people. Moses lauded Met Life's chairman of the board, Frederick H. Ecker, praising his "far-sightedness and courage" to get involved in public works. Not everyone agreed. *The New Yorker*'s architecture critic, Lewis Mumford, wrote that the buildings looked like "the architecture of the Police State."

The project quickly caused a public outcry when it was revealed that Met Life had a whites-only policy. Ecker only added to the firestorm by blatantly revealing his segregationist views. "Negroes and whites don't mix," the Met Life chairman stated, and claimed that if Stuyvesant Town was integrated, it would be detrimental to the city because "it would depress all the surrounding property [values]." It didn't help, in the eyes of many progressive citizens—including the NAACP—that, at Moses' urging, Met Life was also creating a similar apartment complex uptown, the Riverton Houses, which had a blacks-only policy.

Lawsuits were filed, including one by three African-American WWII veterans. Moses dismissed any and all complaints, in particular any objections to Met Life's discriminatory policies, claiming that such lawsuits were the handiwork of citizens who were "obviously looking for a political issue and not for the results in the form of actual slum clearance." In 1947 the New York State Supreme Court sided with Met Life; the insurance company, as the de facto landlord of the complex, could discriminate if they wished since, as the judge declared, "housing accommodation is not a recognized civil right."

Moses was pleased with the decision. As early as 1943, he had added legislation to the city's 1942 Redevelopment Companies Act to make sure private companies, such as Met Life, could do as they pleased when it came to urban renewal. Moses also personally lobbied Ecker not to cave in to Mayor La Guardia, who pleaded with the Met Life chairman to soften his discriminatory stand. To do so, Moses believed, would cede decision-making control to the public and its elected officials, which in turn would curb his own power as the head of the Slum Clearance Commission. And that could not be allowed. When it came to racial issues, Moses was hardly on the side of the angels. While he was a public servant, the public could not be allowed to interfere with his work. He attacked his critics as nothing more than "demagogues . . . who want to make a political, racial, religious, or sectional issue out of every progressive step which can be taken to improve local conditions."

With the passage of the Housing Act of 1949, America embarked on a new urban policy intended to restore the nation's neglected cities, which would dramatically increase Moses' power again. The laws introduced a controversial program known as Title I, a regulation that enabled the government to claim private property—citing eminent domain—and develop the land in partnership with private companies for the benefit of the public good.

A leading force behind the legislation was Ohio's powerful senator Robert A. Taft, the embodiment of the Republican Party's conservative wing, who was both a Moses ally and a fellow Yalie. Moses kept a close tab on the housing law as it worked its way through Congress. When it finally passed, he made sure he had multiple projects that were "shovel-ready." Moses would ultimately claim $65.8 million in Title I funding for New York—more than any other American city (his closest competitor was Chicago, which received $30.8 million in federal largesse). In the decades after WWII, urban renewal would become a much-reviled phrase—Mumford considered the term "a filthy word"—and in the minds of many, Moses would come to personify the expression.

Of all Moses' critics, his most vocal—and eloquent—was Mumford, who opposed nearly every public works project that the Master Builder embarked on. For nearly as long as Moses was a titanic source of power in New York, Mumford used his position at *The New Yorker* to combat Moses' vision of urban America. A true Renaissance man, Mumford's interests were even more catholic than Moses'; his nearly two-dozen books touched upon history, philosophy, architecture, science, art, and literature.

Born in Queens but raised in Manhattan, Mumford celebrated urban architecture that lived in harmony with nature, practicing what he preached. In 1922 he moved his family to Sunnyside Gardens, Queens—the first planned "garden city" community in the United States—where he lived until 1933. Although at first he championed Moses' work, particularly his scenic parkways and Jones Beach (a "masterpiece," he called it), by the advent of the 1939–40 New York World's Fair, the pair were at odds. Mumford was not in the least impressed by "the World of Tomorrow" or the Fair's other attractions. "[The Fair] has no architectural character whatever," Mumford wrote. As for GM's much-celebrated Futurama exhibit, he felt that "what the Futurama really demonstrates is that by 1960 all [rides] of more than fifty miles will be as deadly as they are now in parts of New Jersey and in the

Farther West." Eventually, *The New Yorker* scribe would describe Moses as "the great un-builder."

In 1955, shortly after Moses had begun building the Long Island Expressway, Mumford launched a spirited attack on the project—and on Moses—in the pages of *The New Yorker*. Moses' New York, Mumford thought, had "become steadily more frustrating and unsatisfactory to raise children in, and more difficult to escape from for a holiday in the country." By now, both men were diametrically opposed in their core beliefs. While Moses famously claimed that "cities are created by and for traffic," Mumford firmly believed and repeatedly stated that highways do not mitigate traffic; they create it. "A city exists, not for the constant passage of motorcars, but for the care and culture of men," said Mumford, who in 1961 published his award-winning book, *The City in History*.

Not that Moses cared. He lumped Mumford in with the academic critics "who build nothing." In the meantime, Moses continued to accumulate positions—and power—like trophies; La Guardia's successor, Mayor William O'Dwyer, added Construction Coordinator and Chairman of the Emergency Committee on Housing to his growing portfolio. By the 1950s it was impossible to build anything in New York without Moses' consent. If he opposed a project—as he did when Brooklyn Dodgers owner Walter O'Malley wanted to build a new ballpark in Brooklyn—it never happened; if he wanted a project realized—a baseball stadium in his favored Flushing Meadow Park in Queens—it was built.

But for all his power and influence, Title I almost proved Moses' undoing. Each time he embarked on the construction of new housing, streets and neighborhoods had to be condemned, and the unfortunate souls who called those neighborhoods home had their lives upended. Over the course of his Title I reign, Moses uprooted tens of thousands of New Yorkers, old and young alike, replacing neighborhoods with concrete-slab towers. "There is nothing wrong with these buildings," Mumford wrote after taking a tour of a few newly created housing projects, "except that, humanly speaking, they stink."

In 1959 a scandal revealed that notorious mob boss Frank Costello, button man Vinny "the Chin" Gigante, and other assorted mafiosi were involved in one of Moses' Title I public housing programs. While Moses didn't know of the mob connection, the incident stained his reputation and, most infuriating, allowed his media critics an opportunity to publicly tar and feather him. Costello Pal Got Title I Deal, roared the *New York Post*; Banker Had Warning on Costello Pal, clamored the *New York World-Telegram*.

Moses was incensed. Mayor Wagner and Governor Rockefeller were under pressure to do something with the aging Master Builder, to strip him of some of his titles at least, which wouldn't be easy, as Wagner could testify. In 1954, right after taking the oath of office, Wagner swore in Moses as City Parks Commissioner and City Construction Coordinator. When he was done, Moses stood at attention waiting for Wagner to swear him in as Chairman of the City Planning Commission.

After all the other administration appointees took their oaths, the mayor still hadn't done so. Moses followed Wagner into his private office. What the Master Builder didn't know was that Wagner's aides had been pressuring the mayor not to allow Moses to head the Planning Commission. Holding all three positions would give Moses the power to propose and green-light public works projects with little to no oversight— far too much power in one man's hands.

Behind closed doors, Moses informed Wagner that if he wasn't reappointed the head of the Planning Commission, he would resign his other posts, immediately. Wagner froze. He said it was just a clerical oversight; give it a few days, he promised, and the situation would all be sorted out. Moses walked out, grabbed a blank application form from a nearby office, filled it out, put it on the mayor's desk, and stood there until Wagner signed it. Recalling the incident years later, Wagner said he initially hesitated just to let Moses know that he couldn't control him, the way Moses had dominated other mayors. "[Moses] had done some remarkable things for the city and state of New York," Wagner said. "There was no question that he knew that field well, and that he was going to be retained."

Throughout his twelve years as New York City's mayor, Moses would always be a thorny issue for Wagner, who could never come down hard on him, the way La Guardia would. Wagner grew up around the Master Builder—Moses was a good friend of his father, Senator Robert F. Wagner Sr.—and both Moses and his father would regale him with stories of Governor Al Smith, a beloved figure that all three held in the highest regard. While Wagner wasn't blind to Moses' faults, the elder Master Builder consistently got preferential treatment. "[He] was always a very controversial figure," recalled Wagner. "He was rather arrogant, and he'd irritate you."

Now six years later, in 1960, Moses wanted out. The Parks Commissioner had been following the news of the 1964–65 World's Fair closely. He had, after all, testified down in Washington, DC, earlier in the year on behalf of the exhibition. And the Fair's top acting executive, Thomas J. Deegan, was a Moses loyalist. There was little question that Moses desired the job and that he would move heaven and earth to create a Fair worth remembering; he had even met with members of the Executive Committee, urging them not to cave into the BIE's demands, to keep their autonomy, thus enabling them to control their own destiny. The 1939–40 New York World's Fair was remembered as a wondrous event in the lives of millions, but it was a financial failure. That wasn't Moses' fault; he didn't have complete control over the earlier Fair. The whole experience proved to be a valuable lesson, one he never forgot.

Nine months after the Title I mafia scandal first erupted, Moses resigned from several key positions, including his post on the mayor's Slum Clearance Committee and as Parks Commissioner to become the president of the World's Fair Corporation. Though Moses was "a great man and a good friend," Wagner said years later, "this wasn't one of his great monuments, this Slum Clearance Committee operation." Fate had given Moses his second chance at re-creating the Flushing Meadow. He wasn't about to waste it.

4.

I hold that if your natural weapon is the broadaxe, you should not affect the rapier.

—Robert Moses

In retrospect, it must have seemed like a fait accompli that Moses—the man who built New York into a modern metropolis—would spearhead the 1964–65 New York World's Fair. Not only did he have the credentials and the reputation, he had the backing of New York's ruling class.

Although Mayor Robert F. Wagner Jr. had empowered Robert Kopple to lay the groundwork for the Fair, the sullen-faced mayor had a habit of caving in to Moses. Governor Rockefeller had a much rockier relationship with the Master Builder, but must have seen the benefits that a great New York World's Fair would have for his national reputation, an important consideration since he was positioning himself for a presidential run. If the Fair, as Rockefeller declared, would have "lasting benefits as a magnificent showcase," then who better to make that happen than Moses? Whatever his faults—and few members of the Empire State's ruling elite were blind to the political and personal baggage Moses would bring to the Fair—he had an undeniable and proven track record.

With Moses running the World's Fair Corporation, there would be no question who was in charge. And there was no doubt that he would do his utmost to attract the seventy million Fairgoers from the four corners of the globe, as planners promised. To reach this goal, the Fair would require a daily average of 220,000 visitors over its two six-month seasons in consecutive years; this would yield nearly $100 million in estimated profits—plus millions of dollars in ancillary income to the city coffers from the tourists who would flock to see the spectacle. And with some of those profits, Moses could fund his nearly forty-year-old dream of transforming Flushing Meadow into New York's premier green space, the centerpiece of a string of parks he envisioned extending across Queens.

Despite Kopple's complaints about the Master Builder, he was voted down by the Moses loyalists in the room: William E. Robinson, Coca-Cola's chairman of the board; banker David Rockefeller (and the governor's younger brother); department store magnate Bernard Gimbel; and, of course, Thomas J. Deegan, who had called Moses about the job before the meeting even began. Moses happily accepted the $100,000-a-year position as president of the World's Fair Corporation. However, before beginning his new job in May 1960, he had one condition: Kopple must resign immediately. He explained to Deegan that he could not accept the position if Kopple was his executive vice president. "Having looked up his record, I find nothing in it that justifies his appointment," Moses declared. For his services heretofore, Moses suggested Kopple be paid accordingly and dismissed.

The pair had a history. In 1958, just a few months before his World's Fair epiphany, Kopple had led a crusade of civic groups against one of Moses' pet projects: the Mid-Manhattan Expressway. The $88 million six-lane elevated expressway would have razed Manhattan's 30th Street—from east to west—creating a link from the East Side's Queens Midtown Tunnel to the West Side's Lincoln Tunnel uniting the roadways of Long Island with the highways of New Jersey. The Mid-Manhattan Expressway, the Master Builder promised, would solve "the worst problem of traffic strangulation in history." It was also a missing link in the Master Builder's puzzle of arterial expressways and key to his vision of urban life.

Kopple disagreed. As the executive vice president of the Midtown Realty Owners Association, he said the expressway would be "a sword cutting through the city's heart," destroying two vital Manhattan neighborhoods in the process: the West Side's garment district, a bustling area of small businesses, and the East Side's Murray Hill, an area teeming with historic brownstones and tenement buildings full of working-class families. "Thousands of residents now gainfully employed will be thrown out of work," Kopple told the *New York Times*. "In addition, $40 million in real estate will be taken off the tax rolls—a revenue loss to the city of more than $2 million a year." He also ridiculed Moses' assertion that the expressway would reduce traffic. "Every traffic expert knows that [the expressway] will create bottlenecks in mid-Manhattan that will make today's problems look like paradise," he said.

Although the Mid-Manhattan Expressway wouldn't be stricken completely from New York City's Master Plan for another thirteen years, Kopple's opposition in 1958 dealt it a fatal blow. It was a huge defeat for Moses—a sin he would not forgive. When asked by reporters why he insisted on Kopple's dismissal, Moses was blunt. "These fellows that started [the Fair] had to get out, so I could have a free hand," he said. "They were not the kind of people I would hire. They had to go, and they were paid."

Moses and Kopple also had a mutual friend, whom they both held in particularly high regard: Charles Poletti, the longtime New York political insider, who briefly served as the Empire State's governor for twenty-nine days when Governor Herbert H. Lehman vacated the position early to head up the United Nations Relief and Rehabilitation Administration—a massive international effort to aid civilians in war-scarred Europe—in 1942. A Harvard man and world traveler who spoke multiple languages, Poletti had also been the US Army's reigning governor of Sicily during WWII, after the island was liberated by General George S. Patton's Seventh Army. Tapped by the Master Builder to run the Fair's International Division, even Poletti couldn't persuade Moses to keep Kopple. "I tried to dissuade him from it," Poletti admitted years later. But there was nothing doing. Moses wouldn't budge.

And just like that, Kopple, who had first dreamed of a second New York World's Fair, an exhibition to foster "Peace Through Understanding," was summarily dismissed by Deegan—the man whom he had hired and who all along had been a Moses loyalist. The man who had started the Fair for the most altruistic of reasons—"bringing the nations of the world together"—was reimbursed $35,000 for the expenses he had accrued and given free tickets for his family for the life of the Fair.

Years later, as the Fair he originally conceived of was about to open, Kopple insisted it was his own outspoken nature that irritated Moses. "He simply can't tolerate independent strength in anything he runs,"

Kopple told a reporter. Even then, Kopple couldn't fathom that his 1958 victory over the Mid-Manhattan Expressway had played any part in the behind-the-scenes drama of the World's Fair. "I find it hard to believe that he forced me out because I fought him on the expressway," he said.

Clearly, the man didn't understand Moses.

5

We ... are not subject to any rulings.

—Robert Moses

Robert Moses detested the executives of the Bureau of International Exhibitions. After flying to Paris in 1960, he arrived at the organization's modest office space—"a dingy attic," he deemed it—and quickly clashed with the European bureaucrats. He spoke to the members of the agency in his usual imperial manner, as if they were his personal underlings. "Moses hated the idea that he now had to go over to Paris, 'hat in hand,' and beg for approval of his fair," recalled Bruce Nicholson, an executive in the Fair's International Affairs and Exhibits division. It wasn't personal: Moses resented having to ask for permission from *anyone* for *anything.*

Since its formation in 1928, the BIE had governed international exhibitions; without the bureau's approval, a World's Fair was not—technically speaking—a World's Fair. After the success of London's Great Exhibition of 1851, fairs were all the rage. In the nineteenth century, cities on both side of the Atlantic wanted to host exhibitions to attract business, display their industrial might, and tout their cultural achievements. Fairs were economic boosts that could reenergize a city or announce its arrival on the world stage. Just two years after the London Exhibition, New York held its first World's Fair: the Crystal Palace Exhibition of 1853, which featured its version of the famed Crystal Palace, on the current site of Manhattan's Bryant Park. (Imitative as it might have been, the metal and glass structure, shaped like a Greek cross, was beloved by New Yorkers, including Walt Whitman, who wrote about it in his masterpiece *Leaves of Grass;* it burned down in 1858.) The BIE took its job of controlling the selection of Fair cities and regulating exhibitions very seriously.

Despite the fact that the 1964–65 World's Fair violated a healthy list of BIE bylaws, history was on Moses' side: Unlike European exhibitions, most American World's Fairs weren't government-sponsored; the New

York Fair was officially being run by a nonprofit agency with the blessing of the US government, which would have to foot the bill for its own federal pavilion. Moses was adamant that the New York Fair run for two consecutive years and exhibitors pay for the lots they rented. How else could he generate enough profits to transform the Flushing Meadow into "the finest park in the city"?

A far more significant problem for Moses and his colleagues was the 1962 Seattle World's Fair; no country was allowed to hold a sanctioned fair twice in the same decade. The organizers of that exhibition were seeking the BIE's blessing and were likely to get it, since they were following the organization's bylaws as best they could. They even rented an office in Paris to work more closely with the Europeans. But one thing that neither Moses nor his Seattle counterparts had any control over was the fact that the United States wasn't a member of the BIE, having never ratified the organization's 1928 treaty; to do so would require an act of both the president and Congress, a process that could take years—"If it could be done at all," noted Moses.

But getting it done had been Robert Kopple's intention. Before Moses insisted that he resign, Kopple had been working with New York's Republican senator Kenneth Keating to introduce legislation asking the government to consider signing the BIE treaty. The Master Builder was dead-set against that approach. For one, it would give Congress a voice in the Fair's business (never a good thing, as far as Moses was concerned), and it could potentially transform the Fair into a hotly debated political issue, maybe even poison the public against it. Lastly, an international treaty would have provided the Fair's congressional foes, such as Senator Fulbright, the powerful chairman of the Foreign Relations Committee, plenty of ammunition. As soon as Moses took control of the Fair, he had the legislation squashed.

Despite a number of seemingly irreconcilable differences with the Paris-based organization, none of its bylaws were deal-breakers. Prior to the 1939–40 New York World's Fair, Grover Whalen had managed to finagle his way around each of these same rules and get the BIE's consent. That was what a flamboyant showman—known for his natty suits, easy smile, and interpersonal skills—could do. But Moses was no Whalen; he wasn't interested in the BIE's rules—or anybody else's, for that matter.

A few months before he took over the World's Fair Corporation, Moses asked if anyone had inquired if "the so-called international body has any real jurisdiction or control." He urged the Executive Committee to confront the BIE about hosting a two-year World's Fair in New York. A two-year gate-receipt formula was an issue, Moses argued, that "can't be ducked, dodged or left open . . . the entire financing and revenues plans are dependant on this decision." Moses was not about to let a group of aging French bureaucrats derail his plans for Flushing Meadow Park.

Publicly, the Fair's planners played it cool. In February 1960 they announced their intention of hosting a two-year exposition, and tried to downplay the potential clash with the BIE. Behind the scenes, Moses was gearing up for a fight. He firmly believed that Whalen's handling of the BIE was one of the many missteps his predecessor had taken. "Grover promised a lot of things [to the BIE] which didn't happen," he told one of his executives, "and the whole thing ended with correspondence between the BIE and the Department of State. The tone of which was far from friendly to say the least. It appears we are heading in the same direction."

And so, with all that in mind, Moses had flown to Paris, but not before he had hired a Wall Street law firm to analyze the BIE's treaty to see if it was applicable to an American Fair. The law firm, Whitman, Ransom & Coulson, reported that the European treaty "had no application at all to a free enterprise exhibition." From that moment on, Moses staked out his positions. He would seek an official sanction from the BIE but wouldn't compromise to get one; if they refused his request, then at least they could look the other way—a "gentleman's agreement," as it were—while he and his team appealed to private corporations of BIE member nations to represent their countries on an "unofficial" basis. And, of course, should they oppose him, then he would treat them like he did anyone—politicians, community activists, private citizens—who got in his way: He would steamroll over them.

It didn't take long for Fair executives to understand that Moses' meeting with the BIE hadn't gone well. Still they hadn't anticipated the BIE's vote—twenty-three to zero (with four abstentions)—to officially sanction the Seattle exhibition. The BIE's statement announcing the vote didn't specifically mention the New York Fair, but it reiterated that no country could host two exhibitions in the same decade, nor could BIE members participate in a non-sanctioned exhibition. The message was clear: Thanks to Moses' ham-fisted handling of the situation, the bureau and its thirty member-states were now effectively boycotting New York and Moses, which would make it difficult for foreign nations to sign up for the Fair.

New York's spin machine then went into overdrive, issuing a rebuttal dripping with condescension and contempt. "We could not possibly obey directives of the BIE and allow it to control a private, free-enterprise fair in New York," read the release, which also called the notion of "a one-year fair in New York . . . impossible." Moses' statement openly, albeit subtly, mocked the BIE's authority, declaring "the absurdity of operating a fair here [in New York] under control from a bureau in Paris," and cast its ruling as inconsistent and arbitrary by recalling how the earlier New York Fair was officially sanctioned yet did not "follow [the BIE's] rules and orders." And in one last—and poetically poignant—dig, the statement noted that signing a BIE treaty "would surely do nothing to promote peace and harmony."

Even though the New York planners downplayed the BIE's boycott, within months America's closest allies, such as Britain, France, and Italy, all abided by the bureau's decision. While publicly nonchalant about the brouhaha—"The Fair is going along nicely and does not require the support of the BIE," Moses told the *New York Times*—behind the scenes it was another story.

In the weeks following the BIE's decision, Moses suggested to one friendly newspaper editor that he should assign a reporter and photographer to the bureau's Paris office to give the public "a visual impression of the organization" that wants to run a New York Fair on a shoestring budget. The picture of the bureau's simple offices, Moses suggested, "would be worth 10,000 words." A short while later, he told William Berns, the vice president of the Fair's PR machine, that "the great BIE explosion proved to be a very wet firecracker lighted by punks . . . I don't underestimate the BIE zombies, but they never get far." Either incapable or unwilling to hold his mouth or his temper, Moses even described the Parisian organization to reporters as "three people living obscurely in a dumpy apartment" and "that bunch of clowns in Paris."

By late 1960 he had instructed his staff that "the BIE announcement was a dead issue." Nevertheless, when Moses was preparing for an upcoming meeting with President Kennedy, Charles Poletti urged him to remind Kennedy to have the State Department "put some pressure" on European ambassadors to ignore the BIE's edict. And almost a year later, Moses was still waging a covert war against Leon Barety, the venerable director of the BIE, suggesting that Poletti "take steps to have our friends" in the organization vote him out of office. The truth is, Moses wanted an official sanction for his World's Fair—he just wasn't willing to do anything to get it. Just as Kopple had predicted, Moses was no diplomat.

Moses' real strengths were his organizational skills and his sheer desire to succeed where the 1939–40 World's Fair had failed. He dedicated himself to avoiding the mistakes made by his predecessor, Whalen, who, Moses thought, had been more interested in creating a wondrous event than a profitable one. If someone had a fantastic idea for a pavilion, Whalen would build it and figure out how to pay for it later; he built no less than twenty pavilions with Fair money and then rented them to exhibitors (often taking a loss). Ironically, Moses—New York's Master Builder—would build precious little himself, just a handful of permanent structures including a ten-thousand-seat outdoor theater, the Hall of Science, and the Port Authority Building, which featured a helipad on the roof and a top-floor restaurant with a panoramic view where VIPs could be entertained. Nor would Moses create a large bureaucracy, staffing his World's Fair Corporation with approximately two hundred employees (Whalen's organization had had 3,700 on the payroll).

Another major decision Moses made was to dismiss the World's Fair Design Committee, which was composed of five well-known architects: Henry Dreyfuss, Emil Praeger, Edward Durrell Stone, Gordon Bunshaft, and Wallace K. Harrison. Traditionally international exhibitions had a central plan to create a sense of architectural unity among the dozens of pavilions. Headed by Harrison, who had been chief designer for the 1939–40 World's Fair, the committee proposed one massive square-mile circular structure—essentially a gigantic doughnut-shaped pavilion—1,800 feet in diameter. Exhibitors would rent "slices" of the doughnut. Moses wouldn't hear of it.

The idea was an old one, actually. It had been utilized in the 1867 Universal Exposition in Paris—"That's how new it was," Moses noted dryly—and designed by no other than Baron Haussmann, the legendary urban planner who rebuilt Paris for Napoleon III and whose life and work Moses had studied closely. The Master Builder not only dismissed the committee's idea—"constipating and stultifying" was Moses' take on the plan—he also derided its members as unimaginative. "Such a single giant doughnut would have discouraged all freedom, originality, experiment, color and boldness in form and design," he later wrote, "precisely the qualities which my avant-garde associates in the architectural field and their friends, the critics, always insist must be given free rein in expositions which will determine the pattern of the future."

Moses declared that his Fair would have no central plan. Instead, pavilion creators were free to build whatever they liked, as long as it adhered to the Fair's building codes, which retired Major General William E. Potter, the Fair's executive vice president and Moses' building czar, rigorously enforced. By building little, Moses thought he could save the Fair money, which meant more funds for his park, $23 million or so of which he would use to build his grand playground—"a new sort of super Central Park," he claimed—that would be his "gift to the city." Moses had a thing for Queens. Maybe because it was the direct link between his Manhattan home and his beloved Long Island, where he would go to relax and swim at the state park beaches that he had created; maybe because compared to the steel-and-glass towers of Manhattan and the old winding streets of Brooklyn, full of historic brownstones and church steeples of every denomination, Queens was something of a blank slate, an empty canvas upon which he could draw his master plan.

He even readily admitted that, to him at least, the post–World's Fair Flushing Meadow Park was, ultimately, the "main attraction." And the park he envisioned would be the centerpiece of a seven-mile stretch of parks that would cut across the borough of Queens, the largest—geographically—of New York's five boroughs. "Parks are the big thing in my life, and I decided to turn this dump into a great park," he told an interviewer in 1964. "When they started planning the 1939 World's Fair, I saw my opportunity. Well, I made the fairgrounds all right but the fine park never materialized, because we didn't have the money." Naturally, with the new Fair's profits, he would build the park himself, rather than hand the money over to city coffers. "With all due respect to City Hall," he noted, "if we hand over our profits to the city government and ask them to make the park, the park will never be built."

Paying for pavilions was out of the question, but one area in which Moses would spend freely would be his beloved arterial highway system, particularly the roads right outside Flushing Meadow Park. Even before he assumed the presidency of the World's Fair Corporation, Moses declared that the network of expressways in Queens and the city's transit system needed an $85 million facelift. He initiated construction on the Clearview Expressway, a six-mile-long stretch of highway that connected the Throg's Neck Bridge (for which Moses allocated $120 million in improvement funds) with the Long Island Expressway; he also worked on the Grand Central Parkway, a six-lane highway that stretched across Queens and led commuters from Long Island to Brooklyn (via the Interboro Parkway). Closer to Flushing Meadow, Moses improved the Van Wyck Expressway, a six-lane connecting highway. All of these roads would lead commuters directly to the World's Fair and the new ballpark, Shea Stadium, that was being built at the same time. By lumping the funds that he spent on these projects with the Fair's accounts, plus the money required for preparing Flushing Meadow Park, along with Lincoln Center (the premier cultural center that was under construction on the Upper West Side), the Moses PR team dubbed the Queens exhibition, with some creative calculating, "the billion-dollar Fair."

Naturally, all the massive construction efforts in such a concentrated area of Queens wreacked havoc on traffic. "New Yorkers are most aware of their Fair in terms of the bumper-to-bumper embolisms the highway expansion program is causing in the borough of Queens," an October 1962 issue of *Time* stated. Queens, thanks to Moses, had become "the world's biggest parking lot."

While Moses concerned himself with his massive construction efforts, his deputies flew around the world drumming up foreign exhibitors for the World's Fair. With major European nations sitting out, Poletti and his team went after private foreign companies, who were not bound by the BIE's bylaws since they were not officially representing their national governments. What's more, by necessity, the World's Fair Corporation would have to look outside of Europe and North America and seek pavilions from nations in South America, Asia, Africa, and the Middle East. The postwar world, Poletti pointed out, had changed dramatically. "A whole host of nations have come into existence since the last World's Fair," he said. After all, New York City—in part thanks to Moses—was the site of the United Nations,* which hadn't existed in 1939. Why shouldn't the Fair reflect the geopolitical reality of its time? It would be the peoples of these nations—many of which were dismissed as "small potatoes" by *Esquire* in an October 1963 piece on the Fair— who made the 1964–65 Flushing Meadow exhibition a truly global and multicultural event, a showcase of the postcolonial world.

Even with the BIE's boycott, some of its members were still planning on exhibiting national pavilions at the World's Fair, including Lebanon, Israel, and the Soviet Union (though under the auspices of its All-Union Chamber of Commerce). The latter was the Fair's earliest triumph, the first nation that Mayor Robert F. Wagner Jr., with the permission of the State Department, invited to New York. The Soviet Union readily accepted. But given the temperature of the Cold War at the time, the

---

* While its Manhattan location was being prepared, the United Nations made its home in Flushing Meadow Park—another way for Moses to funnel funds toward his dream park.

Soviet Union's satellite states' decision to build a pavilion in Flushing Meadow seemed, according to Moses and Poletti, doomed from the start. "I can tell you without reservation that the State Department did not want the Soviet Union at the World's Fair," Poletti recalled years later.

The Soviet Union sought multiple variances to build an immense pavilion at the Fair, threatening to steal the show from the United States, just as they had in Brussels in 1958, according to some observers. Then, after beginning their plans for the Fair, the Russians insisted that America commit to building a pavilion at the proposed Moscow World's Fair of 1967; this tit-for-tat policy was officially known as "reciprocity" and it ruled all cultural exchanges at the time between the Cold War enemies. The United States hesitated but ultimately said they would consider it. That was good enough for the Soviets, and in March 1962 they signed an agreement with the World's Fair Corporation to build a pavilion. But much to Poletti's chagrin, the State Department wanted some say over the exhibit in the Soviet Pavilion. "Governor Poletti . . . has been asked by Washington for information and assurances regarding the USSR exhibit which we do not have," Moses wrote Secretary of State Dean Rusk. "We cannot dictate to the USSR what it shall do in its pavilion."

When in April the Soviets dropped their bid for a Moscow Fair, the State Department demanded the United States be allowed to stage a one-nation exhibition for two six-month periods in the Soviet Union. The Russians balked. Negotiations were now moved from Queens to Washington, DC, where the State Department dealt directly with the Kremlin—exactly what Moses did not want.

On September 29, 1962, Moses got a telegram from the Soviet Foreign Minister informing him that the need for a Soviet pavilion "had lost its force." Moses complained to Rusk that the State Department's "ill-advised" negotiations had damaged the World's Fair's chances of securing a Soviet commitment. His protests were ignored, and just as Moses was about to dispatch Poletti to Moscow in October 1962 to see if a deal could be worked out, the Cuban Missile Crisis unfolded and Poletti was barred from traveling to the Soviet Union. Any hope that the World's Fair could remain above the Cold War was gone.

Meanwhile, one of the world's newest nations, Israel, had signed up for the Fair and showed no signs of yielding to BIE pressure to withdraw. Staunch American allies that they were, the Israelis even informed the State Department that Great Britain had sent diplomatic cables inquiring why the Soviets and Israelis weren't adhering to BIE guidelines. However, political instability would ultimately doom Israeli participation, too. Poletti flew to Tel Aviv in January 1962 and secured a verbal commitment from his hosts. Israeli planners then flew to Queens the following month to pick a site and discuss logistics. But while the delegation was still in New York, they received news that the Israeli parliament had voted against participating in the Fair. Then August came, and officials were told the Israeli government had reconsidered: They would erect a national pavilion at Flushing Meadow after all.

Poletti and his group welcomed the Israelis back with open arms. A new site had to be chosen (their previous one had been rented to another nation), but a deal was quickly sorted out. Israel announced that their World's Fair exhibit would display portions of the Dead Sea Scrolls. A week after the announcement, Poletti was informed that the Israeli government had decided the $2 million earmarked for its pavilion "could be put to better use." Israel was out. "We kept a lamp in the window for Israel for a long time," Poletti said, "but now we've pulled down the shade."

Most of the United States' western European allies abstained from the fair; only Spain, still ruled by fascist dictator General Francisco Franco, and Ireland sent government-sanctioned pavilions. Poletti's International Division managed to secure "official" pavilions from Nationalist China* (President Kennedy barred Communist China's participation), Guinea, India, Indonesia, Japan, Jordan, South Korea, Lebanon, Malaysia, Mexico, Pakistan, the Philippine Republic, Sierra Leone, the Sudan, Thailand, the United Arab Republic, and Venezuela. They also secured "unofficial" pavilions from private companies or industrial organizations from Austria, Denmark, France, Greece, Hong Kong, Morocco, Polynesia, Sweden, Switzerland, and, as a symbolic gesture of its strategic Cold War importance, West Berlin.

---

* Now known as the Republic of Taiwan.

A city physically cut in half by the Berlin Wall, erected on Khrushchev's orders in June 1961, West Berlin was the only city on the planet—aside from host city New York—to have its own pavilion. And Berliners insisted on having the lot directly next to the US Federal Pavilion, wanting to be situated as close as possible to their American protectors, symbolic of the link between the Cold War allies. The Germans, perhaps afraid of being overshadowed by bigger pavilions— they were representing only half a city—wanted to show themselves in the best possible light, literally. Planners for the pavilion personally lobbied Moses to use outdoor lighting of their own design after they found the Fair's uniform streetlamps lacking. "So please, let us install our own lamps," they implored Moses, who refused their request. America might, unlike Germany, be a free country, but in Flushing Meadow things were done the Master Builder's way.

Pavilions would also be built by twenty-three states and twenty-eight representatives from corporate America, perhaps the real star of the Fair. The consumer culture that it preached and that would soon dominate every aspect of American life would be on full display in Queens. Many of the biggest names in American industry, including IBM, Travelers Insurance, RCA (which would display a new novelty for Americans: color television), US Royal Tires, Eastman Kodak, Bell, and DuPont, would all build pavilions. And, of course, no single industry was better represented than Detroit's Big Three automakers.

But it wasn't just corporate America that was looking to the future. NASA, then busy planning the Apollo moon mission, would show off its wares at the US Space Park—a critical chess move in the Cold War–era Space Race with the Soviet Union—including a fifty-one-foot-tall replica of the Saturn V Boattail rocket engines, the crucial stage-one propulsion jets that would help various Apollo missions reach outer space. They would also send a life-size Lunar Excursion Module, or LEM, the actual craft that *Apollo 11* astronauts would use to touch down on the moon's surface just four years after the World's Fair was over. The 1939–40 World's Fair might have put the "World of Tomorrow" on display, but its Fairgoers could only dream of a spaceship that actually landed on the moon; in the early 1960s, NASA was working diligently to make it happen.

As popular as these exhibits would prove to be, one of the most enticing draws was more than 450 years old. Crowds would line up to see the dramatic beauty of Michelangelo's sculpture *La Pietà*, which showed an almost lifelike Virgin Mary cradling a crucified Christ, at the Vatican Pavilion. It was the first time the Renaissance masterpiece was permitted to leave Italy since its creation in 1499, thanks to the personal intervention of Pope John XXIII himself and New York's influential Cardinal Francis Spellman, a close ally of Moses and a powerful player in New York and Washington political circles. When the Master Builder bragged months before opening day that "Michelangelo and Walt Disney are the stars of my show," it wasn't an exaggeration. Instead, Moses left the exaggerations to the World's Fair Corporation's chairman and public relations executive, Thomas J. Deegan, who promised that their exhibition would be "the greatest single event in history."

6.

Thanks to some old-fashioned magic we call "imagination," this Ford Motor Company car will be your time machine for your journey. Carrying you far back to the dawn of life on land and transporting you far out into the future.

—Walt Disney

In early 1960, Walt Disney called a meeting with his executives in his Anaheim, California, office. He had been following the news from the East Coast about the upcoming New York World's Fair and saw an opportunity for his Walt Disney Company, especially its design and development offshoot, WED Enterprises, to expand its horizons and reap a serious windfall at the same time.

"There's going to be a big fair up in New York," Disney told his executives. "All the big corporations in the country are going to be spending a helluva lot of money building exhibits there. They won't know what they want to do. They won't even know *why* they're doing it, except that the other corporations are doing it and they have to keep up with the Joneses." That's where WED Enterprises—billed as an "architectural services and engineering company"—came in.

He wanted the group to make pilgrimages to the boardrooms of the country's biggest corporations—General Motors, Coca-Cola, General Electric, Pepsi-Cola, Ford Motor Company, Travelers Insurance, Kodak, IBM, and AT&T—all the blue-chip firms that were going to spend millions on Fair pavilions, and offer the company's services. Disney saw an opportunity to develop new rides, new concepts, and—with the benefit of corporate subsidies—new technologies. In addition, he would charge corporate clients $1 million for the use of his company's name in their pavilions—his surname had become synonymous with his patented, unique brand of American entertainment. (Ever eager to find new revenue streams, after one company agreed to his usage fee, Disney immediately thought he had lowballed himself.

"Don't you think you might have asked for a little bit more?" he asked the executive in charge of negotiations.)

When a company expressed interest, Disney would personally fly in on his private Gulfstream jet for further discussions. However, none of WED's technicians—Imagineers, they were called—thought that money was the real factor motivating their boss: Disney wanted to establish a theme park east of the Mississippi River. He knew that California's Disneyland was only playing to one-fourth of the country's population, and the New York World's Fair would be his testing ground. "He wanted to see if his kind of entertainment would appeal to the more sophisticated eastern audiences, 'sophisticated' in that that's where the nation's leaders, the decision-makers were based," reported an associate.

Soon after Disney gave his executives their marching orders, Robert Moses came calling. He told Disney that he was saving eight acres of the Fairgrounds with the idea of creating a permanent "children's village." Long after the World's Fair was gone, this Disney-designed attraction would be a major draw in Moses' new Flushing Meadow Park. Not only would Moses build the greatest park in all of the five boroughs, but he would also personally import a piece of Disneyland for the children of New York. Moses would show his critics exactly whose side he was on: *the side of the angels.*

Although not one to share the spotlight—or the credit—Moses wanted Disney to have a headlining role at his Fair. From the get-go the Master Builder and the Master Showman hit it off. Although Moses was thirteen years older than Disney, the two men had characteristics in common. Disney had remade the American pop culture landscape, just as Moses had reshaped the actual landscape of New York City—each according to his own vision. Both had outsize imaginations and egos; both were leaders who surrounded themselves with armies of technicians on whom they could rely; and both were intensely driven workaholics. Disney would bring home scripts, poring over them, one after another, in his living room. He would often awake in the middle of the night, unable to sleep because he had an idea. His wife would wake up to find him doodling a sketch, or muttering to himself about a new design.

But the similarities ended there. Born on Chicago's South Side in 1901, Walter Elias Disney was the fourth child of Elias Disney, a hard-working, demanding, and deeply devout father, who despite his best efforts, never found the fame and fortune he so desired. His mother, Flora, was a nurturing, patient woman who doted on her youngest son. The family didn't have an easy life, moving often throughout the Midwest so that Elias could pursue another failed business venture.

For a time they settled in the Windy City, where—before Walt was born—Elias worked as a carpenter at the 1893 Columbian Exposition. (This biographical detail came in handy decades later when Walt Disney had some labor trouble with the New York–based construction crews working on his Fair pavilions. As he chatted up the hard hats, he casually mentioned how his own father had been a laborer at the Chicago fair; after that, his labor issues were solved.) The Disneys also lived in Kansas City, Missouri, for a time, but the place that Walt would always consider his true home was Marceline, Missouri, a rural railroad town that grew in significance to him the older and more famous he became. The celebrated Main Street, USA, at his Anaheim theme park was his idealized version of Marceline's town center.

Quaint Marceline, where the roads were unpaved when the family moved there in 1906, would be the source of Disney's small-town America ethos, and as he rose from the modest circumstances of his Midwestern childhood to become one of the richest, most famous moguls of his day, he was all too happy to talk about it. He favorably compared the family farm he grew up on to big-city life, recalling specific details of languid summer days spent lolling by trout-filled streams, picking apples or gathering wild grapes and hazelnuts from the nearby woods with his older brother Roy.

It was on the farm and in the surrounding forest where Disney developed a love for animals, sitting and watching rabbits and foxes and the meadowlarks and cardinals perched in their trees. "That is what you experience when you go into the country," he would say. "You escape the everyday world—the strife and struggle. You get out where everything is free and beautiful." But more than anything, Disney pitied "people who

live in cities all their lives . . . they don't have a little hometown. I do."
He would spend the rest of his life trying to recapture the magic of his
years in Marceline. Four decades later, when he was a rich man living the
American Dream, he added a studio/office to his California home: It
was an exact replica of the family barn in Marceline.

An admittedly unexceptional student, Disney was a dreamer and
class clown with two early passions that would stay with him throughout
his life: art and entertainment. Schoolmates remembered him always
with paper and a pencil in his hand. He later indulged in his love of acting
by performing in school plays, portraying Abraham Lincoln in the fifth
grade and even committing the Gettysburg Address to memory. When
the First World War broke out, and his older brothers already overseas,
Disney was swept up in the wave of patriotic fervor and enlisted despite
being underage. He finally got shipped to Europe as an ambulance driver
for the Red Cross, just after the war ended.

He returned home to the United States in 1919, and three years
later created his own cartoon film studio in Kansas City. Although he
struggled early, including having to file for bankruptcy, ever the dreamer,
he chased his vision and created the first cartoon shorts upon which
he would build a global multimedia empire, eventually expanding from
cartoon to feature-length animated films to live-action features to theme
parks—and, of course, all the merchandise that went along with it. By the
1955 opening of Disneyland in Anaheim, California, Walt Disney had
reinvented American pop culture, having built a company that would
entertain millions of people around the world.

In August 1960 Disney flew east to dine with Moses at Jones
Beach and discuss his plans for the World's Fair. Disney let Moses
know that the "children's village" wouldn't be practical or profitable
without a financial commitment from New York State to make it
permanent (such an assurance was not forthcoming). Even so, Moses
urged Disney to get more involved with his Fair. There were corporate
pavilions that needed building, Moses told him, and suggested that
Disney could provide the various companies' bigwigs with what they
needed most: ideas.

Disney, of course, was way ahead of him. On that same East Coast trip, he met with executives at GE, IBM, AT&T, American Gas Association, and General Dynamics. By the end of the year, WED had secured a contract with GE worth $50,000 for research alone; more money would be provided to design and actually build the pavilion. But Disney harbored bigger ambitions, the fulfillment of which required lasting relationships with deep-pocketed corporations. He had become obsessed with urban planning—Robert Moses' area of expertise—and sought to build not only a new theme park, but also an ideal city, a futuristic idyll where his employees could live—a location without pollution or urban sprawl that combined the cultural opportunities of an urban center with the small-town community of his youth.

While making plans for the World's Fair, Disney cryptically asked one of his workers, "How would you like to work on a future city?" The employee didn't know what to say, and Disney didn't go into further detail. But he already had a name for this new city: Experimental Prototype Community of Tomorrow, or EPCOT. What it sounded like, more than anything, was a permanent World's Fair, one completely of Disney's own making. Now those ideas and designs could be tested on the millions of Fairgoers who would flock to Flushing Meadow Park.

There was one particular sophisticated concept that Disney wanted to try out at the World's Fair. It was his own brand of robotic technology: life-size and lifelike automated mannequins that could move, speak, stand, or sing, thanks to an internal recording device. He called his creations "Audio-Animatronics," a phrase he had trademarked. It was a concept that Disney had been mulling over since the early 1950s, and for the global audience of the World's Fair he resurrected the idea.

The Ford Motor Company hired Disney to design its Magic Skyway ride, a twelve-minute journey back in time. In a stroke of marketing genius, the company chose the Fair to introduce its latest model, the Ford Mustang, which would go on to become one of the best-selling automobiles in American history. Millions of adult Fairgoers—each a prospective customer—would get a free ride in a Mustang convertible as they were propelled by a conveyor belt–like device, gliding past scenes of

Audio-Animatronic brontosauruses, tyrannosaurs, woolly mammoths, and cavemen. Audiences were dazzled by these special effects—far superior to most Hollywood special effects at the time.

The Magic Skyway even had a Neanderthal hero—"the inventor of the wheel," according to the ride's narrator, Disney himself, who informed his captive audiences, "The wheel gave man a new freedom. Now he could leave the caves behind and travel on to seek his fortune in the wide, wide world." The suggestion that such a journey should be undertaken in a Ford automobile went without saying.

For General Electric's World's Fair pavilion, Disney designed a $10 million Carousel of Progress, which featured an Audio-Animatronic family—complete with a cute dog—inspired by Thornton Wilder's *Our Town*. Fairgoers would watch various decades of American history play out: the 1880s, the 1920s, the 1940s, and up to the present-day 1960s. The auditorium itself shifted—like a carousel—and with each passing decade, the family's life was made progressively easier thanks to ever-improving household products (like the ones GE made). It was typical Disney: a nostalgic look back at a simpler time, brought to you via state-of-the-art technology and all while hawking his corporate clients' products as you were being entertained. "There was more of Walt in 'the Carousel of Progress' than anything else," said one WED Imagineer.

But when Disney informed the GE vice president in charge of the pavilion about his concept, the VP suggested that the company would come up with a different approach. After all, he told Disney, what would a company like GE that sold technological gadgets want with a show that was based on nostalgia for simpler times? Disney flew into a rage. "I spent my whole life telling stories with nostalgia," he shouted, "and this is the way you communicate with people!" He even called his legal department and told them to see if there was any way to terminate the contract.

Although things were quickly sorted out, GE executives would fly to Anaheim occasionally to check in on Disney's progress—and like Moses, he didn't appreciate the oversight. At one meeting, he stood at the head of a conference table and delivered a blunt message. "All right, gentleman, what I want you to do is go down to the Coral Room and have a good lunch. Then I want you to go back to Burbank Airport and get in your Grumman Gulfstream and fly back east where you came from and stay there until I've got something I want you to see. Then, I'll call *you*. Thank you, gentlemen." He then turned around and walked out of the room. Moses couldn't have done it better himself.

It was Moses, in fact, who made it his personal mission to find a place at the World's Fair for one of Disney's pet projects, the Hall of the Presidents. On a trip to New York, Disney had shown Moses a slide presentation of his idea—an exhibit of Audio-Animatronic American presidents. Moses was sold. He was convinced that the Hall of Presidents should go in the US Federal Pavilion. Disney had the same idea. He had even flown down to Washington, DC, with Charles Luckman, the architect of the pavilion, to meet with the Commerce Department and sell them on the idea, but they didn't bite. Moses used his personal influence to convince Undersecretary of Commerce Franklin Roosevelt Jr. to change the department's mind, but he got nowhere, too. Moses then tried to convince Disney that WED should construct its own pavilion for the exhibit, but Disney didn't want to foot the bill. Undaunted, Moses pressed on, believing that the exhibit was "too important to the Fair and to Walt Disney to drop this without exhausting all possibilities."

Then in April 1962, while hosting Moses at Disneyland to review progress, Disney asked Moses if he would like to meet Abraham Lincoln. It seems Disney hadn't completely forsaken his Hall of Presidents concept, devoting a group of Imagineers to work on an Audio-Animatronic version of American's sixteenth president. He quickly ushered Moses into a secret room in his studio's Animation Building, and there a robotic President Lincoln offered his hand in friendship. Moses was completely astonished. "I won't open the Fair without that exhibit!" he shouted. Disney said it would take his team of Imagineers years to perfect Lincoln. It didn't matter; Moses wanted Lincoln at his Fair, and no was not an option.

Eventually Moses convinced the State of Illinois—Lincoln's and Disney's home state—to host a pavilion entitled "The Land of Lincoln."

It would take months of intense work from a small army of Imagineers and dozens of failures before it worked properly; Disney's team would complain that all the traffic due to Moses' highway construction in Queens contributed mightily to the machine's delay. But eventually the Audio-Animatronics would meet Disney's high expectations. "I'd like to not be able to tell them from real people," he said.

It would also take a unique financial arrangement between Moses, Disney, and the State of Illinois to ultimately bring the exhibit to the World's Fair, an arrangement that would eventually blow up in the Master Builder's face. When it came time to negotiate a fee, knowing how badly Moses wanted the robotic Lincoln at his Fair, Disney played hardball with the Illinois legislature, which was allocating the funds for its state pavilion. Disney wanted $600,000 just for Lincoln; more money would be needed to create the entire pavilion. The legislature balked. Although Moses pleaded with Disney, the Imagineer-in-Chief wouldn't budge. He eventually made multiple concessions on various fees for the pavilion and secretly paid the legislature a $250,000 subsidy—an arrangement that no other exhibitor was offered. It worked. On November 19, 1963—the one hundredth anniversary of the Gettysburg Address—Moses and Disney flew to Springfield, Illinois, to announce the Lincoln exhibit beside Governor Otto Kerner. Disney promised a skeptical Illinois audience that Lincoln would seem alive, "maybe more alive than I am."

The last ride that Disney created at the 1964–65 World's Fair was for a special exhibit in the Pepsi Pavilion that was sponsored by UNICEF, the United Nations children's charity. With opening day less than a year away, Disney accepted the commission. While his crews were busy finishing their creations of the Ford, GE, and Illinois pavilions, he gathered his WED staff and told them that he had one more project for them: a "little boat ride that maybe we can do."

Using the same Audio-Animatronic technology as his Abe Lincoln, Disney's concept dovetailed seamlessly with UNICEF's mission and the international flavor of the Fair. On this latest ride, Fairgoers would sail around the globe in a small boat, listening to a collection of pintsize singing puppets of different races and ethnicities, representing the children of the world. At first he envisioned the puppets simultaneously singing their various national anthems, but that didn't work out. He then commissioned Robert and Richard Sherman, the songwriting brothers who had worked on *Chitty Chitty Bang Bang* and other Disney musicals, to create a tune that could be sung in multiple languages—something simple and catchy. During his conversations with the Shermans, Disney remarked, "It's a small world after all."

The Shermans seized on the phrase; it became the name of both the song and the ride, and in a uniquely Disney fashion, it expressed the Fair's lofty goal of "Peace Through Understanding"—and indeed racial integration—in a child-friendly manner. Moses might have been in charge of the World's Fair and its public face, as far as New Yorkers were concerned, but it was Disney and his fantastical machinations that the crowds would pay to see.

7

*You cannot legislate tolerance by constitutional amendment or statute
... social equality is of slow growth and rests on mutual esteem and
respect, not on force.*

—Robert Moses, 1943

Despite the racial goodwill of Disney's "It's a Small World" ride, by
February 1962 Robert Moses and the World's Fair had a race problem. For more than a year, the Urban League of Greater New York had
been lobbying the World's Fair Corporation behind the scenes to hire
more African Americans and Puerto Ricans to the staff of the World's
Fair Corporation. By the Urban League's count, there were exactly
two African Americans among the Fair's staff, both secretaries. After
being largely ignored by Moses, in June 1961 Dr. Edward Lewis, the
Urban League's executive director, went public with the story, complaining to the *New York Times* that he had been getting the "runaround"
from Moses. This was exactly the kind of publicity that Moses detested:
WORLD'S FAIR URGED TO HIRE NEGROES blared the *Times'* headline.

The Urban League again accused Moses of "an apparent pattern of
discrimination" at the Fair. "Our efforts have resulted in conferences and
correspondence but no action," league president Frederick W. Richmond
told the *Times*. "We consider this an intolerable situation and will take
whatever steps are necessary to make the World's Fair a legitimate
showcase of American democracy." In response to the story, the Master
Builder invited Richmond to discuss the issue with him over lunch at
Flushing Meadow the following month.

The meeting, it seemed, went well. The civil rights group asked Moses
to add more African Americans to the World's Fair's board of directors—a
collection of New York luminaries such as David Rockefeller, Time Inc.
publisher and owner Henry Luce, and Dr. Ralph J. Bunche, the Queens-
born United Nations diplomat and first African American to win the
Nobel Peace Prize for brokering the 1949 armistice between Israel and

its Arab neighbors. The next day Moses had his right-hand man Charles Poletti follow up with the Urban League to see if its leaders "really want two additional directors added to our board" and told Poletti "to assure them of full participation." Although he complained that there were already "too many directors," Moses chose one—Lawrence "Judge" Pierce, a former Brooklyn DA turned New York City Deputy Police Commissioner—from a list of four African-American candidates. However, by the end of 1961, the World's Fair Corporation's executive staff, who actually organized and planned the Fair, was still 100 percent white.

The Master Builder had come under fire from civil rights activists before. In fact, he had a long history of opposing the aims of such groups—"professional integrationists," he labeled them. As a delegate to the 1938 New York State Constitutional Convention, Moses wrote to lawmakers arguing against a proposed antidiscrimination amendment, claiming that the civil rights law would only "fan the very flames you seek to quench. Moreover, you will encourage scamps and professional agitators to blackmail not only bigots but those who cannot afford to comply with impossible laws."

Such antidiscrimination laws, Moses stated in a lengthy 1943 *New York Times Magazine* piece, were meant to do nothing more than "amuse politicians, fool the minorities and make the angels weep"; he also wrote disapprovingly of "Negro leaders who will accept nothing but complete social equality." Instead, Moses advocated incremental changes to the social order, and held up Booker T. Washington—who thought that blacks should concentrate on education, securing jobs, and basic political rights but set social equality aside for the time—as an example of the kind of leadership to which the blacks should look. (Washington's famous "Atlanta compromise" speech, which laid out his philosophy, was announced at the 1895 Cotton States and International Exposition in Atlanta.) "The truth is that the path to fair and honorable treatment of our colored citizens," Moses advised, "is a long and thorny one to be traveled slowly and surely with wise and patient leadership." Moses, the impatient modernist who was forever dreaming of new public works projects to build—moving earth, rock, men, and steel according to his vision—advocated a sedate, cautious philosophy toward improving the living conditions of black New Yorkers.

And it was exactly such a conservative, wait-and-see approach to race relations that had run its course by the early 1960s. Now Moses' anti–civil rights stances were tainting the Fair's reputation, a major public relations faux pas for an international exhibition—funded with taxpayers' dollars—that proclaimed to be a symbol of "Peace Through Understanding" for the entire world.

The Urban League knew that the Fair would be a job bonanza. People would be needed to work the exhibits, staff the restaurants, man the ticket booths, and serve as security guards. Most importantly, thousands of good-paying construction jobs would be created. Flushing Meadow Park and its surrounding environs would be one massive construction site for years to come. The Urban League wanted Moses to ensure that the companies involved, both foreign and domestic, respected New York State's antidiscrimination laws. It also wanted to force the building trade unions to hire African Americans and Puerto Ricans—a key strategy of many civil rights organizations' campaigns in the North. However, even Moses' power had limits, and he was loath to pick a fight with the very unions on whom he was depending to build and maintain the structures of the World's Fair. "We would have to attempt to force the trade unions to change their present methods, whatever they may be," he wrote to Poletti. "We could not possibly succeed in this, and . . . we have plenty of problems with the unions."

Columnist James A. Wechsler of the *New York Post,* then a strongly liberal newspaper, slammed Moses for his laissez-faire stance, declaring that "the notion that all employment at the Fair should be left to the vagaries of private business and old-line unionism is a monumental abdication of responsibility." The world will be watching the Fair, predicted Wechsler—no fan of Moses—and "there will be harsh questions asked about its hiring policy."

Moses dismissed the *Post* piece—"completely malicious and inaccurate and which of course we shall not answer"—and clarified the Fair's hiring practices in a memo to his staff the next day. "There is absolutely no discrimination of any kind in hiring help by the Fair, nor is there or will there be any minority quota political system of hiring," he wrote. "As to higher positions, we appoint on merit, not on pressure from any groups whatsoever involving racial, religious, color, political, sex or other extraneous considerations. . . . We don't go looking for directors of Polish, German, Italian, Greek or any other racial or national extraction." As usual, when confronted with external pressure or accused of irresponsibility, Moses attacked his critics, claimed moral indignation, and prepared to wait out the controversy. "My firm conviction is that this agitation . . . will blow over very soon," he promised.

He was wrong. America was changing and the slow growth of public support for civil rights was accelerating. In postwar America, the national movement for black freedom was making an impact upon the nation's collective conscience, thanks to a new generation of leaders as divergent as the Reverend Martin Luther King Jr. president of the Southern Christian Leadership Conference, or SCLC; Black Nationalist leader Malcolm X (who lived just a mile or so from Flushing Meadow Park); James L. Farmer Jr. the cofounder of the Congress for Racial Equality, or CORE; and John Lewis, of the Student Nonviolent Coordinating Committee, or SNCC. By the early 1960s, the movement had organized tens of thousands of anonymous and ordinary African Americans who marched, protested, and resisted the nation's racist policies through civil disobedience, even as they were murdered and brutalized by their fellow citizens for wanting the same protection that American law afforded their white neighbors. And they weren't alone: White Americans—clergymen, nuns, rabbis, college radicals, housewives—were joining the fight.

Moses was now on the wrong side of history. His "separate but equal" position was essentially no different than that of the bloc of Southern segregationist Democratic senators, including Senator Strom Thurmond (of South Carolina), Senator Richard B. Russell (of Georgia), and Senator Fulbright (of Arkansas, and Moses' main senatorial adversary, who tried to kill federal funding for the Fair in 1960). In 1955 this trio, along with sixteen other senators and eighty-two members of the House of Representatives, signed the Southern Manifesto—Russell, in fact, wrote the final draft—attacking the 1954 Brown v. Board of Education decision of the US Supreme Court, which had declared the South's racist "separate but equal" Jim Crow laws unconstitutional.

It didn't matter that Moses actually believed in "separate but equal"; that is, he thought it could work, and sometimes because of his efforts, it actually did. As far back as the late 1930s, Moses had created no less than eleven monumental public pools with New Deal funds across the city's five boroughs. He built two specifically for the then–racially divided Harlem: one in the primarily Italian immigrant neighborhood of East Harlem (Jefferson Park Pool) and one in the heart of predominately black Central Harlem (Colonial Park Pool)—built with "Negro labor," Moses proudly bragged to the twenty-five thousand people who turned out for the elaborate opening-day ceremony. Each pool featured the same art deco architecture and amenities that served thousands of inner-city residents, young and old alike, desperate for recreational facilities. This was Moses' practical separate-but-equal solution to the racial problems of 1930s Uptown New York.

On occasion, and in his own way, Moses would advocate for the victims of discrimination, such as in 1939 when he gave a group of lectures at Harvard University on politics. After discussing the twin pools he had built in Harlem, Moses admitted that "a little honest indignation" was in order for the working folks at the bottom of the social order, whom he described as "Lifschitz the sweatshop worker," "Baccigaluppo the seasonal day laborer," and "Taliaferro the urban Negro, who can't get into a union." What Moses seemed to be confessing in his lectures was that, in his opinion, there was only so much government could—or *should*—do to rectify such social ills.

Two years after the Harvard lectures, Moses and his beloved mentor Al Smith resigned from the Society for the Preservation and Encouragement of Barber Shop Quartet Singing after the organization disqualified a New York all-black barbershop quartet from advancing to the national contest's finals due to their race.

Moses continued to pursue his own brand of "separate but equal," pushing the Metropolitan Life Insurance Company to build the Riverton

---

* Since renamed the Jackie Robinson Pool.

Houses in Harlem, a "blacks-only" middle-class housing development that opened in 1947 (partly, no doubt, to offset the criticism of the company's Stuyvesant Town "whites-only" apartments). Not long after the passage of the Housing Act of 1949, Moses secured more Title I funds for a new project: Lenox Terrace, a $20 million luxury housing complex in the heart of Harlem, designed for upper-middle-class residents. The complex didn't open until 1958 due to financial problems; Moses had to personally intercede to solidify the finances when banks balked at lending money for upscale housing in Harlem.

A decade later, after attracting an eclectic mix of professionals and artists, Lenox Terrace would be declared "Harlem's most fashionable address" by the *New York Times*. "The fiction that the only people who will stay in Harlem are those who can't move and those who are provided for in the lowest rental public housing dies a hard death," Moses crowed at the time. Neither project would have ever happened were it not for the Master Builder. However, at the end of the day, both housing complexes—intentionally or not—perpetuated a separation of the races, keeping whites and blacks on either side of the entrenched "color line."

By April 1962, with the job discrimination scandal still in the papers, Moses caught a break for a few days when the World's Fair publicity machine announced that Pope John XXXIII had granted permission to send Michelangelo's Renaissance masterpiece *La Pietà* to Queens, where it would become the centerpiece of the Vatican Pavilion. Although Moses caught a further break when criticism of the pope in the Italian press for entrusting a priceless treasure to uncultured Americans helped extend the story's lifespan a few extra days, the Fair's race problem wouldn't go away. Harlem's congressman, Adam Clayton Powell Jr., requested a federal investigation into the Fair's hiring practices. Moses could ignore such politicians, but he could not discount criticism from within the Fair itself. The most prominent African American associated with the World's Fair, Bunche, explained to the *New York Amsterdam News* that he planned "to thoroughly investigate these charges and to see that something is done about it."

Bunche was a voice that Moses had to heed, so he instructed Poletti to set up a meeting with the Nobel laureate, even as he lamented the fact that if outside groups started dictating hiring practices at the Fair, he feared a Pandora's box of political problems with exhibitors and unions (which were notoriously racist in their hiring policies). "There will be not a single exhibit of any state south of the Mason and Dixon line if we begin to tell them whom they must employ," worried Moses. "How can we tell the Arab nations whom to employ, or the Russians? Can we tell them we find no Jews among their employees and that they must employ some?"

But Moses' fears were unfounded. In April, after Bunche lodged his complaint—and after the Urban League threatened to bring their grievances to the White House and New York governor Nelson A. Rockefeller—the World's Fair Corporation hired Dr. George H. Bennett, an African-American educator who worked at the UN and had international connections. The sky didn't fall, and no geopolitical fracas ensued. Instead, Bennett went on to become a key member of Poletti's all-important International Division.

What made Moses' adversarial reaction to legitimate civil rights critiques so difficult to understand was that it contradicted other projects he was undertaking while preparing the Fair. While being pilloried in the press for the lack of diversity among his staff, just ten miles away on the long-abandoned Jamaica Race Track in Jamaica, Queens—then the third-largest African-American neighborhood in the five boroughs—Moses was putting the finishing touches on Rochdale Village, the largest integrated housing complex in the world. "One of my babies," he referred to it fondly.

Moses had earmarked the defunct Race Track in the center of Queens for redevelopment by the mid-1950s. From the start, the site had one huge advantage, according to the Master Builder: It had "no people to move." Rochdale Village was conceived as an affordable integrated cooperative for New Yorkers, and to bring it to fruition, Moses teamed with his old ally, Abraham Kazan, the president of the United Housing Foundation.

The pair was the oddest of political couples. Kazan was an idealistic labor leader whose radical left-wing politics, somewhere between anarchism and socialism, were reflective of his humble Ukrainian origins. Yet, he and Moses had collaborated on several successful housing cooperatives since 1950. They also had a genuine and abiding admiration for one another. Moses, never one to bestow praise lightly, deemed Kazan a "working genius," while Kazan admired the Master Builder for his loyalty. "If you got Moses to be on your side," a Kazan associate recalled, "you knew that you didn't need anything more than a handshake to know that Moses would be with you through thick and thin."

Still, due to Rochdale Village's biracial makeup, banks and builders shied away. That didn't stop Moses, who with his usual single-minded focus, steered the project to fruition by personally lobbying financiers and Governor Rockefeller for funding. "Rochdale Village owes its existence to Robert Moses," Kazan later said.

In December 1963, just four months before the opening day of the World's Fair, Moses unveiled Rochdale Village and its fourteen-story buildings (twenty in total) with 5,800 apartments. Soon Rochdale Village's population was 80 percent white (the vast majority Jewish) and 20 percent African American. Quick to show off his vision of what integrated housing could and should look like, Moses planned bus tours from the World's Fair to the site for international and domestic politicians and VIPs.

In 1966 the *New York Times* would rave about Moses' handiwork in a piece titled WHEN BLACK AND WHITE LIVE TOGETHER. While Congress debated "opening housing laws" aimed at ending the kind of discriminatory housing practiced in northern cities such as Chicago—a discussion that threatened to rip the Democratic Party apart—Rochdale Village could legitimately be held up as an example of what integrated housing could achieve. Despite his conservative racial beliefs—and unwillingness to challenge the hiring policies of New York's unions—Moses led the way for publicly financed integrated housing, proving that if nothing else, he was a man whose work was often ahead of his time.

8

We preach freedom around the world, and we mean it . . . but are we to say to the world . . . that we have no second-class citizens except Negroes; that we have no class or caste system, no ghettoes, no master race except with respect to Negroes?

—President John F. Kennedy, June 11, 1963

If I die, it will be in a good cause. I've been fighting for America just as much as the soldiers in Vietnam.

—Medgar Evers

By the end of 1962, President John F. Kennedy had reason to celebrate. Although the 1964 presidential election was more than a year away, he was riding high in the polls, leading potential Republican rivals by thirty points or more. After the dark days of the Cuban Missile Crisis, Kennedy was contemplating ways to reduce Cold War tensions by having the United Kingdom, the Soviet Union, and the United States sign a treaty limiting nuclear testing. Ever the cautious and pragmatic politician, domestically he moved to solidify his position with one hostile constituency, the business community, even as he kept a friendly one, African Americans, at arm's length.

The country was enjoying a buoyant economy with low unemployment and nearly nonexistent inflation, but Wall Street was distrustful of Kennedy. After his appearance at the ground-breaking ceremony for the World's Fair's US Federal Pavilion at Flushing Meadow Park, the president gave a speech to the Economic Club of New York at the Waldorf-Astoria in Manhattan, where he pledged a significant cut in federal and corporate taxes to spur the economy to even greater heights.

Introducing pro-business tax reform one year prior to his reelection bid was a politically astute move. Meanwhile, although Kennedy had pledged his support for civil rights during the 1960 presidential election—as did his Republican opponent, Vice President Richard M.

Nixon—he moved slowly on the issue once in office. On the campaign trail, Kennedy had promised to sign an executive order ending segregation in federally subsidized housing with "a stroke of a pen." But he had waited until November 1962 to issue the order—and only after civil rights activists had mailed dozens of pens to the White House reminding him of his pledge—and even then it was a watered-down version, which left many of his supporters disappointed. "He had at this point, I think, a terrible ambivalence about civil rights," said historian and Kennedy advisor Arthur M. Schlesinger Jr.

Kennedy was all too aware of the bloc of Southern Democratic senators who were militantly opposed to any substantive civil rights measures. The last thing he wanted going into the 1964 campaign was to incite rebellion within his own party. Besides, at the time, Kennedy's advisors told him he could afford to be prudent: One aide stated that African Americans were "pretty much at peace," and while civil rights could be explosive on a local level and were not necessarily relegated to the South—as Robert Moses' problems in New York showed—the issue ranked extraordinarily low in national polls.

In fact, civil rights was so low on the president's domestic agenda that he neglected to even mention the topic during his State of the Union address in January 1963. Louis Martin, a Chicago newspaper publisher, Democratic National Committee member, and one of Kennedy's closest African-American advisors, summed up how many civil rights leaders felt about Kennedy. "The fact is, the President cares more about Germany than about Negroes, he thinks it's more important," Martin complained.

Some civil rights leaders were even considering making new alliances with liberal Republicans such as New York's Governor Nelson A. Rockefeller, Senator Jacob K. Javitz, and Senator Keating—all strong supporters of civil rights, the World's Fair, and Moses. Rockefeller was already sharpening his attacks on Kennedy, as he prepared another run for the White House in 1964. During a February 1963 speech celebrating President Lincoln's birthday, the governor criticized Kennedy for appointing segregationist judges to Southern benches.

Kennedy was infuriated. "Rockefeller gets away with murder. What's he doing for Negroes in New York?" he grilled a *Time* journalist who knew the Republican governor during an informal White House dinner the next night. However, the placid political climate would erupt into a national crisis and force his hand. The trouble had begun in earnest in September 1962, when the Fifth Circuit Court of the United States of Appeals ruled that James Meredith, an African-American Air Force veteran, was allowed to register at the University of Mississippi in Jackson. Meredith had first attempted to enroll in January—after being inspired by President Kennedy's inaugural speech. Despite the court order, it took federal agents, national guardsmen, and high-level negotiations between Mississippi's racist Democratic governor Ross Barnett, Robert Kennedy, and President Kennedy himself to get Meredith enrolled at "Ole Miss" the following month.

The president seemed as shocked by the turn of events as anyone else. He asked Martin, point blank, where young blacks were getting these new ideas from. Martin quickly shot back, "From you! You're lifting the horizons of Negroes." The notion certainly wasn't what Kennedy was hearing from his white advisors, and from a purely political viewpoint, he was anxious to put the civil rights issue—and any talk of a civil rights bill—on the backburner. "We go up [to Congress] with that and they'll piss all over us," he complained to aides.

With the election of Alabama governor George C. Wallace that same month, Kennedy's race problems were about to boil over. As a circuit judge, Wallace had been something of a moderate Democrat, at least by Southern standards. However, after the Supreme Court's 1954 Brown v. Board of Education ruling—and more importantly, after his losing bid to become governor in 1958—Wallace reinvented himself as a hard-line segregationist, running a race-baiting campaign with the backing of the Ku Klux Klan. At his inaugural address in front of the Alabama state capitol building in January 1963, Wallace took an unequivocal stance in support of the Southern way of life. "I draw the line in the dust and toss the gauntlet before the feet of tyranny, and I say segregation *now*, segregation *tomorrow*, segregation *forever!*" The fact that Governor Wallace stood in the exact spot where a century earlier Jefferson Davis was sworn in as the president of the doomed Confederacy was probably not lost on the adoring Dixie crowd.

Wallace was the anti-Kennedy: short, pugnacious (a onetime boxer), and a skilled orator who knew how to work up a crowd; a lawyer who hailed from rural Alabama and who walked and talked like one of his "good ol' boy" constituents. He had served in the Air Force in World War II, flying bombing missions over Japan for General Curtis LeMay—the same trigger-happy general who thought Kennedy had sold out America's interest by negotiating with Khrushchev during the Cuban Missile Crisis.* To Northern Democratic politicians like Kennedy (or to unabashed urbanites like Moses) Wallace and his racist demagoguery were an embarrassment. But without Southern Democrats like Wallace (and the voters they represented) a Northern Democrat like Kennedy couldn't get elected to the White House, which is why the civil rights struggle in early 1963—one year before the Fair's debut—was not a priority for the chief executive.

And leaders like the Reverend Martin Luther King Jr. knew it. King complained that 1962 was "the year that civil rights was displaced as the dominant issue in domestic politics. . . . The issue no longer commanded the conscience of the nation." What's more, King and others knew that to move their cause to the forefront of America's consciousness, something needed to happen, something dubbed Project C. The C stood for Connor, as in Eugene "Bull" Connor, the Commissioner of Public Safety in Birmingham, Alabama, who embodied "the dark spirit of Birmingham, the hellish side of Birmingham," according to one native Alabaman.

A dedicated racist and segregationist, Connor would drive around in a white tank—a heavily armored police car—to instill fear in Birmingham's black populace. Under his tyrannical rule, the Ku Klux Klan had a free hand to intimidate, assault, and murder blacks. In 1961, when the first wave of Freedom Riders made it to Birmingham, their bus was surrounded by local Klansman. Connor made sure the cross-burners

---

* In his failed bid for the 1968 Democratic nomination for president, Wallace would select LeMay as his running mate, forming a sort of dynamic duo of right-wing fanaticism.

had a solid fifteen minutes to beat the riders before his police arrived to break up the melee. His reactionary take on civil rights was hardly out of the mainstream; like FBI director J. Edgar Hoover, Connor thought that the civil rights movement was a Communist plot. But King and his colleagues knew that they could use the Birmingham boss's racism to turn popular opinion against the South. "[Connor] believed that he would be the state's most popular politician if he treated the black violently, bloodily, and sternly," said Wyatt Walker, a King aide, who helped plan the Project C campaign. "We knew that the psyche of the white redneck was such that he would inevitably do something to help our cause."

Walker's plan was simple enough: The SCLC would organize a boycott of Birmingham's downtown business district in hopes of desegregating the whites-only establishments. In April 1963 the first protesters marched, but Connor stayed his hand. Then, on May 3, the SCLC began sending hundreds of youths, mostly teenagers from local high schools, on a peaceful march to the downtown area. As the kids marched and chanted "We Shall Overcome," Connor let his police loose. They went on a rampage, assaulting the protesters with nightsticks while trained K-9 unit German shepherds mauled them and the local fire department unleashed high-velocity water cannons, powerful enough to strip bark off trees. It was a savage attack, orchestrated and perpetuated by local authorities, upon hundreds of youths who only wanted their right to frequent Birmingham's business district; and, as King and his aides had hoped, the bloodbath was captured by television cameras. The images of Connor's police dogs ripping into unarmed young marchers showed the country—and the world—a side of the United States that most Americans didn't want to acknowledge.

They certainly weren't images that helped Moses or the World's Fair any. Exhibitors from non-Western nations no doubt struggled to reconcile "the land of the free and home of the brave" that sought to contain Soviet Communism, even at the risk of a nuclear holocaust, in order to remake the world over in its own image, with a country where police attacked children without remorse. America's enemies were taking note, too. "We have the impression that American authorities both cannot and do not wish to stop outrages by racists," crowed Radio Moscow.

By now even the civic leaders of Birmingham had had enough of Connor and his terrorist tactics; just weeks after the launch of Project C, the city's business leaders decided to desegregate Birmingham's shopping district. However, for some African Americans it was a case of too little, too late; peaceful disobedience had run its course. The sight of defenseless children being mowed down by power-hoses, attacked by baton-swinging police, and mangled by German shepherds was the final straw. Hundreds of indignant blacks rioted, attacking police and white Birmingham pedestrians with glass bottles and rocks, while others torched the whites-only businesses that civil rights leaders wanted desegregated.

To separatists like Malcolm X, the rejection of King's Gandhian nonviolent principles by Birmingham blacks was exactly what he was hoping for. "The lesson of Birmingham," the militant Nation of Islam preacher said, "is that the Negroes have lost their fear of the white man's reprisals and will react with violence, if provoked. This could happen anywhere in the country today."

It was becoming apparent to the Kennedys that they didn't have a handle on what was happening on the streets of black America. If the president and his advisors hadn't noticed Louis E. Lomax's 1962 book, *The Negro Revolt*, the president, at least, took notice of novelist James Baldwin's lengthy *New Yorker* essay "Letter from a Region in My Mind." The following year it was turned into a best-selling book, *The Fire Next Time*, and landed Baldwin on the cover of *Time*, just as all hell was breaking loose in Birmingham.

For a time the mainstream media considered Baldwin the voice of black America, and anyone who wanted to understand black America read him. This included Moses, who sent copies of the book to a dozen friends. Moses, however, had a different take than the president. "A strange, bitter, disturbing and essentially pathetic diatribe, one of those hoarse, out of the depths hymns of hate," he wrote to his close friend Samuel "Judge" Rosenman, a former speechwriter for Franklin

Roosevelt—he coined the term "New Deal"—and now a member of the World's Fair's Executive Committee, who agreed.

Robert F. Kennedy was impressed enough with Baldwin that after meeting him at a Washington, DC, event he invited the thirty-eight-year-old Harlem native to his family's Park Avenue South apartment in Manhattan and asked him to bring other black intellectuals to discuss the problems of northern ghettos. On May 21 Baldwin brought actress Lena Horne, crooner/activist Harry Belafonte, playwright Lorraine Hansberry, and young Freedom Rider Jerome Smith, who, after suffering beatings by Alabama police, wasn't the least bit intimidated by the attorney general. "I want to vomit being in the same room with you," he told the president's younger brother.

Kennedy, growing defensive and angry, mentioned how his Irish immigrant great-grandfather came to America with nothing and how his grandfather faced discrimination back in Boston; now his brother was the leader of the Free World. The comparison between the plight of the American Irish and black Americans enraged Baldwin. "Your family has been here for three generations and your brother's on top," the novelist retorted. "My family has been here a lot longer than that, and we're on the bottom. That's the heart of the problem, Mr. Kennedy."

But it was Horne, the elegant and beautiful singer-actress, who delivered the most shocking message to Kennedy when he tried to defend his brother's administration. "If *you* are so proud of your record, Mr. Attorney General," she said, "you go up to Harlem into those churches and barber shops and pool halls, and *you* tell the people. We ain't going to do it because *we* don't want to get shot."

After two hours, the meeting ended when the guests walked out. Kennedy, not one who liked to be challenged, was furious. True to his ruthless reputation, he degraded Baldwin to his aides for being gay and requested FBI files on the entire group. But despite his petulant reaction, Kennedy must have realized the racial problems in the North were just as complex, if not more so, as in the South. Certainly, Kennedy must have begun to wonder, if his celebrated guests were this angry—and they were successful by any conceivable standard—how must the average man (and woman) on the streets of Harlem feel? It was a question that the White House would eventually have to answer.

In the meantime, the situation in the South continued to unravel. James Hood and Vivian Malone, two African-American students, had won a court order in May to register for a class at the University of Alabama at Tuscaloosa—the alma mater of Governor Wallace, who had promised during his 1962 campaign that he would personally "stand in the schoolhouse door" if the federal government attempted to desegregate Alabama's university system, as they had in neighboring Mississippi.

True to his word, on the morning of June 11, Governor Wallace stood beside a podium in front of the main entrance of the administration building, where Hood and Malone hoped to register for their classes (clinical psychology and accounting, respectively). This would be Wallace's last stand. With the television cameras rolling, Deputy Attorney General Nicholas Katzenbach, backed by a contingent of national guardsman, sought assurances from the governor that the students would be allowed to register since, he said, "after all, they merely want an education in this great university." Wallace then read a four-page statement denouncing "this illegal and unwarranted action" before stepping aside. While the repercussions and the potential for violence were very real, the outcome was predetermined. Robert Kennedy and Katzenbach had been negotiating behind the scenes with Wallace, who had agreed to make sure his police officers kept the peace but demanded he be allowed to make a dramatic stand for the cameras in order to save face with his Jim Crow–loving supporters.

That afternoon, during a civil rights session in the White House, the president discussed his next move. One aide suggested Kennedy make a major speech on national television, taking his case directly to the American public. "I didn't think so," the president demurred. But before he could continue, his brother cut him off. "I think it would be helpful," opined the younger Kennedy. The others didn't know what to say; the brothers didn't make a habit of contradicting each other in public. Then the attorney general, the president's closest advisor, laid out his case for making a televised speech, concluding by saying, "I don't think you can get by without it." The younger Kennedy's evening with Baldwin and company may not have been a total loss after all.

"Well, I suppose we could do it," said the president, warming to the idea.

The speechwriters got to work. Now it was President Kennedy's time to make a dramatic stand for the cameras. After the evening news replayed the day's events at the University of Alabama, Kennedy delivered one of the most powerful speeches in American history. The subject: why the time had come for a comprehensive and meaningful civil rights law, one that would seek to finish what the Emancipation Proclamation had begun a century earlier.

After detailing the day's events in Alabama, the president looked into the camera and into the living rooms of Americans in every corner of the country and announced that the right of equality could no longer be denied to the nation's twenty-two million African Americans. "We face, therefore, a moral crisis as a country and as a people," he continued. "It cannot be met by repressive police action. It cannot be left to increased demonstrations in the streets. It cannot be quieted by token moves or talk. It is a time to act in the Congress, in your State and local legislative body and, above all, in all of our daily lives. It is not enough to pin the blame on others, to say this is a problem of one section of the country or another, or deplore the facts that we face. A great change is at hand, and our task, our obligation, is to make that revolution, that change, peaceful, and constructive for all. Those who do nothing are inviting shame as well as violence. Those who act boldly are recognizing right as well as reality."

Then came the moment that every Southern Democrat who ever whistled Dixie feared most. "Next week," the president said, "I shall ask the Congress of the United States to act, to make a commitment it has not fully made in this century to the proposition that race has no place in American life or law."

The millions of Americans watching from home, or their local bar or church basement, may not have realized it at the time, but a page had been turned in America's history. Not since the Civil War, which raged exactly a century earlier, had the issue of race so preoccupied the nation or an American president. But the country wasn't going to change that easily, or peacefully. Just hours after Kennedy finished, Medgar Evers, a former Army sergeant who had fought in France during WWII and the NAACP's field secretary in Mississippi, pulled into his driveway at his ranch home in Jackson. It was Evers who had counseled Meredith to enroll at Ole Miss and sounded the death knell of Jim Crow's hold on the state's university system.

Getting out of his car, Evers collected a stack of T-shirts with the logo JIM CROW MUST GO! and walked toward his front door. Inside were his wife, Myrlie, and the couple's three small children. She had allowed the kids to wait up to see their father and discuss the president's historic speech. But before Evers could reach the door, he was shot in the back by a Klan terrorist. Evers staggered toward his home and collapsed. His wife and children rushed outside to find him lying in a pool of blood, and watched helplessly as he bled to death.

Just 150 feet away, hiding behind a honeysuckle bush, was the assassin, Byron De La Beckwith, a white supremacist and local fertilizer salesman who murdered Evers with a bolt-action rifle. An ex-marine and WWII veteran, De La Beckwith was charged with the crime, but an all-white jury failed to find him guilty of any wrongdoing. Not that he was repentant in the least. "Killing that nigger gave me no more inner discomfort than our wives endure when they give birth to our children," he later boasted at a local Klan rally. "We ask them to do that for us. We should do just as much."*

Battle lines were being drawn all over the country, not just in Mississippi and Alabama, but even in New York. The summer of 1963 was a long, bitter season for race relations in the Empire State. Inside the gates of Moses' World's Fair, the utopian theme of "Peace Through Understanding" might reign, but outside of Flushing Meadow Park, blood would flow.

---

* In 1994 De La Beckwith was found guilty and sentenced to life imprisonment—a full thirty years after murdering Evers. He died in jail at age eighty in 2001.

9

We will not stop until the dogs stop biting us in the South and the rats stop biting us in the North.
　　　　　　　　—James L. Farmer Jr., August 28, 1963

We must not allow our creative protest to degenerate into physical violence. Again and again, we must rise to the majestic heights of meeting physical force with soul force.
　　　　　　　　—Reverend Martin Luther King Jr., August 28, 1963

By the time of President Kennedy's speech on June 11, 1963, many civil rights groups had already turned their attention northward. Local chapters of CORE, the NAACP, the Urban League, and other groups were staging a sustained campaign of direct-action protests throughout New York City, demanding jobs for African-American and Puerto Rican workers in the building trades—industries that were forever busy in Robert Moses' New York. Despite its having some of the most liberal politicians in the country who all supported civil rights, there was still racial inequality in the Empire State, especially when it came to taxpayer-financed public works programs, which were flourishing throughout the five boroughs.

In June protesters blocked trucks and stopped construction of the Harlem Hospital, chanting, "If we don't work, nobody works!" In July CORE activists marched and clashed with police at the construction site of the Rutgers Housing project on the Lower East Side, and held sit-ins at the Manhattan offices of Mayor Robert F. Wagner Jr. (which lasted forty-four days) and Governor Nelson A. Rockefeller, who took the protests in stride. "I have no objection at all," he said. "This is a free country." At the construction site for the Downstate Medical Center in Brooklyn, protesters marched through the streets carrying a coffin that read BURY JIM CROW and demanded that a quarter of the workers be hired from within the local African-American community.

On July 31 roiling tensions between protesters and police boiled over into a riot. A local preacher, Reverend William A. Jones of the Bethany Baptist Church in Bedford-Stuyvesant, tried in vain to quell the anger of the surging crowd. As violence erupted, Reverend Jones, who would one day succeed Martin Luther King Jr. as the head of the Southern Christian Leadership Council, uttered aloud what many of the younger, more militant civil rights workers were already thinking. "This proves there's no difference between New York and Alabama," he shouted in his resonant baritone as the police attacked the crowd. "No difference between the United States and South Africa. This nation is going straight to hell!"

By the end of July 1963, nearly seven hundred men, women, and children had been arrested at the Downstate Medical Center, including one Brooklyn mother who, as she sat in the back of a police patrol wagon, attempted to calm her crying twelve-year-old daughter. "Don't cry," she told the girl. "We're fighting for freedom. Sing now."

That same month, members of this broad coalition of civil rights groups began targeting Moses' beloved Rochdale Village project in Jamaica, Queens. Although the construction crews building the complex were mixed—some 210 of the 1,350 workers were African Americans—it was hardly a model of integration. Rochdale Village, which would become the world's largest integrated housing complex, was being built in the third-largest African-American neighborhood in New York City and being bankrolled with nearly $87 million of state funds. Even the left-wing chief of the United Housing Foundation, Abraham Kazan, was no help. "We can't tell the contractors whom to employ, and we certainly don't practice discrimination," he said.

Taking matters into their own hands, local activists focused on Rochdale as part of their effort to end discrimination in the building trade unions. During their first day of protests, some two hundred activists formed a picket line blocking workers from entering the site, resulting in twenty-three arrests. The protests continued for months throughout the summer and fall. Several times a week activists would descend upon Rochdale Village and attempt to disrupt the site by blocking traffic with their bodies. In September nine activists caused a stir when they snuck into the site and chained themselves to cranes thirty feet in the air. The protests eventually attracted national attention when John Lewis, the onetime Freedom Rider turned SNCC leader—and eventual Georgia congressman—addressed the protesters at an October rally, claiming now was the "time to put the movement back into the streets." He wasn't the only heavyweight to lend his credibility to the protests. Malcolm X appeared at rallies at the Queens housing complex, too, impressed by the persistence and growing militancy of the protests.

Then, in a brilliant tactical move to elevate their battle against Moses and the World's Fair, protesters marched in the streets outside the United Nations, carrying signs that read END APARTHEID AT THE FAIR and AFRICAN PAVILIONS BUILT WITH LILY WHITE LABOR. It was not lost on the Joint Committee for Equal Employment Opportunity, the coalition of civil rights groups sponsoring the direct-action campaign in New York that summer, that the World's Fair was playing host to many African and Latin American countries. They jumped at the chance to use the Fair's utopian message against Moses, who was unable—or unwilling—to integrate fully the construction crews at the World's Fair or his other projects.

A spokesperson for the group noted that the laborers busy working on the Sierra Leone, Guinea, and Vatican Pavilions were all white, and only two of the sixty-eight workers erecting the Philip Johnson–designed New York State Pavilion were black. "We hope that you will not allow your country to become an unwitting partner to the furtherance of discrimination in any form, at any place," read the letter addressed to the foreign nations erecting pavilions in Flushing Meadow. Although Moses refused to give in to any demands, the UN protests yielded some visible results. One member of the Guinea delegation who traveled to Queens to check on the progress of his country's pavilion received assurances by a subcontractor that five of the six workers that had just began work were indeed African-American.

In early August, Alfred Stern, a noted set designer whose New York–based firm was handling a number of pavilions at the Fair, including the Tower of Light—"the brightest show on Earth"—wrote Moses, suggesting a new pavilion that could solve the Fair's and his racial troubles: an exhibit devoted to "the progress and problems of the American Negro" created with the help of the NAACP, CORE, the Urban League, and other civil rights groups. Such an exhibit would be "compatible with the Fair's theme of 'Peace Through Understanding,'" wrote Stern, and "would tend to neutralize any negative attitudes or activities such groups may contemplate in regard to . . . the Fair." It could also end the picketing that was already wreaking havoc with construction schedules. And should Moses approve, of course, Stern's firm would certainly be happy to design it. Self-interest aside, Stern's idea was loaded with pros and had few—if any—cons.

Moses, however, declined. While noting that such an exhibit "would be of great interest," pulling it together with just nine months to opening day made it "a practical impossibility at this late stage . . . there simply is not enough time remaining." Such an excuse would be readily believable had Moses not sent a telegram to US Secretary of State Dean Rusk four days earlier, pleading with him to pressure the Soviet Union to reconsider making an eleventh-hour return to the Fair. "We know it is possible for them to construct an attractive, suitable and representative building," Moses wrote, after he had asked Rusk to discuss the matter "personally" with Nikita Khrushchev.

By August ongoing protests in the Bronx threatened to erupt after the local CORE chapter picketed two local White Castle restaurants for refusing to hire African Americans. "We are not pressing toward the brink of violence, but for the peak of freedom," CORE's national chairman, James L. Farmer Jr. told the picketers. The Bronx was "a bomb," a policeman warned the *New York Times*, "and it may explode any minute." He wasn't exaggerating: That same month eight members of the National Renaissance Party, a local neo-Nazi outfit, were arrested for conspiring to incite a riot at the Bronx marches. When their homes were raided by police, an arsenal of firearms was found and confiscated. The differences between the Bronx and Birmingham were slowly eroding.

The civil rights movement was changing. Younger, more militant leaders—like the activists in the Bronx and Brooklyn chapters of

CORE—were beginning to break away from the national leaders of their own organizations. These activists wanted more than the ability to exercise their right to vote; they wanted access to better jobs and education, and they wanted an end to police brutality, which was all too common. Like the New York City protests that summer, direct-action campaigns in many northern cities—Boston, Cleveland, Newark, Philadelphia—devolved into violent confrontations with police. Nonviolence was quickly becoming a thing of the past.

This was a reality that the "Big Four"—Martin Luther King, Farmer, Whitney Young (of the Urban League), and Roy Wilkins (of the NAACP)—had been warning the Kennedy administration about for some time. In the months leading up to the World's Fair—one of the largest public works projects in New York City history—these local activists focused their attention on the event that would bring the entire world and, more importantly, the global media to Queens. The Fair provided a once-in-a-lifetime opportunity to capture the world's attention for their cause with one collective act. But they needed a bold new tactic, maybe even some new form of protest.

The idea for their grand gesture would come from Louis E. Lomax, an African-American author and journalist. Lomax understood the desire among young activists to embrace radical tactics and move away from the approach of national civil rights groups. And he was close to the most militant African-American leader in the nation: Malcolm X. It was Lomax who helped create the 1959 television documentary *The Hate That Hate Produced* with CBS's Mike Wallace, which introduced Malcolm X and the Nation of Islam to a national audience. The documentary gave white America a glimpse of a different kind of black leader—proud, strong, charismatic, and unafraid to vent his rage. Speaking with the righteousness of a preacher but with the savvy street smarts of a hustler, Malcolm X didn't believe in the Christian notion of turning the other cheek. Instead, he thought that black men should defend themselves against the blue-eyed white devil "by any means necessary."

Like Malcolm X, Lomax lived in Queens and was all too familiar with the more subtle forms of New York City's de facto segregation.

"The mood of the Negro particularly in New York City, is very, very bitter," Lomax warned. "He is losing faith. The Negro on the streets of Harlem is tired of platitudes from white liberals." Whether those liberals were Rockefeller Republicans or Kennedy Democrats, it didn't matter; for black America, progress was moving too slow. "White liberals . . . have been making a great fuss over the South, only to blind us to what is happening here in the North," Malcolm X told a DC crowd in August.

Lomax had been predicting a split between younger African Americans and their elders as early as 1960. He covered the protests of the Greensboro Four—a quartet of college students who rejuvenated the civil rights movement after attempting to desegregate a "whites-only" lunch counter in North Carolina. The Greensboro Four inspired scores of imitators throughout the South, and Lomax saw the writing on the wall, predicting that such youthful activists would eventually clash with members of their own race, whether it was with "moneyed Negroes in high places" or with the Southern blacks who had grown accustomed to life under Jim Crow.

"The student demonstrators have no illusions," Lomax wrote. "They know the segregationists are not their only enemies. But the students told me they are not prejudiced—they are willing to stand up to their enemies, Negro and white alike." After taking their seats at the "whites-only" counter, the quartet were refused service by a black waitress, who told them, "Fellows like you make our race look bad." In 1962 Lomax expanded his article into a book, *The Negro Revolt,* just months before one of President Kennedy's advisors assured him that African Americans were "pretty much at peace."

It was Lomax who dreamed up a radical and ingenious way to crash the World's Fair, a move that would force the likes of Moses, Mayor Wagner, Governor Rockefeller, and even President Kennedy and his brother the attorney general to finally take heed of their struggle. Just two miles from Flushing Meadow Park, during a lecture at Queens College—then a hotbed of political activism—Lomax introduced the novel idea of a "stall-in."

If Wagner and Rockefeller and Moses chose to ignore the pleas for equitable hiring practices in New York City and at the World's Fair, then

Lomax suggested using the Master Builder's beloved arterial highway system against him and his bosses: Activists could clog all the expressways and highways that led to the Fair on opening day by having hundreds of people run out of gas, or just stop their cars, causing the largest traffic jam in New York history. Moses might be able to keep protesters outside the Fairgrounds, but he couldn't keep them off the highways. "Imagine the confusion which might result if five hundred people get in their cars, drive towards the Fairgrounds and run out of gas," Lomax told the crowd of activists. It was a question the political elites of New York and Washington, DC, were afraid to fathom.

The *New York Journal-American,* a conservative broadsheet closely aligned with Moses and a key paper in the Hearst publishing empire, covered the speech and quickly denounced the idea. The so-called stall-in, the paper wrote in an editorial, was "going too far . . . stalling hundreds of autos on crowded highways is not peaceful assembly. It is a clear threat to law and order which must be prevented." Furthermore, the paper's editorial stated that such a tactic would "only harm their cause by alienating the innocent citizens who would suffer untold hardship."

But while the Brooklyn chapter of CORE considered Lomax's idea to obstruct the World's Fair, King and the venerable A. Phillip Randolph, the Oakland-based union leader and civil rights activist, announced their own idea: They wanted to sponsor a "March on Washington for Freedom and Jobs." Now that President Kennedy's civil rights legislation had been introduced to Congress, King and Randolph wanted to hold a massive rally right in the heart of the nation's capital—the largest biracial plea for racial unity in American history. The idea was close to Randolph's heart; he had first proposed it to President Franklin D. Roosevelt back in 1941 but called the march off after Roosevelt issued Executive Order 8802 desegregating "the defense industries or government because of race, creed, color or national origin."

All the major civil rights groups backed the march; even the militant Brooklyn chapter of CORE proudly supported such a broad appeal for civil rights. The Kennedys, however, were less than enthusiastic about the idea. The president feared that such an event would endanger his civil rights bill in the Senate, where the usual cast of racist Dixiecrats like Senators Russell and Thurmond and their ilk were prepared to kill the legislation by any means necessary.

At a meeting at the White House on June 22, 1963, with the "Big Four," Kennedy was blunt. "It seemed to me a great mistake to announce a march on Washington before the bill was even in committee," he told the group. "We want success in Congress, not just a big show at the Capitol. Some of these people are looking for an excuse to be against us. I don't want to give any of them a chance to say, 'Yes, I'm for the bill, but I'm damned if I will vote for it at a point of a gun.'"

The group's elder statesman, Wilkins of the NAACP, agreed with the president. He thought the timing was dangerous. Wilkins, the urbane New Yorker who lived in the upper-middle-class African-American neighborhood of St. Albans, Queens, was cautious and practical—much more like Kennedy than King. He had long been suspicious of King's nonviolent techniques and his fame. Both men and the organizations they headed were diametrically opposed within the civil rights movement: King's SCLC was Southern, Christian, and dedicated to the principles of spiritual nonviolence, utilizing Gandhi's notion of *satyagraha*—"truth force" or "soul force"—to bring about racial equality; while Wilkins's NAACP was Northern, secular, and dedicated to chipping away at discrimination with lawsuit after lawsuit, one legislative victory at a time. But King had a response for both Kennedy and Wilkins. "I have never engaged in any direct action movement which did not seem ill-timed," he told them.

Realizing that the march was inevitable, Kennedy threw his administration's weight behind the event. "The march has been taken over by the government," complained Malcolm X, who referred to it as the "Farce on Washington," though he would travel to the capital to witness the historic event for himself. "This is government controlled."

Indeed it was. Robert Kennedy's Justice Department managed most of the logistics, the date and time (a Wednesday afternoon, when many potential protesters would be at work), and site (the Lincoln Memorial). Not only was the latter historically appropriate, it would keep the crowds away from DC's commercial centers—easing the fears of shopkeepers and business owners who worried about a riot. The memorial was also surrounded by water on three sides, making it easier to control the crowd should things turn violent. Major League Baseball wasn't taking any chances: The league cancelled two Washington Senators' games. The capital was on lockdown.

The government also paid for the sound system that the march's many speakers and performers would use. Few of the civil rights leaders—if any at all—knew that Jerry Bruno, one of the Kennedys' top Secret Service agents, would sit behind the statue of President Lincoln with a kill switch, ready to silence the speakers in deus ex machina fashion should any orator get carried away.

On the morning of August 28, 1963, a sweltering, muggy day, more than a quarter million people flooded into the nation's capital. The protesters, who had come from all over the country, marched peacefully along the Mall, while inside the White House Kennedy and his advisors discussed another vexing problem that was taking up more and more of the president's time: Vietnam. As they considered their policy options, they could hear the protesters as the march got under way. Kennedy halted his meeting so he and his advisors could watch on television, just as millions of Americans at home did (the major networks had preempted their regular programming). And like the rest of America, Kennedy was amazed as King stood before the Lincoln Memorial to deliver the keynote address and proclaim his "dream."

King made reference to the nation's history, its Declaration of Independence, President Lincoln, and the Emancipation Proclamation, summing up in one speech the colossal contradictions of an America that proudly proclaimed itself the global leader of peace and democracy—a country that was busy organizing a World's Fair in New York City based on the notion of peace through understanding; a country that had less than two decades earlier destroyed Hitler's *Wehrmacht,* liberated a ravaged European continent, and now opposed the threat of global Communism in faraway lands like Vietnam. Yet this same country had never come to terms with its own tortured racial history, which was still being written in the blood of new victims on a regular basis in the North and South alike; a history that everyone involved—from King, the marchers, and the Kennedys to the KKK and their protectors down South to the racists who disgraced the halls of the US Senate—knew would claim more innocent lives in the weeks and months to come.

"And so," King said, looking out at the biracial ocean of humanity gathered around the Mall's reflecting pool, "even though we face the difficulties of today and tomorrow, I still have a dream. It is a dream deeply rooted in the American dream. I have a dream that one day this nation will rise up and live out the true meaning of its creed: 'We hold these truths to be self-evident, that all men are created equal.' I have a dream that one day on the red hills of Georgia, the sons of former slaves and the sons of former slave owners will be able to sit down together at the table of brotherhood. . . . I have a dream today!" Back at the White House, President Kennedy, who knew a thing or two about speechmaking, was suitably impressed as he watched on television from his living quarters. "He's damned good," the president said, turning to his advisors. "Damned good!"

For that day at least, the country seemed united; maybe "Peace Through Understanding" was possible after all. But just in case, the Kennedys had more than 2,500 national guardsman and 4,000 members of the US Army stationed in the capital to supplement DC's police department. The Justice Department also had 14,000 members of the 82nd Airborne on standby in Fort Bragg, North Carolina. But the March on Washington transpired without incident.

The civil rights movement had now gone mainstream. The march attracted a dozen celebrity-activists who wanted to fight the good fight, from gospel singer Odetta, jazz vocalist Mahalia Jackson, and crooner Harry Belafonte to movie stars like Burt Lancaster, Charlton Heston, and the enigmatic Marlon Brando, who carried a cattle prod to show people the kind of weapons Southern police used against African Americans.

There was also a crop of younger folksingers, who were far more influential with the white collegiate members of the crowd. Peter, Paul and Mary sang their No. 1 hit "Blowin' in the Wind." Joan Baez, the stunning ebony-haired beauty with an angelic voice, who was both the darling of the folk music set and its political conscience, had brought along her moody poet-singer boyfriend Bob Dylan, who was creating a body of work that was steadily rewriting the rules of American folk music. Not that Baez had an easy time convincing Dylan, who was suspicious of politics and political movements, to perform. "I had to use Brando's cattle prod to get him up there up, practically," she joked. "But he did it. It wasn't really his thing, but he did it."

When it was his turn at the microphone, Dylan sang a new song, "Only a Pawn in Their Game," that referenced the death of Medgar Evers, and a duet with Baez on his own "Blowin' in the Wind" (from his second album, *The Freewheelin' Bob Dylan,* released that spring). Although the young activists in the folk music scene had already begun referring to Dylan as the "voice of his generation," not everyone at the march was impressed: Lancaster, Belafonte, and Heston all "stood up to stretch and chat" among themselves as he sang. "I preferred to see Odetta up there," said African-American comedian and activist Dick Gregory, who put his hands over his ears during Dylan's set.

Despite the generational differences, by any measure it was a triumphant day for the forces of progress in the country. Something was indeed changing in America. To the tens of thousands who participated in the momentous event, and to the millions who watched on television at home, it certainly seemed that way. But not to Dylan. Looking in the distance at the Capitol, where segregationist senators went about their normal business in an attempt to ignore the March, Dylan wasn't optimistic about the future at all. "Think they're listening?" he asked before answering his own question. "No, they ain't listening at all."

Come round by my side and I'll sing you a song
I'll sing it so softly, it'll do no one wrong.
On Birmingham Sunday the blood ran like wine
And the choir kept singing of Freedom.
　　　　　　—"Birmingham Sunday" by Richard Fariña

Two weeks after the March on Washington, the nation and the world were reminded why Birmingham, Alabama, had earned the nickname "Bombingham." Since 1945 some fifty bombings had occurred in the city, each targeting the homes or gathering places of civil rights activists. Reverend Fred Shuttlesworth, one of the founders of the Southern Christian Leadership Conference, had his home destroyed and his church attacked on multiple occasions. No one was ever caught or prosecuted for the crimes.

That was life in Birmingham; if you were black, you never knew what might happen. "From the time I was very small, I remember the sound of bombs exploding across the street, our house shaking," recalled Angela Davis, the author and Black Power activist, years later. "I remember my father having to have guns at his disposal at all times because of the fact that at any moment . . . we might expect to be attacked." Davis recalled how Birmingham's Commissioner of Public Safety, Eugene "Bull" Connor, might be heard on the radio announcing, "Niggers have moved into a white neighborhood; we better expect some bloodshed tonight." Added Davis: "And sure enough there would be bloodshed."

Connor was so volatile, his power so absolute, even some of his fellow segregationists feared him. "I didn't trust the man . . . he was unpredictable," admitted former Alabama governor James Paterson. "Frankly, I was a bit afraid of him." When Paterson ran for governor in 1958, he did so without Connor's endorsement, so in order to win he ran *to the right* of his opponent, George C. Wallace, bragging to voters how, as the state's attorney general, he got the NAACP kicked out of Alabama. It would be the last time that anyone outflanked Wallace on the segregation issue. With men like that in charge, the black citizens of the Yellowhammer State had good reason to fear for their lives.

On Sunday, September 15, 1963, the world at large would understand. That morning was a busy one at the 16th Street Baptist Church, the same church where back in May, hundreds of children had begun their peaceful march to downtown Birmingham only to be met by Connor's police dogs and fire hoses. It wasn't any ordinary Sunday: The annual Youth Day services were to begin promptly at eleven. The black children of Birmingham were very much on everyone's mind; the state's schools had been desegregated by federal order just a week before. Inside the church four hundred people, including some eighty children, were preparing to take part in that celebration after months of struggle. The theme of the day's sermon was "The Love That Forgives."

No one got to hear it. At 10:22 a.m. as four young girls—fourteen-year-olds Addie Mae Collins, Cynthia Wesley, and Carole Robertson and eleven-year-old Denise McNair—were changing into their finest Sunday clothes for the occasion, a dozen sticks of dynamite planted by KKK terrorists ripped a hole in the eastern side of the church, exploding the stone staircase, killing all four girls and injuring another twenty-two people. From out of the dust and rubble staggered an elderly man, holding a shoe that had belonged to his granddaughter, the rest of her bloodied body buried among the ruins. The blast had blown out the windows of cars parked blocks away. Soon a crowd of two thousand gathered at the destroyed church, where only one stained-glass window remained—depicting Christ surrounded by a group of small children.

The horror and rage boiled over into a riot, as the black citizens of Birmingham fought with the city's racist police, bombarding them with rocks and bottles. Governor Wallace, who only a week earlier had said that what was needed to stop desegregation was "a few first-class funerals" and got what he had asked for, called in the National Guard. Before the day was over, more young blacks would die: Johnny Robinson, age sixteen, was shot in the back after running away from a police officer; and Virgil Ware, a thirteen-year-old heading to his suburban home with his brother, was shot twice by Larry Joe Sims, a sixteen-year-old white Eagle Scout who was returning with a friend from a segregationist rally. Neither assassin would ever face jail time.

"When an American city is ruled by the police dog, the high-pressure fire hose, the shotgun and the bomb, then it no longer can be considered a city ruled by law," declared a *New York Times* editorial. "The massacre of innocents in a church" and the murder of Robinson "were bestial acts," the editorial continued. Martin Luther King Jr. arrived in Birmingham before nightfall and sent a telegram to President Kennedy predicting "the worst racial holocaust this nation has ever seen" unless federal troops intervened. Kennedy, while decrying the murders, refused. The black citizens of Birmingham were on their own; and in at least one neighborhood, where one of the little girls had lived, they took matters into their own hands. "In my neighborhood all the men organized themselves into an armed patrol," Davis said. "They had to take their guns and patrol our community every night because they did not want that to happen again."

The following week the nation expressed its rage. More than ten thousand people gathered at a Washington, DC, rally where Bayard Rustin, deputy director of the recent March on Washington, called for a nonviolent "uprising" in a hundred American cities. James L. Farmer Jr. of CORE, who had sat in the Oval Office with the Kennedys, now told the angry crowd that if the administration didn't double its civil rights efforts, it "will be replaced." At the rally, members of the Brooklyn Chapter of CORE were seen carrying signs calling on President Kennedy to fire FBI director J. Edgar Hoover for his refusal to prosecute racial murders in the South.

There were similar rallies and demonstrations all over the country that day: Boston and Philadelphia; Houston, Texas, and Shreveport, Louisiana; Des Moines, Iowa, and Fort Wayne, Indiana; Lexington, Kentucky, and Kansas City, Missouri; as well as Milwaukee, Seattle, Salt Lake City, and Portland, Oregon. But perhaps the most astonishing event of the day took place in Birmingham, where two white pastors participated in the funeral services of the two black teenagers who had been murdered in the chaotic aftermath of the church bombings.

In New York City, where the racial tensions of the summer of '63 threatened to boil over into a dramatic stall-in on the highways to Robert Moses' World's Fair, thousands of people demonstrated, showing Moses, Mayor Wagner, and Governor Rockefeller that the battle for civil rights was far from just a Southern problem: In the Bronx, a thousand people, including eight children who carried coffins for Birmingham's dead children, marched to the borough's courthouse; in Queens, 2,500 people gathered at St. Alban's Memorial Park; and in Brooklyn, 4,500 New Yorkers from eighteen different churches marched to Brownsville's Betsy Head Memorial Playground—transformed by Moses into a magnificent public pool in 1937. Now Moses' handiwork had become a gathering place for citizens who had had enough of the empty promises of their leaders in New York and Washington. No doubt, it had never occurred to Moses that one of his parks or his pools could become a stage for the "professional integrationists" that he often ridiculed. However, it was a sign of the times and one that would have serious repercussions for the World's Fair.

The New York World's Fair is a misnomer; it is a trade mart, no more and no less.

—Hugo Geller, artist and activist

There are no substitutes for courage and loyalty and no way of making everybody happy.

—Robert Moses

By September 1963, with the opening day of the World's Fair just months away, the "Countdown Clock" inaugurated by President John F. Kennedy back in April had become an object of scorn at the massive construction site that was Flushing Meadow. Dubbed the "Ulcer Clock" by staffers, it served as a constant reminder of all the unfinished tasks at hand. Robert Moses made sure it wasn't the only reminder: An exact count of the days left until opening day—April 22, 1964—was typed at the bottom of every memo, letter, report, and daily correspondence on Fair stationery. Moses wanted everyone to remember exactly what they were striving for: to stage the most successful World's Fair in history.

To the Master Builder, anything that distracted from this goal was an attack against the "Olympics of Progress." He wouldn't tolerate even the slightest criticism. By the fall of 1963, this meant he was in a state of open war with the media, whether print, television, or radio, and in particular the half-dozen metropolitan daily newspapers. Moses never passed up an opportunity to lodge his complaints in "URGENT" hand-delivered memos to the top brass of New York's media, many of whom where long-standing associates, if not old friends. He constantly worked his personal connections to influence the news in his—and the Fair's—favor, and he made a habit of disparaging the work of any reporter whose prose was not to his liking.

On September 9, 1963, the *New York Times* ran a friendly front-page article—WORLD'S FAIR GAINS IMPETUS DESPITE SNUBS—that jumped inside to a full, eight-column story. Of the article's thousands of words, Moses took umbrage with a few sentences that implied he doled out contracts to favored firms. He immediately fired off a memo to Arthur Ochs "Punch" Sulzberger, the paper's newly installed president and publisher. "Why this stuff about employing pets who have worked for me before and profited through me in the past?" he demanded. "The effect is to suggest to the average reader that there is considerable suspicion of patronage and private profit." Moses denied any and all charges, insisting that nearly three-quarters of the Fair's work was being done by subcontractors and almost all other contracts were related to the vast highway or park construction he was overlooking, leaving "perhaps 2 or 3%" to his discretion.

The following month, when he found a WCBS radio editorial "totally inaccurate," he immediately informed William S. Paley, CBS's chairman of the board. He requested an investigation and lectured Paley, who was a member of the Fair's Executive Committee, about his responsibility to the Flushing exhibition. "You are a Director of the Fair," Moses chided him, "and I assume continue to be interested in its progress and success."

For all of his thin-skinned paranoia toward the press, Moses wasn't completely off base. While on friendly terms with those at the top of the New York media world, his standing with the rank-and-file reporters who covered his various projects—almost all of them newsworthy—could hardly have been worse. "The mood of the media seemed against him, tired of him, not only the *Times* but the other newspapers as well, plus radio and television," wrote author Gay Talese, who covered the World's Fair as a young Timesman. "It was not that they reported the news incompletely or anything inaccurately. If anything they were *too* complete, *too* accurate, they overlooked nothing. . . . They had fun with Moses, this cranky old man trying to ballyhoo the Fair, and they picked it apart before its flimsy construction was complete, and they continued to downgrade it through the next two years."

Even if the reporters on the city's metropolitan dailies largely detested Moses, the Master Builder still held sway with top editors and publishers of many newspapers, particularly the *New York Times*, where he was close with the Sulzbergers, who owned the paper. "Moses was a power and the *Times* is responsive to power and powerful people," said Talese. The *Times'* only potential rival, the *New York Herald Tribune,* however, could afford to take a more strident tone with Moses, since by the early 1960s it was "a sinking ship with declining ad revenue." What the *Trib,* as it was known, did have were innovative writers like Tom Wolfe, Jimmy Breslin, and Dick Schapp, who would go on—along with Talese—to pioneer a new form of writing dubbed the "New Journalism."

Still, for a beat reporter covering the World's Fair, there was no shortage of stories to report. Several controversies threatened to overshadow the Fair's progress throughout the autumn of 1963; each was played out in the papers, and every story was helped along by Moses' insistence to counterattack his enemies, therefore keeping the story in the headlines for weeks or even months.

The first scandalous story had to do with the price of tickets for New York City's 1.4 million schoolchildren. Tickets to the World's Fair cost $1 for children age twelve years old and younger; adults paid $2. By February 1963 the World's Fair Corporation had sold $28 million in discounted tickets. But now some officials—like labor lawyer and City Council candidate Paul O'Dwyer (and brother of Moses' ex-boss, the former New York mayor William O'Dwyer)—picked up the rallying cry for a reduced fee for schoolchildren, first sounded by the Board of Education. O'Dwyer was soon joined by a chorus of politicos who found it all too easy to pontificate to newspapers, which loved a good Moses controversy, especially one that portrayed the septuagenarian Master Builder as a miserly bully who wouldn't cut children—particularly poor schoolchildren—a break to come see his "Olympics of Progress."

Unable to resist lashing out at his critics, or to engage in good-hearted negotiations with the enemy, Moses fell right into their trap. Deriding his critics as "assorted Santa Clauses" who didn't have their facts or figures straight, he flatly refused any discount, claiming it would be detrimental to the Fair's financial health. The World's Fair, he claimed, could lose as much as $9 million if it cut prices. And he noted that it was his stated intention of using the exhibition's profits to "leave a great legacy to the city—another Central Park for the future—wholly without cost to the public." To create this post-Fair Flushing Meadow Park that he had dreamed of for so long would cost at least $23 million, according to Moses' in-house figures.

The war of words filled the pages of the daily papers. "It should be brought to the attention of Mr. Moses by the appropriate bodies," O'Dwyer told reporters, "that the World's Fair is not an exclusive club. Millions of dollars of our taxpayers' money has gone into it." Amos Basil, seeking the same City Council seat as O'Dwyer, out-quipped his opponent on the campaign stump. "Moses thinks he's God," Basil joked, "but fortunately he's just Moses."

The brouhaha wouldn't go away. Soon City Council passed a resolution demanding a price decrease for schoolchildren; eventually Mayor Robert F. Wagner Jr. joined the fray, and in a rare public instance sided with the anti-Moses forces. Moses, perhaps sensing that his hard-line stance was damaging the Fair in the eyes of New Yorkers, who after all were intrinsic to the exhibition's success, put the matter to a vote by the Executive Committee. As he told Bernard Gimbel, a key ally and one of the committee's eighteen members, this was no time for getting weak in the knees. "The Executive Committee will simply have to stand up and be counted," Moses declared.

On October 16 the committee voted and sided with their leader. Their counterproposal was to allow children age two to twelve to pay only twenty-five cents on Mondays in July and August. But their offer didn't please the critics, who were growing in number—now the New York State legislature in Albany was considering a vote on the matter. By the end of October there were threats to revoke the Fair's 5 percent state admissions tax exemption and a serious threat by City Council to have the Fair's books audited (which Moses denied they had the authority to do).

Moses kept a brave face publicly but privately sounded the alarm. He sent a telegram to top deputy Charles Poletti, who was in Jordan on one of his frequent international trips, asking him to return immediately. "There are serious threats to the integrity of the Fair," Moses wrote. (Poletti, who had stipulated in his contract that his wife, Jane, could travel with him at the Fair's expense, stayed put in Jordan.) By December, Moses sensed the tide of popular opinion turning against him. Wanting to avoid further damage to the World's Fair's image in a "rather pointless and destructive argument," as one committee member put it, he conceded the fight: Groups of schoolchildren from the Tri-State area could purchase tickets for twenty-five cents throughout the school year.

While Moses lost that battle, he played to his advantage another controversy that erupted. Back in 1961 the World's Fair Corporation had sought the services of eccentric right-wing billionaire H. L. Hunt, reportedly the fourth-richest man in the world, to take over three and a half acres of prime real estate at the Fair for a Tivoli Gardens–inspired children's playground. The idea was a favorite of Moses, who held the Copenhagen park in the highest regard. The seventy-four-year-old Texas oil tycoon paid $1.1 million up front to seal the deal, but by October 1963 he was holding a press conference at the Waldorf Towers to announce that he was getting "evicted" from the Fair. The Dallas-based free-market fundamentalist, who during the 1950s had supported Senator Joseph McCarthy, the disgraced red-baiting demagogue, read a rambling eight-page statement, repeatedly referring to himself in the third person and announcing that he had been "pressured and taken in" by Moses, whom he referred to as "the ruler of the World's Fair."

Soon after Hunt had gotten involved with the Fair, he had started to rub Moses the wrong way. For starters, he was concerned about the type of amusement rides Hunt was building; there would be absolutely no Coney Island–style entertainment at the World's Fair—"Coney Island" being Moses' oft-repeated catchphrase for low-end, déclassé amusement parks. He told Hunt that the Fair wouldn't tolerate anything "gaudy" or high-priced. The Texan reportedly wanted to charge a fifty-cent entrance fee for each of his proposed eleven rides—at the exact time that the newspapers, the City Council, and Albany were pressuring Moses to reduce the entrance fees for schoolchildren.

Hunt denied both charges, insisting to the reporters during his press conference that his rides would neither be expensive nor gaudy. In fact, he bragged that his mini amusement park would have included "a very ancient carousel said to be of 1900 vintage and something called a 'Wild Mouse Ride.'" The *New York Herald Tribune* noted dryly, "Those last three words were not further explained."

The New York reporters didn't know what to make of the rotund bow-tie-wearing billionaire who was apt to interrupt his speech with his outside-the-mainstream political views, which Moses described as "absolutely free old-fashioned, capitalistic enterprise, reminiscent of the late nineties of the last century." Noting that the New York papers, including his least favorite of the dailies, the *Herald Tribune*, didn't seem to take Hunt or his charges seriously, Moses, for once, let the matter fade into oblivion. "Old boy H. L. Hunt has gone down the drain," he wrote a friend. "Thank God we seem to be rid of him."

But the most enduring controversy of autumn 1963 dated back to the earliest days of Moses' tenure at the Fair: the amount of art—or the lack thereof, according to his critics—on display in Flushing Meadow. This controversy was rekindled when Emily Genauer, the highly regarded art critic for the *Herald Tribune*, who would go on to win a Pulitzer Prize for her criticism, lashed out at Moses in August. An outspoken champion of modernism and artists such as Pablo Picasso, Marc Chagall, and Diego Rivera—precisely the kind of art that ran afoul of Moses' more conservative tastes—Genauer had established herself in the 1930s as the art critic for the *New York World-Telegram*. In 1949, after a red-baiting congressman mentioned her by name, the paper's conservative owner, Roy S. Howard, told her to stop writing about "Communists and left-wingers" like Picasso. Genauer quit on the spot, then used Howard's phone to call an editor she knew at the *Herald Tribune*. By the time she hung up, she was the *Trib*'s new chief art critic, a position she still held in 1963 when Hugo Geller, a painter, printmaker, and activist, came to her office to discuss his attempts to create a pavilion for contemporary American artists at the 1964–65 World's Fair.

Geller was the chairman of the Committee of Artists' Societies, a collective of more than a dozen groups. Their goal was to erect a forty-thousand-square-foot, $1.5 million pavilion designed by the architect August Sak and made of aluminum and rubberized plastic, which could be built in a mere ninety days, if only Moses would foot the bill. Instead, Moses was offering free rent but per Fair policy, he insisted exhibitors pay for their own pavilion.

Geller had fought—and won—this battle before. A quarter of a century earlier, he had been part of another cooperative that successfully pressured Grover Whalen, the president of the 1939–40 World's Fair, to create the Contemporary Art Building on the Fair's dime. When he handed Genauer a yellowing newspaper article extolling his earlier efforts, it took her a few moments to realize that the February 5, 1938, clip she was reading was, in fact, her own. "If you want to see an art show," Genauer had written twenty-five years earlier, "they will tell the millions who visit the Fair, you must leave this great exposition of everything important in contemporary American life and go eight miles away to the Metropolitan [Museum of Art]." Genauer recapped all of these details in her 1963 article and added, with derisive déjà vu: "Absolutely nothing has changed in twenty-five years."

While Genauer's article didn't provoke Moses—though it surely irritated him—Geller's group did make some headway with August Heckscher, a former cultural advisor to President Kennedy. Heckscher requested a meeting with Moses at Flushing Meadow to discuss the matter. "Back of these Washington people and their associates are a number of critics and writers who have been anything but friendly to the Fair," Moses complained to a top staffer. "They picture us as barbarians not interested in the finer things."

Moses set up the meeting and made sure that there was "a record of the proceedings" and a final report; he wanted to be able to use his critics' words against them, if necessary. But like so many other of the various proposals from artist coalitions or wealthy patrons that had been discussed over the previous three years, nothing came of it. Moses had insisted all along that there was room for such a display of contemporary American art—albeit, a smaller one—in the Federal Pavilion. Not only was this pavilion the Fair's largest, but Heckscher was also a key player in developing its exhibits. "He has had opportunities right along to take care of the art and cultural exhibits there," Moses sniffed.

On November 17 the Committee of Artists' Societies fired another salvo. At a press conference held at the Whitney Museum, Heckscher, playwright Arthur Miller, conductor Leonard Bernstein, and others joined Geller and Genauer in denouncing Moses and the Fair. "It's a disgrace that there is no pavilion for contemporary American art at the World's Fair," lamented Miller. "It shows the world that this is a nation of blind men without culture, that we just live for money, and that we are gross—without any spirit."

Genauer charged that Moses had wasted an opportunity for the World's Fair to host the immense modern art collection of multimillionaire investor Joseph H. Hirshhorn—a Latvian-born, Brooklyn-raised immigrant who owned some of the great masterworks of nineteenth- and twentieth-century art. According to Genauer, Moses insisted on breaking up the collection and distributing Hirshhorn's abstract sculptures, including pieces by Alberto Giacometti, Pablo Serrano, and Henry Moore, throughout the Fairgrounds in an ill-conceived sculpture garden. "This shows what Moses knows about art," she huffed.

Heckscher, who was unable to secure any space for contemporary art in the Federal Pavilion, where real estate was as politically complicated as the US Senate, put the blame squarely on the shoulders of the man behind the Fair. "Mr. Moses," he said, "was not interested in art." If Moses, the president of the Fair, wouldn't help them, then Geller insisted they would go over his head and petition President Kennedy, a vocal supporter of the World's Fair.

The next day, the story hit the papers. Not only did the *New York Times* give it prominent coverage, but it also ran another piece about art at the Fair, which only added fuel to the critics' fire. According to the *Times,* there was a brand-new oil painting hanging prominently on a wall at the Top of the Fair restaurant in the Port Authority Building depicting various images of New York, including a number of Moses' works, such as the Verrazano Bridge (which would open in 1964), the Robert Moses Dam, and Jones Beach, among others. It was seemingly an artistic tribute to the Master Builder, who regularly entertained VIPs there. Hanging in the same restaurant was a large-scale reproduction of a cartoon by Rube Goldberg, a funny papers regular whose name would become synonymous with homemade contraptions.

Neither was an example of high art or what his critics had in mind, but Moses insisted the cartoon—titled "How to Cure World's Fair Tired Feet"—stay put, much to the dismay of the restaurant's staff. "It is vulgar," the eatery's art director complained. "It is the most ugly comic caricature I have ever seen. . . . [Moses] is a genius in some ways but he knows absolutely nothing about art."

Moses' counterattack appeared in the papers the next day. The *New York Times* quoted liberally from his statement addressing both articles, which he said didn't possess "a suspicion of the truth." While Moses insisted he knew nothing about the mural depicting his handiwork until after it was hanging on the Top of the Fair's wall, he wasn't about to move the Goldberg, for which he said, "I will go down the *Times'* artistic drain." Moses attacked the accusations one at time, calling Grenauer's version of the Hirshhorn story "fiction." He offered to print the Fair's entire, voluminous correspondence with Hirshhorn, which he noted couldn't have been any more "cordial." Said Moses, "We begged him to come into the Fair."

In fact, he had. For more than two years, Moses had doggedly pursued Hirshhorn and his vast collection of art, hoping to lure the aging speculator to bankroll a pavilion that would eventually become "a permanent endowed building" in the future Flushing Meadow Park. Unfortunately, Hirshhorn and his people had balked at the notion of having his collection of sculptures, as well as his contemporary paintings by Jackson Pollock, Willem de Kooning, and Larry Rivers, plus works by Auguste Rodin and Henri Matisse, among dozens of others, permanently housed in a park in the middle of Queens. Instead, Moses noted, "Mr. Hirshhorn talked of Fifth Avenue." (Eventually the collection and endowment would find a home at the Smithsonian in Washington, DC.)

The continuous attempts by Moses to get Hirshhorn's collection rendered his critics' claims of "Fair antagonism to modern art and design . . . manifestly ridiculous." Fair officials, he noted, may have their individual tastes—as he most certainly did—"but these don't enter into the determination of the Fair to give every possible encouragement to every school, period, academy and fashion," he lectured the *Times*. And apparently those tastes included James N. Rosenberg, a painter of expressionistic landscapes, who joined Genauer and the others in their attack on the Fair. "It is sad when late in the game old friends become mere acquaintances," Moses responded in a private letter to the artist. "I guess I shall have to turn your landscape to the wall."

Moses laid the blame for any lack of art pavilion on Heckscher or the various art groups that demanded the Fair bankroll their ventures. Multiple attempts, both inside and outside the Fair, were made to secure funding from a variety of sources and organizations such as the Ford Foundation. Ultimately, each fell through. Fair executives worked with New York City's cultural institutions—from the newly opened Lincoln Center (which Moses played a major role in creating) to all the major museums (including the Museum of Modern Art and the Guggenheim)—to hold World's Fair–affiliated exhibitions, becoming, in a sense, cultural annexes of the Fair. Both city and state officials were counting on the millions of tourists who would flood Flushing Meadow to explore Manhattan's cultural and tourist attractions, thereby boosting New York's tax coffers.

But what Genauer, Geller, and the rest seemed to miss—or ignore—was a story in the *New York Times* in early October announcing some extraordinary radical art that would be on display at the New York State Pavilion. The architect Philip Johnson had designed the pavilion, itself a strange, new, postmodern work of art. Heralded as "the architectural delight of Flushing Meadow," by the *Times'* architecture critic Ada Louise Huxtable, Johnson's pavilion was a series of festive circular towers, a rounded theater, and a large open-air oval with a roof shaped like a giant bicycle tire, complete with suspension rings. Johnson, a prolific art collector, had commissioned ten artists, almost all of whom were working in the new style known as pop art (sometimes called the new realism), to create twenty-by-twenty-foot murals that would be mounted outside the pavilion's theater like a "charm bracelet."

Johnson hired some of the most controversial young sculptors and painters—almost are were in their thirties—working in New York City, or the rest of America, in the early 1960s: Robert Indiana, Roy Lichtenstein, James Rosenquist, John Chamberlain, Ellsworth Kelly, Robert Rauschenberg, and a former graphic artist named Andy Warhol. The article even highlighted some of the controversial works that were being created specifically for Moses' World's Fair. According to the *Times,* millions of Fairgoers would see art that included a painted comic strip of a laughing redheaded woman; a collection of crashed car parts; a sculpture of black tuxedos made "rock hard" with resin; a sculpture of stone balloons; a collage of photographic images and oil paint showing contemporary scenes of American life; and a silk screen depicting the "Thirteen Most Wanted Men" in New York State. This was as contemporary and controversial as American art got in 1964, but none of the critics who were lambasting Moses for his lack of aesthetic grace seemed to take note; apparently pop art wasn't to their liking.

However, at least one conservative critic did take note. Wheeler Williams, the president of the American Artists Professional League, lodged his complaints in a letter to Moses, Mayor Wagner, and Governor Rockefeller—who was ultimately in charge of the pavilion and who had commissioned Johnson to design it—protesting "the use of the avant garde art" at the New York State Pavilion. "This Fair is not a circus or *jahrmarkt,*" he wrote, using the German word for amusement park, "and such a presentation is unworthy of the ideal and accomplishments of the citizens of this great State. It cannot possibly enhance the American image in the eye of any foreign or native visitor." He added that he hoped Moses would stand his ground and not lower ticket prices for children, "so that as few as possible will see" the Johnson-commissioned works.

Williams ridiculed the pop art pieces to reporters. The artists, he told the *Long Island Star Journal,* were "way out, like man, say Beatnik Land or some haven for Bohemian artists." A spokesperson for the Museum of Modern Art retorted that Williams's complaints were nothing more than a case of sour grapes, while Johnson defended his commissions, adding that they were not picked "at random" but because they represented the "best" of the current generation of artists. Williams was also surprised to find that the avant-garde artists had another unlikely defender: Moses, the only public official who responded to his letter. "As to what you term the 'avant garde art commissioned for the New York State Pavilion,' I have no opinion and express none," wrote Moses, "except to remark in passing that your letter seems to be just a bit intemperate."

While Moses wasn't a fan of such work, he was true to his word that there was room for all schools of art at his World's Fair, despite what his foes—whom he dismissed as the "long-haired critics, fanatics, and demagogues, perfectionists and daydreamers"—said. And like some of his most vocal critics, he spoke highly of Johnson's handiwork, defending the New York State Pavilion as a building "that grows on you." By early 1964, he would put the postmodernist structure on his short list of Fair buildings that he wanted to grace the post-Fair Flushing Meadow Park.

The controversy over art at the World's Fair was over for now. But by the time opening day rolled around, many New Yorkers who had never heard of pop art or Warhol before would soon get their first glimpse of this odd, downtown hipster and his work that would capture so many imaginations and revolutionize art, and perhaps even more importantly, the art market. And they could thank Moses and the World's Fair for that.

Americans are the youngest country, the largest country, and the strongest country, we like to say, and yet the very notion of change, real change throws Americans into a panic.

—James Baldwin, November 1963

Robert Moses arrived at his office in the Administration Building at Flushing Meadow early on the morning of Friday, November 22, as he always did—driven to work in a chauffeured car. After quickly getting down to work, he dictated a number of memos on a range of issues, including the ongoing controversy about modern art at the World's Fair. He happily noted that the previous day's edition of the *New York Times* ran a story about the priceless paintings by El Greco, Goya, and Velázquez from Madrid's Prado Museum that would be exhibited in the Spanish Pavilion; it was exactly the kind of press he hoped would silence his critics.

As he scoured the morning papers, scores of hard-hat workers labored in the late November weather to finish the dozens pavilions that were in various stages of construction. The World's Fair would open in exactly five months and there was much—perhaps too much—to do. Shea Stadium, the new baseball park that existed because Moses wanted a ballpark in Queens, was, as it had been for months, behind schedule. More than one hundred electricians were working seven days a week to ensure that the stadium, with its fifty-six thousand seats, would be open in time for the New York Mets to play the 1964 season in its new state-of-the-art home.

As far as Moses was concerned, the stadium was one more pavilion at his World's Fair, an ingenious way of attracting tens of thousands of fans throughout the long baseball season, which, like the Fair, extended from April to October. Shea Stadium was also a key component of Moses' post-Fair Flushing Meadow Park, which he promised would become "the most important park in the entire City, measured by size, usage, or any other yardstick." Although Moses was instrumental in having the stadium built, he wasn't directly involved in its construction and could only watch as others realized his vision, a position he never relished. Earlier that week he had confided to an associate that "the stadium may be completed by April 15," but he wasn't holding his breath.

Meanwhile, across the Atlantic in Moses' beloved England, screaming teenagers and youths were agog over a new musical quartet calling themselves the Beatles. The youth of England besieged record shops that morning to purchase the band's second LP, *With the Beatles*. The album, which featured a moody black-and-white photo of the band gazing straight ahead with deadly seriousness, as if they were the possessors of some joyless knowledge, immediately topped the British charts, where it finally dislodged their own debut album *Please Please Me*, released exactly seven months earlier.

The four Liverpudlians with matching custom-made suits, identical mop-top haircuts, irreverent attitudes, and, perhaps most shocking to the class-conscious British, working-class accents, had produced a series of chart-topping hits—"Please Please Me," "From Me to You," "She Loves You," "I Want to Hold Your Hand"—that had, seemingly overnight, destroyed and resurrected the British pop industry in their own image. One journalist even created a new name for the mass hysteria that the band was creating among the younger portion of Her Majesty's royal subjects: Beatlemania.

Earlier that month Her Royal Majesty got a chance to hear the band in person at the Royal Variety Performance at London's Prince of Wales Theatre. Queen Elizabeth, Princess Margaret, and the Queen Mother—the latter two seen snapping their fingers and clapping along to the beat—attended the black-tie affair among other well-heeled Brits. As the Beatles were about to end their set with their roaring take on the Isley Brothers' "Twist and Shout," John Lennon was unable to resist mouthing off in front of his social betters. "For our last number, I'd like to ask your help," he informed his diamond-flashing, tuxedo-wearing audience. "Would the people in the cheaper seats clap your hands? And the rest of you, if you'll just rattle your jewelry."

The concert and the pandemiclike spread of Beatlemania reached journalists in America, despite the fact that Capitol Records, the American subsidiary of EMI, the band's British record label, had refused to release any of its music stateside. "American Top 40 in those days was bland white artists, and that's the way the American record companies wanted it then," recalled Paul White, a Capitol Records A&R executive. "There were the Fabians"—as in Fabian, the clean-cut teenage pop star—"and ordinary types of things that didn't offend anybody." Still, *Time* and *Newsweek* covered the Beatles' unprecedented popularity in the United Kingdom and Lennon's cheeky comments at the Royal Variety Performance.

Soon NBC's *Huntley-Brinkley Report* aired a segment on the group. By chance, Ed Sullivan, the TV impresario who hosted his self-titled variety show on CBS—the most important half-hour of television in show business—was at London's Heathrow Airport on October 31 where he witnessed Beatlemania firsthand, as thousands of screaming teens gathered to glimpse their heroes returning from a Scandinavian tour. Within weeks he had negotiated three appearances by the group for his show in February 1964.

The Sullivan deal helped CBS land exclusive rights to Beatles appearances for one year. The network aired its first story on the band with a four-minute segment on *Morning News with Mike Wallace* in the early hours of November 22, with plans to re-air it that evening on the CBS *Evening News* with Walter Cronkite.

While the Beatles were making news on American televisions, Ken Kesey, an athletic, golden-haired, twenty-nine-year-old novelist, was on the road in Texas headed back to his ranch in La Jolla, California. Kesey had driven cross-country to New York City with a friend to see the Broadway adaptation of his novel, *One Flew Over the Cuckoo's Nest,* starring Kirk Douglas. While in New York, he was curious to see what the World's Fair was about and drove out to Queens to glimpse the pavilions being erected. "Wow, this is spectacular," Kesey said, suitably impressed by the oddly shaped buildings in Flushing Meadow. "We're gonna want to come see this." Next time, though, he thought, he would bring some friends.

As his car sped westbound on a Texas highway, Kesey heard news that would erase all the other events of the day. On a campaign trip to Dallas, in preparation for the upcoming 1964 election, America's young, charismatic president was assassinated as he sat in the backseat of a black open-air limousine, next to his wife, First Lady Jacqueline Kennedy, while their car passed through Dealey Plaza in the bright midday sun. Although doctors at Parkland Memorial Hospital reportedly fought to resuscitate him, nothing could be done for the forty-six-year-old president. "Everywhere you went you looked in people's eyes and they all felt the same thing," Kesey said. "It wasn't just sadness, it was the loss of an innocence, the loss of the idea that good is always going to prevail."

Back in Flushing Meadow, after Cronkite informed the nation shortly after 2:30 p.m. eastern standard time that the President of the United States was dead, Moses released a short statement in honor of the commander in chief who had visited the Fairgrounds just twelve months earlier. "The World's Fair had counted confidently on the international leadership, support, and encouragement of President Kennedy," wrote Moses, who sent both staff and workers home for the weekend. "We shall have to go on without his support but with his inspiration ever in mind."

The World's Fair, which Kennedy had promised to attend, would open five months to the day after his assassination. To millions of Americans, whether they loved or hated Kennedy, his shocking murder—and the eventual official and questionable government explanation of it—was undeniable evidence that something had gone terribly wrong with the country. What they did not and could not know was that the events of November 22, 1963, were just the beginning: An era in the nation's history was over, and the new one that had just begun would prove to be far beyond the imagination of most Americans.

13

The time has come for Americans of all races and creeds and political beliefs to understand and to respect one another. So let us put an end to the teaching and the preaching of hate and evil and violence.
—President Lyndon B. Johnson, November 27, 1963

For four days the entire nation was riveted to their televisions; the only news transmitted over the airwaves was coverage about President Kennedy and his funeral. On Sunday, November 24, just two days after the president's murder, his alleged assassin, Lee Harvey Oswald, was shot dead by shady Dallas nightclub owner Jack Ruby while in police custody and in full view of live television news cameras.

Anyone watching that Sunday morning—young or old—witnessed another mysterious assassination unfolding in real time, another unprecedented shock to America's collective psyche, just one in a series of indelible, tragic images over those four days that would haunt the country for decades to come: the grief-stricken First Lady, her delicate features covered in a black veil; the president's seven-year-old daughter, Caroline, kneeling with her mother at her father's casket as it lay in state in the Capitol; and her little brother, John F. Kennedy Jr.—who turned three on the day of the president's funeral—saluting the coffin carrying the father he would barely remember. "It just didn't seem like America this weekend," one New Yorker complained to the *Times*.

Vice President Lyndon Baines Johnson took the Oath of Office aboard Air Force One as it sat on the runway at the Dallas airport just hours after Kennedy's murder. A shell-shocked Jacqueline Kennedy looked on at the untimely and succinct transition of power. She was still wearing her wool Chanel strawberry pink dress, splattered with her husband's blood. "One leg was almost entirely covered with [blood] and her right glove was caked—that immaculate woman—it was caked with blood," remembered the new First Lady, Lady Bird Johnson, who comforted her predecessor in the back of the airplane. "And that was somehow one of the most poignant sights . . . exquisitely dressed, and caked in blood." But when Mrs. Kennedy was asked if she wanted to change into new clothes, she refused. "I want them to see what they've done to Jack," she said with a fierce determination.

Two days after the funeral, the new president addressed Congress and the nation. Three years earlier, during his inaugural address, Kennedy had told the country, "Let us begin"; now here was Johnson, America's new and unelected president, offering a grieving nation the new refrain: "Let us continue." Then Johnson declared how "no memorial, oration or eulogy could more eloquently honor President Kennedy's memory than the earliest possible passage of the civil rights bill for which he fought so long. . . . We have talked long enough in this country about equal rights. We have talked for one hundred years or more. It is time now to write the next chapter, and to write it in the books of law."

If the leaders and members of the civil rights movement were suddenly dumbstruck as they watched Johnson's speech at home that Thanksgiving Eve, suddenly perplexed at the sight of the Texan, they could be forgiven. Every black man or woman who had suffered the savagery of attack dogs, fire hoses, and beatings or endured jail for seeking their constitutional rights had plenty of reasons to distrust the new president. As a congressman and then US senator, Johnson had either failed to support or, when he became the Senate Majority Leader, personally gutted civil rights legislation—as he did in 1957 and 1960. Yet there he was, the one-time protégé of segregationist senator Richard B. Russell of Georgia, architect of the Southern Manifesto (which Johnson never signed), picking up the fallen standard of Kennedy and throwing his thirty-two years of political muscle behind the civil rights movement, just as he had promised two of Kennedy's closet aides, Kenneth O'Donnell and Larry O'Brien, he would aboard Air Force One shortly before he took the Oath of Office.

While America's political equilibrium twisted on its axis, letters requesting that Robert Moses do something dramatic to honor the fallen president who had supported the World's Fair began arriving at Flushing Meadow within days of the funeral. One writer suggested that

Moses erect a John F. Kennedy Pavilion; another man, from Forest Hills, Queens, sent Moses a letter, enclosed with five dollars, suggesting the Master Builder ask all Americans to donate one dollar each to erect a suitable memorial. Moses promptly sent the money back, suggesting that a more appropriate honor would be to name the new National Arts Center then being planned for the banks of the Potomac—designed by Moses associate Edward Durrell Stone—after Kennedy. Moses also supported the renaming of Idlewild Airport in southern Queens to John F. Kennedy International Airport, as some New York City officials had already suggested.

The Master Builder wasted no time in attempting to win the new president's support for his World's Fair. On December 5 he sent a formal invitation to President Johnson requesting the thirty-sixth President of the United States deliver the keynote address on opening day, just as Kennedy had promised to do. It would be months before Moses would receive an answer, unfortunately, leaving his opening day plans in limbo.

Meanwhile, as the World's Fair drew closer, preparations of another kind were under way in New York City. Authorities there had begun a coordinated campaign to "clean up" the Fair's host city in anticipation of the millions of tourists that were expected to flood Gotham over the next two years. After all, the mayor and other officials were hoping that Moses' exhibition would inflate municipal coffers by millions of dollars. They wanted to be certain nothing—or no one—the tourists encountered would offend them. One of the primary targets of the campaign were the denizens of lower Manhattan, particularly the more bohemian elements of its flourishing art scene.

While Greenwich Village and its adjacent district, the West Village, had been an area populated by artists, writers, and bohemians of every kind since the mid-nineteenth century, its burgeoning populations expanded in the postwar years to the tenement buildings east of Broadway. This area of expansion, which roughly stretched from 14th Street (exactly where Moses' Stuyvesant Town towers began) to Houston Street and from Broadway to Avenue D, had once been the domain of generations of immigrant families seeking the American Dream.

Hailing from some of the Continent's poorest locales—including Sicily, Poland, and the Ukraine—these immigrants settled on what was known as Manhattan's East Side, bringing their food, culture, and artisan skills to the New World and, in the process, creating a dynamic neighborhood with a Europeanlike feel.

When their children grew up and married, many fled their former tenement homes and headed further east, for houses in the less crowded districts of Queens and the burgeoning suburbs of Long Island—now readily accessible thanks to the expressways, parkways, and bridges that Moses had been building for decades. In their wake, artists, poets, filmmakers, and assorted scenesters repopulated the former East Side apartments, transforming the neighborhood into a bohemian enclave that would eventually be known as the East Village.

It was only fitting that downtown Manhattan should come under attack by city authorities as Moses entered the final stages of World's Fair preparation. Moses had been trying, in one way or another, to raze various downtown areas or reshape their streets to fit his own master plan. But Greenwich Village was in many ways a fortress that Moses could not penetrate: Time and again he was stopped by the activists and artists, bohemians and intelligentsia, who, led by writer Jane Jacobs, illustrated that there were indeed limits to the Master Builder's supposedly unlimited power. (In 1962 while working on the World's Fair, Moses had one of his staffers investigate Jacobs, in an attempt to dig up anything he could use against her.)

Jacobs repeatedly foiled Moses' plans to slice the historic Washington Square Park in two; she fought him when he declared a large portion of the West Village—including her home on Hudson Street—a slum area; and in 1962, perhaps most painfully to Moses, she led the charge to finally kill his proposed Lower Manhattan Expressway, an elevated ten-lane highway that would have stretched from south Manhattan, slicing through historic neighborhoods like Chinatown, Little Italy, SoHo (then called the Cast-Iron District for its distinct facades), and Greenwich Village. This last crusade earned the attention and support of Bob Dylan. He wrote a song about the downtown streets he loved and offered it to the activists as a *cri de guerre*. "It had a lot of street names in it that we sang at rallies," Jacobs later remembered.

By the early 1960s, as surely as Moses was transforming Flushing Meadow into the World's Fair, a wide range of artists were transforming the East Village into an important outpost of the great cultural shift that had begun to take root in America—from Julian Beck and Judith Malina's Living Theatre; to the Peace Eye Store on East 10th Street, owned and operated by poet/activist Ed Sanders; to the cutting-edge underground cinema of filmmakers Jack Smith and Kenneth Anger, which were shown at various downtown venues by Lithuanian-born poet/critic Jonas Mekas, who created the Film-Makers' Cooperative. Alongside these underground artists flourished nationally known talents like comedian Lenny Bruce, part of the new generation of "sick comics," who never heard of a sacred cow that he didn't want to slay, and who, when he wasn't making the rounds on television, was busy filling Greenwich Village coffeehouses. And just on the other side of Washington Square Park was Dylan's West Village apartment.

If anyone sold the idea of living in downtown Manhattan to millions of disaffected youths who had never even been to New York, it was probably Dylan. The cover of his 1963 breakthrough album, *The Freewheelin' Bob Dylan,* featured an iconic photograph of the songwriter and his then-girlfriend, Suze Rotolo, strolling down a snow-covered Village street near their apartment, lending its beaten-down neighborhood considerable hipster cachet. Like the Beatles' second album, *With the Beatles,* the cover was unusual for its time. It became "one of those cultural markers that influenced the look of album covers precisely because of its casual, down-home spontaneity and sensibility," recalled Rotolo decades later.

Then at the end of 1963, almost as if to bestow cultural validity on the vibrant and multidimensional art scene that was happening downtown, poet Allen Ginsberg—the celebrated author of "Howl" and "Kaddish" and Beat Generation writer who had helped create a media storm in the staid, conservative 1950s—returned to New York after several years of incessant travel. He eventually settled in an East Fifth Street apartment with his lover, Peter Orlovsky. It may not have been obvious right at the time, but the downtown art scene was about to explode.

The changes to New York in the early sixties were noticed by another prodigal son of Gotham. Bronx-born A. M. Rosenthal, the newly installed Metropolitan Editor of the *New York Times*, had been a Pulitzer Prize–winning foreign correspondent for the paper, filing stories from Eastern Europe, India, and Japan, among other foreign locales, before resettling in New York in the summer of 1963. In an attempt to modernize the Paper of Record's coverage of his hometown, Rosenthal and his deputy, Arthur Gelb, would go on frequent walks in the neighborhoods that usually didn't benefit from coverage in the *Times*.

During one such stroll through Manhattan, Rosenthal noticed that some men were not hiding their homosexuality in public. Rosenthal thought the paper should do a story about this new sexual boldness. Wanting their reporters to cover New York City with "the curiosity of a foreign correspondent in an unfamiliar city," Rosenthal and Gelb selected Robert C. Doty, the *Times*' former Paris bureau chief, and gave him a month to report the piece.

The result was an incendiary front-page *Times* story on December 17, 1963—Growth of Overt Homosexuality in City Provokes Wide Concern—which claimed in its opening line that "the problem of homosexuality in New York" was a top concern of both the police and the State Liquor Authority. Earlier in the year, the police had raided known gay hangouts such as Fawn in the West Village and the Heights Supper Club in Brooklyn, and revoked their liquor licenses in an attempt to curb "the city's most sensitive open secret— the presence of what is probably the greatest homosexual population in the world and its increasing openness." This "open secret," as the *Times* explained, concerned not only the police but psychiatrists and religious leaders. "Homosexuality is another one of the many problems confronting law enforcement in this city," Police Commissioner Michael J. Murphy told the *Times*, while stressing that the "underlying factors of homosexuality are not criminal but rather medical and sociological in nature."

In the article, experts estimated that at least a hundred thousand homosexual "deviants" or "sexual inverts" lived in New York and have "colonized" certain areas of the city, including portions of the Upper West Side and Upper East Side, a large swath of Midtown, and Greenwich Village, which was now "a center for the bohemians of the homosexual world." More than a thousand men were arrested each year since 1960 for "overt homosexual activity," the majority of them busted for soliciting sex.

Again and again throughout the article, homosexuality was presented as a New York problem, both in the five boroughs and its outer environs, where a homosexual "can find vacation spots frequented by his kind—notably parts of Fire Island, a section of the beach of Jacob Riis Park, and many others." The *Times* earnestly examined the then-prevalent viewpoint of psychologists who thought that homosexuality was the product of "parental misdeeds and attitudes" and that such men could be "cured by sophisticated analytical and therapeutic techniques." What's more, the *Times* warned that it wasn't just men embracing a "deviant" lifestyle throughout New York City—"lesbianism is also on the rise."

Some greeted the article with acclaim, a new direction for the staid "Old Gray Lady," but to others it was the opening salvo against New York's gay community—the *Times* article had explained that "gay" and "straight" were now words of choice among homosexuals to describe sexual identities—and it was much discussed in the ensuing weeks. And it certainly fueled the city's oppressive clean-up campaign downtown, carried out with the help of Police Commissioner Murphy and under Mayor Robert F. Wagner Jr.'s watch.

To someone like Frank O'Hara, a prominent member of the New York School of Poetry and an openly gay man, it was a malicious attack against him and his friends. O'Hara wrote John Ashbery, his friend and fellow poet, who was then in Paris, a sarcastic, angry letter informing him of the shifting atmosphere in New York: "You may be interested to know that the *New York Times* had a front page (and a full page continuation inside) story on how New York is the world center of homosexuality, with somewhere between 100,000 and 600,000 of *THEM* prowling the areaways of fair Gotham. Kind of exciting, isn't it?" By spring, O'Hara characterization of the situation to friends wouldn't be so tongue in cheek.

As America attempted to restore its social equilibrium, across the Atlantic, Great Britain seemed on the verge of losing its own: Beatlemania wasn't just sweeping the charts, it was akin to a seismic shift of the nation's tectonic plates; riots and melees erupted in any city or town where the Liverpool quartet appeared. A December 1 article in the *New York Times Magazine*—the first appearance of the band in the pages of the Paper of Record—began like a dispatch from the front lines of war: "They are fighting all over Britain. Rarely a night passes without an outbreak in some town or other. Sometimes it is a mere skirmish involving a few hundred police, but more often there is a pitched battle with broken legs, cracked ribs and bloody noses."

The band's fans were hardly criminals or even dime-store leather-clad juvenile delinquents—known as "Teddy Boys" in England. In Carlisle, the historic English town near the border of Scotland, a four-hour-long melee erupted between police and four hundred schoolgirls as the distraught youngsters tried to buy tickets to the band's show. When the Beatles arrived in Dublin, there was a mad rush among the young teens resulting in injuries and broken bones. "It was all right until the mania degenerated into barbarism," complained a Dublin police chief.

There had been teen idols before: Frank Sinatra in the 1930s and the Beatles' favorite, Elvis Presley, in the 1950s. But this was different. Unlike Sinatra and Presley, the Beatles were a group that wrote, recorded, and played its own songs; they were a self-contained unit and didn't have to rely on anyone besides themselves to create their music. Then add to the mix their Northern England working-class cheekiness and rebellious attitude toward any form of authority—they refused to adhere to Britain's rigid, traditional class system; they were utterly authentic both onstage and off.

The Beatles were something entirely new on the pop landscape. The *Times* declared the band to be spokesmen for "the new, noisy, anti-Establishment generation, which is becoming a force in British life." It seemed that all at once, the youth of Britain had new idols to worship, new role models to emulate, and soon enough American teenagers—and much of the rest of the Free World's youth—would follow. "We came out of the fucking sticks to take over the world," Lennon would later say.

The Beatles were not the only rising stars with big dreams. In December, back in New York, folk hero Dylan was having a different kind of impact on the youth of America. Already deemed a poet, a prophet, and "voice of his generation," Dylan was a bit lost. Earlier in the month he had accepted a Tom Paine Award by the National Emergency Civil Liberties Committee at their annual Bill of Rights Dinner at the Americana Hotel. It was a prestigious honor by the group, a product of the battle-scarred Old Left, who had fought McCarthyism and other progressive-smearing tactics. Dylan, it would seem, was in good company; that same night novelist James Baldwin, whom the mainstream press treated as if he were the spokesman for black America, was also honored.

But Dylan wasn't having it. He didn't want to be the voice of his generation. Seemingly drunk—or high—Dylan accepted the award and then proceeded to insult the crowd. Like Lennon in front of the British Royal Family and their blue-blooded, moneyed kin, Dylan couldn't accept being *accepted* by the Establishment, even if it was an Establishment that he was, at least politically, simpatico with. "I only wish that all you people who are sitting out here today or tonight weren't here and I could see all kinds of faces with hair on their head," he bellowed. "You people should be at the beach. You should be out there and you should be swimming and you should be just relaxing in the time you have to relax."

At first the crowd laughed uneasily. Dylan's rambling speech got odder and more belligerent, and the crowd didn't know what to make of this young baby-faced folksinger. Then, to make sure his older audience understood just where he was—or wasn't—coming from, Dylan committed an act of political heresy. "I got to admit that the man who shot President Kennedy, Lee Oswald," he said. "I saw some of myself in him." Here was the man-child who wrote "Blowin' in the Wind" comparing himself to a man who, just three weeks earlier, had murdered a president. After a smattering of boos, Dylan said he accepted the award on behalf of James Forman, one of the founders of the SNCC, and left.

Although the Tom Paine episode was the beginning of Dylan's public rupture with the political activists who bought his records, he was still, in his own way, committed to their cause. At the end of the month, Dylan attended a national council meeting of the Students for a Democratic Society, or SDS—the national organization of student radicals that would in a short time become a national political force—in Brooklyn Heights. After listening to what the organization's top tacticians like Tom Hayden and Todd Gitlin had to say, the folksinger pledged his support. "I don't know what you all are talking about, but it sounds like you want something to happen, and if that's what you want, that's what I want," he told them.

Two weeks after the meeting, Dylan released his third album in less than two years, *The Times They Are a-Changin'*, a record that would further cement his reputation as a songwriter of unparalleled talent and only amplify the roar of the critics who labeled him the voice of his generation. As one critic would comment, the title track was sung by "a prophetic voice trumpeting a changing order." Whatever people thought of Dylan, no one who had witnessed the surreal, tragic, bloodstained events of 1963 could argue with the veracity of the album's title.

PART TWO

SOMETHING NEW

14.

"When the modes of the music change, the walls of the city shake."
—Allen Ginsberg

Robert Moses found himself dealing with the same old problems in the new year of 1964. He had been complaining loudly—and to anyone who would listen—for the last two years about the US Federal Pavilion, the largest of the World's Fair's buildings. He was unimpressed with architect Charles Luckman's clean and sleek modernist design—it was nothing more than "a square doughnut on stilts" in his estimation—and, try as he might, he was unable to influence the pavilion's exhibits.

Moses had little faith in the Commerce Department, including Under Secretary of Commerce Franklin D. Roosevelt Jr. the son of his bitter enemy. He detested Herb Klotz, the coordinator for the pavilion, and had little time even for his old ally, New York–based developer Norman K. Winston. Moses worried that the host country's pavilion would be "second-rate." (By the end of the Fair's first season, one Flushing Meadow executive said "third-rate" was more like it.)

Winston contacted Moses early in the new year with a request: The US Federal Pavilion owed $223,000 in electrical contracting expenses but was cash-strapped, so he wanted to know if Moses would "deobligate" the pavilion of the payments it owed the World's Fair Corporation. Moses wouldn't hear of it. "It is certainly no fault of the Fair that you are short of funds," he shot back in a memo. Moses said he would take the matter under consideration, but being unable to resist a cheap dig at his friend, insisted on imposing "one condition . . . namely that you cease to use the word *deobligate*. It's not in the dictionary." He also made sure his written response was carbon copied to top World's Fair and Commerce Department executives. Maybe he felt guilty or maybe he was just in a more generous mood, but a few weeks later, Moses allowed Winston to defer in his other Fair payments so the pavilion wouldn't default on its bills.

There were other lingering concerns, such as a memorial to President Kennedy. Although the public had been writing the World's Fair chief with their suggestions since the assassination, Moses was not about to make the delicate process of choosing an appropriate memorial to the slain president a democratic one; he would handle it privately and in own his way. He told his friend Gilmore D. Clarke, a respected landscape artist who had designed Moses' beloved Unisphere, in mid-January that he wanted a sculpture or bust of Kennedy, but something that would not offend public tastes. "A really fine objective piece of portrait sculpture in the conservative tradition," he instructed. "No distorted Epstein, Moore or Lipchitz stuff to become the subject of public controversy." The last thing that the World's Fair needed was another uproar regarding art, particularly one that risked incurring the wrath of an American public still mourning its fallen leader.

At the end of the month, Moses got the news that he had been fearing: President Johnson wouldn't be able to attend the opening day ceremonies. It was a severe blow to the prestige of the Fair. Moses knew that any New Yorker old enough to remember the 1939–40 World's Fair could recall that President Franklin D. Roosevelt had addressed the crowds at Flushing Meadow; what's more, the speech was broadcast on a new technological device called a television, two hundred of which were strategically positioned around the city, allowing citizens to actually hear and—more importantly, *see*—their president. Moses also knew that when the New York newspapers found out, they would have a field day.

In the meantime, he received friendly cooperation from one of the most powerful men in show business: Ed Sullivan. The television impresario, whose eponymous-named Sunday-night variety show was one of the most-watched programs in the nation, contacted Moses in early February regarding the special World's Fair–themed show he was preparing; if there was any aspect of the Fair that Moses wanted specifically promoted, Sullivan said, he only had to ask. The Master Builder trusted Sullivan's showbiz instincts implicitly and responded that anything the TV host thought would "contribute to the exposition's success" was fine with him. Sullivan's was exactly the kind of carte blanche cooperation that Moses expected from all of New York's media elite but, much to his endless chagrin, rarely, if ever, received.

Moses need not have worried about the presidential snub flooding the press, however: The New York media was about to become preoccupied for the next several weeks with the arrival of the Beatles, who would capture the hearts and minds of the nation's teenagers, who would then buy their 45 singles and LP albums by the millions. The same day that Sullivan wrote Moses—Friday, February 7—the TV showman was expecting his special guests, the Beatles, to arrive via transatlantic Pan Am jet at John F. Kennedy International Airport in Jamaica, Queens, shortly after 1:00 p.m. They were coming to New York to perform on *The Ed Sullivan Show* on Sunday night, as they would for the next two weeks.

The Beatles were still something of a gamble. The previous October Sullivan witnessed Beatlemania firsthand when he happened to be at London's Heathrow Airport at the same time that the band returned from a tour in Scandinavia. He immediately got in contact with the band's manager, Brian Epstein, and booked the group on his show. However, his crosstown rival, Jack Paar, had secretly obtained a concert clip of the band and played it for his bemused audience in early January. Paar's audience hadn't been impressed. Neither had the *New York Times'* television critic, Jack Gould, who wrote the next day that the Beatles were like "[Elvis] Presley multiplied by four, their calisthenics were wilder, and . . . might prove infinitely more amusing." Gould predicted the band would flop, doubting that Beatlemania would be "successfully exported. On this side of the Atlantic, it is dated stuff."

He had a point. In the early 1960s, rock 'n' roll had flamed out. The proof, as Gould noted, could be found on the charts: The week that Paar aired his Beatles clip, the top song in the United States was "Dominique" by the Singing Nun—an actual Belgian nun—who became an international recording sensation (and also landed a spot on *The Ed Sullivan Show*). The year 1963, according to music and cultural critic Greil Marcus, was a low point for the music he grew up listening to. "Rock 'n' roll—the radio—felt dull and stupid, a dead end," he later wrote.

The golden age of rock 'n' roll of the 1950s and the media sensation that had ensued was over. After his discharge from the US Army, Presley had gone mainstream, recording forgettable songs ("Kissing Cousins") and starring in even more forgettable motion pictures (including 1963's *It Happened at the World's Fair*, filmed at the 1962 Seattle Fair). Chuck Berry's star had faded after he was jailed for transporting a fourteen-year-old girl across state lines; Little Richard returned to the church; Jerry Lee Lewis married his thirteen-year-old cousin; and Buddy Holly, Eddie Cochran, and Ritchie Valens were dead. So it seemed was rock 'n' roll.

The Beatles knew it, too. "We were new," John Lennon confessed to *Rolling Stone*, rock's paper of record, years later. "When we got here you were all walking around in fucking Bermuda shorts with Boston crewcuts and stuff on your teeth. The chicks looked like fuckin' 1940s horses. There was no conception of dress or any of that jazz. I mean we just thought, 'What an ugly race.' It looked just disgustin'." But Lennon and his bandmates knew that the roots of the Beatles sound—rock 'n' roll, R&B, Motown, soul, pop, even flashes of country and western, all crafted with Tin Pan Alley–like polish—were anything but new. They were here to preach the gospel of American music to the country that had invented it.

The Beatles had a unique vision of American music, one that was untainted by the country's great historic stain of race. In February 1964 music was segregated like everything else in the country. The color line in music had black music on one side (Berry, the Drifters, Smokey Robinson, Marvin Gaye, the Isley Brothers) and white music on the other (Presley, the Everly Brothers, the late Holly). Others, most importantly Elvis, a country boy from Tupelo, Mississippi, had blurred the line before, but the Beatles were different; they unabashedly and openly loved the music of black America.

"We used to really laugh at America, except for its music," Lennon confessed in the same *Rolling Stone* interview. "It was the black music we dug. Over here even the blacks were laughing at people like Chuck Berry and the blues signers. . . . The whites only listened to Jan and Dean and all that. . . . Nobody was listening to rock 'n' roll or to black music in America. We felt like [our] message was, 'Listen to this music.'. . . We thought we were coming to the land of its origin. But nobody wanted to know about it."

They soon would. By the time the Beatles' jet landed at JFK, the band's single "I Want to Hold Your Hand" was the No. 1 song in the country and would be for the next six weeks. In fact, the band would have a monopoly on *Billboard*'s top spot for the next fourteen weeks—an unprecedented feat at the time—with two more No. 1 songs: "She Loves You" and "Can't Buy Me Love." Sullivan's gamble would pay off beyond anyone's wildest imaginations.

America would get its first taste of Beatlemania in early 1964, the lads becoming, in many ways, their own four-man World's Fair. If Moses wanted to know what would attract young teenagers, whom he expected to be repeat customers at his exhibit, he only had to observe the scene at JFK Airport. Waiting for the English youths—two of the mop-tops were twenty-one years old; the other pair, twenty-three years old—were three thousand teenagers who had been whipped into hysteria by a barrage of record label hype: Capitol Records had plastered posters and bumper stickers all over proclaiming messianically "The Beatles Are Coming!" Local deejays encouraged kids to "cut school" and make a beeline for the airport to "see the Beatles." But Murray the K, who spoke in a brash, pseudo-hipster slang, turned his Queens-based AM station, WINS, into a self-styled Beatles headquarters, proclaiming February 7 "B-Day" and referring to himself as "the *fifth* Beatle." Airport officials were shocked at the spectacle. "We've never seen anything like this here before," one told the *New York Times*. "Never. Not even for kings and queens."

After landing, the Beatles were shuffled into a makeshift press conference with a roomful of cynical New York newspapermen, many of whom were wondering just what all the hysteria was about. They soon found themselves getting played by the quick-witted Brits, each of whom could hold their own with the most grizzled reporters. The questions came at the band rapid-fire. The answers were just as fast.

Q: "Are you for real?"

A: "Come have a feel." (Lennon)

Q: "Do you ever have haircuts?"

A: "I had one yesterday." (Harrison)

Q: "How about the Detroit campaign to stamp out the Beatles?"

A: "We've a campaign of our own to stamp out Detroit." (McCartney)

Q: "What do you think of Beethoven?"

A: "I love him. Especially his poems." (Starr)

In one brief, spontaneous, noisy, off-the-cuff press conference, the four lads from Liverpool did what Moses had rarely (if ever) done in four decades: They charmed the abrasive and jaundiced New York press corp. Two days later, when the Beatles played their five-song set on *The Ed Sullivan Show*, seventy-three million Americans tuned in to watch—a record audience for an entertainment program. That was three million more than Moses was promising to attract to his World's Fair over two years. Someone in Flushing Meadow should have seen the writing on the wall.

New York music promoter Sid Bernstein certainly did. He had booked the band into Carnegie Hall based solely on glowing reports from the British press. Fortunately for Bernstein, the Carnegie dates were in the same month as the band's *Ed Sullivan Show* appearances. "That practically ensured my dates," Bernstein recalled, "because anything on *Sullivan* twice in a row was tantamount to being a superstar."

Bob Dylan noticed, too. In February 1964 he was driving cross-country with four friends in a sky-blue Ford station wagon, trying to escape himself. Dylan was still reeling from a November 1963 exposé in *Newsweek* revealing his true origins—he wasn't the half-Indian high plains drifter he pretended to be, but a Jewish kid from a working-class family in Hibbings, Minnesota. Needing a change of scene, Dylan and company left New York on February 3, meandering their way to California, where he was scheduled to play a concert in Berkeley at the end of the month. Along the way, they stopped in Virginia (where the singer's road manager, Victor Maymudes, donated clothes to striking miners), North Carolina (Dylan knocked on poet Carl Sandburg's door, only to be turned away), and New Orleans, where they partied during Mardi Gras. It was the festive atmosphere of the Big Easy that inspired Dylan to write a new song with stream-of-consciousness kaleidoscopic lyrics called "Mr. Tambourine Man."

They were driving somewhere in California when "I Want to Hold Your Hand" came over the radio. "Did you hear that?" Dylan asked his friends. "Fuck! Man, that was great! Oh, man—fuck!" When the song ended, Maymudes flipped the knobs as he drove, looking in vain for another station playing the Beatles. "Don't worry about it, man," Dylan told him, as he stared out the window in silence for miles. "We kept driving along," recalled Maymudes, "but we lost Bob somewhere back on Route 1."

At seventy-five, Moses was hardly hip enough to hear what Dylan was hearing. His musical tastes included the insipid stylings of bandleader Guy Lombardo and his Royal Canadians, not only a close friend, but one that Moses made sure played weekly concerts at the World's Fair. Just as Beatlemania was about to hit New York City like an invading army, Moses was writing liner notes for Russian-born conductor and arranger Andre Kostelanetz's April 1964 album *Wonderland of New York*—a record which he thought served as "an excellent medium to invoke the spirit of our town." Kostelanetz's popular radio broadcasts of light classical music and lush orchestral recordings of the American songbook helped pioneer a new musical genre: easy listening.

A week after the Beatles' *Ed Sullivan* debut, Mary C. Dillion of Ridgefield, Connecticut, a young fan of both the Beatles and the World's Fair, mailed Moses a suggestion: Wouldn't the Beatles make "a wonderful addition" to the Fair? She noted how their Carnegie Hall concert was sold out—20,000 fans were turned away from the 2,870-seat concert hall, in fact. Perhaps, she wanted to know, could Moses use his enormous clout and "ask them" to play the Fair? "Please write me and tell me what you think of my idea." He did.

Two days later, Moses mailed his curt response:

Dear Miss Dillion:

Absolutely nothing doing.

Sincerely,
Robert Moses

But before the World's Fair was over, Moses would realize that his young correspondent was right. The Beatles would eventually play Flushing Meadow and prove two things in the process: One, that they were, without question, the biggest pop stars on the planet; and two, they wielded far more influence among young audiences than Moses or his World's Fair.

15.

I don't have to be who you want me to be. I'm free to be who I want.
—Cassius Clay/Muhammad Ali, February 27, 1964

I don't care what Cassius Clay says, "You are the greatest!"
—Fan letter to Robert Moses, April 1964

In January 1964 Robert Moses, in a moment of uncharacteristic humility, told the *New York Herald Tribune* that "the most I can possibly expect is to be remembered for a very short time as the Archie Moore of public works." The simple, innocuous comment, like many things Moses did, served multiple purposes. In one sentence he paid homage to his friend Moore, the former light middleweight boxing champion who had a prestigious career that spanned decades, while also passing subtle judgment on the current state of boxing, a sport that was then still a beloved American pasttime. By 1964 Moore had hung up his gloves after a lifetime in the ring; he was part of the sweet science's old guard, representative of another era. Moore had been defeated in November 1962 at the hands of boxing's future: a young brash pugilist unlike any other named Cassius Clay.

For millions of Americans, the twenty-two-year-old bronze-skinned Clay was a nightmare; for millions of others, he was the realization of a dream whose time had finally come. A former Olympic gold-medalist, at six feet, three inches and two hundred pounds, Clay was graceful in the ring and entertaining outside of it. He was handsome, even beautiful, and full of pseudo-poetic bravado, a man who playfully—and repeatedly—referred to himself as "the Greatest."

While in Miami, during a brief break in their tour, the Beatles filmed their third consecutive appearance on *The Ed Sullivan Show* before dropping by the Fifth Street Gym, where Clay was training. Like the Fab Four, Clay was an ascendant star never far from a microphone. But when the Beatles arrived for a quick photo op with the boxer, they were annoyed to be kept waiting. "Where the fuck's Clay?" Ringo shouted to no one in particular. As the quartet headed for the door, the Louisville Lip appeared, winning over the Liverpool Lads with his infectious wit.

"Hello there, Beatles!" he boomed as he entered the gym. "We ought to do some road shows together. We'll get rich." As photographer Harry Benson recalled, "Clay mesmerized them." Used to being the most irreverent guys in the room, the band had met their match. Not that Clay was impressed. After the Beatles left, the young boxer turned to a reporter and asked, "So who were those little faggots?"

Whatever he thought of them, Clay was *new,* just like the Fab Four. Clay was no Jackie Robinson. As the second basemen for the Brooklyn Dodgers and the first African American to break Major League Baseball's race barrier in 1947, Robinson endured the worst racist taunts imaginable from both fans and players, at times even his own teammates. And he endured them mostly in silence. The Dodger executives who had signed him insisted that was the only way, which ultimately made him a target of criticism by Black Nationalists. "Robinson was the white man's hero," Malcolm X pointedly told reporters with Clay at his side.

But 1964 America was a new era, and Clay was a new type of sports hero. He would not—he seemingly could not—keep quiet. He had fought—and talked—his way to a shot at the heavyweight championship of the world in late February. To claim the title, however, he had to defeat reigning champ Sonny Liston, who was as mean and vicious inside the ring as out. A surly illiterate gambler and ex-criminal with connections to the Philadelphia mob, Liston, it was said, could also punch harder than anyone else. If most Americans didn't know what to make of Clay, they knew what to think of Liston: He was a thug.

In 1962 he had squashed the reigning champ, gentleman pugilist Floyd Patterson—who had the backing of both President Kennedy and the NAACP—in a first-round knockout. Liston epitomized everything that was ugly about the sweet science. "We have at last a heavyweight champion on the moral level of the men who own him," *New York Post* columnist Murray Kempton wrote. Considered "the meanest man alive," Liston was photographed in a Santa Claus cap for the December 1963 cover of *Esquire*. It was meant to be both a thought-provoking comment on race in America and a joke, but some Americans weren't ready for such humor—not even *Esquire*'s sophisticated readers, many of whom wrote angry letters or cancelled their subscriptions. "We got a ton of hate mail," recalled George Lois, the Bronx-born Madison Avenue maestro who had conceived and shot the cover, one of dozens he would create throughout the 1960s to ensure that *Esquire* was the most important journalistic chronicler of what was *new* in American culture.

No one gave Clay a chance. By February 25, the day of the fight, Liston was an eight-to-one favorite. Maybe that's why Clay avoided his opponent for most of the fight, dancing around the ring, using his superior speed. By the third round, he had landed enough shots to slice open the skin above Liston's right eye. However, by the fourth, Liston had nearly punched Clay into submission. Fighting on, Clay made his opponent chase him around the ring again, wearing him out; by the sixth, Clay had taken the lead. Then the unthinkable happened. As the seventh round started, Liston refused to continue. He spit out his mouth guard and just sat in his corner, giving up. Cassius Clay was now the heavyweight champion of the world.

The shock of Clay's victory would quickly be overshadowed. Two days later, when a reporter asked him if he was a "card-carrying member of the Black Muslims," Clay, as expected, spoke his mind. "I believe in Allah and peace," he declared. "I don't try to move into white neighborhoods. I don't want to marry a white woman.... I'm not Christian anymore."

The next day, while he and Malcolm X ate breakfast at the Hampton House, a black motel in segregated Miami, he elaborated to a group of white sportswriters: Yes, it was true, he was a member of the Nation of Islam, and as the heavyweight champion of the world, that meant he was rejecting white American society and its God. What's more, he was rejecting the entire concept of integration, the prize that the civil rights movement had been fighting and dying for, just a month after President Johnson had met with Martin Luther King Jr. and Roy Wilkins at the White House to reaffirm his personal commitment to pass the stagnant civil rights bill—"without a word or a comma changed," Johnson told them. (King and the others feared the president had called the meeting to tell them he was watering down the bill.)

Now, at this pivotal moment in race relations in the United States, the newly crowned boxing world champ was rejecting leaders of both races and embracing a religious group on the fringes of American society, an organization that many considered a hate group—*The Hate That Hate Produced*—and feared was bent on overthrowing the government. What's more, Clay had forsaken his Christian name; from now on, as the world would soon learn, he would be known as Muhammad Ali. In just two years, the world of boxing—a sport still at the heart of American life—had gone from the gentlemanly Patterson to the thuggish brute Liston to Ali, the disciple of a black separatist sect. "[He] is the finest Negro athlete I have ever known, the man who will mean more to his people than any athlete before him," Malcolm X told reporters. To many whites, the prediction sounded like a threat.

If it was all just a bit too much for many Americans, maybe it was because there were so many other cultural touchstones challenging the status quo. The same month, February 1964, that introduced the Beatles and Clay/Ali to the nation, American institutions and traditions were seemingly under attack in movie theaters, on the bestsellers list, and on Broadway. A new movie had recently opened, one that took a humorous take, an extraordinarily *dark* humorous take, not only on the American military and the Cold War, but on the very notion of nuclear war—the prospect of which had been horrifyingly real during the Cuban Missile Crisis just fifteen months earlier.

Stanley Kubrick's *Dr. Strangelove or: How I Learned to Stop Worrying and Love the Bomb* reduced Cold War anxieties and America's containment policy toward Soviet Communism to pure theater of the absurd. The film challenged—and openly ridiculed—Americans' notion of themselves. They were the nation that had won World War II, defeating Hitler and his Fascist cronies, and now were in the process of stopping the worldwide spread of Communism. In 1964 American soldiers were holding the line in Berlin, and a decade after having stopped totalitarianism at the border of North Korea, were now in the process of doing the same in Vietnam. Just as President Kennedy had promised to the world, America was paying any price, bearing any burden, and opposing any foe. Americans were the good guys. *Weren't they?* In 1964, that last rhetorical question was as new to millions of Americans as the music of the Beatles or the bravado of Ali.

The film's cowriter, Terry Southern, had also made headlines with his best-selling novel *Candy,* a modern retelling of Voltaire's *Candide.* The novel's young, all-American heroine isn't asking what she can do for her country. Instead, she has sex for sex's sake, like millions of American women utilizing the birth control pill, which had become available just a few years before. *Candy* was another humorous take—a satire really—on a largely verboten topic: sex.

Candy was published by Grove Press, the same New York City publishing house that had issued the first uncensored American version of D. H. Lawrence's 1929 novel, *Lady Chatterley's Lover,* in 1959, provoking a lawsuit that eventually ended the US Post Office's ban of the book. Grove was run by a literary-minded provocateur from Chicago named Barney Rosset, who would wage a seemingly one-man war on censorship in the United States, publishing *Naked Lunch,* William S. Burroughs's dystopian dreamscape of a novel, in 1962. The *Naked Lunch* saga would end in another victorious court case for the publisher and for freedom of expression.

The year before *Lunch,* Rosset had published Henry Miller's banned 1934 novel, *Tropic of Cancer,* which was considered obscene by US authorities for its unabashed depiction of sex, and no doubt for its rejection of American values. Miller, like the protagonist in *Cancer* (also named Henry Miller), left his native New York broke and utterly disgusted with the American way of life. Living in Paris, Miller leads the life of an art-(and sex-)obsessed bohemian. ("What really got me," Rosset confessed decades later, "was the anti-American feeling that Miller had. He was not happy living in this country and he was extremely endowed with the ability to say why.") The book was a talisman and inspiration for disaffected postwar writers like the Beats and Norman Mailer, who viewed it as a serious work of literature. Then in June 1964, after sixty court cases in twenty-one states, the US Supreme Court agreed, ruling that the book had "redeeming social value."

Walls were being broken down in American society, and quickly. On Broadway James Baldwin's play, *Blues for Mr. Charlie*, loosely based on the killing of Emmitt Till—a fourteen-year-old black boy who was kidnapped, mutilated, and murdered in Mississippi in 1955 by two white men for allegedly flirting with a white female shopkeeper—also opened in February 1964. The horrific case—Till's mother insisted on an open coffin so the country and the world could see what the murderers had done to her son—was a transformative moment in the civil rights movement. The shocking death inspired poems by Gwendolyn Brooks and Langston Hughes, an essay by novelist William Faulkner, and a 1962 song from Bob Dylan. But now here on Broadway—the Great White Way—was a painful drama picking at the scab, so soon after the shocking deaths of the four little girls in Birmingham (to whom the play was dedicated, along with Medgar Evers).

But the far more controversial play of the season was *The Deputy*, which opened around the same time. Written by German playwright Rolf Hochhuth, the drama questioned Pope Pius XXII's silence during the Holocaust, portraying the aristocratic pontiff as indifferent to Nazi war crimes. Conservative Catholics were outraged. Leading the charge was New York's powerful Cardinal Francis Spellman, who had become a one-man crusading army against the blasphemies and moral degradations of Hollywood dating back to Elia Kazan's 1956 film, *Baby Doll*, and against Roberto Rossellini's *Il Miraclo* (*The Miracle*), in which a peasant woman is impregnated by an itinerant wanderer that she believes is a saint. Spellman, who was at one time powerful enough to earn the moniker "the American Pope," saw *The Deputy* as "an outrageous desecration of the honor of a great and good man." Here was another form of popular entertainment—the Broadway play—fronting an attack on another venerable institution: the Roman Catholic Church.

Although Catholics were a minority religion in America—only four years earlier, John F. Kennedy's Catholicism had been seen as a massive obstacle to his chances at winning the White House—Spellman had been a dominant force in New York City for decades. He wielded immense influence among Gotham's ruling elite. He was a close political ally of both Mayor Wagner, who appointed the cardinal's cronies to his administration, and Moses, who was instrumental in helping the cardinal acquire the Manhattan real estate to create Fordham University's Manhattan campus near Lincoln Center (even though the move forced the eviction of hundreds of working-class families). Without Spellman, there wouldn't have been any Vatican Pavilion or *La Pietà* in Flushing Meadow.

Spellman hadn't seen *The Deputy* (nor would he), and although the publicity-seeking cardinal tore into the play, the protest never achieved critical mass: Only 150 people picketed the Brooks Atkinson Theater when it opened. Even Boston's Cardinal Richard Cushing, a close personal friend of the Kennedy clan, disagreed publically with his fellow Prince of the Church, declaring that maybe Spellman should see the play before damning it. Powerless to stop its Broadway run, or the drama's publication in book form that same year (by Rosset's Grove Press), Spellman, like his good friend Moses, was beginning to seem like a man from another age.

They weren't alone. Others manned the barricades against these seemingly endless assaults on the culture. One eloquent critic, English journalist and historian Paul Johnson, knew exactly whom to blame for these sorrowful turns of events: the Beatles. Just weeks after the band's triumphant introduction to America, Johnson tried to warn his fellow countrymen—and the English-speaking world—of "The Menace of Beatlism."

Johnson thought the Beatles—their music, their modish suits, their disrespect for authority, and everything they stood for—were an assault on Western culture and the existing social order. Like other forms of "pop culture," which to his mind included jazz virtuosos like Charlie Parker and Duke Ellington, "the growing public approval of anti-culture is itself . . . a reflection of the new cult of youth." The young, screaming teenagers in the throes of Beatlemania formed "a collective portrait of a generation enslaved by a commercial machine." He declared Beatlism as another "mass-produced mental opiate."

Ironically, Johnson, the conservative anti-Communist, sounded like a Marxist zealot lamenting the undue influence of religion among the proletariat. However, one certainty that Johnson had the foresight to realize was that the stagnant postwar ancien régime of England—and America—was under attack. And the Beatles, along with their like-minded cultural avatars like Ali were leading the charge.

16.

*Revolutions are never peaceful, never loving, never nonviolent. Nor
are they compromising. Revolutions are destructive and bloody.*
                              —Malcolm X, December 1, 1963

Malcolm X was evolving. By early 1964 his political ideas, his spiritual
foundation, even his racial philosophy—everything that had turned a
small-time hustler named Malcolm Little into one of the most dynamic
and charismatic leaders in American history—seemed to be up for grabs.
Although his metamorphosis had actually been a gradual process, like so
much else in American life, in the aftermath of the Kennedy assassination, his transition reached critical mass. Malcolm was morphing into
something new.

On December 1, 1963, less than two weeks after the events of Dallas,
the dynamic orator was scheduled to speak at New York's Manhattan
Center, filling in for Elijah Muhammad, the spiritual leader of the Nation
of Islam. Muhammad issued direct orders to his National Minister just
a few days earlier: Under no circumstances was Malcolm to discuss the
assassination or even mention Kennedy by name. The Nation had always
been apolitical, but more importantly, Muhammad was well aware of
Kennedy's popularity among African Americans. He did not want a
backlash against his sect, or more antagonism from white reporters in
the mainstream press who would be attending Malcolm's talk, which was
dramatically titled "God's Judgment of White America." The stakes for
all involved were much too high.

Malcolm, with his strong independent streak, was already chafing
under the strict edicts of the Nation. But even he must have understood Muhammad's reasoning: Malcolm had regularly criticized the
Kennedy administration for its gradualist approach to civil rights. The
president's historic primetime speech on race back in June had done
little to change the fiery minister's mind. In fact, just two days before the
assassination, Malcolm had ridiculed Kennedy and his policies during a

talk at Columbia University. "Any time a man can become president and after three years in office do as little for Negroes as [Kennedy] has done despite the fact that Negroes went for him 80 percent," he told the audience. "I'll have to say he's the foxiest of the foxy."

Despite his orders, Malcolm took little time before veering from his script at the Manhattan Center. The killing of the president wasn't just random violence, he said, it was a violent act in a violent country that exported violence. Then, comparing Kennedy's death to the US-backed November 2 assassination of South Vietnam president Ngo Dinh Diem, he said the events in Dallas were nothing more than "the chickens coming home to roost." Inspired by the enthusiastic reaction of the crowd, mostly Nation faithful, he pushed the rhetorical envelope further. "Being an old farm boy myself, chickens coming home to roost never did make me sad; they've always made me glad," he remarked. The audience roared with laughter and applause.

The fallout was immediate. Malcolm was suspended from all Nation activities for ninety days. He was forbidden from speaking at his spiritual and political headquarters, Mosque No. 7 in Harlem, and no Muslim in good standing with the Nation could speak to or be seen with him. Accepting his sentence obediently, Malcolm hoped to reconcile with Muhammad, a man he loved like a father, a man revered by Nation members as no mere mortal but the divine Messenger. Despite their increasing differences—Malcolm had been struggling spiritually since hearing of Muhammad's infidelities (the Messenger had a penchant for the attractive, young secretaries at the Nation's Chicago headquarters)—he hoped their fractured relationship could be mended.

During the early months of 1964, however, Malcolm came to the realization that the split was permanent. In fact, it was his close, personal relationship with Muhammad that had endangered Malcolm's role in the secretive Black Nationalist group. Muhammad's family members and closest advisors in Chicago were envious of Malcolm, fearing he would be named the Messenger's successor. In the end, petty jealousies and palace politics had played a critical role in sending Malcolm X into exile.

By March he was moving on, no longer shackled by the Nation's strict separatist or apolitical stances, which forbade members from participating in the white devil's political system or joining the civil rights movement. Seeing how the civil rights cause was fueled largely by Southern black Christians, Malcolm began to explore a more secular and practical approach to the liberation of black Americans. He was ready to "cooperate in local civil rights actions in the South and elsewhere," he told the *New York Times,* announcing his split with the Nation of Islam. He was now entering a new phase of his life. "It is going to be different now," he said. "I'm going to join in the fight wherever Negroes ask for my help." However, he soon realized that this new, inclusive approach was dangerous, too: His former spiritual brethren in the Nation of Islam now viewed him as a traitor. In their eyes he was a heretic, and he knew they would stop at nothing to silence him if his voice grew too loud or his influence too large.

Malcolm founded a new organization, the Muslim Mosque, Inc. and commuted each day from his home in East Elmhurst, Queens, to the Hotel Theresa in Harlem, which served as the group's headquarters. In the poisonous atmosphere of race relations in New York City in early 1964, controversy immediately ensued. After reaffirming to local media his belief that blacks should arm themselves in self-defense—"by whatever means necessary," in his famous words—taking full advantage of their Second Amendment rights, New York City Police Commissioner Michael J. Murphy immediately condemned him. "Nobody will be allowed to turn New York City into a battleground," the commissioner warned, claiming Malcolm X and other local activists were driven by "a lust for power" and "other sinister motives."

Maybe Murphy feared that the newly liberated Malcolm X would become the truly revolutionary figure that many activists had hoped for, or that Malcolm would rival, perhaps even overshadow, the nonviolent wing of the civil rights movement. Maybe the pressure of the job was getting to the police commissioner. Since the summer of 1963, the daily street protests and sit-ins in New York City had been threatening to boil over into a full-scale race riot. The World's Fair, which was set to open in just weeks, had become a central focus for local radicals, like the Brooklyn chapter of CORE, who were promising a citywide stall-in to ruin Robert Moses' opening day.

Throughout March and April, Malcolm stayed in the spotlight, accepting speaking engagements in the Northeast. He visited the Capitol to witness the civil rights debate in the Senate. Historically, the US Senate was where civil rights legislation went to die or get watered down until it was largely meaningless. It was not lost on Malcolm that the person most responsible for gutting those previous laws was then Senator Lyndon B. Johnson of Texas, who was now the President of the United States. Malcolm refused to believe that this man, this Texan—who called the Democrats' 1948 civil rights plank "a farce and a sham"—was sincere when he met with Roy Wilkins, James Farmer, or Martin Luther King Jr. It was a leap of faith that Malcolm was not prepared to make.

But at least one aspect of his Washington, DC, trek would make the whole trip worthwhile. While leaving the Senate gallery, Malcolm and King—whom he had critiqued again just the week before, saying, "Martin Luther King must devise a new approach in the coming year or he will be a man without followers"—came face-to-face for the only time in their abbreviated lives. The meeting was short, just a minute or so, but the resulting iconic photo of the two men, laughing and shaking hands like old friends, would have a lasting historic significance. "I always had a deep affection for Malcolm," King would later say, "and felt that he had the great ability to put his finger on the existence and root of the problem." Although Malcolm continued to question the legitimacy of King's nonviolent approach, he began to speak of his rival as someone who had fought in the same wars, acquired the same scars, even if they continued to differ on tactics.

Soon after their historic meeting, Malcolm would lay the rhetorical foundation for his new approach, melding his unrepentant revolutionary ideas with the practical political strategies of King and other civil rights leaders. Instead of erecting philosophical walls between himself and other in the struggle for black freedom, Malcolm wanted to build bridges. "Unity is the right religion," he told a New York audience, just three days after meeting King. "Black people must forget their differences and discuss the points on which they can agree." This was something new indeed.

Then on April 3, at Cleveland's Cory Methodist Church, Malcolm would deliver one of the most important speeches of his life in front of a multiracial crowd of more than two thousand people. Invited by the local chapter of CORE, and sharing the stage with his friend, author and activist Louis E. Lomax. The evening was devoted to the topic "The Negro Revolt—What Comes Next?" For Malcolm, this wasn't much of a question at all; the choice facing African Americans—indeed America itself—was evident in the title of the speech: "The Ballot or the Bullet." He had first unveiled the speech at various engagements in New York at the end of March, and sounding every bit like the new man he was, he crafted the words for weeks until he perfected its every cadence and grace note.

Malcolm began with another plea for unity as he extended an olive branch to King and other leaders. "If we have differences, let us differ in the closet." As Malcolm pointed out, if Kennedy had found a way to work with the Soviets, then African-American leaders could come together, too. "We certainly have more in common with each other than Kennedy and Khrushchev had with each other," he said. The scenario Malcolm painted was stark, but the choices surprisingly simple: It was either going to be the ballot—that is, twenty-two million black Americans would be able to exercise their constitutional right to vote—or it would be the bullet. "It's one of the other in 1964," he said. "It isn't that time is running out—time has *run out!* Nineteen sixty-four threatens to be the most explosive year America has ever witnessed."

For Malcolm, black Americans would be treated as full and free first-class citizens, with all the protections of the US Constitution, or there would be an armed and bloody revolution where both black and white blood would flow. To put it in World's Fair terminology, there would be no peace through understanding unless America had a historic shift of its political axis.

Malcolm quickly explained to his audience why he didn't believe such a shift would happen: The Democratic Party itself was rotten to its Southern core. The coalition of voters—Northern liberals, urban ethnics, African Americans, and Southern segregationists—that Franklin D. Roosevelt had patched together for his unprecedented four terms as president was torn and frayed; the civil rights bill threatened to destroy it once and for all. And he named names: Senator Richard B. Russell—"that's [President Lyndon B. Johnson's] boy, that's his pal, that's his buddy"—and Senator James O. Eastland, two of the Senate's most notorious racists, who along with their senatorial kin were keeping the civil rights bill from getting anywhere.

Malcolm was airing the hypocrisy that was the heart of the Democratic Party. "A Dixiecrat is nothing but a Democrat in disguise," he said. "A vote for a Democrat is a vote for a Dixiecrat." Malcolm's political logic was hardly deniable: The Democrats held a massive majority in the Senate—sixty-five to thirty-five—and still a Democratic president couldn't get a civil rights bill through Congress. Malcolm didn't believe that Johnson would follow through on his promises. Although Malcolm X reinvented himself repeatedly, he had no faith in the president to do the same.

It was this intraparty civil war that Malcolm based his choices on. In the ten years since the US Supreme Court's historic Brown v. Board of Education decision that declared segregated schooling unconstitutional, Malcolm wanted to know one thing: "Where's the progress?" It was for all these reasons that he declared the American political system hopelessly and morally bankrupt; *that's* why younger activists were growing militant and choosing confrontation over nonviolence. Younger blacks "don't want to hear that 'turn-the-other-cheek' stuff," he said, noting that rioting teenagers in Jacksonville, Florida, had thrown Molotov cocktails at police during a recent melee. "It'll be Molotov cocktails this month, hand grenades next month, and something else next month. It'll be ballots or it'll be bullets. It'll be liberty or it'll be death." Malcolm spoke of the struggle of black Americans in the universal language of revolution.

Malcolm wanted to bring America's racial crimes before the United Nations. It wasn't the first time such a demand was made: William Paterson, a black communist leader, charged the United States with genocide before the world court in the 1940s; and just months earlier, the NAACP and the Urban League, fed up with the impotent promises of Governor Rockefeller and Mayor Wagner and the silence from Moses, had marched outside the UN—the very international body that the Master Builder helped bring to New York—to complain about job discrimination at the World's Fair.

Seeking to unite the oppression of black Americans with the oppressed people of the world—"our African brothers and our Asian brothers and our Latin-American brothers"—was Malcolm's way of circumventing the hypocrisy of the American government and of tapping into the revolutionary energy that fueled so many former colonies in the Third World. And now these very same countries were coming to America to participate in the World's Fair as *free men*. For Malcolm— who like everyone living in Queens, had to be aware of the Fair—the irony had to be overwhelming. (Like millions of other New Yorkers, Malcolm had to navigate the same arterial highways that Moses was in the process of rebuilding in preparation for the Fair.)

Malcolm wanted people to stop seeing their struggle as a battle of *civil rights* and to start demanding their *human rights*. Explaining the difference, he said, "Civil rights means you're asking Uncle Sam to treat you right. Human rights are something you were born with. Human rights are your God-given rights . . . any time anyone violates your human rights, you can take them to the world court." But if this approach, the ballot approach—lawful, peaceful means—did not work, then justice must be sought with the bullet and revolutionary means would have to suffice. "Uncle Sam's hands are dripping with blood . . . of the black man in this country. He has the audacity—yes, he has—imagine him posing as the leader of the free world. The free world!—and you over here singing 'We Shall Overcome.'"

He pointed to the victories of the rebels that had brought Castro to power in Cuba, that had chased Europeans from Africa and defeated de

Gaulle in Algeria, and of the peasants that were battling the US Armed Forces to a standstill in the jungles of Vietnam. All over the world, black and brown and yellow Davids were besting white Goliaths. America's winning days were behind it. After all, hadn't Uncle Sam lost in Korea, settling for a negotiated truce? "America's not supposed to sign a truce," Malcolm said. "She's supposed to be *bad*. But she's not *bad* anymore. . . . This is the day of the guerrilla . . . nowhere on this earth does the white man win in a guerrilla warfare. It's not his speed." It would take the US government another decade and tens of thousands of dead American soldiers to grasp the logic of Malcolm X's argument.

Pledging to work with any group of any race or religion or political persuasion, Malcolm wanted a united front in the fight for black freedom. "We want freedom now," he said, "but we're not going to get it saying 'We Shall Overcome.' We've got to fight until we overcome." But in the end, he seemed to say the choice was really up to the president. What President Johnson did—or did not do—would determine whether millions of African Americans chose the ballot or the bullet. Johnson had to decide. But Malcolm warned that Johnson had better act, and fast. "Let him go in there right now and take a moral stand—right now, not later," he said.

Then Malcolm made a prescient prediction that in just a few months would come true. "If [Johnson] waits too long, brothers and sisters, he will be responsible for letting a condition develop in this country which will create a climate that will bring seeds up out of the ground with vegetation on the end of them looking like something these people never dreamed of." By the end of the summer of 1964, as parts of New York erupted in flame, everyone in America, including President Johnson, Moses, and the other backers of the World's Fair, would understand what Malcolm was talking about.

17

"I didn't want to get involved."
"I was tired. I went back to bed."
"I don't know."

> —Reasons witnesses gave when asked why they
> didn't call the police when they heard Catherine
> "Kitty" Genovese being attacked

The month before Malcolm X made his bold prediction, urban crime had already begun to lay waste to parts of New York City. In Kew Gardens, Queens, a sleepy neighborhood not far from the East Elmhurst home where the fiery Muslim preacher lived with his wife and five daughters, on a quiet street lined with immense sycamore and Norway maple trees and dotted with Tudor-style buildings, the most shocking murder in the history of New York City took place on March 13, 1964, just five weeks before opening day of the World's Fair.

Not that anyone knew it at the time. The murder was originally recorded in the *New York Times* as a mere four-paragraph story: QUEENS WOMAN IS STABBED TO DEATH IN FRONT OF HOME. The gruesome details would only appear later. The fact that the world would come to know how Catherine "Kitty" Genovese spent the last moments of her short life at all was in large part due to the *Times'* A. M. Rosenthal. In his quest to reacquaint himself with his hometown after a decade abroad as a Pulitzer Prize–winning foreign correspondent, Rosenthal, the *Times'* new Metropolitan Editor, made it his business to get to know New York's VIPs. In order to do his job, Rosenthal said, he needed to know the people who have "anything significant to do with the life of the city."

A perfect case in point was New York City Police Commissioner Michael J. Murphy. On March 23, Rosenthal, along with his deputy editor, Arthur Gelb, lunched with the commissioner at the lawman's favorite spot, Emil's in downtown Manhattan. Murphy, as usual, sat with his back against the wall, agreeing to answer any question the editors had, although the commissioner, who looked every bit like the tough Irish cop he was, wasn't giving away any classified secrets; the session was off the record.

But as the meal and conversation wore on, Murphy casually mentioned a recent murder in his native borough of Queens, where he still lived, that had left him, a twenty-five-year veteran of the force, flabbergasted. "That Queens story is something else . . . [it's] one for the books," the commissioner said. The Timesmen didn't know what he was talking about. Thirty-eight people, Murphy informed them, had watched—or heard—a young woman get murdered in the illuminated city night, and no one could be bothered to call the police. "I've been in this business a long time," Murphy said toward the end of meal, "but this beats everything."

Rosenthal couldn't believe it. Certainly Murphy had gotten the number wrong. Still, he thought, even it if were less than ten eyewitnesses, it was a story—a big story. But thirty-eight? Immediately Rosenthal told the commissioner that this account needed to be on the record. Murphy agreed. The *Times* would look into it.

The very fact that the *Times* was venturing into Queens to investigate a nearly two-week-old murder was itself a story. The borough didn't get much space in the Paper of Record. Although Robert Moses and the World's Fair would soon change that, the Fair was a once-in-a-generation undertaking. Besides, the *Times* was interested in the actual Fair, not its host borough. Despite the fact that Queens was the fastest-growing county in New York at the time, it was "probably the least exotic place" in the city, as Rosenthal freely admitted. "It can be shown statistically, I believe, that in the past few years *Times* reporters have spent more time in Antarctica than in Queens," he wrote in 1964.

The story that eventually ran in the *Times* would paint Queens as a nightmarish urban landscape—one that should be avoided at all costs, and just in time for Moses' "Olympics of Progress."

Around 3:20 a.m. on March 13, Genovese, a twenty-eight-year-old single woman, returned to her Kew Gardens neighborhood after a long day at Ev's 11th Hour, the tavern in nearby Hollis where she worked. Kitty, as she was known to her friends and family, pulled her red Fiat into the parking lot of the Long Island Rail Road, adjacent to her Austin Street apartment, which was just a half block away. As she got out of her car and stood near the lighted LIRR station, she noticed a man parked on the far side of the lot watching her. What she didn't know was that Winston Moseley, age twenty-nine, had been following her for at least ten blocks, thinking only of murder and death. Moseley, who had a decent job fixing calculating machines, had left the comfort of his South Ozone Park, Queens, home at 1:20 a.m. and snuck out of his house as his wife and two children slept. He had one thought coursing through his mind, he later told the police: He was going to find a woman and kill her.

Genovese walked nervously to a nearby police call box, which was connected to the local precinct, but when she saw the man emerge from his white Corvair with a hunting knife, she ran for her life. It didn't take long for Moseley to catch up with her. When he did, he stabbed Genovese twice in the back, then the chest, and in the stomach.

"Oh my God, he stabbed me! Please help me! Please help me!" she cried out.

Almost immediately, her blood-curdling screams woke some neighbors. On a top floor of a large apartment building across the street, a window went up, a light flicked on, and a man's voice shouted out in the frosty night air: "Leave that girl alone!" Moseley stopped his attack and walked away, leaving Genovese lying in the street. Frightened that a witness had seen him get out of his car and would be able to describe it, Moseley halted his attack and returned to his automobile, driving it a short distance away. He switched hats, choosing a fedora to better disguise himself, and returned to hunt Genovese. As he later admitted, he didn't think any of the people who opened their windows "would come down to help her." He was free to do as he wished.

Genovese had managed to stumble toward the street near the police call box, where she had first glimpsed her attacker. Bleeding from at least four wounds, she struggled to stand and turn the last corner to make it to her doorway on Austin Street.

"I'm dying! I'm dying!" she shouted into the still winter night. Now many lights went on and neighbors opened windows, craning their necks to get a better look at what was happening on the street below; some kept the lights off to see more clearly.

When Moseley returned, however, Genovese was nowhere to be found. He walked along Austin Street, opposite the tall apartment building from where the first neighbor had shouted. The entire block of Tudor buildings here were only two stories high; on the ground floor were stores, and above them apartments. He tried the first door but it was locked. The second was ajar and inside he could see Genovese, bleeding and lying at the bottom of the staircase, unable to make it up the stairs to the safety of her second-floor apartment.

Seeing her assailant again, Genovese screamed. This time Moseley wasn't taking any chances: He stabbed her in the neck, slashing her vocal cords. "She only moaned after that," he later explained. And there, just down the stairs from her home, Moseley cut off her clothes and attempted to rape her. If her groans grew too loud, he told the court at his trial months later, he stabbed her again. Having finished his crime, Moseley put his pants back on and left his victim for dead, but not before searching her wallet. Inside was $49, which he took.

"Why would I throw money away?" he calmly noted to prosecutors during his trial.

Despite having been stabbed seventeen times and sexually assaulted for thirty-five minutes, when Genovese was abandoned by Moseley on the bottom of her stairwell, she was still alive. The police arrived at approximately 3:55 a.m., five minutes after one of her neighbors had finally called. The man later explained that after much indecision and only after he woke up a friend in the middle of the night to seek advice, did he come to her aid and phone for help. By then it was too late.

It wasn't the fact that a young woman was stabbed and assaulted in two separate attacks in a respectable Queens neighborhood where violent crime was a rarity that shocked detectives; it was the number of neighbors who admitted—after the fact—that they saw or heard at least one of the attacks that stunned them: thirty-eight people according to police; thirty-eight law-abiding, decent, ordinary, middle-class citizens, many of them elderly—old enough to remember the 1939–40 World's

Fair, and probably many were grandparents thinking of taking their grandchildren to the World's Fair set to open in just five weeks. Thirty-eight, and only one came forward.

"The people came out," a detective told the *Times,* at 4:25 a.m. only when the ambulance took Genovese to Queens General Hospital. An hour later, she was pronounced dead. Had someone—anyone—called them earlier, the police told reporters, Genovese might have survived. "A phone call," a detective said, "would have done it."

The outcry from the *Times'* follow-up article—THIRTY-EIGHT WHO SAW MURDER DIDN'T CALL THE POLICE—was immediate. The New York papers seized on the sensational story, as the populace of Kew Gardens now had to answer for the actions—or lack thereof—of its three-dozen silent witnesses. The article, assigned by Rosenthal to a young reporter named Martin Gansberg, prompted New Yorkers throughout the five boroughs to ask some difficult questions about themselves and their metropolis. When had New York devolved into a bloody battleground of life and death? When had America's most modern and cultured urban society become so depraved? What was wrong with New York?

Citizens, clergy, politicians, journalists, and psychologists offered numerous opinions in an attempt to explain the horrible crime, and the larger issues it invoked. President Johnson mentioned it in a radio address, as the murder of Genovese quickly became a symbol of all that was wrong with America's cities. The silence of those thirty-eight witnesses would be debated for decades to come; sociologists even gave a name to this new disease that was infecting urban America: Genovese syndrome.

The perception of New York—among its own eight million citizens, the nation, and the world—would never be the same. Newspapers from Moscow to Istanbul recounted the indifference to human suffering that was on display in Queens, the home borough of the World's Fair, whose self-proclaimed mission was to foster a new era of "Peace Through Understanding." The murder of Genovese mocked such utopian schemes.

As the weeks and months passed, long after the Fair's opening day, the story refused to die; radio and television, newspapers and magazines delivered a constant barrage of "apathy" stories. "It's as if everybody in New York were watching to see how apathetic everybody else was," Rosenthal told *The New Yorker*, after publishing a short book on the crime. "Maybe 'apathy' isn't the right word after all. Maybe it should be 'callousness' or 'dissociation.' Whatever it is, there seem to be an awful lot of people who have been turning away from this or that. People don't seem to be connected to other people any more."

With 1964 being an election year, it was only a matter of time before crafty politicos seized upon the story to drive the narratives that benefited their ambitions. Alabama's segregationist governor, George C. Wallace, who entered the Democratic presidential race in a bid to wrest the nomination from President Johnson, began to allude to urban America's soaring crime rates. The fact that Genovese's assailant—who quickly confessed to murdering two other Queens women—was black, a fact the *Times* left unreported, was used by Wallace and the defenders of Jim Crow to inflame tension between the races.

Back at his Flushing Meadow office, Robert Moses began receiving letters from frightened Americans too scared to travel to New York to see his Fair. Moses assured them that, yes, terrible crimes did transpire in New York, but that local journalists had overplayed such tawdry tales in a bid to sell newspapers. Accusing his enemies in the press of sensationalism in order to sell more copies of their ailing newspapers, such reporting "creates a picture of conditions in New York City at variance with the facts," Moses explained in a letter to a gentleman from Virginia. "This does the city, the Fair and the Country a great disservice." Crime in New York, he noted, was less than other "large cities."

That wasn't saying much. Violent crime had doubled from 1963 to 1964, and urban violence would continue to soar from coast to coast throughout the 1960s and beyond. And despite Moses' warnings, the specter of Genovese—and the silent eyewitnesses to her death—would haunt New York long after the World's Fair and all its wonders were just distant memories.

18

I feel I'm very much a part of my times, of my culture, as much a part of it as rockets and television.

—Andy Warhol

On April 28, 1963, Andy Warhol found himself at a small dinner party at a friend's downtown loft. Over a meal of coq au vin and white wine, the artist informed his fellow guests that he had a won a new commission from one of his collectors, the architect Philip Johnson, to create a twenty-by-twenty-foot mural for the 1964 World's Fair. It would be his first foray into public art and in the most public of settings: An estimated seventy million people—maybe more—were expected at the Fair. Millions would see his work. That was the good news; the bad news was that he lacked inspiration.

"Oh, I don't know what to do!" he complained.

Luckily for Warhol, his friend, the painter Wynn Chamberlain, who was hosting the dinner party, had a suggestion. "Andy, I have a great idea for you," he said. "The Ten Most Wanted Men! You know, the mug shots the police issue of the ten most wanted men." Not only did Chamberlain give Warhol the idea, but he would supply the source material: Wynn's boyfriend was a cop—a half-Irish, half-Italian, third-generation NYPD officer (and presumably deeply closeted)—who had access to mug shots, crime photos, anything Warhol needed.

"Oh, what a great idea!" Warhol said. However, the pop artist could already imagine the fallout with Fair officials over a mural of mug shots that was meant to hang on Johnson's postmodern New York State Pavilion—destined to be one of the Fair's most celebrated structures and signature attractions. What's more, he knew *exactly* which Fair official might object to such a mural. "Robert Moses has to approve it or something," Warhol said. "I don't care, I'm going to do it!"

Warhol was one of ten New York–based artists that Johnson hired to create original works for the Fair; it was a veritable Who's Who of the pop art world, which by then was remaking the landscape of the New York art scene: Robert Rauschenberg, Roy Lichtenstein, Ellsworth Kelly, John Chamberlain, James Rosenquist, Robert Indiana, Peter Agnostini, Alexander Liberman, Robert Mallary, and Warhol would bring their silk screens and collages, their comic book–inspired paintings and abstract sculptures, that celebrated—or mocked, depending on your point of view—commercial culture. By October 1963 news about the ten Johnson-commissioned "avant-garde" works had hit the papers. The *New York Times* gave brief descriptions of the pieces, including Warhol's most wanted men painting.

At the time, all Warhol had was a concept. Finally, in January 1964, the promised package from Chamberlain's cop boyfriend finally arrived at Warhol's West 47th Street silver-walled studio, the Factory. Inside a large manila envelope, he found archival material—a vast array of photos and a small booklet from the NYPD titled *The Thirteen Most Wanted Men*. With the World's Fair only months away, Warhol got down to work.

Work was something that Andy Warhol was never shy about. Born Andrew Warhola in 1928 in Pittsburgh, the youngest and sickly son of Carpatho-Rusyn immigrant parents, Warhol grew up as a working-class outsider in a city best known for steel production. His family managed to send him to college, and he graduated from the Carnegie Institute of Technology with a degree in fine art before moving to New York City in 1949. He quickly shortened his name and just as quickly established himself as a reliable, if eccentric, commercial artist.

Warhol's first taste of success was illustrating shoe ads—whimsical, ornate drawings of women's footwear—for the I. Miller Shoe Company. Soon he had an impressive range of corporate clients, including Tiffany's, Bergdorf-Goodman, and Columbia Records, as well as important fashion bibles like *Vogue* and *Harper's Bazaar*. By 1957 his work was celebrated enough that *Life* featured a spread of his shoe drawings. However, Warhol's commercial work, while lucrative, wasn't deemed sophisticated. According to the prevailing sentiment at the time, commercial art was a fine day job but it wasn't Art. Other artists had toiled in the commercial art world to earn a living, but the artists on the pop vanguard seemed to excel at it: Lichtenstein dressed windows (as did Warhol on occasion), while Rosenquist painted billboards.

Another reason Warhol's work won few accolades at the time was that the art world was still under the sway of abstract expressionism. The drip paintings of Jackson Pollock and the layered and colored abstractions of Willem de Kooning and others were considered the next great leap forward in painting after the great flourishing of modernism in the early twentieth century.

By 1958 the Museum of Modern Art was featuring a traveling exhibition titled *The New American Painting* (curated by poet Frank O'Hara); soon thereafter New York was seen as the center of the art universe. Warhol made the most of the city's art scene, frequenting galleries, making connections with major players, and beginning to collect art, including works by Larry Rivers and Jasper Johns. At one show, Warhol considered buying a Rauschenberg collage but balked at the $250 price tag.

"I can do that myself," said Warhol.

"Well, why don't you?" his friend replied.

He apparently took the advice to heart. By 1960 Warhol had created a series of paintings of comic strip characters: Superman, Popeye, and Dick Tracy. He also painted two large canvases, six by three feet, of Coke bottles in two different styles: The first had elements of abstract expressionism—hash marks, heavy globs of dripping black paint—while the other was a simple, straightforward, almost line-drawing of a Coke bottle. One afternoon he showed both to his friend, filmmaker Emile de Antonio, who dubbed the first "a piece of shit." The second, de Antonio said, was different. It was something *new*. "[The second] is remarkable," he told Warhol. "It's our society, it's who we are, it's absolutely beautiful and naked, and you ought to destroy the first one and show the other." Years later, Warhol would write: "That afternoon was an important one for me."

While turning such ephemeral or banal objects like Coke bottles and comic book characters into artistic subject matter may have seemed new, Warhol wasn't the first to do it. Rosenquist had painted images of 7 Up bottles, among other consumer products, on his canvases, and

Lichtenstein had already created bold new paintings based on comic characters. (Lichtenstein's *Image Duplicator* was based on a comic panel drawn by Jack "The King" Kirby, the maestro of the Marvel Universe; soon thereafter the company's comics bore a new tagline: "Marvel Pop Art Productions.")

Even before them, Rauschenberg—who along with Johns was considered pop's "old master"—had incorporated postcards, photographs, bits of wood, and fabric into his paintings he called "combines." Meanwhile, Johns had painted familiar objects like the American flag and made bronze sculptures out of used Ballantine Beer cans. Now, however, such objects were worthy, serious subject matter. "I feel sorry for people who think things like soap dishes or mirrors or Coke bottles are ugly," Rauschenberg once explained, "because they're surrounded by things like that all day long, and it must make them miserable."

Soon Warhol was painting the ultimate commodity: the dollar bill (and according to his critics, the object he cared about most). He then created a series of paintings based on a Campbell soup can, which he first displayed at the Ferus Gallery in Los Angeles that October. By then Warhol's lineage to pop art had been cemented in the pages of *Time* magazine. But Warhol wasn't content to be part of a movement that was already in motion: He pushed the envelope even further with his life-size silk screens of Elvis Presley (painted silver) and portraits of Marilyn Monroe, the celebrities that Warhol—like millions of other Americans—were so enamored with.

His Monroe pictures, including *Gold Marilyn Monroe*—a silk-screened publicity shot painted with a bright splash of color and surrounded in glittering gold like a Byzantine icon—were shown in November 1962 at Manhattan's Stable Gallery, Warhol's first solo New York show. The painting would become part of a larger series called "Death and Disaster" that was perfectly attuned to the times: images of movie stars and celebrities like Monroe (who had already died); Elizabeth Taylor (who was ailing and reportedly near death at the time); and Jackie Kennedy (both just before the assassination and later as a black-veiled, grieving widow at her husband's funeral). These images hinted at the dark reality of American life in the early 1960s: On the surface was affluence and fame; below, death and suffering.

By 1963 Warhol was creating iconographic silk screens of still darker elements of the nation's life: car crashes, electric chairs, and police dogs attacking black activists in Birmingham—literally appropriating the day's news into his artwork. Sometimes, he took images directly from the media, as with his 1962 *129 Die in Jet (Plane Crash)*, a silk screen of the actual front page of the June 4, 1962, edition of the *New York Mirror* tabloid. By the time Johnson commissioned him to create a new original piece for the 1964 Fair, Warhol had established himself as an important practitioner of pop.

Not that everyone in Warhol's ever-expanding circle wanted him to take the job. Warhol got into "a real disagreement" with his friend Soren Agenoux, who thought that he should decline Johnson's commission because essentially it meant "working for Robert Moses," remembered Billy Linich (better known by his Factory nom de plume, Billy Name). "Soren wanted him to refuse the commission, and Andy would just say, 'Oh, Soren, I'm doing it, I need the money.'"

When the work was done, *Thirteen Most Wanted Men* consisted of twenty-five Masonite panels featuring silk-screened images of twenty-two black-and-white mug shots of genuine thugs (three were intentionally left blank, perhaps to represent the "wanted men" who were exonerated or who were not yet hunted by the authorities); each was wanted for crimes like murder, assault, and burglary. Although the warrants for their arrest were old, as of February 1962 they were all on the NYPD's list. Shortly before opening day of the World's Fair, the piece, along with all the other pop artwork, was mounted onto the circular outer wall of the Theaterama of Johnson's pavilion—hailed as "the architectural delight of Flushing Meadows" according to Ada Louise Huxtable, the *Times*' acerbic architecture critic.

This was a prestigious pedestal for public art, particularly something as new and radical as pop art. Johnson was one of the most famous architects in America; by displaying these ten artists so prominently, he was giving pop his stamp of approval—and, in essence, the stamp of approval of New York

State and the World's Fair. He even managed to win a few converts to his way of thinking. John Canaday, the contrarian art critic for the *New York Times*, noted that by the spring of 1964, pop's staying power was causing "chronically advanced critics, who at first just couldn't see Pop" to reconsider their previously harsh judgment "as quickly as dignity will allow."

Canaday was apparently one of the critics taking a second look. The inclusion of pop art on the New York State Pavilion, "potentially the most influential piece of architecture" at the Fair, he wrote, implied that "Pop is as legitimate to our situation as the statues of saints on the exteriors of Gothic cathedrals were to that of our ancestors." From downtown renegades to mainstream sainthood in just a few years.

Not everyone was enamored with the pavilion's artwork, however . . . at least with Warhol's piece. On April 14, just eight days before the Fair threw open its gates, the *New York Journal-American*, the Hearst-owned evening paper—and one of the most pro-Moses papers in town—ran a front-page story that took aim squarely at Warhol's painting. Under a provocative tabloid headline—MURAL IS SOMETHING YEGG-STRA—the *Journal-American* stirred up another World's Fair art controversy. "Unabashedly adorning the New York State pavilion at the World's Fair today, resplendent in all their scars, cauliflower ears and other appurtenances of their trade—are the faces of the city's 13 Most Wanted Criminals," the story reported.

A member of the city's Art Commission complained to the *Journal-American*: "I don't know who's in charge out there." Since scores of New York City schoolchildren could tell any reporter who asked just who was in charge at Flushing Meadow, such a sentiment was a deliberate dig at Moses. A spokesman for New York's Finest confirmed the photos were real, but didn't know how Warhol had gotten his hands on them. Regardless of the complaints, Johnson told the paper that he was "delighted" with the work, dubbing it "a comment on the sociological factor in American life." Furthermore, the famed architect explained, the carping of bureaucrats or policemen didn't matter. There was "no question about official complaints from any Fair authorities," he claimed. "And if there were, we would not do anything about it."

But just three days later, Johnson had an abrupt change of mind. Now the architect told reporters that Warhol's painting would be replaced, claiming that it was the artist himself who made the request. "[He] claims that the work was not properly installed and felt that it did not do justice to what he had in mind," Johnson told the *Herald Tribune's* critic, Emily Genauer. "I've asked him to do another mural for the spot and knowing how quickly Warhol works, I'm sure we'll be able to put it up in time for the opening next Wednesday."

The same day that Johnson was informing reporters of the mural's fate, Warhol wrote a letter to the New York State Department of Public Works authorizing Fair workers to paint over his mural "in a color suitable to the Architect." Someone chose aluminum silver (a most Warholian choice) and covered the entire mural under a coat of house paint. Shortly thereafter Warhol trekked out to Queens to see what had become of his creation. "We went out to Flushing Meadow one day to see it, with the images just showing through like ghosts," recalled Mark Lancaster, an assistant to Warhol at the time. *Thirteen Most Wanted Men* would continue to hang on the New York State Pavilion in a sort of ethereal half-life—its images erased, but not quite, by a coat of silver paint—for months. In its new form, the mural now seemed to become yet another painting, a sort of *Thirteen Most Wanted Men Painted Over*—a descendent of sorts of Rauschenberg's 1953 work *Erased de Kooning*.

Warhol's mural and its audacious subject matter should have come as no surprise to anyone; its contents were public knowledge as far back as October 1963. Some more conservative critics had even lodged complaints with Moses, Mayor Robert Wagner, and Governor Nelson Rockefeller. But it wasn't until *Thirteen Most Wanted Men* was hung on the facade of Johnson's pavilion that anyone seemed to notice the incongruity of displaying the stiff-necked mugs of hardened criminals and alledged mafiosi—at least one of whom claimed that he "would never be taken alive"—on a structure created to extol the cultural and ecological virtues of the Empire State to millions of tourists. Like all pavilions at the World's Fair, the $11 million New York State Pavilion had something to sell: *itself*.

Johnson's series of circular towers was one gigantic, albeit artful, advertisement for New York State. The truth was, New York's reputation was sinking fast in 1964: Crime was on the rise; and only one month earlier, the Kitty Genovese murder had made headlines around the world. Intended or not, Warhol's *Thirteen Most Wanted Men* created yet another link between New York, criminals, and crime at a World's Fair dedicated to "Peace Through Understanding."

Whatever had happened behind the scenes at Flushing Meadow, Warhol knew whom he blamed for the fiasco: Moses. The World's Fair Corporation president had the authority to censor art—or any exhibit—"in cases of extreme bad taste or low standard." And Moses had just exercised his presidential veto power when he had an oil painting by American artist Walter Keane removed from the Hall of Education. Keane's *Tomorrow Forever* depicted scores of haunted, vacant-eyed young children. It was one part creepy and two parts kitsch.

Warhol clearly felt that Moses was involved in his work's removal, too. When Johnson said he could create another work, Warhol already had one in mind. Instead of twenty-five portraits of wanted criminals, the artist silk-screened twenty-five images of a broadly smiling Moses, using a black-and-white photograph of the World's Fair Corporation's president gleaned from the pages of *Life*. He called it *Robert Moses Twenty-Five Times*. It would illustrate for the millions who flocked to the Fair what many believed the exhibition was really all about anyway: Robert Moses.

Warhol quickly set about creating silk screens of Moses' image on Masonite panels at the Factory, where Lancaster found him busy at work. "Andy couldn't have been doing this out of anything but anger—Moses wouldn't have gone for it in a million years," said Lancaster. When he was asked about the painting years later, Warhol deadpanned, "I thought [Moses] would like it."

Actually, Moses never even heard about the new mural; Johnson censored the idea quickly. "I forbade that," the architect later confessed, "because I just don't think it made any sense to thumb our noses. . . . I don't like Mr. Moses, but inviting more lawsuits by taking potshots at the head of the Fair would seem to me very, very bad taste. Andy and I had a little battle at the time." Despite his anger at being censored—again—Warhol never complained to the media. When he was asked about the painted-over mural, he claimed yet another reason for its demise. "One of the men labeled 'wanted' had been pardoned, you see," he explained offhandedly. "So the mural wasn't valid anymore."

The real truth was that the mural became a political issue within days of being mounted. New York governor Nelson A. Rockefeller, who had hired Johnson to create the pavilion, demanded Warhol's work be removed. Rockefeller, an avid—and deep-pocketed—collector of modern art (Warhol would eventually paint his portrait), had political reasons for censoring the mural: 1964 was an election year and, once again, Rockefeller was seeking the Republican nomination for the presidency.

After losing to Richard M. Nixon in 1960, the popular governor was considered the GOP front-runner for the 1964 election—President Kennedy had considered Rockefeller to be his toughest potential opponent. But then Rockefeller committed what was then a cardinal sin in politics: He got divorced. What's more, he quickly got remarried to his former mistress, who gave birth to a son, Nelson Jr.

By the fall of 1963, Rockefeller still had a chance, but was considered damaged goods. Now the unlikely candidate Senator Barry Goldwater, whose right-wing conservatism was far outside the political mainstream, seemed destined to become the Republican candidate who would face President Lyndon B. Johnson in the fall of 1964. Rockefeller could ill afford another controversy. Nor could he risk alienating a key voting bloc like Italian Americans, who might be offended that Warhol's painting reinforced ethnic stereotypes (seven of the thirteen most wanted men were of Italian descent). There were also claims that some of the men had beaten the charges, making them, in the eyes of the law, innocent.

It would be years before Johnson came clean about Rockefeller's orders. "Andy's was the one the governor turned down," he later admitted. "It was a very sad story. I gave each artist the chance to pick his own subject, and [Warhol] picked—impishly—the most wanted men. And I thought, 'That would be an absolutely delicious idea. Why not?'"

Postmodernist visionary that he was, Johnson couldn't foresee any controversy erupting. However, when René d'Harnoncourt, the director of the Museum of Modern Art, informed him the governor wanted the mural removed, Johnson immediately capitulated to his powerful patron.

Johnson once admitted his greatest ambition was to be *l'architecte du roi*—the king's architect, the person responsible for creating public architecture, the kind that lasted decades, if not centuries. In 1964 alone, Johnson opened three major works in New York City: the State Pavilion in Flushing Meadow, the New York State Theater at Lincoln Center, and a new wing at the Museum of Modern Art. The Rockefellers had played important roles in all three. Johnson was not about to speak truth—or defend censored art—to power. "Whoever commissions buildings buys me," he once claimed. "I'm for sale. I'm a whore. I'm an artist."

For all these reasons, Warhol's *Thirteen Most Wanted Men* and the work that he created to replace it, *Robert Moses Twenty-Five Times*, were rejected, making Warhol the only artist to have two works—both specifically created for the World's Fair—censored. For someone who didn't like Moses, Johnson certainly had a couple of Moseslike traits: an outsize ego and even larger ambition. But there was one key difference between the two men: Moses spoke truth—or his version of it, anyway—to whomever he damned well pleased.

In the end, Warhol would have the last laugh. The controversy surrounding his World's Fair mural gave an extra bit of publicity to his latest show, which debuted at the Stable Gallery on April 21—the night before the World's Fair opened. Now Warhol's fame was spreading outside downtown hipster cliques and art world sophisticates. The line to get into the Stable stretched down West 58th Street as viewers waited to glimpse the four hundred sculptures of painted plywood boxes carefully stacked almost all the way to the ceiling: Some looked like boxes of Brillo pads, Campbell's tomato juice, and Heinz ketchup; others were painted to look like Mott's apple juice, Kellogg's Corn Flakes, and Del Monte peaches. Despite some of the inevitable carping ("Is this an art gallery or Gristede's warehouse?" quipped one attendee) and critical complaints ("Anti-Art with capital A's" lamented one reviewer), collectors snapped up the "sculptures," which ranged from $200 to $400; one collector plopped down $6,000 for twenty boxes.

Ironically, the artist who had designed the original Brillo box in 1961, painter Jim Harvey, a commercial artist by day and abstract expressionist by night, attended the opening show. He didn't think much of Warhol's sculptural simulacrums of his design as *serious* art. "A good commercial design," he told a reporter of his original Campbell soup can label, "but that's all." Not that Warhol cared. That night after the opening he cele-brated his triumph with a party at the Factory, where he held court along with his fellow pop stars such as Lichtenstein and Rosenquist.

Whatever the critics—or Moses and Rockefeller—thought of his art, Warhol was breaking boundaries and creating works that, like the best pop art, forced his audience to reconsider the very definition of art and corporate consumer culture; the same corporate consumer culture that the World's Fair would put on display in Flushing Meadow. Moses' World's Fair and Warhol's art were more alike than probably either would care to admit. But thanks in part to the controversy his art caused at (or rather, just *before*) Moses' "Olympics of Progress," Warhol was well on his way to superstardom, which would last for far longer than his allotted fifteen minutes.

19

What does it mean to be found obscene in New York? This is the most sophisticated city in the country. . . . If anyone is . . . found obscene in New York, he must feel utterly depraved.

—Lenny Bruce

By the spring of 1964, the crackdown on homosexual bars that had begun the year before had bloomed into a campaign of political persecution of the downtown cultural scene and its iconoclastic denizens. In an attempt to "clean up" New York City before millions of tourists arrived for the World's Fair, the administration of Mayor Robert F. Wagner Jr. heeded the voices of the city's most reactionary religious authorities and began busting artists, performers, and bohemians of every stripe.

By the time the Fair opened its gates on the morning of April 22, New York was waging an all-out war on nonconformists such as Jack Smith, the underground filmmaker; Jonas Mekas, the director, archivist, and film critic; Julian Beck and Judith Malina, the founders of the politically radical Living Theatre; Lenny Bruce, the most outrageous of the new so-called sick comedians; and Greenwich Village coffeehouses such as Le Metro Café, where poets Allen Ginsberg and Frank O'Hara, among others, frequently read.

By April O'Hara, who had just published his most celebrated work, *Lunch Poems*, the month before, had had enough. "In preparation for the World's Fair, New York has been undergoing a horrible cleanup (I wonder what they think people are *really* coming to NYC for, anyway?). All the queer bars except one are already closed," he complained in a letter to his on-again, off-again lover, the painter Larry Rivers. "The Fair itself, or its preparations are too ridiculous and boring to go into, except for the amusing fact that Moses flies over it in a helicopter every day to inspect progress. And CORE has promised to totally stop traffic the first day by lying down on the highway. I hope they do."

O'Hara's frustration with New York's oppressive climate and his joy that the proposed stall-in by the Brooklyn chapter of CORE would upstage Robert Moses' opening day were perfectly blended in a playfully surreal poem he wrote around the same time, titled "Here in New York We Are Having a Lot of Trouble with the World's Fair."

This moral crackdown had actually been in the works since 1960, when Mayor Wagner, egged on by religious leaders, instigated a fight against "obscene magazines." That December, in cooperation with the city's five district attorneys and the License Department, the mayor had ordered 140 police officers to serve legal papers throughout the city—to distributors, publishers, and point-of-sale businesses (from luncheon-ettes to newsstands)—making it illegal to sell "girlie magazines" such as *Adam Bedside Reader, Cloud 9, Bare,* and *Mr. Cool* to anyone under the age of eighteen. It was all part of a plan, Wagner said, "to rid our city of those publications which, in my opinion, have contributed significantly toward juvenile delinquency and have played a major part in encouraging criminal acts and the increase of crime."

By October 1962 the city's antipornography campaign had led to the creation of Operation: Yorkville, a new advocacy group formed by a trio of religious leaders from Manhattan's Yorkville neighborhood, the same Upper East Side district where Wagner had grown up. Founded by Reverend Morton A. Hill, SJ, a Roman Catholic priest; Rabbi Julius G. Neumann; and Reverend Robert Wiltenburg, a Lutheran minister, the group aimed "to keep obscene literature out of the hands of children." By 1963 the New York Police Department had launched its own Operation: Pornography, a coordinated attempt to battle the growing number of porn shops, strip clubs, and bathhouses in the city, particularly in Times Square. From April to August 1963, the police made 166 obscenity-related arrests—all but 36 of them in or around Times Square. But for some religious leaders, Wagner's efforts weren't enough.

On Sunday, May 5, 1963, an irate Monsignor Joseph A. McCaffrey took to the pulpit of Holy Cross Church, on West 42nd Street, at that morning's 11:15 mass to berate "broad-minded" judges who, he said, were obstructing attempts to cleanse the city of smut. The result of such malicious jurisprudence, he told his parishioners, resulted in "the disgrace that is Times Square." No sooner had New York's Finest—whom McCaffrey absolved from blame—executed raids and arrested filth peddlers, than judges set them free or liberal defense attorneys claimed the First Amendment was being trampled upon. The Founding Fathers, Monsignor McCaffrey claimed, did not "anticipate giving free rein to the publication of pornographic literature when they established the principle of a free press."

Monsignor McCaffrey wanted Times Square cleaned up *now*. Aiming squarely at the jugulars of the mayor and the World's Fair management, he noted that in a year's time, millions of tourists would descend upon New York City—with millions of dollars in their pockets—only to come face to face with the smut of Times Square. The worst thing that could happen, McCaffrey said, was that visitors would think New York "is wide open"—an amoral town where anything goes. Without being explicit, he got his point across: Smut and obscenity would damage the World's Fair and its bottom line.

The mayor got the message. Within two months of McCaffrey's outburst, Wagner announced that he was ratcheting up his antiobscenity campaign into a crusade that would include a *new* four-pronged attack, which featured an antipornography police unit and even "a special court" devoted to dealing with such cases. But like many of Wagner's announcements, there was little to no follow-up. Wagner's father, the late Senator Robert F. Wagner Sr., had often cautioned his son, "When in doubt, don't"; it was sage advice that the mayor had turned into a political art form.

Political inaction—creating a committee to placate unhappy constituents and then just hoping the problem would go away—was Wagner's specialty. Although he was a liberal Democrat and a strong supporter of civil rights, young militant members of CORE grew so frustrated with Wagner's inaction that they staged an audacious bit of political street theater and "arrested" him on the steps of City Hall in July 1964. Likewise, the religious leaders of Operation: Yorkville understood it would take a grand gesture to force Wagner's hand.

Five months later, dissatisfied with Wagner's efforts, Reverend Hill made just such a gesture. On Sunday, October 27, during his sermon at St. Ignatius Loyola on 84th Street and Park Avenue, Hill announced that he was on a hunger strike—"a black fast" he called it. Since 6:00 p.m. the previous Friday, he had subsisted solely on water and would continue to do so until Wagner made good on his promises. The mayor had done nothing, declared Reverend Hill, while he had been busy screening *Perversion for Profit*, a thirty-minute film about the dangers of exposing children to pornography, to local community groups. The sale of pornographic literature to children was a violation of "parental civil rights" said the Jesuit, who believed that nude or even seminude photos could lead impressionable minds down the path of sexual violence and even drugs. "[It] sows the idea of perversion that soon leads to experimentation and finally fixation," he claimed.

The hunger strike was a public relations disaster for Wagner, a popular Democrat and a Catholic. With the next mayoral election just two years away, such actions and charges by a moral crusader like Reverend Hill could eat away at Wagner's electoral base. The mayor immediately released a statement that he was directing Deputy Mayor Edward F. Cavanagh Jr. to head up the city's antiobscenity efforts. He also made it clear that his administration welcomed the help of Operation: Yorkville or any "religious or civic leaders in rooting out this evil."

The next day Reverend Hill ended his seventy-five-hour fast, and the following week the members of Operation: Yorkville were invited to City Hall. But the deputy mayor wanted to stress that although the city was embarking on a theologically fueled crusade against *evil*—specifically the evil of selling porn to minors—adults were free to do as they like. "We are not out to trample on civil liberties," he told reporters. "We are not book burners."

It didn't seem that way to some. Ralph Ginzburg, the Bronx-born journalist and publisher of *Eros*, a high-end erotic literary magazine that had published the work of Norman Mailer and Salvador Dalí, among others, announced on October 28 that he too was going on a hunger strike to dispute "the obscenity panic that is plaguing our city and the country.'" Just five months earlier Ginzburg had been sentenced to five years in prison by a Philadelphia federal court for mailing obscene materials. The charges had been leveled against him in 1963 by US Attorney General Robert F. Kennedy after *Eros* printed a photo essay featuring a pair of nude dancers—a black man and white woman.

Kennedy found it offensive; he was certain this was a plot to derail his brother's civil rights legislation, then dying a slow death in the Senate. Miscegenation, or the mixing of the races, after all, was what segregationist senators feared most; in fact, antimiscegenation statutes were still the law of sixteen states in the nation (and would be until a 1967 US Supreme Court decision). "We are really dealing with something akin to witchery because obscenity is neither measurable nor definable nor worthy of the law," argued Ginzburg, who was appealing his conviction. Other antiobscenity leaders heaped scorn on Ginzburg. Dr. William P. Riley, the New York–based vice president of the National Organization of Citizens for Decent Literature, declared Ginzburg a "homegrown leftist," who along with *Playboy* publisher Hugh Hefner wanted "to destroy the Judeo-Christian concepts upon which the world has been built."

Ginzburg, who would serve two years in jail, was hardly the only victim of New York's—and the nation's—politically motivated morality campaign. Manhattan bookstore owner John Downs was facing criminal charges for selling illicit material to a minor that same month. At the behest of Operation: Yorkville members, sixteen-year-old Kathleen Keegan purchased a hardcover copy of *Fanny Hill: The Memoirs of a Woman of Pleasure,* an eighteenth-century erotic novel, at Downs's Lexington Avenue bookstore. While she never read the novel, she took it home to her mother, who after perusing just two pages, proclaimed it "horrible filth." The next day Downs and the clerk who sold her the book were arrested and charged with selling illicit materials to a minor.

New York Criminal Court Judge Benjamin Gassman agreed. A short, stern, religious conservative who had fled his native Kiev in 1903 after an anti-Semitic pogrom, Gassman favored Talmudic literature; he wasn't impressed by *Fanny Hill.* "While it is true that the book is well written," he wrote in the court's unanimous decision, "such [a] fact does

On February 1, 1961, John F. Kennedy met with Robert Moses, President of the World's Fair Corporation, and Thomas J. Deegan, the World's Fair Executive Vice President. Kennedy was an enthusiastic Fair supporter from the earliest days of his administration.

Kennedy's shocking assassination cast a dark shadow over the World's Fair and his successor President Lyndon B. Johnson, who was heckled by college students on the Fair's Opening Day.

The US Federal Pavilion was one of the largest buildings at the World's Fair and one of Robert Moses' least favorite. He called the Charles Luckman–designed, modernist structure "a square doughnut on stilts."
PHOTOGRAPH COURTESY OF BILL COTTER

Philip Johnson's New York State Pavilion, hailed as "the architectural delight" of the Fair, was embraced by Moses as well. Defending it against conservative critics, he described it as a building "that grows on you." It was one of the few Fair buildings selected by Moses to have an afterlife in his post-Fair Flushing Meadow Park.
PHOTOGRAPH COURTESY OF BILL COTTER

There was no shortage of corporate pavilions at the 1964–65 World's Fair, and one of the most popular was the General Motors Pavilion, which housed the Futurama II exhibit, a sequel to the carmaker's "World of Tomorrow" Futurama exhibit at the 1939–40 World's Fair.
PHOTOGRAPH COURTESY OF BILL COTTER

Inside Futurama II fairgoers saw a glimpse of "Tomorrow-Land"—a futuristic city of sleek modernist skyscrapers and smart superhighways, which bore a striking resemblance to the bustling—some would say soul deadening—urban landscapes that Robert Moses had devoted his life to creating.
PHOTOGRAPH COURTESY OF BILL COTTER

One of the most interesting structures at the Fair was the IBM Pavilion by Charles Ames and Eero Saarinen. On the outside, the pavilion looked like a giant industrial egg nestled atop a forest of metallic trees.
PHOTOGRAPH COURTESY OF BILL COTTER

Inside the IBM Pavilion, visitors were treated to the "People Wall"—a 500-seat indoor theatre—that rose several stories. Once airborne, the audience watched a multi-screened film projected onto numerous walls of the Pavilion.
PHOTOGRAPH COURTESY OF BILL COTTER

The General Electric Pavilion housed Walt Disney's Carousel of Progress, one of the World Fair's most popular exhibits. The show featured an Audio-Animatronic family throughout the 19th and 20th centuries, whose lives were made progressively easier through the wonder of household gadgets (much like GE's own).
PHOTOGRAPH COURTESY OF BILL COTTER

The Electric Power & Light's Tower of Light was a series of aluminum-covered rectangular panels that illuminated in a rainbow of pastel hues equaling some 12-billion-candlepower, reportedly the world's largest (and presumably, most expensive) searchlight.
PHOTOGRAPH COURTESY OF BILL COTTER

The heated controversy surrounding the mural in the Jordan Pavilion quickly became one of Robert Moses' biggest headaches, and for a time, put Middle Eastern politics at the center of a World's Fair devoted to "peace through understanding."

Andy Warhol's mural *Thirteen Wanted Men* (silkscreen ink on masonite; 1964), commissioned by Philip Johnson for the World's Fair, briefly hung on the architect's New York State Pavilion along with several other Pop Art murals. But the controversial work was quickly painted over before being removed at Governor Rockefeller's request.

Although Moses preferred the easy listening sounds of Guy Lombardo and disdained the amateur rock bands that played at the World's Fair, Beatlemania was an unstoppable cultural phenomenon. The immensely popular Johnson & Johnson Wax Museum exhibit featured a replica Fab Four before the real band played Shea Stadium in August 1965, solidifying their dominance over the worlds of pop and rock.

PHOTOGRAPH COURTESY OF BILL COTTER

While the World's Fair was a financial failure, it was—and remains—a seminal event in the lives of millions, occurring at a crucial moment in the history of New York and the nation, when the tectonic plates of American society were shifting rapidly.

not condone its indecency. Filth, even if wrapped in the finest packaging, is still filth." When Downs was found guilty in mid-November 1963, Reverend Hill called the ruling "a ray of hope that the corruption of youth in our land will be speedily halted and a fair warning to cesspool publishers and dealers that our youth is protected by law."

That same month, the Wagner administration's antiobscenity crusade began shuttering downtown cinemas that screened underground films. As promised, the city used any legal technicality at its disposal. The Pocket Theatre on Third Avenue and East 12th Street was closed in December for showing films without New York State's censor's seal of approval. In early 1964 Mekas, a Lithuanian-born poet, archivist, and *Village Voice* film critic, began screening avant-garde filmmaker Jack Smith's *Flaming Creatures* at the Gramercy Arts Theatre on East 27th Street. The controversial forty-five-minute feature was a campy piece of black-and-white celluloid depicting male and female genitals, transvestites, and a cunnilingual rape scene. The film broke barriers and was seemingly all things to all people: City officials considered it obscene; Smith called it "a comedy set in a haunted music studio"; and Mekas waxed poetic about it in the *Village Voice*, calling the film the "most luxurious outpouring of imagination, of imagery, of poetry, of movie artistry."

For three consecutive Mondays, Mekas showed the film at the Gramercy without a problem. Then on February 15, 1964, police issued a summons to the venue's owner, ending its run. Undeterred, Mekas began showing the controversial feature at the New Bowery Theatre on St. Mark's Place in the East Village. However, on March 3 the police interrupted the movie, arresting Mekas and several moviegoers and seizing the film's print and the projectors. Mekas was held in jail overnight and released.

But Mekas didn't scare easily. In the early 1940s, he and his brother Adolfas ran an anti-Nazi underground paper in their native Lithuania, and both escaped a German labor camp before landing in New York in 1949. Once there, he established himself as a patron of avant-garde art. In 1955 he started a magazine, *Film Culture*, and four years later became a film critic for the *Village Voice*. He even overcame his own homophobia, recanting earlier critical comments that New York's avant-garde film scene was falling prey to "the conspiracy of homosexuality" (he blamed his reactionary ideas on his Marxist views at the time).

In 1962 Mekas created the Film-Makers' Cooperative, which lent out film equipment to avant-garde filmmakers like Stan Brakhage, Ronald Rice, and Kenneth Anger—all artists whose work would eventually run into censorship issues. One of the aspiring filmmakers that Mekas helped out was Andy Warhol, who had begun to make movies in 1963, inspired by the East Village underground film scene, and Jack Smith in particular. "He's the only person I would ever copy," Warhol said of Smith. "I just think he makes the best pictures." Warhol's early films included *Kiss* (various shorts of Warhol hangers-on kissing), *Sleep* (literally eight hours of an actor sleeping), and *Empire State* (an eight-hour static shot of the Empire State Building, for which Mekas operated the camera).

Mekas was also a filmmaker. After seeing a performance of the Living Theatre's play *The Brig*, an antimilitary drama about the inhuman conditions inflicted on soldiers in the Marine Corps' prison (aka the brig), Mekas filmed the group's final performance of the show in January 1964. The film would go on to win the Grand Prize at the 1964 Venice Film Festival and bring the left-wing radicalism of the Living Theatre to a wider audience.

And Mekas the filmmaker also continued screening avant-garde films. Just a week after his arrest for showing *Flaming Creatures*, he was busted again for screening the 1950 French film *Un Chant d'Amour* (*A Song of Love*), about the unconsummated affair between two male prisoners and the guard who spies on them. *Un Chant d'Amour*, written and directed by novelist Jean Genet, is a bold depiction of homosexuality that includes full-frontal nudity and masturbation. Although made fourteen years prior in France, it was an extraordinarily provocative work for 1964 America and exactly the type of film that the Wagner administration and Operation: Yorkville considered obscene. Ultimately the case was thrown out on a technicality, but not before French writer and intellectual Jean-Paul Sartre, who would win the Nobel Prize in Literature later that year, and his partner, Simone de Beauvoir, author of the landmark feminist work *The Second Sex*, wrote protesting Mekas's arrest as an act of censorship.

Mekas received a six-month suspended sentence for screening *Flaming Creatures* and appealed the case all the way to the US Supreme Court in 1967. Although the court refused to hear the case, it would have a lingering political half-life. Associate Justice Abe Fortas, a liberal who was appointed to the High Court by his longtime friend President Lyndon Johnson, wrote in his minority opinion that Mekas's conviction should be overturned, essentially declaring that *Flaming Creatures* was not obscene. In 1968, when Johnson nominated Fortas to become Chief Justice, Senator Strom Thurmond used Fortas's vote to paint him as a protector of pornographers (it was his way of getting even with Johnson for his civil rights legislation). Due to his support of *Flaming Creatures* and financial improprieties that Congress uncovered, Fortas withdrew his nomination. Instead of having a liberal-leaning Fortas court in place, incoming president Richard M. Nixon named the next Chief Justice, thus altering the ideological makeup of the Supreme Court for decades.

While the city was closing theaters, it was also harassing owners of East Village coffeehouses that frequently staged poetry readings, places like Lé Cafe Metro. On February 10, 1964, Lé Cafe Metro was given a summons for operating without a cabaret license. Obtaining one was expensive, but without it, such cafes like it were sunk. The move was the Wagner administration's attempt to put establishments that catered to the downtown bohemian set out of business. For Ginsberg, the bard of the Beat Generation, whose 1955 poem "Howl" changed the course of American poetry, this was all a case of déjà vu.

In 1957 Ginsberg's friend and fellow Beat poet Lawrence Ferlinghetti was put on trial for publishing *Howl and Other Poems*, which, due to its celebration of gay sex, San Francisco city officials dubbed "obscene." Ferlinghetti owned and operated San Francisco's City Lights Bookstore, the first all-paperback store in the country, and its publishing division, City Lights Books. *Howl* and O'Hara's *Lunch Poems* were part of City

Light's popular Pocket Poetry Series, whose avid fans frequented establishments like Lé Cafe Metro and underground cinemas.

Although Ferlinghetti eventually won the case seven years later, the same strain of American Puritanism was rearing its ugly head in New York. "I'm in the middle of struggle with license dept. on poetry reading in coffeehouses, now Jonas Mekas been arrested twice, once for showing *Flaming Creatures* and once for showing Genet film," Ginsberg complained in a letter to Ferlinghetti. Uniting with fellow downtown poets like Diane di Prima and Ed Sanders, Ginsberg formed the Committee on Poetry, or COP, to fight Mayor Wagner and the city, who, they argued, were trampling on their First Amendment rights.

Ginsberg and his committee worked their way around the city's various agencies—albeit peacefully, as per Ginsberg's suggestion—including the mayor's office and the Cultural Commissioner's office. COP got help and advice from their local congressman Ed Koch, the future mayor of New York, and Henry Stern, member-at-large for the City Council. Ultimately their peaceful work-the-system strategy succeeded: On April 3 the License Department backed off, leaving Village coffeehouses and the New York poetry scene alone to flourish.

But that very same day, New York opened a new front in its war against art or speech that it considered obscene. This battleground would see action for years, even after its main protagonist was dead. Just hours after Ginsberg and his fellow activists won their victory, thirty-eight-year-old comedian Lenny Bruce was in his dressing room at the Café Au Go Go, a Greenwich Village club on Bleecker Street. As he prepared to go on for his 10:30 p.m. show, plainclothes police arrested him and the Go Go's manager, Howard Solomon, for obscenity. The charges were based on a tape recording undercover cops had made of a show at the same venue earlier that week. Bruce, who had already faced criminal charges in San Francisco and Chicago, was no stranger to the law and wanted to know which statute he had violated. The policeman cited Section 1040 of the Criminal Code.

"But that's prostitution," Bruce protested.

"Aww, Lenny, don't be technical," the cop complained. "It's one of them numbers."

Released on $1,000 bail the next day, Bruce and Solomon pleaded not guilty before New York's Supreme Court. The trial was set to begin April 23—the day after the World's Fair opened. Now freed, Bruce returned to the Café Au Go Go's stage that very night to perform his act, which included the same skits that were considered obscene: "Eleanor Roosevelt's Tits," an extended comical riff about the former First Lady's breasts, and "Hauling Ass to Save Ass," a fearlessly tasteless commentary about the Kennedy assassination, which had transpired barely five months before. Bruce's skit was based on the widely seen *Time* magazine photo of Jackie Kennedy, who moments after her husband had been shot, reached across the trunk of the presidential limo to assist a Secret Service agent. Rather than see the former First Lady performing an act of bravery, Bruce claimed she was running for her life, or "hauling ass to save ass."

This time, though, rather than utter the words that New York City officials deemed obscene, Bruce spelled them out. It worked for the moment. But his luck didn't last. On April 7, while once again performing at the Café Au Go Go, Bruce was arrested again, this time in the middle of his set, along with Ella Solomon, who co-owned the Go Go with her husband, Howard.

Ginsberg was infuriated. First gay bars, then the arrest of Mekas for showing films, the attempt to silence the coffeehouse poets, the harassment of the politically radical avant-garde Living Theatre on charges of tax invasion, and now Bruce, who had transformed nightclub comedy into social satire spiked with as many four-letter words—or ten-letter or twelve-letter words—as he could squeeze in. For Ginsberg, the city's antiobscenity crusade had morphed into an all-out assault on artistic expression.

The poet quickly organized the Emergency Committee Against the Harassment of Lenny Bruce, eventually enlisting a hundred esteemed artists and intellectuals like Ferlinghetti; theologian Reinhold Niebuhr; Lionel Trilling, Ginsberg's old Columbia University mentor (who believed Bruce was "a very remarkable and pointed satirist"); cultural critic Dwight Macdonald (who called Bruce's language "rough" but said he used it in "a witty, sophisticated and parodic way"); and novelists like Mailer, Terry Southern (of *Candy* fame), James Baldwin, Joseph Heller, and Henry Miller, among others. The group released a statement, noting that Bruce continued the tradition of such literary satirists as "Swift, Rabelais and Twain." Bruce certainly appreciated the support, even if he admitted he had never read any of the literary lights with which the committee associated him. But the poet's crusade still made him nervous. "The problem with people helping you with protests is that historically they march you straight to the [electric] chair," he quipped.

Born Leonard Alfred Schneider in Mineola, Long Island, Bruce was raised by various relatives until the age of sixteen, when he joined the Navy. After getting discharged he moved to Hollywood and attended acting school on the GI Bill. He began working the club circuit, traveling around the country before landing back in Tinsel Town and establishing himself (along with Mort Sahl) as one of the new so-called "sick comics." Working his way up the show business food chain, Bruce found important benefactors in comedian and TV host Steve Allen ("Lenny Bruce is literally a comic genius, a philosopher" Allen told *The New Yorker*) and *Playboy* founder and editor Hugh Hefner.

For Bruce, there was nothing sacred in postwar America: not sex, not religion, not language, not motherhood. How could there be in a country that lived with Jim Crow and under the omnipresent threat of an atomic mushroom cloud? Bruce loved to expose the hypocrisy of the political establishment, moralistic censors, and, of course, religious leaders—preferably with as many obscene words and scatological references as possible. His comedy was fueled with rage against the Establishment. As jazz composer Stan Kenton once told Bruce, "You're really a preacher, and the nightclubs are becoming churches because of your moralizing."

Admittedly, Bruce's shtick-as-sermons weren't for everyone. The *New York Times* cautioned that his nightclub act amounted to "shock therapy" for the audience. The *Daily News* was more pedestrian in its criticism, labeling the comic "The Man From Outer Taste."

Given the climate in the country, particularly in New York City, it was only a matter of time before Bruce made powerful enemies, including the head of the New York Archdiocese, Cardinal Francis Spellman, another target of his blasphemous barbs ("Spellman does *it* with the nuns"). After the cardinal reportedly complained to officials, Bruce's troubles in New York began in earnest. The comic and his defense team, then headed by free-speech lawyer Martin Garbus, drew a direct line between the cardinal and Bruce's legal woes. "It was rumored that Spellman was behind the trial," Garbus said. "We wanted to believe desperately that Cardinal Spellman was behind the whole thing. Lenny firmly believed it and that raised it to the level of truth in many people's eyes."

There were plenty of reasons to think so. Just six days before the Bruce trial was about to begin in Manhattan's Criminal Court—one of the most costly antiobscenity fights in New York City history and paid for by taxpayers—Spellman sought to publicly take control of Wagner's antiobscenity crusade. Speaking at Fordham University's commencement ceremony in early June 1964, he suggested the creation of a citizens' commission to battle the sale of "salacious literature." Clearly, Spellman thought Wagner's efforts weren't "effective" and the theocrats of Operation: Yorkville too "silent." The cardinal's speech demanded that a stronger, more experienced hand was needed to guide the city's collective antiobscenity crusade, and what better hand than that of the man called the American Pope?

But as Spellman marshaled the troops in New York, and the Bruce trial dragged on, the US Supreme Court handed down two landmark decisions later that same month. In the first, Jacobellis v. Ohio, the court struck down the Buckeye State ban of the French film *The Lovers* (*Les Amants*) in a six–three vote; with the second, Grove Press, Inc. v. Gerstein, the court voted five–four to lift the ban on Henry Miller's *Tropic of Cancer*, a book that had been outlawed by twenty-one states for decades. These decisions, which set new standards for the legal definitions of obscenity—declaring that neither *The Lovers* nor *Tropic of Cancer* were obscene—incensed Cardinal Spellman, who said the High Court had now allowed an "acceptance of degeneracy and the beatnik mentality as the standard way of American Life." The Cardinal declared a crusade was needed in "every city, town and village of this great nation" to combat the cancerous effects of smut, filth, obscenity, and pornography.

The same day the cardinal ripped into the Supreme Court, Mayor Wagner announced his creation of the Anti-pornography Committee, for which Spellman had lobbied. The new committee would have twenty-one members, including civic, educational, business, and labor leaders. New York's vast right-wing crusade, launched ostensibly to battle obscenity—and laced with a powerful undercurrent of homophobia—was working. During Mayor Wagner's administration, New York's religious leaders and city officials consistently and repeatedly persecuted avant-garde artists and East Village poets, and shuttered gay bars. When it decided to persecute Bruce, it took on the First Amendment itself.

Ironically, this was all happening at the same time that the US Supreme Court redefined obscenity and empowered the freedom of speech for all Americans, while out on the West Coast at the University of Berkeley, a Queens-born ex–New Yorker named Mario Savio was leading a student revolt that would ultimately become known as the Berkeley Free Speech Movement. Thanks to its myopic leaders, New York—the unabashed capital of the nation in so many ways, as Moses bragged to the World's Fair Committee in 1960—was falling behind the times.

Even as Mayor Wagner and Cardinal Spellman worked diligently with Moses to ensure the success of the World's Fair, they were two of the architects behind a crusade against free speech and artistic expression—a crusade that was certainly at odds with the message of the World's Fair, once again proving that the glittering pavilions of Flushing Meadow's manicured Fairgrounds and its utopian slogans had little—if anything—to do with the political turmoil of the city around it.

20

Negroes are fed up and there's going to be a revolution.

—Dick Gregory

In the early months of 1964, militant activists in New York who had grown disillusioned with the city's political establishment and the civil rights movement's national leaders planned to disrupt the World's Fair. The citywide protests throughout the summer of 1963 had done little to improve the lives or job prospects of black New Yorkers and had poisoned the city's already precarious state of race relations. Despite saying all the right things, the collected efforts of Mayor Robert F. Wagner Jr. and Governor Nelson A. Rockefeller had yielded few tangible results.

As 1963 ended, both politicians were preoccupied with matters other than racial justice: Wagner was more concerned with purging New York streets of gays, poetry-loving beatniks, and any book or film that religious authorities deemed obscene; while the governor was—once again—seeking the White House. And both had one eye on Queens, where after five long years, Robert Moses was overseeing hundreds of construction workers putting the finishing touches on scores of World's Fair pavilions in Flushing Meadow Park.

The Fair was expected to enrich city and state coffers and would surely be the greatest in history, Moses and his public relations staff repeatedly reminded New Yorkers. Wagner and Rockefeller could only hope so; there was a lot riding on the two-year exhibition. Regardless of the mayor's and governor's tense personal relationship with the Master Builder, each man gave him free rein to do as he wished with the Fair. The pressure was on: Not only would portions of the opening ceremonies be televised, but the White House also informed Moses just a couple weeks before opening day that President Lyndon Johnson would attend the festivities to deliver the keynote address after all. New York's political leadership would be in the spotlight, which could be particularly beneficial to Rockefeller, who hoped to challenge Johnson at the polls in November.

While New York and its leaders prepared for the influx of tourists anxious to see the Fair's gleaming space-age pavilions, life in the ghettos of Harlem and Bedford-Stuyvesant went unchanged: crumbling tenements, violent crime, joblessness, rundown public schools, and police brutality, which often went unpunished and unreported (with the notable exception of the black press, which covered such cases extensively; without police brutality incidents, noted Louis E. Lomax, "Negro newspapers would have considerable blank space"). Young activists, many of whom hailed from such neighborhoods, grew more militant as disillusionment set in. "They don't want us on the streets because the World's Fair and all their friends are coming!" complained one young Harlemite.

The movement's long-cherished dream of racial integration was beginning to seem as far-fetched to many black Americans as the futuristic predictions of the Fair. And perhaps more disconcerting to leaders like Martin Luther King Jr. (who was once heckled in Harlem as "Martin *Loser* King") and CORE national chairman James L. Farmer Jr. the Gandhian principles these men cherished were becoming passé; the notion of meeting the "physical force" of hatred with the "soul force" of nonviolence—as King exhorted activists to do during the March on Washington—was anathema to many activists who were now working for the cause.

In Washington, President Johnson was utilizing every trick in his political playbook to get the civil rights bill through the Senate and signed into law. But all along there were some black Americans, including many in the urban North, who had been asking themselves if maybe a *separation* of the races wasn't the better solution to America's racial nightmare. "The people in the black community who didn't want integration were never given a voice," Malcolm X claimed in 1962. "[They were] never given a platform. [They] were never given an opportunity to shout out the fact that integration would never solve the problem." That same year, James Baldwin asked pointedly in *The*

New Yorker (later reprinted in *The Fire Next Time*): "Do I really want to be integrated into a burning house?"

There was no simple answer to Baldwin's question, and mainstream civil rights leaders knew it. "Deep in the heart of every black adult, lives some of Malcolm X and some of Martin Luther King, side by side," noted Farmer, whose organization, CORE, seemed to embody the schizophrenic feelings of the movement in 1964. And nowhere were those feelings more conflicted than among the radical members of CORE's Brooklyn chapter.

The turning point for these young activists, who were mostly under thirty, had been the disappointing campaign at Brooklyn's Downstate Medical Center, which they had helped organize with local religious leaders. Construction jobs for members of the largely black community where the center was being built seemed like a reasonable and fair request for a taxpayer-funded public works project—hardly revolutionary by any standard. After weeks of protests, nearly seven hundred arrests, and a near-riot, Governor Rockefeller and Mayor Wagner had met with activists and union leaders. Goodwill expressed all around; committees formed; promises made; and then nothing. "[We have] used every means at our disposal to awaken the City Fathers of New York to the crying needs of their city," Isaiah Brunson, the twenty-two-year-old former auto mechanic who eventually became the chairman of the Brooklyn chapter, explained months later. "We have picketed, boycotted, sat-in, lied-in, etc. All of our efforts have been in vain." Up until this juncture, Brooklyn CORE had mostly gone along with the direction of the organization's national leadership—they marched, they protested, they wrote letters. But the lack of results militarized the organization.

One of the chapter's most active and strident members was public relations officer Arnold Goldwag, who often acted a provocateur, particularly when writing to the nation's leaders. In March 1963, after the Ku Klux Klan attacked civil rights workers in Greenwood, Mississippi, Goldwag repeatedly sent telegrams to Attorney General Robert Kennedy, demanding he order federal troops to protect them:

ATTEMPTED MURDER; ORGANIZED GENOCIDE; KLAN TERRORISM IN
GREENWOOD, MISSISSIPPI AND YET YOU WAIT. THE GERMAN PEOPLE
WAITED TOO—UNTIL HITLER BECAME A FRANKENSTEIN. WHAT ARE
YOU WAITING FOR TILL GREENWOOD BECOMES AUSCHWITZ?

This wasn't how King and Farmer—frequent guests in the Kennedy
White House—usually addressed the attorney general or his brother, the
president. But Goldwag didn't care: He called out Kennedy for being
soft on the KKK, just as Kennedy's father, Joseph P. Kennedy Sr. had
been soft on the Nazis while serving as Roosevelt's Ambassador to the
United Kingdom (a historical fact that the Jewish Goldwag was probably keenly aware of). A few months later, when President Kennedy made
his landmark civil rights speech, Goldwag struck a more conciliatory
tone, congratulating the president's stand: "Carry on the good fight," he
encouraged the president, "and we'll all be free in '63!"

Goldwag had a knack for provocative commentary. He would generate significant media attention for Brooklyn CORE (and a slew of
press clippings for his collection). In December 1963, when Baldwin and
actors/activists Ruby Dee and Ossie Davis called for a ban on Christmas
gift buying in memory of the four young victims of the Birmingham
Church bombings, Goldwag explained their position to the media: "And
to those who talk about traditions—and who live by the credo of 'Yes,
Virginia, there is a Santa Claus'—we say No Santa Claus because there
is a Virginia, there is a Mississippi and there is a Birmingham!"

A short man with a round baby face and deep-set, intense eyes,
Goldwag was a college dropout from Williamsburg, Brooklyn, raised
in a religious Jewish family and expected to become a rabbi like his
older brother. Against his parents' wishes, he got involved with the
civil rights movement after learning about it while attending the
Jacob Joseph Yeshiva on Manhattan's Lower East Side. "That's when
I first learned about democracy," he said. He joined the local chapter of CORE in 1961 and became a regular fixture at their office
on Nostrand Avenue in Bedford-Stuyvesant, even sleeping in the
cramped quarters.

By 1964 Goldwag, who smoked four packs of cigarettes a day, slept only four hours a night, and whose diet consisted of cake and black coffee, had been arrested nearly thirty times in various campaigns, including at the Downstate Medical Center protests, where he and several other protestors climbed on top of a construction crane; a photograph of the scene—with Goldwag front and center—was featured in the *New York Times*.

It was clear to Goldwag and the members of Brooklyn CORE that a new kind of direct action, a new form of protest, was needed to address the city's racial problems. Other radical New York activists, such as the outspoken Reverend Milton A. Galamison of Bedford-Stuyvesant's Siloam Presbyterian Church, had come to the same conclusion. National leaders of CORE, the NAACP, and the Urban League organized a February 3, 1964, school boycott to desegregate the New York Public School System. By all accounts it was a success—nearly half of the city's students skipped school that day. Unfortunately for the proponents of integration, their solidarity was met with stony silence from the New York City Board of Education.

Reverend Galamison, who had supported the boycott, now declared the city's public education system beyond redemption, claiming it should be "destroyed." His militant and violent rhetoric—a radical departure from mainstream civil rights groups—wasn't necessarily meant to get results, but it did grab attention from politicians, the media, and white New Yorkers, especially those with school-age children.

Allying itself with Reverend Galamison, the Harlem chapter of CORE organized a blockade of the Triborough Bridge—built by Moses in 1936—linking themselves arm-in-arm and dumping bags of garbage on the road, grinding traffic to a standstill. Although their action was nonviolent, it was deliberately provocative, and drew no distinction between ordinary citizens and those elected (or unelected) officials who promoted—or did nothing to change—New York's discriminatory practices. Yet this protest that was meant to draw attention to the poor quality of Harlem schools really only resulted in numerous arrests, considerable anger from the public, and condemnation from editorialists (the *Times* claimed the protests did "a disservice to civil rights"). It also drew a line across the city, as distinct as Fifth Avenue: On one side was a new style of civil rights activists; on the other was everyone else. When Galamison called for a second school boycott, city officials braced themselves for anything.

Senator Hubert H. Humphrey, one of the most passionate supporters of civil rights in either political party—he wrote the Democrats' 1948 civil rights plank that Johnson had called "a farce and a sham"—chimed in, afraid that the events in New York would derail the struggling civil rights bill. Along with Senator Thomas Kuchel, a Republican from California, the senators lectured the New York activists that "civil wrongs do not bring civil rights."

It was in this atmosphere that members of Brooklyn CORE continued with their plans of a grand gesture, one immense act of civil disobedience that would command the attention of not only Mayor Wagner, Governor Rockefeller, and Moses, but also of the media and *all* of New York City. If their gesture were grand enough—and yes, theatrical enough—it would grab the attention of the president and Congress, indeed the entire political establishment of the nation, the very people who had so egregiously ignored the demand for racial justice for so long.

Lomax had first raised the notion of a World's Fair stall-in back in July 1963, during a speech at Queens College. He called for five hundred drivers to make their way to the Fair in their automobiles and, by running out of gas or simply stopping on the way there, create a traffic jam of historical proportions. Moses' beloved network of newly renovated highways would be used as a roadblock, preventing tens of thousands from attending his Fair. Brooklyn CORE now seized on Lomax's suggestion: the World's Fair would be their target.

Zenlike in its simplicity, the plan also brought the World's Fair full circle: Twenty-five years earlier at the 1939 World's Fair, GM's Futurama exhibit mesmerized millions with its vision of the World of Tomorrow—a world of automobiles and highways; an imaginary Tomorrow-Land that Moses had spent his life making a reality; a world that, he bragged shortly after taking charge of the World's Fair, "was already in the process of being realized." Now, in 1964, civil rights activists would transform the automobile and the highway—those two potent symbols of the Modern Age—into weapons of mass disruption. From the protesters' point of view, the timing couldn't be better: World leaders would be at the Fair, and some seventy-five television cameras would be positioned around the Fairgrounds to capture the excitement of opening day; the world would—quite literally—be watching.

In a joint statement on April 4, the Brooklyn and Bronx chapters of CORE announced their plan to disrupt the opening of the World's Fair on April 22 unless the city addressed the problems of job discrimination, police brutality, slum housing, and poor schools—*immediately*. "While millions of dollars are being spent on the World's Fair, thousands of Black & Puerto Rican people are suffering," the statement read:

> *There will be no peace or rest until every child is afforded an opportunity to obtain high-quality education, and until significant changes are made in all areas mentioned. The World's Fair cannot be permitted to operate without protest from those who are angered by conditions which have been permitted to exist for so long—conditions which deny millions of Americans rights guaranteed them by the Constitution of the United States. We want all our freedom!!! We want it here!!! We want it Now!!!*

Five days later Goldwag sent a telegram to Mayor Wagner, Governor Rockefeller, and Moses with another ultimatum:

> THE PEOPLE OF THIS COMMUNITY ARE FED UP WITH EMPTY PROMISES AND PIOUS PRONOUNCEMENTS. UNLESS YOU FORMULATE AND BEGIN TO IMPLEMENT A COMPREHENSIVE PROGRAM, BY APRIL 20, WHICH WILL END POLICE BRUTALITY, ABOLISH SLUM HOUSING AND PROVIDE INTEGRATED QUALITY EDUCATION FOR ALL—WE WILL FULLY SUPPORT AND HELP ORGANIZE A COMMUNITY-BACKED PLAN TO IMMOBILIZE ALL TRAFFIC LEADING TO THE WORLD'S FAIR ON OPENING DAY.

Although civil rights groups had been lobbying Moses to appoint more blacks to executive positions at the Fair—to date there were two, Dr. Ralph J. Bunche and baseball icon Jackie Robinson—and to use his considerable power to force union leaders to hire more African Americans and Puerto Ricans for several years, Brooklyn CORE wasn't interested in such simple objectives. They wanted to make a symbolic point: that the World's Fair was being hosted in a city that was anything but *fair*. "Our objective is to have our own civil rights exhibit at the World's Fair," noted Oliver Leeds, another leader of the Brooklyn chapter. "We do not see why white people should enjoy themselves when Negroes are suffering."

Although Brooklyn CORE's rhetoric was belligerent and confrontational—radically different than that of mainstream activists—the stall-in would be an act of pure nonviolent civil disobedience. When asked why they would disrupt the World's Fair just to make their point, the activists claimed they had no choice. "The Power Structure of this City, State and Country must be made to realize that we will accept palliation no longer," Brunson, the Brooklyn CORE chairman explained. "Empty promises, investigatory committees, and such have done nothing to alleviate the problems that exist."

Few honest New Yorkers could disagree.

However, the backlash began immediately. The first to react was Farmer, CORE's national chairman, who called the notion a "harebrained idea." After a contentious meeting with the Brooklyn activists at his Manhattan apartment that went until four in the morning, he suspended the group on April 11, a move that brought indignation from several of CORE's other New York chapters. "We are not splitting with them," Farmer told the *New York Times*, "they are splitting with us."

While Farmer struggled to gain control of his organization—as one member of CORE's steering committee quipped, the stall-in "won't end segregation but it might end CORE"—other national civil rights groups tried to make light of the proposed protests. The NAACP's Roy Wilkins, who lived in Queens, dismissed the stall-in organizers' rhetoric as "strictly Brooklynese"—a snobbish comment that only amused the

Brooklyn chapter. "Oh, you're so right, baby!" laughed a Brooklyn activist after hearing Wilkins's snide remark.

City officials were outraged. Police Commissioner Michael J. Murphy declared that New York's Finest would "protect the constitutional rights" of anyone "to peacefully assemble and petition," but he had an obligation to protect "all men to the pursuit of happiness . . . the World's Fair should be a happy occasion in a somewhat far from happy world. No unlawful acts by any groups will be allowed to mar it." Traffic Commissioner Henry A. Barnes—one of Moses' favorite punching bags—quickly added a new law to the books making it illegal to intentionally run out of gas on a New York City roadway. Although he announced the law days after the Brooklyn group's announcement, Barnes told reporters with a straight face that the new rule had nothing to do with the stall-in. And then, just to keep the city's thermostat at a roiling temperature, Goldwag announced that his Brooklyn unit was planning on wasting millions of gallons of water by turning on New York City faucets just in case the stall-in didn't yield the desired results.

The media's condemnation of the activists was swift. "The projected traffic tie-up can win few converts to the civil rights banner," complained the *New York Post*. "It will provide new ammunition from racists—here and in Washington . . . it will in short be a form of sound and fury, carrying no clear message to most of the populace." As *Time*'s Theodore H. White memorably quipped, the traffic jam would amount to a "grab at the groin of a community of 10 million" New Yorkers.

Ordinary citizens flooded newspaper editors with letters. Some were from liberals concerned that the protest "would turn many people against the Negro cause," while others wrote that protesters should be arrested for "loitering, inciting to riot, and being plain fools." Some letters, sent directly to Brooklyn CORE's office, were unabashedly racist. "The colored people of Brooklyn want to be and act like parasites that should be exterminated," one anonymous writer wrote, adding "YOU WILL BE JUDGED BY YOUR ACTS." Another note, written on NYC Board of Education letterhead, read, "Why you miserable *blacksonofabitch!* How dare you threaten the World's Fair and the Christian White

Power structure of this City? You nigger bastards belong in Africa not here among genteel white Christian folk! We hope the police break your black ape heads on [opening day]! So drop dead!" One black woman from Manhattan wrote to the *Daily News* to express her disdain for the plan, suggesting that every car used in the protest should be towed away, and every driver's license suspended for one year. "I was hired to work at the Fair," she wrote. "I am a Negro, and I think this tie-up stuff is just too much."

The threats of a stall-in ruining the World's Fair filled the liberal political establishment with fear. Like Senator Humphrey, President Johnson worried any disturbance at the World's Fair would empower the Senate's bloc of Dixiecrats, who at that very moment were staging their own stall-in by making sure the civil rights bill didn't get anywhere. Such extreme measures in the streets of New York, Johnson told reporters, would "do the civil rights cause no good."

On April 16, at a meeting of the American Society of Newspaper Editors in Washington, DC, Farmer continued to condemn the actions of his organization's rogue chapter. But he told the largely white editors in the audience that while he disapproved of their methods, he understood their viewpoint; there was a "growing frustration, anger, militancy" among young blacks throughout the country, he warned, and unless action—real action rather than more broken promises—was delivered, the future didn't bode well for America.

Speaking at the same conference, Attorney General Kennedy struck a similar note, condemning the stall-in as irresponsible and urging the Senate to pass the civil rights bill his late brother had introduced the previous June. If the Senate didn't act soon, Kennedy predicted, young African Americans might start to believe that "there's no future for [them] in this system." What Kennedy either didn't know or failed to acknowledge was that many young activists in New York and elsewhere had already come to that conclusion.

It was apparent to anyone who was watching that the civil rights movement was hardly united under one banner or philosophy: A fissure exposed its warring factions, and the NAACP's Wilkins, one of the most moderate of the national leaders, wanted it fixed, and quickly. He sought a consensus from the top civil rights groups, and joined by Farmer, the Urban League's Whitney Young, and the SNCC's John Lewis, issued a statement that same day, declaring the stall-in a "revolutionary proposal" that was not in "the broad interests and needs of the Negro people," and characterizing the protest as "neither orderly or nonviolent."

While it is hard to imagine a mammoth New York traffic jam being orderly, declaring the protest as something other than nonviolent was pure spin. Lewis, one of the original Freedom Riders, apparently agreed. The next day Lewis, who was as devoted to Gandhian principles as Farmer or King, and who had sustained severe beatings at the hands of Southern racists, withdrew his name and organization from the hastily organized statement. There was "no evidence," he stated, that the stall-in violated "the time-honored tactics of civil disobedience."

Wilkins and the others told reporters that King, who had not signed the anti-stall-in statement, would eventually join them in condemning the actions of the rogue CORE activists. But King, the personification of the civil rights struggle for millions of Americans, had other ideas. In a plaintive letter to Wilkins, King admitted that he considered the stall-in a "tactical error," but flatly refused to condemn the young activists. "Which is worse, a 'Stall-In' at the World's Fair or a 'Stall-In' in the United States Senate?" he pointedly asked. "The former merely ties up the traffic of a single city. But the latter seeks to tie up the traffic of history, and endanger the psychological lives of twenty million people."

Sensing the seismic shift in the civil rights movement he had helped lead for nearly a decade, King attempted to explain the tactics of the Brooklyn activists to a broader audience. "The World's Fair action must be viewed in the broader context of 20,000,000 Negroes living in an unfair world," he wrote in a statement to the press, "facing grinding poverty and humiliating denial of elementary and fundamental rights to equal accommodation, voting, housing, education and jobs."

The split stance of the mainstream civil rights leaders only bolstered the militant posturing of Brooklyn CORE, who quickly found allies rallying to their side. Already aligned with CORE's Bronx chapter as well as

Reverend Galamison's organization, Brooklyn CORE accepted pledges of support and the promise to send drivers from other local chapters—Manhattan, Long Island, Columbia University—and SNCC activists from Washington, Maryland, and Pennsylvania. "You do not stand alone," one supporter wrote to the group. And at least one New York union leader, John J. Felury, president of the Sanitation Men's Local 831, told reporters that none of his ten thousand sanitation workers would report to work on April 22 if the city ordered them to tow cars. "We're not going to scab on anyone fighting for freedom or civil rights," he said.

Meanwhile, activists around the city passed out leaflets, many of them handwritten with drawings of the Unisphere, to rally drivers for their cause. "Drive awhile for freedom," exhorted one flyer. "Take only enough gas to get your car on EXHIBIT on one of these highways," it read, and listed the five roadways they would target: the Grand Central Parkway, the Brooklyn-Queens Expressway, the Belt Parkway, the Interboro Parkway, and the Van Wyck Expressway—every one of them built or refurbished by Moses.

Throughout the hectic weeks leading up to the World's Fair, when every day brought a new drama to the stall-in saga, Moses was curiously quiet. Perhaps, after decades of spouting off at his enemies—both real and imagined—the Master Builder had learned that silence could be the better side of valor. With his historical unfriendliness toward civil rights activists and his combative nature, his usual pontifications in the press could only make things worse. Already, unbeknownst to Moses, one of the activists had circulated a flyer with his picture (cut out from the *New York Times*) accentuated by several hand-drawn arrows pointed at his image and the words: THE TARGET APRIL 22 1964.

Privately, Moses used his connections with his friends in the media elite to write editorials coaxing city officials to come down hard on the would-be protesters. Writing his friend Jack Flynn, publisher of the *Daily News,* he suggested any driver whose car stalled on April 22 should have his license, registration, and liability insurance revoked—permanently. "A fine is *not* the answer," Moses declared. "The penalty of forfeiting the right to drive seems the best suggestion made." At a preview of the Illinois Pavilion, which would soon mesmerize Fairgoers with its animated Abraham Lincoln, Moses sat silently as his friend Adlai Stevenson, the former governor of Illinois, former great liberal hope of the Democratic Party, and at the time US Ambassador to the UN, criticized the stall-in as a "civil wrong" and declared that there must be "respect for law and order."

But ultimately and quite uncharacteristically, Moses felt powerless as the threat of the stall-in grew. When his friend Robert Daru, a well-connected lawyer, offered his legal assistance to battle the activists, Moses politely declined. "The trouble is that the main part of this problem lies outside of the Fair and is directly under the city administration and the Police Commissioner," Moses complained. "I have no doubt of Commissioner Murphy's ability and courage but some of the others who ought to be heard from have been singularly silent." He closed the letter by stating he was confident his Pinkerton police force could meet any challenges inside the Fair but that what happens outside the Fair's gates was beyond his control. "There are indeed a number of things which could be done," he lamented, "but I am not in a position to advocate, much less do them."

All along Moses had been preoccupied with the press coverage of the World's Fair. Now, here was a story that couldn't be ignored: a traffic jam intended to prevent tens of thousands of Fairgoers from reaching their destination. Given the city's roiling racial turmoil of the past year, it wasn't hard to imagine that such an undertaking—even if it was a nonviolent act of civil disobedience—could touch off a full-blown race riot. And Moses' worst fears were realized when one would-be Fairgoer from Clayton, Ohio, wrote him to say that after reading reports about the civil rights activities in New York, he had decided against subjecting "our children to such unhuman [sic] like actions, this degrading spectacle . . . we have decided to cancel our reservations and take our vacation in a more human atmosphere somewhere else."

By now the players in the stall-in drama were busy ratcheting up their rhetoric. Farmer announced that he would lead activists from National CORE in a "positive" counterdemonstration *inside* the World's

Fair, specifically targeting the exhibits of Jim Crow–supporting Southern state pavilions like Louisiana. Farmer would brandish a cattle prod, just like the ones that Louisiana police used on civil rights workers, and some of his activists might attempt to scale the twelve-story Unisphere. This new CORE protest would illustrate "the contrast of the glittering fantasy of the technical abundance" of the World's Fair with "the real world of discrimination, poverty and brutality faced by the Negroes of America, North and South." Millions of people would be attending the Fair; millions, Farmer noted, who remained neutral on the issue of racial discrimination. "We hope to get them off the fence," he said.

But for all Farmer's high-handed talk, his real motivation for leading this new protest was to reclaim control of CORE. "The success or failure of the stall-in loomed as a test of my strength within CORE," he later admitted.

Meanwhile, his erstwhile members held a press conference at the Hotel Theresa in Harlem—Malcolm X's de facto office after his split with the Nation of Islam—announcing they had 1,800 drivers pledged to stall on the roadways. In fact, they claimed, they had so many volunteers that they were now planning on having people block various bridges, and tunnels around the city with their bodies and stacks of garbage and other debris as well as block subway cars and the Long Island Rail Road. The whole thing now was beyond their control, they claimed. "It's not so much that CORE is planning [the stall-in] but that the man in the street is going to do it," Leeds told reporters. "From what I've heard in Bedford-Stuyvesant, neither CORE nor anyone else is going to be able to stop him. That's the beauty of this whole operation." A last-minute effort by the Queens DA, who met the stall-in leaders for a half hour in his office at the Kew Gardens courthouse to get them to reconsider, led to nothing. Later that day he served the stall-in leaders with papers declaring their proposed protest illegal.

As opening day approached, Mayor Wagner announced that the city wasn't taking any chances. All roads leading in and out of Queens, he said, would be swarming with 1,100 officers in police cars, accompanied by dozens of tow trucks; three command centers would be set up; and there would be a police presence on every subway. That was on terra firma; from the sky, police helicopters would be hovering, including one that was capable of lifting an automobile into the air. As far as the city was concerned, this was war.

Mayor Wagner engaged in his own histrionics when, on the eve of opening day, he called the activists' plans "a gun to the heart of the city"—exactly the kind of violent imagery that Moses thought did nothing to counter New York's growing reputation as a savage city or benefit the World's Fair. Later that night, the *New York Times* put together a story about a meeting of stall-in leaders who claimed drivers from Philadelphia and New Jersey were in New York already, prepared to risk their cars. "[The stall-in] is planned to dramatize the Negroes' dissatisfaction with the pace of civil rights progress," the *Times* reported on its front page the next day. "No power on earth can stop it now."

21

Unless we can achieve the theme of this fair—"Peace Through Understanding"—unless we can use our skill and our wisdom to conquer conflict as we have conquered science—then our hopes of today—these proud achievements—will go under in the devastation of tomorrow.

—President Lyndon B. Johnson at the
World's Fair opening ceremony

After five long years of negotiations and toil, the opening day of the World's Fair—April 22, 1964—finally arrived. As millions of New Yorkers awoke that morning to an unseasonably chilly day and rainy skies, more like late autumn than early spring, crowds gathered at the Fair's gates, anxious to roam the 646 acres of manicured Fairgrounds where oblong-, pylon-, and ziggurat-shaped pavilions had been taking shape for more than a year.

When the gates opened at 9:00 a.m., the first visitor of the day was ushered in: eighteen-year-old Bill Turchyn, a freshman from St. Peter's College in Jersey City, who had been waiting—first in line—for nearly two days, braving the rain and cold. Standing behind him, along with thousands of others, was Michael Catan, who twenty-five years earlier had been the first customer at the 1939–40 World's Fair.

Third in line that blustery morning, and equally intent on making history, was a big-band jazz drummer from Chicago named Al Carter, an admitted fair buff. Carter loved being first; in fact, he had made an art of it: He had been the first paying customer to enter Chicago's 1933 Century of Progress exhibition, as well as Seattle's Century 21 Exposition two years before (and he would be the first paying customer at Montreal's Expo '67 three years later). "I like to participate in moments of history," Carter told the *New York Times*. "That's my hobby. Is it any crazier than those people who collect little pieces of paper—stamps?" That was exactly the kind of enthusiasm and dedication that Robert Moses was banking on.

Despite the weather, the festivities went along as scheduled. The opening parade featured five thousand people marching in the rain before the reviewing stand, where the Fair's executive vice president, General William E. Potter, saluted them. The paraders were a microcosm of the World's Fair itself, in all its multicultural glory: bagpipers (from three countries); a Chinese drum and bugle corps; Montana cowboys; Japanese geishas; Spanish guitarists (plus flamenco dancers); the University of Pennsylvania's 101-piece marching band; a horse-drawn beer wagon from Germany; a steel-drum troupe from the Caribbean; an Israeli accordionist; a soaked-to-the-bone Miss Louisiana, who smiled bravely in her strapless sequined dress while perched in a slow-moving red convertible; and several Walt Disney characters.

Unbeknownst to the paraders and revelers, a short distance away at the 74th Street and Broadway station in Jackson Heights, the first protests of the day had already taken place. After threatening to bring New York's arterial highway system to a halt, the activists of Brooklyn CORE and their cohorts opted to target the city's subway system. In response, Mayor Robert F. Wagner Jr. and Police Commissioner Michael J. Murphy had stationed a cop on every subway car; all twenty-five thousand members of New York's Finest had been activated for duty, like a heavily fortified army ready to defend its homeland from foreign marauders.

The No. 7 Train in Queens, the "official" World's Fair subway—*Just pay 15 cents—hop aboard!—and you're on your way / Yes, part of the fun of the World's Fair is the Subway Special that takes you there*" promised a Metropolitan Transit Authority TV commercial—provided an easy and inexpensive way for millions of travelers to get to the Fairgrounds and Shea Stadium. It was also an obvious target for protesters.

The trouble started around 6:00 a.m. when four teenagers—three boys and a girl—blocked the subway doors from closing on a Fair-bound train at the 74th Street station. The police quickly surrounded the youths, who refused to budge while clutching the doors. Officers pried their hands loose by bashing their knuckles with nightsticks, and the quartet was promptly arrested. About an hour later, at the same station in Queens, a crowd of fifty teenagers rushed another train, holding open its doors and shouting "Freedom Now!" and "Jim Crow must go!" Dozens of police moved in. When the protesters refused to move, officers dragged them away by their feet.

"This is America!" one black youth shouted as he was carried away. "Look what they're doing to a sixteen-year-old boy who wants freedom!"

Another black protester asked his arresting officer, also black, if the white policemen called him a "boy back at the station." His response was to bash the protester with his club. An older black woman thought the cops were going too easy on the teens. "What they need is bayonets stuck in them," she said.

When it was over, seven people were injured in the melee, four protestors hospitalized for head wounds and three police officers. Twenty-three people were arrested in all, four of them charged with felonious assault. A CBS reporter saw the whole thing. "The police did their job but it required a great deal of force," he told the *New York Times*, "and a number of people got hurt quite badly."

The incident illustrated how the racial dynamics in the North differed from its Southern counterpart. These weren't Bull Connor's racist Southern policemen happily beating peaceful protesters chanting "We Shall Overcome"; this was Queens, New York, already one of the country's fastest-growing melting pots—a pastiche of cultures and ethnicities—with both an integrated police force and a subway system. In New York's racial landscape, black policemen faced not only on-the-job discrimination, but also taunting from young activists, as subway riders—black and white—nodded their consent as they watched those same officers use brute force against civil rights protesters.

For many Northern Democratic voters, using civil disobedience to end the South's Jim Crow laws was one thing; using similar tactics to end discrimination in New York was something else entirely. Somewhere Connor and Senator Richard B. Russell were smiling, while ensconced at his Wall Street law firm former vice president Richard Nixon was taking notes—and calculating the political benefits of a potential "backlash" among white working-class voters—while plotting his political comeback.

Despite the disruptions to the No. 7 Train, the highways outside the World's Fair were nearly empty—at least by New York City rush hour standards. So were the bridges and tunnels. As police stood in the rain wearing yellow slickers or patrolled the roads in black-and-white cruisers, tow trucks roamed nearby and helicopters hovered overhead. In fact, there was nary a traffic problem to be found—only a dozen drivers were arrested when their cars stalled. Firebrand preacher Reverend Milton A. Galamison and comedian/activist Dick Gregory drove to Queens but quickly realized the stall-in wasn't happening. For all their ballast, the Brooklyn activists couldn't pull it off. With nothing else to do, Galamison suggested they head back to the church and regroup. "Regroup what?" quipped Gregory, who would use the stall-in as a punch line in his comedy routine.

But if Moses and the political elite inside the World's Fair thought that the day's troubles were over, James L. Farmer Jr. had other ideas. Although the national CORE chairman only planned his "counter-demonstration" as a last-minute rebuttal to the stall-in, he had managed to put together a contingent of highly motivated veteran activists, including Bayard Rustin, the co-organizer of the March of Washington. Earlier that morning Farmer had gathered his troops at Community Church on East 35th Street and reiterated that their demonstration had clear and precise goals—unlike the stall-in. Their mission, he would say throughout the day, was to illustrate "the contrast between the glittering world of fantasy and the real world of brutality, bigotry and poverty." They then traveled down to Penn Station—the magnificent neoclassical building that would by year's end be torn down in an act of architectural vandalism—and boarded the 8:43 a.m. Long Island Rail Road for Flushing Meadow.

Debarking the train, Farmer strode up to the Fair's gate, where he and his group encountered members of Moses' Pinkerton private police force. The guards readily spotted the nationally known Farmer—hard to miss with his barrel-chested frame and linebacker build. Prepared for any contingency, the CORE leader already had advance troops inside the Fair equipped with walkie-talkies to scope out the scene.

As Farmer stood at the gate, one of his young troops listened in on the Pinkertons' wavelength, overhearing the Fair's official plan: Farmer would be stopped at the gate, and thus unable to lead a demonstration. Such a calculated move seemed to have Moses' fingerprints all over it. But improvising on the fly, the young activist imitated a guard and barked into the walkie-talkie. "Correction! There are new orders. Let Farmer and his group come in. Repeat. *Do* let them come in. That is all." Just like that, Farmer, with his group in tow, entered the Fairgrounds. Whatever happened next at the World's Fair, one thing was certain: The fate of CORE as a national civil rights organization hung in the balance.

Born in Texas in 1920, Farmer was the grandson of a slave. His father, James L. Farmer Sr. was a preacher and professor who taught literature in three ancient languages—Aramaic, Hebrew, and Greek—and was reportedly the first black man in Texas to earn a PhD. Following in his father's footsteps, Farmer earned a degree in theology from Howard University. With his deep baritone and intellectual mind, he was well-suited for preaching but in 1942 cofounded CORE, an interracial civil rights group. It was during his college years—he began his undergraduate studies at age fourteen—that he first encountered Gandhi's philosophy of nonviolent protest, which CORE would help make a hallmark of the civil rights movement.

After working as a journalist for a time, Farmer labored to integrate the public school system in the South. In February 1960, when four black college students sat at a whites-only lunch counter in Greensboro, North Carolina, they turned to CORE for support. A year later Farmer became CORE's national director, and that summer he pushed for the first Freedom Rides to desegregate the South's public transportation system. After angry white mobs assaulted the riders again and again, Robert Kennedy suggested CORE postpone their protests so that both sides could "cool off." "We have been cooling off for 350 years," Farmer told Kennedy. The Freedom Rides continued.

Now, three years later, he was defying the Northern liberal establishment again. He and Rustin headed to the Louisiana and Mississippi pavilions, where they joined other protesters. Farmer brandished a three-foot-long electric cattle prod—to inform Fairgoers that it was a weapon of choice of the Louisiana police to use on black activists. Unfortunately for Farmer, the pavilion was empty, one of several that weren't ready for opening day. Heading over to the New York City Pavilion, Farmer and Rustin sat in the doorway, blocking entry. It didn't take long for the Pinkertons to find Farmer and politely ask him to move. When he refused, the guard in charge tried pleading with the civil rights leader.

"Mr. Farmer, you know you're blocking entrance to the building," the guard said. "Won't you please move over."

Farmer still refused.

"Mr. Farmer, Robert Moses, who is in charge of the World's Fair, does not want you arrested," the Pinkerton informed him. "We don't want to arrest you. So please move. Your picketing is all right and quite legal, but blocking the entrance is illegal." While Moses might have advocated behind the scenes to throw the book at the would-be stall-inners, when it came to the politically connected Farmer—who had sat in the White House opposite presidents—he used kid gloves.

Ordinary Fairgoers had mixed feelings about the protesters that ranged from hate to sympathy. One mother grew annoyed with her six-year-old girl as they passed in front of the New York State Pavilion because the youngster walked around the prone protestors. "When I say step on them," the mother reprimanded the child, "step on them." One older woman was moved by what she saw. "There's a part of me that feels like joining them," she said. A Pakistani couple who viewed the display of civil disobedience were aghast. "I think we should move on. I do not like to look at this."

Still refusing to move, Farmer was asked by one Pinkerton guard if he would speak to him privately. Again he reiterated how Moses did not want to have the civil rights leader arrested. When Farmer defiantly reclaimed his spot in front of the entrance, the Pinkertons had little choice but to arrest him. It took three guards to carry the heavy Farmer away. "Gee, Mr. Farmer," one of them said as they lifted him to the paddy wagon, "you got to lose some weight." Even Farmer got a laugh out of that.

Years later, the CORE leader recalled that unlike in his Southern campaigns, he and his fellow activists weren't breaking a "bad law" at the World's Fair—blocking entrance to a building was, after all, hardly a misappropriate use of the legal code. But Farmer noted they were purposefully violating it "in order to bring the spotlight of public attention on other evils in New York such as employment discrimination, housing discrimination, and de facto segregation in the schools," which was, contrary to what Farmer or anyone else claimed, exactly what Brooklyn CORE's proposed stall-in meant to do, only on a far grander scale.

However, the Brooklyn group was unable to pull it off. The hundreds of cars promised by fellow activists from outside New York City never arrived. Most were scared off by the court injunction obtained by Queens District Attorney Frank D. O'Connor against Brooklyn CORE for threatening the stall-in; many were afraid that the radical chapter lacked the funds to bail them out if they were arrested.

Arriving in the afternoon at the 110th Precinct in Elmhurst, Queens, where the arrested teenage activists from the subway protests were being held, Brooklyn CORE chairman Isaiah Brunson told reporters that despite the stall-in's failure, there would be other protests in the future. "We are not stopping here," he said, "and there will be no peace in New York City until Mayor Wagner meets our demands." It was bold talk but only talk; within a few days Brunson, troubled by his inability to stage the stall-in, went into hiding.

Brooklyn CORE and its allies were in disarray. Arnold Goldwag was arrested at the Willet Points subway station just outside the Fair on a court-issued bench warrant (he had never bothered to appear in court to answer charges stemming from his arrest at the Downstate Medical Center). Herbert Callender of Bronx CORE appeared at the Elmhurst precinct, insisting he speak with the arrested activists, and was promptly arrested himself. Reverend Galamison appeared there, too, disappointingly telling reporters that he never doubted Brunson's "sincerity" but that the twenty-two-year-old auto mechanic "is no Bayard Rustin."

Back at the World's Fair, as Farmer, Rustin, and their group were being hauled away, other activists—many of them white college students—had fanned out through the Fairgrounds. A group of fifty protesters targeted the Florida Pavilion, where they squared off with police. One attempted to scale the building's 110-foot orange tower as Governor C. Farris Bryant spoke with reporters inside. The protesters were arrested, including the would-be tower-climber, who required a quartet of officers to restrain him as he screamed and kicked, booting one policeman square in the face.

Some protesters carried signs and marched silently; others tapped their feet along with the music of the opening parade; still others took breaks from their picketing to do some sightseeing. "I've been running off to see something whenever I get relieved on the line," said one New York CORE member before heading to the GM Pavilion. Another Maryland activist took a break from picketing his home state's pavilion to see the Ford show. "I think it's an interesting Fair," he said. "I hope I will be able to come back."

The parade ended at the Singer Bowl, the newly constructed ten-thousand-seat open-air stadium where the Fair's VIPs and international dignitaries had gathered for the invitation-only opening ceremony. Sitting on the stage, underneath a blue-and-orange canopy, were former president Harry S. Truman, Governor Nelson A. Rockefeller, Mayor Wagner, and Moses. They were joined by the United Nation's Dr. Ralph J. Bunche and UN Ambassador Adlai Stevenson, eight state governors, eleven congressmen, and twenty-three ambassadors. As the audience took to their seats, doing their best to protect themselves from the rain, speakers took to the podium, decorated with the presidential seal, in anticipation of President Johnson's arrival.

It didn't take long before they began lavishing Moses with praise. Messages were read from former presidents Herbert H. Hoover and Dwight D. Eisenhower, who had awarded the Fair to New York nearly four years earlier. President Truman joked that there "is only one Moses and it's not the one in the Bible." Governor Rockefeller lauded his most infamous employee—"the fabulous Bob Moses has done it again," he said. Mayor Wagner poignantly predicted the Fair's opening day represented a historic event, a before-and-after moment that would grow in importance over time. "Today," he noted, "we may be marking the end of one era and the beginning of another." The mayor had no idea of just how right he was.

Moses stood at the podium, hatless despite the chill and wearing his customary suit and tie and a thin raincoat. While obviously pleased with the accolades and verbal wreaths being laid at his feet, he acknowledged the silent shadow that hung over the Fair, lamenting the fact that President John F. Kennedy—who had been assassinated exactly five months before—wasn't "here to give [the Fair] his blessing." It was, uncharacteristically, a gracious note to strike, and one that Robert Kennedy expressed his thanks for in a handwritten note weeks later.

Representing the family of nations that were participating in the Fair was Indira Gandhi, the daughter of Indian Prime Minister Jawaharlal Nehru. As Gandhi, who in two years would be elected prime minister, spoke, Johnson's military green presidential helicopter swirled overhead, creating a commotion and bringing her time at the podium to an end. (The new president's handlers had made sure to fly directly from the airport just in case the stall-in clogged the highways.) Emerging from the helicopter as the band played "Hail to the Chief," Johnson was surrounded by Secret Service. The events in Dallas were fresh in everyone's mind, nor was it lost on political insiders that President William McKinley had been assassinated at the 1901 Buffalo Fair.

Addressing the crowd, President Johnson spoke of the dual paths that stood before the world, "abundance or annihilation—development or desolation," and characterized the World's Fair as "the promised land of Mr. Moses," borrowing poet Ogden Nash's phrase. The president and the VIPs then moved to the US Federal Pavilion, where Johnson dedicated the Charles Luckman–designed modernist structure that his predecessor had taken such a personal interest in (and the planning for which had elicited so many complaints from Moses). One set of protesters sat down on the rain-soaked grass on either end of the building while the president declared, "Peace is not only possible in our generation but I predict it is coming much nearer."

What Johnson didn't know was that the protests were already under way while he was speaking to the VIP crowd inside the Singer Bowl; during his first speech a few hundred protesters, mostly college students, carried signs and shouted "Jim Crow Must Go!" whenever they heard his Texas twang broadcast over the Fair's PA system. Now the demonstrators, held at bay by a throng of police, shouted "Jim Crow Must Go!" and "Freedom Now!" directly at the president, often drowning out his amplified voice. Three of the college activists sat on the shoulders of their peers and held up signs that were visible not only to Johnson, but for the entire crowd of politicians to see. A World's Fair Is a Luxury but a Fair World Is a Necessity read one; See New York's Worse Fair—Segregated Schools for Negroes, Puerto Ricans and Rats read another.

For Moses and Wagner, this might have been worse than an actual stall-in. They could do nothing but sit and watch helplessly as scores of college students drowned out Johnson, who was making one of his very first public speeches since an assassin's bullet had made him the thirty-sixth President of the United States.

Another group that arrived from nearby Queens College, where Louis E. Lomax had first floated the idea of the stall-in the year before, reinforced the activists who had arrived with Farmer. Queens was a politically active campus with a CORE chapter, including a twenty-year-old activist named Andrew Goodman, who arrived in time to continue on the "official" CORE protest after Farmer and Rustin had been carried off.

Ignoring the rowdy crowd that was shouting him down as if he were some local City Council speaker as best he could, Johnson laid the groundwork for a vision of what by the following month he would call "the Great Society": an America in which "no man need be poor" and where "no man is handicapped by the color of his skin or the nature of his belief." When the college students heard this, they laughed out loud, openly mocking President Johnson for all to see. The crowd—including Moses, Wagner, ambassadors, congressmen, governors, and foreign dignitaries—was horrified at this generational display of disrespect.

The activists looked every bit the part of young collegiate rebels: Some wore jeans and collared shirts, affecting the plebeian look that would make Pete Seeger proud; others affected longish hair a la the Beatles. The most rebellious—and hip—among them were decked out in suede jackets and jeans, their angry eyes hidden by shades—a look that Bob Dylan would soon make famous. Some, perhaps less image-conscious, looked earnest in their black horn-rimmed glasses and pleated skirts.

The new president, who was congenitally sensitive to public embarrassment, could only mask his outrage. Lacking the polished grace and wit of his predecessor or the respect of the Free World commanded by Eisenhower, the former Supreme Allied Commander of WWII, or even Truman's down-home, tell-it-like-it-is charm, Johnson seemed remarkably un-presidential. Hailing from humble origins, Johnson desperately wanted to win the White House on his own and emerge from the slain Kennedy's shadow. He wanted to prove to all the naysayers—the Eastern establishment that never accepted him, the Northern liberals who were horrified that this rough 'n' ready Texan was now the keeper of the Camelot flame—that he, Lyndon Baines Johnson, Landslide Lyndon, as the local reporters dubbed him after the extremely narrow (and stolen) election of 1948 that sent him to the US Senate, was indeed a liberal New Dealer at heart. He would muster all his Machiavellian strategies to accomplish what Kennedy and every other president had failed at: He would sign the most far-reaching piece of civil rights legislation into law.

Yet, here he was, in working-class Queens, province of labor union workers, immigrants, and blacks—natural Democratic voters—and he was being embarrassed and ridiculed by nearly two hundred socially engaged college students, who also should have been his natural constituents. And they were doing it to him at the World's Fair in front of the national and international press; members of the political elite, and one of his potential Republican rivals for the White House—Nelson Rockefeller.

Attempting to reclaim the moment by addressing the students' concerns, Johnson told them that American freedom was an act-in-progress:

"We do not try to mask our national problems. We do not try to disguise our imperfections or cover up our failures. No other nation in history has done so much to correct its flaws." He was met with more contemptuous laughter from the activists. Johnson had been looking forward to the New York trip to open the World's Fair—it was one of the most non-partisan acts a president could perform—and they made a laughingstock out of him.

"I felt sorry for them," he said the next day after returning to Washington, where the White House press corps questioned him about his teenage torturers. Sounding like the disapproving father of the nation's wayward youth, Johnson said that their disruption of his speech served "no good purpose . . . of promoting the cause they profess to support." New York Senator Jacob K. Javitz, a Republican, was so horrified by the demonstrators that he apologized personally to the president. The mayor apologized publicly, saying that "as the city in which this took place, we must be ashamed." But of all the officials who witnessed the public humiliation of a president, only Police Commissioner Murphy seemed to grasp the real significance of the historical event. He noted that the Fair's opening day was "a day in which the President came to the world of fantasy and encountered the world of fact, a day millions will never forget."

Although Moses had predicted that more than 250,000 attendees would pass through the Fair's ninety-five turnstiles on opening day, the official tally was only 92,646—and of those, only 63,791 actually paid the $2 price of admission (the others being well-connected and/or VIPs). Never one to admit a mistake, Moses blamed the low turnout on the Novemberlike weather, the weather being one of the few aspects of life in Gotham that even the Master Builder could not influence—not that he didn't try. Moses would write to local news stations urging them to downplay gloomy weather reports in their nightly broadcasts so that Fairgoers wouldn't be scared off.

But the weather was only half the story. The proposed stall-in—even though it hadn't actually happened—had done its job: Tens of thousands of people had stayed away from the World's Fair. The myriad demonstrations that had transpired—on the subway, the Farmer-led sit-ins at the New York State Pavilion, and the shouting down of an American president in front of political leaders and television camera crews—would not have happened had not a small group of militant Brooklyn CORE activists, with nothing more than bravado and home-made flyers, upped the ante. Although their planned stall-in failed, the day was hardly a failure for the group. President Johnson, Moses, Mayor Wagner, and Governor Rockefeller had all heard their message, even if the Brooklyn activists themselves had not delivered it.

What they and the nation heard that day was that for some civil rights activists, the time for deliberation was over; now was a time for action. "Freedom Now!" was not a polite request; it was a demand. "Jim Crow Must Go!" was not a wish; it was an order. "Peace Through Understanding" was a worthy slogan, but they were empty words against the backdrop of the nation's tumultuous political and psychic landscape. There would be no peace—not at the World's Fair, not in New York City, and not in America—until their voices were heard.

Outside the gates of Flushing Meadow, America was changing far more rapidly than Moses or any of his allies could fully comprehend. The 1964–65 World's Fair marked the beginning of the end of an epoch in American history, the final vestige of the black-and-white conformity of Eisenhower's 1950s and the brief so-called Camelot of Kennedy and his New Frontiersmen. It was all slipping away into the past and being replaced by the new vivid—and even garish—Technicolor of the 1960s.

The future had arrived.

22

The 1939 fair was a promise. The 1964 fair is a boast. . . . And some-how, in its jostling, heedless, undisciplined energy, it makes a person happy to be alive in the 20th century.

—*Time*, June 5, 1964

Shortly before the World's Fair opened, Robert Moses and a reporter from the *Saturday Evening Post*, then one of the nation's most popular magazines, stood on top of one of the Fair's tallest buildings. The Master Builder, obviously pleased with himself and his handiwork, looked around, surveying the mesmerizingly diverse assortment of pavilions and space-age structures that now stood erect in Flushing Meadow Park—which, as he reminded many a journalist, he had created after clearing the soiled wetlands of the debris and garbage of Brooklyn. Then he spoon-fed his interviewer the article's opening. "Well, I guess they'll just have to say, 'The old SOB did it again,'" he said.

Despite the relentless hyperbole emanating from Flushing Meadow ("the single greatest event in history!"), few would dispute that Moses had essentially delivered on his promise to create a World's Fair that had "something for everyone." From Michelangelo's Renaissance masterpiece *La Pietà* to the Walt Disney Audio-Animatronics that brought the past to life—Jurassic age dinosaurs, wheel-building cavemen, and the slain sixteenth US president, Abraham Lincoln, the last of which was so lifelike that when it stood up to speak, one shocked five-year-old shouted, "But Daddy, I thought you said he was dead!"—to introducing the latest in consumer products, including color television, the Picturephone (preceding Skype by almost fifty years), and an IBM computer, something few people had ever seen up close before, the past and the future could be seen at the Fair. And right from the start the Fair seemed to be on solid financial ground: The exhibition had sold $35 million in advance tickets, making many New York officials involved with the project—Moses in particular—wonder if their stated goal of seventy million visitors was too low.

There was much to choose from at the Fair. Despite the earlier outcry of critics, there was plenty of art representing several centuries and an impressive variety of styles: the aforementioned Michelangelo; Spanish old masters like Goya, Velázquez, and El Greco; modernist icons like Picasso, Miró, and Matisse; the landscape romanticism of the Hudson River School painters (which fittingly decorated the interior of the New York State Pavilion); a healthy sampling of the abstract expressionists; as well as the pop art stylings of Robert Rauschenberg, Roy Lichtenstein, and John Chamberlain, whose work—preoccupied with consumer culture as it was—seemed right at home among the Fair's corporate pavilions.

There were nearly seventy foreign nations (eighty including municipalities like West Berlin and city-states like the Vatican) that truly represented the world—not just the West. With most of the major European nations, including America's key NATO allies (the United Kingdom, France, Italy, West Germany), sitting out, as well as its Cold War antagonists staying home (the USSR and its Warsaw Pact puppet states of Central and Eastern Europe), and other Communist enemies uninvited (the People's Republic of China was off-limits, as was Cuba), the free nations of Asia and Africa, South and Central America, the Middle East and the island nations of Oceania, all answered Moses' call to come to the Fair.

Many of these countries were newly independent nations; some had just recently overthrown former colonial European masters. The 1964–65 New York World's Fair presented the world in all its multicultural splendor: Korea, Japan, Hong Kong, Taiwan (then called the Republic of China), Indonesia, Polynesia, the Philippines, and Samoa all built pavilions, as did Venezuela, Honduras, Panama, Mexico, and a slew of Caribbean countries which gathered under one roof in the Caribbean Pavilion. Other South American countries wanted to participate but were made to feel unwelcome. Moses all but kicked out Argentina when he discovered that the main investor was a Canadian company (he never forgave America's northern neighbor for sitting out the Fair, in particular since the US government had decided to build at pavilion at the upcoming Montreal Expo '67). Chile had intended on coming, but after Charles Poletti embarrassed their delegation at a press conference, the offended South Americans decided to stay home.

Saudi Arabia, Jordan, Lebanon, India, Pakistan, Sierra Leone, and Morocco were represented, along with fifteen other independent African republics which united to form the African Pavilion, a project in which Moses took a personal interest. "We've devoted a lot of time to the new republics," Moses said at a ground-breaking ceremony for the American-Israel Pavilion in 1963. "They are new, they are ambitious, they are enthusiastic. They want to send their new image around the world."

A few European nations—Austria, Denmark, Switzerland, Sweden, Ireland, and Greece—ignored the Bureau of International Exhibitions' boycott of Moses' Fair and built pavilions anyway, most of which were sponsored by private, nongovernmental organizations—chamber of commerce–type groups—passing through a technical loophole in the BIE's bylaws.

One major European nation that did not care about the BIE or its laws was Spain, which at the time of the Fair was still under the rule of the fascist regime of General Francisco Franco—former ally of Hitler and Mussolini (and now a staunch ally of the anti-Communist West). Franco, anxious to strengthen his political and economic ties with the United States, spared no expense in creating the celebrated Spanish Pavilion—hailed as one of the Fair's architectural masterpieces—and filled it with cultural and artistic treasures ranging from Spain's Golden Age to its twentieth-century masters.

The world's religions held court, too: The riches of Catholicism were on full display at the Vatican Pavilion thanks to Pope John XXIII, who had died in June 1963. John's successor, Pope Paul VI, was equally enthusiastic about the World's Fair and its potential for fostering cooperation among the nations of the world. The Protestant and Orthodox Pavilion showcased a number of Christian sects, and Billy Graham, the most famous and beloved preacher in the United States, had his very own pavilion, where every night, seven days a week, he held court, trying to win hearts for Jesus. The Mormons built a scaled-down replica of their Salt Lake City Tabernacle, which represented a major public relations push for the enigmatic Utah-based church.

The ancient culture of Judaism and its millennia of history were represented at the American-Israel Pavilion, a joint venture of American Jewish organizations, which symbolized the special relationship between the two nations. The pavilion also commemorated a bit of local history: In Flushing Meadow Park, Queens, in 1948, while its Manhattan headquarters was completed, a nascent United Nations made its historic vote to recognize the fledging state of Israel, just three years after the demise of Hitler's Third Reich. The UN's temporary housing was the old New York City Pavilion from the 1939–40 World's Fair.

Nearly half of the US states built pavilions for the World's Fair. The South was represented by Louisiana, Texas, and Florida; the West by Oregon, Alaska, Montana (which sent an old steam locomotive carrying $1 million of gold across country to Flushing Meadow), and New Mexico; the Midwest by Wisconsin, Minnesota, and Missouri; the East by New Jersey, Maryland, and the various states that formed the New England Pavilion.

But, by far, the most popular and celebrated state pavilions were those from Illinois and New York. The first featured the pride of Disney's technical staff, President Lincoln's robotic doppelgänger, and the latter was an example of Philip Johnson's postmodern architecture, a series of circular shapes with its three towers, the tallest of which allowed vistas of the entire Fair (and Queens) from 212 feet in the sky and was accessible by outdoor elevators. Even Moses—no fan of postmodernism in any form—was taken with the structure and earmarked it for his post-Fair park. "An outstanding example of originality in design, structural, and material experimentation and ingenuity in the selection and display of exhibits," he proclaimed in front of the thousand invited guests at the pavilion's official opening on the second day of the Fair.

While the world and all of its racial diversity were exhibited at the Fair, corporate America and the gospel of consumerism it preached were really the stars of the show. This was, of course, the height of America's postwar boom, and the American economy and its seemingly limitless horizons were the envy the world over. Many of the biggest names in American industry created eye-popping attractions, such as the IBM Pavilion, which looked like a huge industrial egg nestled among a forest of metallic trees. The structure was a collaboration between Finnish-American architect Eero Saarinen (who famously created the TWA Flight Center at John F. Kennedy Airport, a paean to space-age architecture) and Charles Eames, the designer, architect, and filmmaker, who conceived of the pavilion's "People Wall," a five-hundred-seat indoor theater that, once "loaded" with an audience, lifted the crowd fifty feet into the air, where they were entertained by a multiscreen film.

The Travelers Insurance Pavilion looked like a flying saucer from a 1950s sci-fi film, while US Royal Tires decided to make their product into an amusement park ride: a six-story Ferris wheel shaped like a gigantic rubber tire, a bit of marketing savvy and at the same time a nod to the baser commercialistic aspects of pop art. (Perhaps corporate executives understood Andy Warhol and his contemporaries better than some leading art critics.) Electric Power & Light's Tower of Light was a series of rectangular panels that bore a striking resemblance to a child's building blocks. However, once darkness fell, the scores of panels were illuminated in a rainbow of pastel hues that equaled some twelve-billion candlepower, reportedly the world's largest (and presumably, most expensive) searchlight.

But perhaps no industry was better represented than Detroit's Big Three automakers. The Ford Motor Company chose the Fair to introduce its latest model, the Ford Mustang, which would go on to become one of the best-selling automobiles in American history, coupling it with the Walt Disney–designed Magic Skyway ride. For its pavilion General Motors gave a nostalgic nod to its legendary Futurama exhibit from the 1939–40 New York World's Fair, proclaiming in an ad that their pavilion would transport customers to "Tomorrow-Land." Millions of adults who had visited the earlier fair remembered being dazzled by its prediction of the future—"the World of Tomorrow" that, according to the exhibit, would exist by 1960. Now inside its towering tailfin pavilion (a shape that would be recalled decades later in NASA's Space Shuttle) there was a new ride titled Futurama II, which offered 1964 audiences a newer, twenty-first-century vision of "the City of Tomorrow."

According to GM, twenty-first-century cities would feature sleek modernist skyscrapers and smart superhighways—computers would regulate traffic and keep cars safely away from each other. But the great Metropolis of the future would allow for a relic of the past: A Gothic cathedral held a place of honor on one of the few people-populated plazas in the busy city. (Apparently, one of the few places that people walked to in the future was church.) Futurama II's Tomorrow-Land was a lot like the world as it already existed in 1964, only an updated version of the landscape that Moses had been building since the end of the Second World War.

Fairgoers sat three-abreast in slow-moving chairs as they viewed space-age daydreams of roving lunar vehicles, underwater hotels, and rotating space stations. They also saw an improbable gigantic highway-creating machine: a technological Leviathan that could convert Mother Nature, literally pulverizing earth and rock and tearing out trees, as it slowly crawled along its path, leaving only a smooth, paved highway—an earth-eating computerized Moloch that would have given Lewis Mumford nightmares (and put Moses out of work). This was the kind of sci-fi fantasy that fueled the very real Apollo missions to send a man to the moon and "return him safely to Earth," as President Kennedy had declared. According to GM's vision of the twenty-first century, even deserts were overgrown with vegetation, as they became the beneficiary of rerouted and desalinated ocean water.

And if Fairgoers wanted to see what NASA was really up to, they simply had to walk over to the US Space Park. A fifty-one-foot-tall replica of the Saturn V Boattail rocket engine, the stage-one propulsion jet that would help various Apollo missions reach space, mesmerized crowds. NASA also sent a life-size Lunar Excursion Module, or LEM, the actual craft that *Apollo 11* astronauts would use to touch down on the moon's surface. If that wasn't enough for Fairgoers, the Transportation

& Travel Pavilion had a huge half-moon dome as its roof, complete with a crater-encrusted lunar landscape. Although it wasn't completed on opening day, the Hall of Science (which would eventually become a permanent museum in the post-Fair park) would continue the Fair's space exploration theme decades after the Fair permanently closed.

New Yorkers also got a glimpse of their own future: The World Trade Center and its "Twin Towers" were first displayed in miniature in the Port Authority Building, a modernist rectangular box that sat on four stilts, where the much-maligned "Top of the Fair" restaurant was held, its roof serving as a helipad. Designed by Japanese-American architect Minoru Yamasaki, who had created the US Science Pavilion for Seattle's Century 21 Exposition, the 110-story Twin Towers would have fit seamlessly into GM's Futurama II exhibit. Many critics would lambast the architect's Twin Towers when they were completed in April 1973. Moses, however, was a huge fan of them, marveling at their sleek modern design that seemed to recall the geometric abstractions of the Trylon and Perisphere, iconic symbols of the 1939–40 Fair.

Many shows—especially Disney's—were sentimental and aimed to entertain, especially the swarms of children who attended. One such child was seven-year-old Caroline Kennedy, daughter of the recently slain president, who was so convinced that the puppy in the Carousel of Progress was real, she pleaded with her mother, former First Lady Jacqueline Kennedy, to take it home. Still grieving and clad uniformly in black, Mrs. Kennedy's visit to the World's Fair was one of the first public appearances she had made with her family since the murder of her husband in Dallas five months earlier. Her former brother-in-law, Robert Kennedy, in the midst of a Senate race (trying to unseat New York's Republican Senator Kenneth Keating), also visited the fair with his family. Ever the campaigner, Kennedy allowed photographers to snap away as he planted a kiss on each of his kids as they boarded a ride.

The Kennedys weren't the only politicians at the fair. Their old nemesis, Richard Nixon, added the exhibition to his busy itinerary. After losing his 1960 bid for the White House and then being humiliated by Governor Pat Brown in the 1962 California gubernatorial race, Nixon was in political exile. By April 1964 the former vice president was working as a corporate lawyer in a Wall Street firm, making frequent trips abroad to keep his name in the papers and slowly rebuilding his political base. But even Maurice Stans, one of his top fund-raisers and most loyal friends, didn't believe Nixon could ever redeem himself in the eyes of the American voter. That is, until September 1965, when Stans would accompany Nixon to the World's Fair and witness the mobs in Flushing Meadow—the same conservative-minded, middle-class citizens that Nixon would later dub "the silent majority"—pleading with the former vice president for his autograph. Right there in Queens—literally the center of Democratic New York City—Nixon was treated like a hero. After that Stans began a massive fund-raising effort, and launched Nixon's 1968 presidential campaign in the process.

Although Moses was pleased with his own handiwork, his many critics were less than enthusiastic. *Time* devoted a cover story to the Fair, and despite the seemingly disapproving title—THE WORLD OF ALREADY—it was a balanced piece detailing the Fair's many highs (the Ford, GM, and Spanish Pavilions) and undeniable lows (the number of unfinished pavilions and the plethora of uninspiring exhibits). Moses, of course, was incensed by the piece and, as he was apt to do, wrote to Time-Life Inc. founder Henry Luce, a World's Fair director, to register his displeasure. "Henry Luce is a strange character," Moses complained to a friend, refusing to understand Luce's strict separation-of-church-and-state editorial policy. Many more such letters, over the course of the Fair, would find their way to Luce's desk. "Henry Luce didn't give a damn what people said, he loved his magazines and he loved his writers," said Richard J. Whalen, a former writer for *Fortune*.

Architectural critics were less than kind. They had begun sharpening their knives years before when Moses disbanded the Design Committee and rejected its industrial doughnut design. At the time, one critic promised that the Fair would be "the most horrendous hodgepodge of jukebox architecture." Years later, others rendered the same judgment: "Disconnected, grotesque, lacking in any unity of concept or style," opined the *New York Times'* Ada Louise Huxtable. Her assessment did allow, however, for the genius of Philip Johnson. "The architectural high-light of the Fair," she declared the New York State Pavilion in the *New York Times Magazine.*

Life ran a scathing review by renowned Yale architecture historian Vincent J. Scully Jr. titled IF THIS IS ARCHITECTURE, GOD HELP US. The article was even more belligerent than the headline. "I doubt whether any fair was ever so crassly, even brutally conceived as this one," penned Professor Scully. Ironically, one of the handful of buildings that he found enticing was Chrysler's kitschy Autofare, a sort of mini theme park. The main building was built in the shape of giant, colorful car engine, and the exhibit also featured a space rocket that doubled as a fountain and a larger-than-life assembly line, illustrating the ingenuity of Detroit. For the coup de grâce, there was a building some three stories tall, eighty feet long, and fifty feet wide in the shape of a car. "It is the surprise of the Fair," said Scully, who called it "pop art at its best." (An assessment that probably made Johnson, and the pop artists he collected, cringe.)

Aesthetic assessments aside, the critics were right: The Fair *was* a hodgepodge of architectural styles, lacking any unifying theme—and that's exactly how Moses wanted it. "In a fair like this one, you've got to have plenty of variety," he told *Reader's Digest.* "Five people coming here from five different parts of the country are looking for five different things." In the end, according to Moses' vision, the Fair allowed world-class architects to bring their artistic fantasies to life for millions to see; the result was a staggering mixture of immense highs (the IBM, New York State, Spanish, and Japanese Pavilions) and tacky, lowbrow lows (of which the Chrysler exhibit was surely one, as well as a good number of the state pavilions). And some critics even marveled at Moses' handi-work, including world-renowned Italian architect and engineer Pier Luigi Nervi, who after visiting Flushing Meadow was so impressed, he wanted to tell the planners of Montreal's upcoming Expo '67 to forget it. "I'm going to tell them to think twice, because I think everything has been done here," he said. "I don't see how anyone can do anything better."

But one of the most surprising critics to defend Moses was John Canaday, ornery and outspoken chief art critic of the *New York Times,* and one of Moses' least favorite. When the other top art critics in town were putting together committees to denounce Moses the previous autumn, Canaday hadn't joined the fray. Instead, a month before the opening of the Fair, he penned a defense of Moses' decision to not include an art pavilion—even if he disagreed with the Master Builder's reasons. (Canaday must have known he was swatting at a hornets' nest; the piece was titled PARDON THE HERESY.)

When the Timesman finally visited the Fair, he was pleasantly surprised by the amount of art that could be found in Flushing Meadow. "Art is all over the place at the fair, in such quantities as to negate the outcry that went up when an art pavilion was vetoed," he wrote. For Canaday, the artistic highlights included the New York State Pavilion with its Hudson River landscape paintings and its pop art murals, and El Greco's masterpiece *The Burial of the Count of Orgaz* (a painting specifically requested by Moses). But he saved his most lavish praise for Masayuki Nagare's abstract stone sculpture that doubled as the walls of the Japanese Pavilion. "This is high art by standards tested over centuries," he wrote, "and it is contemporary art by the strictest contemporary standards."

Not that Canaday liked everything about the World's Fair. "The only way to keep from crying at the fair is to keep laughing," he wrote. "But I sort of love it. We have to . . . we're stuck with it." By the time the much-delayed Pavilion of Fine Arts finally opened in what would have been the Argentina Pavilion, Canaday pronounced the collection "perfectly respectable and lifeless." It was exactly the kind of review that would send Moses into a tizzy. Before long he fired off another angry letter to *New York Times* publisher Punch Sulzberger.

Regardless of what critics proclaimed, the public soon began to discover the Fair. As the weather improved throughout the spring, the number of visitors steadily increased—the second day of Fair was bright and sunny and 163,152 people visited—70,000 more than opening day. Along with more people came more controversy. The trouble began with the Protestant and Orthodox Pavilion, as Moses had feared. The pavilion was screening a film, *Parable,* in which Christ was depicted as a mime and the Apostles as circus performers. Clearly meant as an attempt to modernize the Christ narrative and provide an entertaining story with a moral to audiences of the sixties, the film gave Moses misgivings. While he didn't see it, he had a trusted Fair executive, John V. Thornton, screen the film and issue a brief report. Although Thornton didn't think *Parable* should be shown, he didn't think "it was bad enough for us to veto."

Afraid of yet another series of negative stories in the press, and a backlash from Fairgoers, Moses wrote to the Protestant Pavilion's board of directors urging them to drop the film, claiming that the Fair Corporation had "grave misgivings about the propriety, good taste and validity of the film." But Reverend Dr. Dan M. Potter, the pavilion's executive director, refused. "We are going ahead with it," he told the *Times*, "because people want to see it." A disappointed Moses neverthe-less resisted the urge to invoke the veto power afforded to him in Article 27 of the Fair charter, which gave him "the right to censor all projects at the Fair site." *Parable* evoked a wide range of reactions from viewers. In the end, despite the steady diet of complaints from religious groups and individuals, Moses dropped the issue, allowing the pavilion to maintain its own affairs as if it were a mini-corporation or a city-state.

Further Holy Land troubles had been brewing ever since Moses and his international staff had tried desperately to get Israel to invest in a pavilion at the Fair. It would have marked the first time that the nascent nation exhibited at a US-based Fair. When efforts failed, a group of influential Jewish Americans banded together to create the American-Israel Pavilion. The handsome circular structure was forty-two feet tall, with a sloped roof extending into a ramp that reached ground level and finished in rectangular red mahogany panels; the 14,438-square-foot lot was landscaped with stones from Jerusalem. The pavilion—like the nation and people it represented—was modern and ancient at the same time. Inside visitors could see gold from the mines of King Solomon, view fragments of the Dead Sea Scrolls, and eat at a kosher restaurant for the observant (or gastronomically curious).

Just down the Avenue of Asia and Africa from the American-Israel Pavilion lay the Jordan Pavilion, created with the consent of King

Hussein I of the Kingdom of Jordan, a sworn enemy of the Israeli state. Built as a series of raised domed roofs and covered in gold mosaic, the Jordan Pavilion looked like a cross between some ancient subterranean desert dwelling and a space-age structure. Like its Israeli neighbors, the Pavilion of the Hashemite Kingdom of Jordan—its official title—also displayed a portion of the Dead Sea Scrolls. The various interior exhibits featured colored-glass windows (by Spanish abstract painter Antonio Saura) depicting the Passion of Christ, while the story of the heavenly ascent of the Prophet Mohammed from the Dome of the Rock was told in bas-relief (thereby emphasizing the link between Christianity and Islam, while snubbing Judaism—the other major Abrahamic faith). There were also television monitors screening photos of the ancient city of Petra, hewn from the sandstone cliffs, as well as belly dancers and a restaurant featuring Middle Eastern cuisine.

On April 23, the second day of the Fair, news began to spread of a painting featured on the wall adjacent to the Jordan Pavilion's exit. Titled plainly *The Mural of a Refuge,* it depicted a poor Palestinian woman cradling her young son and illustrated the story of the birth of Israel from the ideological lens of Palestinian refugees. "Before you go, have you a minute to spare, to hear a word on Palestine, and perhaps to help us right a wrong?" read the poetic polemic, before claiming how "Christians, Jews and Moslems . . . lived in peaceful harmony" for centuries before "strangers from abroad" entered the Holy Land and "began buying up land and stirring up the people." Despite its obvious anti-Israeli propaganda and selective view of history, the mural touched upon an inescapable fact: Far too many Palestinians were exiled to refugee camps, the collateral damage of the historical birth of modern Israel. "Many like my mother," the text read, "wasting lives in exiled misery, waiting to go home."

The executives of the American-Israel Pavilion were incensed, quickly lodging a complaint with Moses. The existence of such an openly anti-Israeli polemic, they said, was an improper "use of the fairgrounds for the dissemination of such propaganda" and one that made a mockery of the Fair's theme of "Peace Through Understanding." It also cited Article 16 of the Fair's constitution, which stated that no exhibit will be allowed that "reflects discredit upon any nation or state."

Moses was quick to respond, informing the American-Israel officials that despite his veto power, he would not use it. "The Fair cannot censor the mural you refer to, even though it is political in nature and subject to misinterpretation," he wrote in a telegram the next day. "We believe no good purpose would be served by exaggerating the significance of this reference to national aims or attributing racial animus to it."

The New York City Council disagreed, and the following month they denounced both the mural and Moses. It didn't take long for Mayor Robert F. Wagner Jr. to see where this was headed, and so he issued a statement that Moses had agreed to remove the offensive mural. That was news to the Master Builder. He fired back with a statement that he had never asked for its removal and would not do so. A spokesman at the Jordan Pavilion told the *New York Times* that they would close the pavilion before removing the mural. "We are in the United States, a country of freedom, not Israel," he said. "We are here to show the American people what our problems are."

Americans, it turns out, wanted to make up their own minds. The controversy was box-office gold for the Jordanians, as people—including many Jews who wanted to see the artwork for themselves—lined up to pay the fifty-cent admission. "It leaves me with the feeling that I don't know what the truth is," one man from Chicago told the *Times*. A Baptist preacher from Valley Forge, Pennsylvania, said, "Let's give them the right to state their case." However, at least one New Yorker wasn't impressed. "What chutzpa. First they charge you 50 cents. Then they insult you. Then they thank you for listening to their story. Typically Jordanian."

The tension only escalated from there. In May, Dr. Joachim Prinz, president of the American Jewish Congress, requested the right to stage a protest demonstration outside the Jordan Pavilion. Moses, as he did with all such requests, refused. Then Dr. Mohammed Mehdi, secretary general of the Committee on American-Arab Relations, wrote the Master Builder insisting on the right to picket the American-Israel

Pavilion that same month. "We would not have raised the issue except for Zionist totalitarianism which is as intolerant as fascism or communism," he wrote. Moses also refused his request and urged him to drop the issue and instead "work for friendship and peace."

In May the Anti-Defamation League of B'nai B'rith filed a lawsuit to have the Jordan Pavilion closed on the grounds that the disputed mural was "anti-Semitic." Then, ignoring the Fair's "no demonstration" policy, Dr. Prinz led a group of one dozen protesters to the Jordan Pavilion on May 25 and was arrested (although well-behaved, the group was charged with disorderly conduct and resisting arrest; all charges that were dismissed the following month). Meanwhile, his lawyers filed a suit alleging that the Fair's no-pickets-allowed law was unconstitutional, which they eventually won. There would be protests outside both pavilions, much to Moses' chagrin.

And just to add a dose of true international tension to the problem, the Israeli premier, Levi Eshkol, cancelled his scheduled May 11 official visit to the Fair to protest Moses' refusal to remove the mural. A month later, someone removed the national flag of the Kingdom of Jordan flying from the flagpole outside its pavilion, replacing it with a blue-and-white flag inscribed with the words "American Israel." This prompted the Jordanian ambassador to the United Nations to lodge a formal complaint with the UN.

It was in this atmosphere that the World's Fair Corporation's board of directors met for the first time since opening day. On June 22 they gathered inside the Beech-Nut Theatre in the Better Living Center. Despite the headlines, there was actually good news: The Fair was averaging one million visitors a week, and fixes for general problems were being developed. Charles F. Preusse, the Fair's lawyer, quickly asserted that due to the two outstanding lawsuits regarding the Jordanian mural, a motion be adopted to not discuss the matter. Moses, gavel in hand, quickly accepted the motion.

However, Alex Rose, vice chairman of the Liberal Party of New York and a union leader, wouldn't hear of it. He stepped up to a microphone and declared the Jordanian mural "a war slogan against Israel." The two men testily exchanged words, until Senator Jacob K. Javitz, one of the Fair's (and Moses') original backers, took the microphone from Rose and suggested that the matter deserved a vote. Board members fidgeted in their seats or sighed, making little to no effort to hide their displeasure. A vote was taken and Moses' no-discussion faction (which included all of the Fair's top executives and General John J. McCloy) easily won.

Just then Harry Van Arsdale, a powerful union leader, stepped forward to offer his still unvoiced vote to the minority "if I thought that my vote would help Israel." Moses repeatedly slammed his gavel, drowning him out, and instructed General William E. Potter, the Fair's executive vice president, to issue his report. When New York State Senator Joseph Zaretzki interrupted Potter again, Moses repeatedly banged his gavel.

"You can't gavel this resolution down!" Zaretzki shouted as Moses ignored him. "I'm raising a point of order. Under Article Six of—" But gaveling him down is exactly what Moses did. Potter went on to give his report, and that was the end of the meeting. Within a week, Zaretzki had resigned from the board and began referring to the Master Builder as "Boss Moses." "Although he is a benevolent despot," Zaretzki told the *Times,* "[he] is a despot just the same."

With the situation rapidly devolving into a political blood sport, the New York City Council couldn't resist the urge to jump into the fray (1964 was an election year, after all). They passed a unanimous resolution demanding the mural's removal because it was "gratuitously insulting." Moses released a statement saying the City Council "asks suppression of free speech" before going on to say that the US Constitution "assumes that ideas will be tested in the intellectual marketplace. Opinions are not to be blue-penciled because some censor, however well intentioned, finds them 'controversial,' 'irritating' or 'offensive.'" Moses argued, essentially, that there are two sides to every story—even preferred historical narratives of a nation's birth. Noting that the American-Israel Pavilion was now planning a parody of the Jordanian mural in its courtyard—free of charge to the public—that was unabashedly pro-Israel, Moses pointedly asked the City Council if it would "now demand that an iron curtain be drawn around the unofficial American-Israel pavilion?"

Regardless of who asked him to reconsider—including his friend Senator Keating—Moses refused. When it came to censoring pavilions, Moses was remarkably consistent. Just as he had when the US State Department demanded to know the details of the Soviet Union's exhibit, Moses refused to get caught in the middle of a political tug-of-war. No lover of Communism by any stretch of the imagination, Moses noted that if the Soviets were paying for their pavilion, then they could put on any exhibit they wanted, a remarkably laissez-faire approach for such a renowned micromanager.

Up until the early summer of 1964, Moses was reluctant to veto anything or be seen choosing one side over another, particularly when it came to religion or politics. Choosing sides meant alienating someone. And with his designs for Flushing Meadow Park, he would need millions of dollars in public funds and profits from the Fair; there wasn't time to alienate anyone who could be in a position to help him.

To date, the only exhibit that Moses had censored was Walter Keane's haunting painting of zombie-eyed children titled *Tomorrow Forever*, which bizarrely enough was chosen to hang in the Hall of Education despite the painting's reminiscence of the 1960 British horror film *Village of the Damned*. "His product has become synonymous among critics with the very definition of tasteless hack work," Canaday wrote in the *New York Times*. Moses thought so, too, and on the grounds that the painting was in "bad taste," had it removed. But what upset him even more was realizing he was simpatico with his least favorite art critic. "I hate like hell to agree with that crab Canaday who never loses a chance to toss mud at the Fair," Moses complained to a friend, "but this time he's right."

23

When the terrorists murder with the complicity of the police, and
when a society supports and cannot condemn them, then the society—
or the state itself—may be guilty. This was Nazi Germany's crime at
Auschwitz . . . it was Mississippi's crime at Philadelphia.
—William Bradford Huie, *Three Lives for Mississippi,* 1965

On April 23, the day after the World's Fair opened, Andrew Goodman had returned to his studies at Queens College. A junior, the twenty-year-old Goodman was working on a sociology paper about the Black Muslims, trying to understand the social forces that had created the segregationist religious organization. Goodman didn't buy into the Nation of Islam's racist rhetoric that all white men were blue-eyed devils, but he thought he understood what was fueling their anger. "The white man (and by this I mean Christian civilization in general)," he wrote, "has proved himself to be the most depraved devil imaginable in his attitudes toward the negro race." He went on to conclude that "people must have dignity and identity. If they can't do it peacefully, they will do it defensively."

Although he had enrolled in Queens College for its strong Drama Department—Goodman was a sometimes actor who performed in off-Broadway plays—he was getting serious about the social sciences, particularly sociology. Whatever his future held, he knew one thing for certain: He was going down to Mississippi to participate in what was being hailed as the Freedom Summer, a massive push—manned by Northern college students and orchestrated by the SNCC and CORE—to register Southern blacks to vote. Goodman had been attending the political lectures at the school. He was in attendance when Louis E. Lomax had first suggested a stall-in to disrupt the World's Fair. After the talk, he was one of fifty students who, motivated by what they heard, approached Lomax to ask him what they should do to help.

After another lecture at Queens College on April 9, Goodman had found his answer. The talk was given by Allard Lowenstein, a veteran organizer who had helped launch the Students for a Democratic Society, or SDS, at Queens College. Protesting job discrimination at the World's Fair was a just cause for Goodman, but Mississippi was on the front lines in the battle for black freedom.

Mississippi was, Lowenstein told his Queens College audience, "the most totalitarian state in America." Essentially a police state run by hate-filled politicians who made a living by appealing to their constituents' racist tendencies, Mississippi exploited the "hate vote" for all its electoral value. And like many Southern states—and even a few Northern ones—Mississippi had its own homegrown terrorist organization, the Ku Klux Klan, that did as it pleased.

Lowenstein wasn't trying to sugarcoat the situation. Going to Mississippi would be dangerous. Race violence in Mississippi was as prevalent as summer humidity, and no one, including Governor Paul B. Johnson Jr. seemed to mind. A Democrat who was elected in 1964 on a campaign of racial hatred, Johnson's stump speech contained the line: "You know what NAACP stands for—niggers, alligators, apes, coons and possums." Plenty of Mississippi's sheriffs were friendly with the Klan, if not active members themselves. As syndicated political columnist Joseph Alsop wrote in early June: "Southern Mississippi is now known to contain no fewer than sixty thousand armed men organized to what amounts to terrorism. Acts of terrorism against the local Negro populace are already an everyday occurrence." Goodman had no illusions about what he was getting himself into. "I'm afraid," he told a friend before his departure, "but I'm going."

By the time Goodman left in mid-June, fellow New Yorkers Michael "Mickey" Schwerner, age twenty-four, and his wife, Rita, twenty-two, were already in Meridian, Mississippi. They had been there since January 17, after driving their Volkswagen all the way from their apartment in Brooklyn Heights. So optimistic about human nature was Schwerner, that he, a conscientious and outgoing young man, had bought a German car, something that many Jewish Americans—particularly ones that had lost family members in the Holocaust like Schwerner had—actively avoided.

On April 23, the day after the World's Fair opened, the married couple and another CORE worker wrote a letter to their organization's national office requesting that James Chaney, age twenty-two, get added to the group's payroll. Chaney, a local African American from Meridian, was central to their work. He also drove the blue Ford station wagon that CORE had given the group, racing his way around every back road in Meridian and the local counties like he had hellhounds on his trail. It was an important survival skill for a black Mississippian—or a Northern college student: Getting pulled over by a white police officer on a back-country road with only the moonlight as a witness could be a death sentence. And Chaney was unafraid to recruit blacks in the toughest areas where the Ku Klux Klan reigned supreme. "Chaney was one of our best men," James L. Farmer Jr. would later say. "He was a native of Mississippi. He was a child of the soiled. . . . He was invaluable."

Most importantly, he was their link to the local black community, who were well aware of young, white Northerners and the hell they would catch if local whites or the police heard they were talking to out-side "agitators." Someone might burn a cross on their lawn or firebomb their house. There were eyes watching them everywhere, including the "Big Toms"—local blacks who spied for the police. Sometimes called "Judas niggers" by their fellow black Mississippians, they were often well-to-do black locals who had a stake in the status quo and were expected to keep their poorer black brethren in line and away from these young civil rights workers and their Northern ideas about integration. Chaney knew better than anyone else what local blacks were up against; he understood their pain and fears; he knew what their lives were like. And he knew that state-sanctioned organizations such as the KKK were all but immune from punishment.

In mid-June the Schwerners and Chaney traveled to the Women's College in Columbus, Ohio, for three days of training, and met Goodman for the first time. They had plenty in common: Goodman and Mickey had attended the prestigious Walton School on Manhattan's Upper West Side, where Goodman had grown up; and Goodman was a student at Queens College, where Rita was finishing up her BA in English. "He was such a fine, intelligent, unassuming young man," Rita would later say. "He and I had much to talk about."

While they attended conferences and seminars, word reached them that Mount Zion Methodist Church in Longdale, Mississippi, a rural district outside of Meridian, was burned to the ground and several of its members—including an elderly man—were pistol-whipped and beaten by Klansmen who had discovered that the churchgoers had met with Mickey Schwerner. Long before Goodman had ever met him, Schwerner was on the KKK's hit list. To those who wanted him dead, he was simply known as Goatee.

Schwerner's regular uniform of blue jeans, T-shirt, sneakers, a blue New York Mets cap, and Beatnik-esque facial hair made him stand out like a thicket of weeds on fresh-cut Mississippi grass. Schwerner was a social worker back in New York, having graduated from Cornell University in 1962. He had a disarming nature that put people at ease—no easy feat for a white Northerner in the rural South. He had become fast friends with the soft-spoken Chaney, whom he affectionately dubbed Bear, often eating home-cooked meals at Chaney's house. In time, Fannie Lou Chaney would come to think of Schwerner as another son.

Everywhere Schwerner went outside his activist family, white bigots shouted at him "Communist nigger-loving Jewboy!" and the like. Many of his verbal tormentors were, by day, law-abiding, church-going citizens. Under the cover of darkness, they wore elaborate costumes, burned crosses, firebombed black churches and homes, and did much worse.

It was exactly this kind of hatred that drew Schwerner and Goodman to Mississippi. After reading about the September 15 murders of the four little girls at Birmingham's 16th Street Baptist Church, Schwerner knew he wanted to do more. As a Jew who believed the kind of hatred that produced Nazi Germany wouldn't happen again, he went down to Mississippi to make sure that it didn't. Then he heard about the beatings in Longdale and how their church was burned to the ground. He refused to stay in Ohio any longer. By 3:00 a.m. on Saturday, June 21, Schwerner, Chaney, and Goodman were driving back to Meridian, while

Schwerner's wife, Rita, stayed behind to teach new trainees for another week. After they arrived, Schwerner reminded Goodman that things might get ugly; he needed to be ready.

"I'm no child," Goodman told him. "I want to get into the thick of the fight."

Things were happening fast. Just hours before the trio took off for Mississippi, a momentous event in the history of the American republic had occurred: The US Senate finally passed President Johnson's civil rights bill by a margin that, in the end, wasn't even close: seventy-three to twenty-seven. The bill had passed after the longest filibuster in the chamber's history, courtesy of the "Southern bloc" of racist Dixiecrats led by Senator Richard B. Russell, who declared: "We will resist to the bitter end any measure or any movement which would have a tendency to bring about social equality and intermingling and amalgamation of the races in our states."

On the morning of June 10, 1964, the resistance faltered. Senator Robert Byrd, a Democrat and former Klansman from West Virginia, then in his first term, was the last hold out. There would be no more delay to the most important legislative achievement in America of the twentieth century. No longer could the Dixiecrats, including the ignoble signers of the Southern Manifesto or the handful of Republicans who had joined them—including the man who would soon represent the Grand Old Party as its presidential candidate, Senator Barry Goldwater of Arizona—hold back the tide of history. For the first time in America, discrimination in the public square was illegal.

In New York, where the Empire State's pair of liberal Republican senators, Jacob K. Javitz and Kenneth Keating—both friends of the World's Fair and Robert Moses—proudly voted for the bill, the passage of the Civil Rights Act of 1964 was viewed as the momentous event that it was. In Meridian, Mississippi, and elsewhere in the South, the passage of the Civil Rights Act was just the latest offensive by the North. The *Dallas Morning News* wrote an editorial claiming that the real trouble wasn't Jim Crow but "the unjustified, uncalled for invasion" of Mississippi "by a bunch of Northern students schooled in advance in

causing trouble under the guise of bringing 'freedom' to . . . Negroes."
Mississippi's Governor Johnson predicted "turmoil, strife and bloodshed
lie ahead" for his state. After signing the bill into law, President Johnson
lamented to an aide that "we just lost the South for a generation." In fact,
it would be a lot longer than that.

The same day that Southern newspapers and radio lamented that
their "way of life" was now illegal—June 21, 1964—was the day that
Schwerner, Chaney, and Goodman arrived in Meridian. The next morning they drove out to Longdale to meet with the victimized members
of the burned-out Mount Zion Methodist Church. But before he left,
Schwerner reminded Sue Brown, a young black woman who worked
at the center, that they would be back by 4:00 p.m., as per standard
operating procedure. If they weren't back by 4:30 p.m. then, according
to procedure, she should start calling every police station, jailhouse, or
courthouse in the surrounding areas. "Don't worry," he said, "we'll be
back." When 4:30 came and went and no one had seen the three of
them, Brown began a frantic round of phone calls, including one to the
jailhouse in nearby Philadelphia, on which she was informed that no one
by those names had been arrested.

That was a lie.

In the same blue Ford station wagon that they drove from Ohio,
the trio had headed toward Meridian on Route 491 around 3:00 p.m.
That's when Deputy Sheriff Cecil Price saw them, and promptly arrested
them. Some witnesses said that the Ford station wagon tried to outrace
Price, but that the deputy shot their tire out. Price charged Chaney, who
was driving, with speeding; he claimed the other two were being held
"for suspicion of arson" for burning the Mount Zion Methodist Church,
an utter fabrication. After they had been put in jail—Schwerner and
Goodman with white prisoners and Chaney with a black prisoner—
it wasn't long before someone made a phone call informing local
Klansmen that Goatee was in custody in Philadelphia. The plan to murder Schwerner was quickly set in stone. The only question that remained
was what to do with the other two. Soon enough, the Klansmen decided
their fate: They would have to die with Goatee.

The plan was simple. The police let the three go on Sunday, June 22, after 10:00 p.m., telling them to hightail it out of town. Then they followed them and pulled them over again. This time, they forced the three "agitators" into the backseat of a car and drove down a dark, dirt road, where the KKK were waiting. As the trio sat in the car wondering what would happen next, the Klansmen jeered them with chants of "If you stayed were you were, you'd be safe, but now you're here with us."

They pulled Schwerner out of the backseat and shoved him against the car, pointing a gun at his chest.

"You think a nigger is as good as me?" one of them asked.

Before Schwerner could answer the question, his assailant blew a hole in his chest. Then they grabbed Goodman, who had barely been in Mississippi twenty-four hours, and the same assailant blasted him with the same gun—one shot to the chest.

"All you left me was a nigger to kill," Chaney's assailant lamented as they grabbed him from the backseat. After seeing what had happened to his good friend Schwerner and Goodman, Chaney struggled, trying to make a break for it. But after being shot three times, the native Mississippian fell. Then, according to forensic evidence, they beat him so savagely, his skull and shoulder were crushed.

The attackers dumped the bodies at the bottom of a ditch on a farm three miles south of Philadelphia. After tossing the three in the Mississippi earth in the wee hours of June 23, amidst the silence of a hot and humid summer night in the middle of nowhere, a bulldozer covered the spot where the bodies were buried, pouring cement over the makeshift dirt grave, yet no one heard a thing. The ditch would be flooded over just as soon as the new dam was finished. Nobody would ever see the three again, they thought.

At home in New York, Farmer got a call about the missing men at 2:30 a.m. In Ohio, Rita Schwerner received the news, too. By Tuesday, President Johnson was getting briefings about the case. One of the first things he did was call Mississippi Senator James O. Eastland, head of the powerful Judiciary Committee and one of the Senate's most rabid segregationists. Eastland told Johnson that the whole thing wasn't true, suggesting to the president, a fellow Southerner, that there was no Klan activity in that part of his state. The trio was probably off somewhere having fun; it was all just a plan to disgrace Mississippians.

Soon the media, national and international, were reporting the story. In no time at all, Meridian was flooded with reporters. Eventually, J. Edgar Hoover would reluctantly send his FBI men down to Mississippi—the only state where the bureau had no full-time office. Hoover had made no secret of his contempt for civil rights organizations or the likes of Schwerner, Chaney, and Goodman; all of them, according to America's top cop, were Communist stooges.

On July 2, while President Johnson signed the Civil Rights Act of 1964, surrounded by Martin Luther King Jr. and Farmer and Robert Kennedy, reporters and FBI agents were flooding the back roads of Mississippi, talking to anyone who might have seen something; their questions were met with stony silence. According to many Mississippi officials, the three men had faked their own disappearance so that the federal government would "invade" the South; in their eyes, it was the Civil War all over again. Even those whites in Meridian who hated the Klan and what they represented didn't want all these *foreigners* around.

As FBI agents and newspapers reporters collected information in Neshoba County, on July 18 another racial disturbance was exploding in New York City. After all the riotous tension of the previous year, it was only fitting that it should happen in Harlem, the epicenter of black life in New York and a prime example of what was wrong with the city's urban centers. "Overcrowded and exploited politically and economically, Harlem is the scene and symbol of the Negro's perpetual alienation in the land of his birth," wrote novelist Ralph Ellison, author of *Invisible Man*, in an essay that appeared in summer of 1964, just before Harlem burned.*

Two days earlier on East 76th Street, a confrontation between an Irish immigrant superintendent and three black youths would leave New York's political class, national civil rights leaders, and many Americans shaking their heads in disbelief. What's known for certain is this: The

---

* Although the article appeared in the August 1964 issue of *Harper's*, making it seem uncannily prescient, it was actually penned in 1948, five years after the Harlem Riots of 1943.

superintendent was watering the flowers and sidewalk in front of the building where he worked. The black teenagers were attending summer school at Robert F. Wagner Sr. Junior High School—namesake of Mayor Wagner's father—in the mayor's old Yorkville neighborhood on Manhattan's Upper East Side. The teens didn't live in the area; they were from further uptown. But the local school board—perhaps in an attempt at desegregation—had sent the youths to the overwhelmingly white district, which still maintained a strong German-American flavor. The teens, for whatever reason, decided to sit down on the building's stoop and relax a while. The superintendent said he asked them to move. They either didn't, or didn't move fast enough.

What happened next remains murky. Either by accident or by design, the superintendent sprayed the three youths with the hose. Some reports said the teens had provoked the superintendent; others said it was just an accident; still others said the superintendent, in his thick Irish brogue, taunted the teens by shouting "I'll wash the black off you!" In the summer of 1964, with memories of Birmingham police pummeling black children with powerful fire hoses still fresh, such an innocuous instrument as a garden hose was viewed by young blacks as a weapon rife with symbolism. The teens reached for the most obvious weapons they could find: garbage can lids and the debris stacked inside. Soon bottles and other detritus were being thrown at the Irishman, who fled into the building behind him. The garbage and bottles shattered the building's glass front door.

According to the official police account, one of the black teens, James Powell, age sixteen, produced a pocketknife and went after the superintendent with the intention of cutting him. Others said there was no knife and that Powell never threatened to cut anyone. But by then, an off-duty policeman, Lieutenant Thomas Gilligan, had arrived and drew his gun. Witnesses said Powell and the other teens ran. Gilligan said Powell lunged at him with the knife, giving him no choice but to defend himself. He opened fire, shooting Powell dead. Some people claimed that Gilligan shot Powell in the back as the teen ran away; some said the officer emptied his weapon into the young man's body until Powell was riddled with bullets and lay bleeding to death on a New York City sidewalk.

Gilligan then reportedly flipped the body over with his foot. Although a knife was found on the body, that was hardly proof to most black New Yorkers. (CORE's Farmer would later say that black police had told him white cops always carried knives to plant on the bodies of their shooting victims, just in case evidence was needed.) Many people questioned the likelihood that a 122-pound black teenager would charge a 200-pound white policeman—who was armed and had a license to kill—with nothing more than a penknife.

Soon enough, the other kids in the school program—as many as eight hundred students—heard about the shooting and rushed over to the scene. So did police reinforcements. In no time at all, the two opposing sides squared off. Black teens threw bottles at the white policemen, taunting them, "Come on, shoot another nigger!" One teen, standing in the glass-splattered streets of Mayor Wagner's old neighborhood, screamed what many black New Yorkers had been thinking for a long time: "This is worse than Mississippi!"

Two days later, on July 18, uptown New York exploded into open warfare. It started just hours after a peaceful CORE rally in Harlem for the missing Schwerner, Chaney, and Goodman, whose trail, aside from the burned-out blue Ford station wagon that the trio had last been seen in, had gone cold. As far as the crowd was concerned, the missing Freedom Summer workers in Mississippi and the Harlem teenager shot to death on the streets of New York were victims of the same vicious hatred. Whether that hatred was born in Ol' Dixie or in the Northern ghettos didn't matter. Southern racist sheriffs or racist New York cops—in the minds of many Harlemites, there was hardly any daylight between the two.

Reverend Nelson C. Dukes, the pastor of the local Fountain Spring Baptist Church, had had enough. He stood on a chair and angrily addressed the crowd. A crime had been committed, and the guilty party—Officer Gilligan—was still free. Reverend Dukes said they would march to the nearby police precinct and demand that Gilligan be arrested and charged with murder. As they roamed the streets of Harlem, the mob took on a life of its own. By the time they arrived at the station, they were shouting "Killers, murderers, Murphy's rats!"—as in Commissioner Murphy, who by now was a regular target of activists' ire and frustrations. The crowd tried to get inside. A human wall of policemen, arms interlocked, held them back.

The police pushed the crowd back out to the pavement. Bottles, rocks, and anything else that could be thrown hailed down to the street from local rooftops. Soon a bus with a special unit of judo-trained police officers arrived: Each was at least six feet tall, young, and prepared to fight hand-to-hand combat. The citizens of Harlem started turning on their own neighborhood, smashing windows, especially those of white-owned stores, which forced black proprietors to hastily make signs to hang in their windows—BLACK OWNED—or stand and protect their shops with their lives.

More police arrived, some wearing riot gear, many wielding nightsticks and swinging them at anything that moved—men, women, teens—as bottles shattered on the streets, rocks pelted the police, and Molotov cocktails exploded. ("It'll be Molotov cocktails this month, hand grenades next month and something else next month," Malcolm X had said. "It'll be ballots or it'll be bullets.")

In response, police emptied their guns into the open air, firing warning shot after warning shot, trying to disperse the crowd. They ran into tenements with their weapons drawn to reach the roof and occupy it, as if each rooftop was a Viet Cong stronghold that had to be neutralized.

"Go home!" police shouted, attempting to clear the streets.

"We are home, baby!" came the response.

At one o'clock in the morning, the phone at Farmer's downtown apartment rang. A voice told him, "You'd better get your ass up here fast! Harlem is blowing up like a volcano! . . . The cops are shooting like cowboys." Farmer took the subway to Harlem, and when he got there, he found out that description was accurate. Seeing the tragedy unfolding before his eyes, Farmer did his best to calm the crowd down. When he told a throng of angry Harlemites that great strides were being made down south, they booed.

"We don't wanna hear *that* shit!" someone shouted back him.

When Farmer said, "Now I'm bringing the movement north, so we can deal with the problems of the northern ghettos," he received cheers. He got their attention by recounting meetings with City Councilman Paul Screvane (who was also a member of the World's Fair Executive Committee) demanding more black cops in Harlem (reportedly a difficult assignment to get due to the potential for lucrative bribes and payoffs that police extracted from Harlem's criminal class). More cheers.

But even Farmer couldn't keep the peace. He marshaled a crowd into a protest march, in the hopes that as the crowd moved through the Harlem streets, he and his CORE workers could convince them to return to their homes. "If we pass by your house, man, drop out and go home," he told the marchers. It was working until gunfire erupted. Who fired—and at whom—was unknown. At the first sound of gunfire, those stationed on rooftops resumed tossing bricks and bottles; cops responded by firing in the air, unable to see their assailants. The crowd scattered; even Farmer wanted to run for cover. Joe Overton of the NAACP, who was leading the march with him, quickly reminded him that as the leader, he couldn't run away.

Another civil rights leader, Bayard Rustin, who had devoted his life to left-wing causes and nonviolence, was there that night and had been shouting into a bullhorn, telling his fellow Harlemites to stay calm. For his efforts he was shouted down as an Uncle Tom. "I am prepared to be a Tom if that's the only way I can save women and children from being shot down in the street!" replied the organizer of the March on Washington—which young Powell had attended. "And if you're not willing to do the same, you're fools!"

The Battle of Harlem raged all night. Finally, as dawn rose over the city, a ghostly quiet filed the glass-covered streets. Shops were destroyed; fifteen people had been shot, while scores were injured, including a dozen cops. More than two hundred people were arrested. And the battle would continue for the next two nights. The crowd that gathered in front of the funeral parlor holding Powell would attack three *New York Times* journalists—one *Times* photographer was beaten so brutally that he almost lost an eye—and other whites who happened to wander into the war zone.

The insurrection quickly became a problem for President Johnson. The Republicans had just selected the ultraconservative Senator Goldwater from Arizona as their presidential nominee the week before at their National Convention in San Francisco. Goldwater, who had voted against the Civil Rights Act, was courting the racist vote, while Southerners now added Lyndon Johnson to their most-hated list, which included the likes of Earl Warren, John F. Kennedy, and Martin Luther King. Goldwater would hit Johnson hard if the president failed to intervene in New York City but had sent Hoover's FBI men into Mississippi.

Johnson had no choice but to have Hoover work up a report on the New York City disturbances. Naturally Hoover thought the riot was the work of Communists, while Governor Nelson A. Rockefeller, in a phone call to the FBI director, suggested that it might have been the work of right-wing groups. After all, Rockefeller said, Goldwater supporters had taunted him at the Republican convention, a riotous and raucous affair with no love lost between activists from Rockefeller's liberal wing of the Grand Old Party and the conservative zealots of the Goldwater wing. His own party deemed that race riots would soon embarrass the New York governor, who for the second consecutive presidential cycle failed to secure the Republican nomination.

And it wasn't just Harlem. Soon Brooklyn's Bedford-Stuyvesant district, New York's second-largest black neighborhood, was burning, as well as Rochester, New York. Insurrection spread to Jersey City and to Philadelphia, too. Forced to choose between the ballot and the bullet, many urban blacks chose the latter, just as Malcolm X had predicted they would. Many observers felt that the Muslim preacher was behind the riots—the thought certainly crossed President Johnson's mind—but, in fact, Malcolm was traveling through Africa and the Middle East, encountering Islam in its purest form, in the part of the world where the Prophet Muhammad originally preached it. When Malcolm returned to the United States, he would undergo self-transformation once again.

When the US government's final report was issued in September, the *New York Times* cited it as characterizing the riots as a series of "attacks on authority," not a racial disturbance. The NAACP's Roy Wilkins was pleased—he had feared the uprisings would damage the greater cause of civil rights. Intentional or not, Hoover had helped the movement by airbrushing the racial component of the conflict out of the picture. But by doing so, the FBI and the nation's political leadership missed the point entirely.

Urban ghettos were repositories for a slew of social problems: rundown housing, rat-infested streets, horrible public schools, sub-par hospitals, and rampant crime, including the crime that dare not be named—police brutality. Such places were prime examples—Exhibit A, in fact—of the death knell of American cities. Their very existence was proof positive that America was failing to provide real opportunities for all its citizens. And the irony, of course, was that these ghettos existed in the North, where blacks were free to vote.

The Harlem riots were the latest example that New York City— home and host of the 1964–65 World's Fair—was imploding. Race riots, the murder of Kitty Genovese, pollution, soaring violent crime—all were the mark of a great metropolis in decline. Or as a *Fortune* magazine cover story put it shortly before the FBI report was released, New York was "a city destroying itself."

While a young black teen was shot dead under extremely question-able circumstances, and while Harlem and Bedford-Stuyvesant burned, Mayor Robert F. Wagner Jr. vacationed on the sunny Mediterranean island of Mallorca. Cautious as ever, the mayor didn't think it was neces-sary to fly home while the two largest black neighborhoods in his city burned. "New Yorkers scarcely missed him," wrote Richard J. Whalen, the author of the *Fortune* story. "They have come to expect deep silence from City Hall in any emergency."

When Wagner finally returned, ahead of schedule, he immediately met with King at City Hall on July 29, in the hopes of finding a solu-tion to the root causes of the Harlem riots. More jobs were needed. New York slums had only grown worse since the end of the war and the emergence of Title I and "slum clearance"—the details of which Wagner, like his predecessors, had left in the hands of Moses. Wagner knew—and just about everyone in New York City and in Albany knew—that giving Moses an enormous task meant giving the Master Builder license to do whatever he wanted. It mattered little if Moses' solutions—invariably erecting soulless high-rise slab towers in once bustling, if poor, neighborhoods—worked or not. Few had the fortitude to challenge the Master Builder, least of all Mayor Wagner.

The mayor and King agreed on just about everything except Lieutenant Gilligan. King argued that the New York policeman should be suspended or, at the very least, put on leave. But Wagner and his staff wouldn't go for it. Such a move would only encourage those who wanted a civilian police review board and, in their view, undercut police authority. Wagner was dead-set against such measures. A review board made up of citizens, he would later tell President Johnson and the First Lady at a private meeting at the White House, would kill New York's Finest's morale, dropping it to "zero overnight." King was unconcerned about police morale, singling out Police Commissioner Michael J. Murphy as "utterly unresponsive to either the demands or the aspirations of the Negro people" and claiming that Murphy was doing all he could to block any civilian review board from trying to "investigate charges of police brutality." And, in fact, the police commissioner was.

As New Yorkers pondered the meaning of the riots, down south the urban disturbances were all the proof that the anti–civil rights forces needed. Mississippians who resented the presence of the Freedom Summer workers, the reporters from around the nation, and the scores of FBI agents felt vindicated that just weeks after the Civil Rights Act was signed into law, blacks in New York had erupted in a frenzy of destruction, burning down their own neighborhoods and turning parts of New York into a war zone. "It is a sad commentary that while mobs stalk the streets of New York," said one Mississippi US representative, "... some 15,000 so-called civil rights workers and troublemakers are in Mississippi—a state with the nation's lowest crime rate—subjecting innocent, law abiding people to insult, national scorn and creating trouble." There were still those in Mississippi who denied that Schwerner, Chaney, and Goodman had been murdered—such as Senator Eastland, who even in late July was still claiming the disappearance was "a hoax" and the work of Communist spies. Bloodshed and shame, these people argued, were only to be found in New York.

That farce ended on August 4. While the World's Fair welcomed its twenty millionth visitor in Queens—the winners were a family of six from Bedford, Indiana—down in Philadelphia, Mississippi, FBI agents chased down a few leads. And although comedian Dick Gregory had offered a $25,000 reward for anyone who could provide information that led to a conviction, it was only after the FBI was said to open up its checkbook that the "cotton curtain" loosened and people in the small town started talking. "Blood, in the deep south of all places, is thicker than water," wrote Louis E. Lomax, "but greed, particularly among poor Mississippi white trash, is thicker than blood."

The federal agents had arrived early that morning to start digging through the top of the dam with heavy machinery. It took a few hours in the airless summer heat, but the stench of death was soon apparent. They used shovels before digging with their hands. Some smoked cigars to mitigate the smell of decaying flesh.

And there they found them, lying buried in the Mississippi soil. The first body was Mickey Schwerner, naked except for his Wrangler jeans and his wedding band. Below him was Andrew Goodman, found face-down, his left hand in a tightened fist clutching the red clay that would be his burial ground, and raising the specter that he had been buried alive. Then, at last, they unearthed James Chaney, whom the terrorists couldn't resist beating senseless, very likely whipping him with chains, breaking his bones and body before he finally bled to death from his wounds. When the bodies were wrapped in plastic and sent to the coroner's office, in a sadistic twist of fate, Deputy Sheriff Price was on hand to help carry them. By all accounts, Price had been one of the last people to see the trio alive.

The news that the three were dead was hardly shocking to the citizens of Meridian, Mississippi, or Neshoba County. Three civil rights workers arrested midday and released late at night? Two of them Jewish New Yorkers, the other a local black man, the blue station wagon they were driving was found, burned out and abandoned, and no one had seen them for weeks? It didn't take a weatherman to know which way the wind had blown.

But even now, with the dead bodies uncovered, some whites still felt that somehow *they* had been betrayed. "Somebody broke our code," one complained. "No honorable white man would have told you what happened." Some blacks complained, too. The simple fact was that there were at least a dozen unsolved murders of blacks in Mississippi at the time and no one was in a rush to solve them; it took the death of two white liberal New Yorkers for the world to pay attention.

Such was the sentiment that Rita Schwerner voiced. "My husband did not die in vain," she proudly proclaimed. "If he and Andrew Goodman had been Negro, they would have taken little note of their death. After all, the slaying of a Negro in Mississippi is not news. It is only because my husband and Andrew Goodman were white that the national alarm has been sounded."

For all the hope and optimism that the Freedom Summer and the passage of the most significant civil rights legislation in the history of the republic had ignited in the hearts and minds of Americans, the decaying bodies of three young men in the mud of Mississippi and the human wreckage of Harlem and the blood-stained pavement of East 76th Street defied the notion put forth by President Johnson that America was moving toward a "Great Society" or operating with the World's Fair's utopian purpose of peaceful coexistence among nations. Before America could end the Cold War with the Soviet Union, it had to end the civil war with itself. And by August 1964, it showed no signs that it was capable of doing so.

24.

Many citizens of the United States who have planned a visit to the World's Fair in New York City are much concerned for their safety from mob violence.

—Letter from a would-be Fairgoer to
Robert Moses, June 15, 1964

The chaos engulfing New York City was the worst possible news for the World's Fair: Race riots, civil rights protests, the public ridicule of the President of the United States by college students, charges of police brutality, and every day more horrific crime stories with headlines that dared you to look away. Just two days after the Fair opened, the papers had described another tragic murder involving two minors—BOY, 16, THROWS GIRL, 12, FROM ROOF—and that was from the high-minded *New York Times,* hardly one of the city's "if-it-bleeds-it-leads" tabloids. All of these events invited the question that Robert Moses once asked in a *New York Times Magazine* article back in 1943: What's wrong with New York? Twenty-one years later, many Americans and would-be Fairgoers pondered the same question.

In late July, Moses sent a sample of the letters he had been receiving for months to Mayor Robert F. Wagner Jr. The first was from a Marshall, Texas, man who feared for the safety of his daughter and three grand-daughters, who were planning to visit the Fair. His letter quoted a maga-zine article about Genovese, recounting how thirty people "witnessed the rape of a defenseless woman by a sex maniac without rendering any assistance." He went on to say: "This would not have happened in this part of the country." He wanted Moses' personal assurance that New York City was safe.

Another man from St. Paul, Minnesota, expressed similar reser-vations. "The news stories concerning racial incidents, muggings, and actual killings have done much to cool our feelings for the Fair," he told Moses. Another wrote the Master Builder asking if it were true that cars with Alabama plates were being targeted by vandals, ostensibly in retaliation for the sins of Bull Connor and Governor George C. Wallace, now a presidential candidate.

"I'm sure you will be perfectly safe here," Moses assured any out-of-towner who asked. And while he admitted that violent crimes occurred in New York and other big cities—"this is true of . . . rural districts as well"—the real problem, he claimed, lay with the New York media. "The metropolitan press unfortunately plays these incidents up," he explained.

Despite these concerns, just four months into the Fair's first season, Moses had already turned his attention to improvements for Season Two, which would begin on April 21, 1965. There was no shortage of problematic pavilions to fix: There was the unofficial French Pavilion (shut down by Moses because the business group that organized it hadn't made the exhibit suitably French enough); the struggling American Arts Pavilion (which managed to aggravate the critics who had lobbied for it and inspire only apathy from the public); the cash-strapped Louisiana Pavilion, with its old-time riverboat-style revue *America Be Seated*, which was too close to a minstrel show for the NAACP, whose complaints ended the show after two days; and the Texas Pavilion, which despite its acclaimed *To Broadway With Love* show—which won praise for its integrated cast from Fair director Dr. Ralph J. Bunche—had red-stained balance sheets and was losing a reported $130,000 a week by early summer.

But by August, Moses' biggest problem was the Lake Amusement Area—the square mile of Fairgrounds adjacent to Meadow Lake that was accessible by a footbridge. He had built a small amphitheater and a marina that would anchor the area, but the surrounding Fairgrounds were ultimately populated with a zoo and a circus, as well as various sideshows and rides. From the get-go, Moses had instituted a no "midway" policy—referring to the traditional seedy entertainment areas of World's Fairs where one could find barkers luring customers into Coney Island–style funhouses, penny arcades, cheap games of chance, or circus freaks shows (like Olga the Bearded Lady, who was famous enough to earn a profile in *The New Yorker* in 1940). When the lights went down and the kids went home, these same venues would become more risqué and were strictly for "adults only."

Not at Moses' Fair, though. The Master Builder flatly refused to allow anything ribald or what he judged "bad taste" anywhere near Flushing Meadow. As Judge Samuel Rosenman, one of Moses' most trusted confidants, told *The New Yorker* months before the Fair opened, "You can have gaiety and amusement without any obscenity." By the summer of 1964, many of the producers of the Lake Amusement Area blamed Moses and his "ban-the-bust, no girlie show" dictum for their failing shows. "Moses is running the Fair as if it were a state park," complained a producer to the *New York World-Telegram*. Said another: "Moses isn't a showman. He has created a public image of the Fair as a serious place and has taken the fun out of it."

For Moses, that was the final straw. "We can do nothing further for the noisy whiners, kickers and mud throwers in the so-called Amusement Area who have attacked the Fair because we won't pay their advertising and other bills," he complained in a letter to his friend Roy S. Howard, who owned the paper: "I see no reason for us to spend any more time and money on shills, barkers, and Coney Island promoters who guessed wrong and really mean nothing to the success of the Fair."

But tradition and history were on the promoters' side. World's Fairs had long incorporated less idealistic and baser entertainments to attract adult customers. The 1933 Chicago Century of Progress Exposition was best remembered by many for Sally Rand's "Streets of Paris" routine where she wiggled and danced to Chopin's "Waltz in C-Sharp Minor" and Debussy's "Clair de Lune" until she was covered only by carefully placed ostrich feathers. The striptease was such a hit that she repeated it at the Fort Worth Frontier Centennial Exposition three years later, renaming it "Sally Rand's Dude Ranch" (when she revised it yet again for the 1938 Golden Gate International Exposition in San Francisco, it was known as "Sally Rand's Nude Ranch"). Not to be outdone, producers at the 1935 Pacific International Exposition in San Diego dreamed up Zoro's Nudist Gardens, which featured a male actor dressed up as a robot who cavorting in a pastoral setting with a half-dozen fully nude female performers, in what could best be described as sci-fi soft porn.

Inspired by the ever-mounting risqué acts in the American expos of the 1930s, set designer Norman Bel Geddes wanted to up the sex ante once again for 1939–40 New York World's Fair. Having already masterminded GM's Futurama exhibit—the Fair's "World of Tomorrow" centerpiece—he now envisioned something less exemplary: a Crystal Gazing Palace (a playful riff on the legendary Crystal Palace after "Sexorama" was rejected). Bel Geddes's "glorified peep show" featured a G-string-clad dancer on a stage in a room full of mirrors, thus allowing one seminude dancer to appear like a platoon of naked performers, while men sat in two rooms gazing on. Bel Geddes also created "The Living Magazine" show, in which seminude models posed as if they were part of a 3-D magazine cover. Customers were allowed to photograph the women as much as they liked. For all its utopian visions of the future, when it came to women, the World of Tomorrow was as sexist as the World of Yesterday.

Moses wanted no such exhibits at his 1964–65 World's Fair, his "endless parade of the wonders of mankind." His Fair was "essentially educational" he said again and again, and had no room for the cheap, puerile, and déclassé. His conservative stance won him praise from like-minded citizens and clergy, like the Reverend John P. Cody, a high-ranking priest from the New Orleans Archdiocese, who within a few years would become Cardinal of the Chicago Archdiocese, one of the most important positions in the US Catholic Church. "Can we survive without vulgarity, just escaping censorship and police intervention?" Moses wrote to Cody. "We have chosen the side of the angels."

If you wanted to sell something, then keep it clean, Moses believed. And all World's Fairs were selling *something*. Nowhere was this more evident than in the series of American World's Fairs held throughout the 1930s. As the Great Depression devoured the nation's self-respect and economic might, every year of that turbulent decade saw a Fair in a different corner of the country: North, South, East, and West. Those Fairs—including New York's 1939–40 World's Fair—were selling capitalism and the free market system, which, thanks to the economic misery of the Depression, had plenty of detractors at the time. After all, it was the unbridled free market fundamentalism of the 1920s that had laid waste to the American economy.

Moses' Fair was selling the notion of *progress*: the kind of progress that had created a National Highway System and enshrined skyscrapers as a new form of American art; the kind of progress that had successfully split the atom and was now close to putting a man on the moon; the kind of progress that unleashed the single-minded directives of a Master Builder who could—and did—mold and shape the largest and greatest metropolis on earth according to his whim, filling it with expressways and block towers, bridges and tunnels that led millions outside of its shadows and into vast pastoral settings of parks and beaches. This was the ethos of postwar America, and it was the personal philosophy—almost a religion, really—of Moses. "Big things happen to cities that make big plans," Moses said. And when the Fair was over, he had very big plans for Flushing Meadow Park. Stripteases and peep shows didn't figure into his calculations.

But while Moses stuck to his strictly family entertainment policy, the Lake Amusement Area offered few, if any, amusements that could attract customers either young or old. "Why spend time at the circus when you were at the World's Fair?" asked Bill Cotter, who attended the Fair dozens of times as a child. "You could go to the circus anytime." The truth was, the Lake Amusement Area, with its county fair–style rides, had to compete against the Fair's most popular attractions, such as Walt Disney's "It's a Small World," the Vatican Pavilion's *La Pietà*, the panoramic views offered by the observation towers at the New York State Pavilion, or the old-world charms of the Belgian Village. And when the Lake Amusement Area did garner media attention, it was for all the wrong reasons. On July 6 several Fairgoers, including a number of children (the youngest was just five years old), were stuck a hundred feet in the air in a gondola for three and a half hours when a ride malfunctioned. As emergency workers labored to fix the ride, a crowd of nearly seven hundred people gathered and watched in anticipation until the families were rescued. "This is the biggest crowd we've had in the Lake Amusement Area all year," noted one worker.

The area was also in a remote location, far from the Fair's popular attractions and its main avenues that fanned out in every direction from its centerpiece, the Unisphere. A visit to the Lake Amusement Area required that Fairgoers walk over a footbridge. At night the poorly lit district was hardly inviting to already jittery tourists fearful of New York's soaring crime rates. (By summer, Moses reluctantly approved $100,000 worth of new lighting for the area.) What's more, throngs of teenagers congregated there, away from the Fair's more populated areas; no doubt many of them were harmless, hormone-laden teenagers, but there were enough of them to garner a piece in the *New York Times* a week after opening day.

The interests of the American teenager occupied a blind spot for the seventy-five-year-old Moses, a particular problem for the Lake Amusement Area, which regularly featured musical shows and concerts. Moses' most daring tastes in music ran to the easy-listening styles of his close friend Guy Lombardo and His Royal Canadians, and Mitch Miller, whose sedate style and popular "Sing Along with Mitch" routines had made him a TV star. Moses was also a fan of swing-era bandleader Benny Goodman, still active in 1964 but synonymous with a style of jazz that was popular during the previous New York World's Fair. Some of the biggest draws at the Fair in the summer of 1964 were shows by the timeless jazz maestro Duke Ellington and the Dave Brubeck Quartet. Brubeck, who was at the height of his popularity, had achieved a mass audience thanks to his crossover hit "Take Five," had landed on the cover of *Time*, and had been savvy enough to name two tracks on his 1964 LP, *Time Changes*, "Unisphere" and "World's Fair."

Though popular, these artists still didn't appeal to teenagers. Moses, however, thought differently. He was sure his friend Guy Lombardo would reach the youthful crowds who had the potential to become repeat customers. "Guy Lombardo would appeal to the somewhat older and more conventional nostalgic group," Moses wrote in a memo marked URGENT to World's Fair director Rosenman, "but I have noted that he is also a favorite with many of the kids, if not the wildest ones."

Even marketing experts trained in reaching young audiences couldn't change Moses' mind. "Our experience tells us, however, that Guy Lombardo's music is not the dance music for Americans today, except for a relatively few people," an executive with the Thom McAn shoe company (which was interested in sponsoring a musical dance) had written to Moses in March. Instead, the executive proposed three different bands to attract a wide variety of Fairgoers but cautioned "the distinct sound of Guy Lombardo is not one of them. We don't think that his is the right music, the right image for a 1964 World's Fair or for us." Regardless, Moses rushed through a contract with his friend Lombardo in early April due to "extreme urgency" under the assumption "that it will have the endorsement of the committee."

But in between headliners like Goodman and Lombardo, who played six nights a week at the Taparillo band shell, plenty of other bands and performers had a chance to play the World's Fair, including a number of rock 'n' roll acts. One of the groups included two local musicians, guitarist-keyboardist Al Kooper, and bassist Harvey Brooks, who had grown up in the same Queens neighborhood just a few miles from the Fair. Their group played forty-five-minute sets, twice a day, seven days a week, performing covers of the Beatles' "A Hard Day's Night" or whatever songs were topping the charts. Kooper, who would soon kick-start his long rock music career by playing with Bob Dylan, loved the steady World's Fair gig. "Until I played with Dylan, the Fair gig was the best-paying job I ever had," he recalled.

By early summer, as the Lake Amusement Area struggled to turn a profit, Moses insisted on seeing what kind of music was being played at his Fair. It didn't take him long to decide he didn't like what he saw. "I want the cheap Rock n' Roll trash at the Amphitheatre *out* immediately," he instructed. What he wanted in its place was crooner Harry Belafonte "and others appearing at Forest Hills Stadium." Moses admitted that Belafonte was probably too busy—besides being at the height of his musical career, he was an activist and a confidant of Martin Luther King. But Moses' point was that he wanted world-class talent at his Fair, not this amateur stuff.

The Forest Hills Tennis Stadium had been the site of the US Open for more than thirty years, and by the summer of 1964, it had also become one of the most prestigious outdoor concert venues in New York. At fifteen thousand seats, it was also one of the largest. Besides Belafonte, acts like big-band jazz maestro Count Basie and crooner Johnny Mathis were playing Forest Hills, as well as younger, hipper acts like folk superstar Joan Baez (who would share her stage and spotlight with her boyfriend, Dylan) and, for two sold-out shows, the Beatles.

After one of their shows, the Beatles themselves came face-to-face with one of Moses' musical heroes, Goodman, who had agreed to interview the band for a local radio station in order to promote his upcoming World's Fair concert. The meeting, however, went nowhere; it seems the generation gap between the lads and the King of Swing was far too wide to bridge. "The Beatles had no interest in meeting Benny Goodman, and Benny Goodman had no interest in the meeting the Beatles," said Rachel Goodman, the jazzman's daughter, who wrote a piece about their intergenerational summit for *Esquire*. "They literally had nothing to say to each other."

But while the dry British humor of the Beatles didn't work on Goodman, it was starting to appeal to Anglophile Moses. As out of touch as he was with pop culture or the mood of teenagers, he came around to the band. Moses even wrote to a friend that he liked the scene in the band's film *A Hard Day's Night*, when a reporter asked, "How do you find America?" "Turn left at Greenland," shot back John Lennon. (Moses mistakenly accredited the one-liner to Ringo, but then he was hardly the only American over the age of thirty who had trouble telling one Beatle from another.)

Although six months earlier he had turned down a young fan's suggestion for the Beatles to play at the World's Fair, by mid-August Moses was open to the idea. "Would it be smart to invite the Beatles to the fountain fireworks and Tiparillo [band shell] or the Singer Stadium on some evening when they are around?" he asked a top aide. "They would probably turn up anyway with their own publicity and the crowd would be hard if not impossible to control unless the whole thing is programmed in advance."

What Moses didn't realize was that by August 1964—just six months after their Sullivan debut—the Beatles had outgrown both the Fair and its Tiparillo Band Shell or its ten-thousand-seat Singer Bowl. For now the Forest Hills Tennis Stadium was the smallest arena that they could play. No rock band had ever been in such demand before. In August 1964 Dylan wasn't headlining Forest Hills. He was just sharing the stage and basking in Baez's stardom; she graciously invited him out to sing a few songs, helping him reach a wider audience.

But while radio deejays and the performers' fans thought the English mop-tops and the protest-song singer were worlds apart, each had a strong appreciation for the other. Ever since he first heard the Fab Four on his cross-country trip in February 1964, Dylan had fixed his imagination on the Beatles—not that he told anyone about his new obsession. "They were doing things nobody was doing," he told a biographer in 1971. "Their chords were outrageous, just outrageous, and their harmonies made it all valid."

The Beatles' arrangements—two guitars, bass, and drums, plus three-part harmonies—got Dylan thinking of his own music, but set in a band context, another thought he kept to himself. "I really dug them," he said. "Everybody else thought they were for teenyboppers, that they were gonna pass right away. But it was obvious to me that they had staying power. I knew they were pointing the direction of where music had to go."

With that epiphany rumbling through his head, Dylan wrote a slew of new songs while on vacation in Greece that May. More personal and inward-looking than his previous material, the songs that formed the crux of his next LP, *Another Side of Bob Dylan*, poured out of him in a week. Released in early August 1964, the album contained no generational anthems like "Blowin' in the Wind" or "The Times They Are a-Changin'"; instead, songs like "All I Really Want to Do," "My Back Pages," and "It Ain't Me Babe" had little, if anything, to do with the topical songs his fans wanted. But the songwriter had grown disillusioned with the political orthodoxy of the folk scene. Dylan had complained to a friend that all anyone wanted from him were political-minded protest songs—"finger-pointing songs," he called them. He didn't want to speak for anybody other than himself. "There aren't any finger-pointing songs in here," he warned *The New Yorker*'s Nat Hentoff about his new LP. "Me, I don't want to write *for* people any more—you know, be a spokesman. From now on, I want to write from inside me. . . . I have to make a new song out of what I know and out of what I'm feeling."

The disillusionment flowed both ways. The album, along with Dylan's headlining performance at that year's Newport Jazz Festival, where he debuted some of the material, inspired Irwin Silber, the editor of *Sing Out!* magazine, to reprimand the singer in an "open letter" published a few months later. "Your new songs seem to be inner-directed now, inner probing, self-conscious. . . . Now, that's all okay—if that's the way you want it, Bob. But then you're a different Bob Dylan from the one we knew. The old one never wasted our precious time."

But Dylan had lost interest in what the editor of *Sing Out!* or any other publication thought about him or his work. He was interested in a different scene now. On August 28—exactly one year to the day after standing with King at the March on Washington, where he sang "With God on Our Side"—Dylan met up with the Beatles at their hotel suite at the Delmonico on Park Avenue and 59th Street, hours after they played the first of two sold-out shows at Forest Hills Tennis Stadium in Queens. After studying each other's records for months, the British pop stars and the Greenwich Village hipster now stared nervously at each other from across a table. The Beatles tried to break the ice by offering their guest their drug of choice: pills. But Dylan, wearing his now omnipresent black shades, turned them down. "How about something a little more organic?" he asked and began to roll a joint. "A skinny American joint," McCartney later complained.

The Beatles, no stranger to chemical substances, hadn't had much experience with marijuana by then. Dylan was confused. "But what about your song—the one about getting high?" he asked before singing in his nasally rasp, *"and when I touch you, I get high, I get high . . ."* It was Lennon who set the record straight. "Those aren't the words," he informed Dylan. "It's 'I can't hide, I can't hide.'"

Undeterred, Dylan finished rolling the joint and handed it to Lennon, who passed it to Ringo, calling him "my official taster." The drummer repaired to the bathroom only to emerge minutes later with an absurd, goofy grin on his face. Intrigued, all the Beatles took a hit and the mood in the room shifted dramatically as the pop stars and their entourages grew more relaxed under the pacifying influence of marijuana. "We were smoking dope, drinking wine and generally being rock 'n' rollers, and having a laugh," recalled Lennon. "It was party time." Dylan got into the joking spirit, too, and repeatedly answered the suite's phone by saying "This is Beatlemania here."

The night was the rock 'n' roll equivalent of a US–USSR summit. In August 1964 the Beatles and Dylan were at opposing ends of the musical spectrum. The Beatles were world-famous British pop stars, outsiders who had arrived on American shores preaching the gospel of rock 'n' roll, which was all but dead in the United States; and unlike racially segregated Americans, the Beatles didn't see—or hear— the difference between Elvis and Chuck Berry, between the Everly Brothers and the Marvelettes. (During their American tours in the 1960s, the band refused to play to segregated audiences.) Beloved by teenyboppers, the band got panned by music critics—Beatles Stump Music Experts Looking for Key to Beatlemania read one *New York Times* headline. Despite their unprecedented success, the Beatles and the mania they elicited were expected to fade.

Dylan, on the other hand, had all the credibility the Beatles lacked. He was the acclaimed avatar of the folk music revival—a "Homer in denim"—revered by his young college-educated audience (many of whom disdained pop bands like the Beatles) as their generational spokesman. He didn't have any hit singles, though others—like Peter, Paul and Mary—turned his songs into hits. He was heralded by living folk legend Pete Seeger, a genuine hero to the Old Left, and through his association—both musically and romantically—with Baez, became a hero to the New Left. While many in the mainstream media deemed the Beatles' music lacking of any redeeming qualities, many journalists—most notably the *New York Times*' Robert Shelton—championed Dylan as a uniquely talented songwriter, whose art stood at the crossroads of American music: a blend of Woody Guthrie and Lead Belly mixed with healthy doses of Hank Williams and lyrics that drew inspiration from the life-affirming and beatific poetry of Kerouac, Ginsberg, and Ferlinghetti.

But Dylan and the Beatles had more in common than most realized: They were rebels with plenty of causes. Each hailed from the provinces (from Northern England and Northern Minnesota, respectively); they were outsiders in the moneyed capitals of London and New York, which they dreamed of winning over. They were talented songwriters, first inspired by rock 'n' roll but drawing upon a wealth of musical influences. They were wildly ambitious. And like countless bohemians, jazzmen, artists, and free sprits before them, both would embrace pot, not only as a creative tool, but as a rebellious way of life. From this point on, both the Beatles and Dylan, inspired by one another, would blur the lines between folk and rock and reinvent pop music, elevating its importance and forever changing American—and global—pop culture.

While Dylan was turning the Beatles on to pot, American bohemians and intelligentsia were already consuming other, more potent forms of drugs. One in particular would, over the next few years, become a source of life-altering inspiration to many, including the Beatles: LSD. That same summer, the harbingers of America's Great Stoned Age, as it would later be remembered, would make a pit stop at the World's Fair, giving Fairgoers a glimpse of the nation's psychedelic future.

25.

These are the stakes: To make a world in which all God's children can live, or to go into the dark. We must either love one another, or we must die.
—Voiceover narration read by President Lyndon B. Johnson
for his 1964 "Daisy" campaign ad

Setting off from his La Honda, Northern California, ranch in June 1964, novelist Ken Kesey and his friends had no idea what would happen during their cross-country trip to New York City. But one thing was for certain: Their destination was the World's Fair.

The exhibition had fascinated Kesey since the November 1963 day when, after seeing the Broadway production of his best-selling novel, *One Flew Over the Cuckoo's Nest,* he and a friend had traveled out to Queens to see the World's Fair taking shape. "We vowed next year we'd come back to New York to see the World's Fair," Kesey promised. A book party planned by his publisher for his new novel, *Sometimes a Great Notion,* in the summer of 1964 gave him the excuse he needed to travel to New York and check out the Fair.

But before leaving La Honda, things had changed. The number of people heading to New York grew too numerous for the Volkswagen he and his friend Ken Babbs intended to use. So, they acquired and outfitted a 1939 Harvester school bus with five hundred pounds of equipment: an elaborate stereo and PA system (with indoor and outdoor speakers); sleeping quarters for roughly a dozen people; a platform on the roof (with a mounted drum kit, just in case anyone should be moved to bang out some grooves as the they made their way down some lonely highway); and film cameras, lights, and microphones. Kesey and company had decided to document their road trip, to create a cinematic diary of their journey. They even came up with a working title: *The Merry Pranksters Search for the Kool Place.*

There was just one last thing to do: paint the bus every color under the sun with Day-Glo paint—blues, oranges, reds, yellows, pinks, and greens—a phantasmagoric array of hues. They dubbed their four-wheel chariot "Further." As a gag—it was the middle of a presidential election cycle—Kesey painted on the side A VOTE FOR BARRY (as in Goldwater, the Republican presidential candidate) IS A VOTE FOR FUN on the side of the bus.

And then Neal Cassady, the real-life muse of Jack Kerouac and the inspiration for Kerouac's *On the Road* hero Dean Moriarty, turned up at Kesey's door unexpectedly. Cassady had read *One Flew Over the Cuckoo's Nest* and saw himself in the novel's hero, McMurphy, the rebel without a cause who fatally clashes with the authoritarian Nurse Ratched. Kesey took Cassady's arrival as a sign of the gods, a blessing for the psychedelic odyssey. When asked by a reporter in New York what had inspired his trip, Kesey replied, "For a lot of us it started when we first read *On the Road*." Now here was Cassady, sprung from the pages of the novel that had changed everything, driving their bus. He would be their amphetamine-induced Virgil and nonstop narrator, giving his endless "rap"—which Kesey called a "careening, corner-squealing commentary on the cosmos"—as they visited the four corners of the nation.

It was all very romantic, and in its rebellious rejection of authority and the status quo, very American. Kerouac's vision of America was romantic, too—all open roads and endless horizons. "Everyone I knew had read *On the Road*," Kesey recalled. Both literati and songwriters alike were affected by the Beat author's work. Reading Kerouac had changed everything for a young Robert Zimmerman. "Someone had handed me *Mexico City Blues* in St. Paul in 1959," Dylan told Kerouac's brother-in-arms, the poet Allen Ginsberg, after the pair met in early 1964 at an East Village bookstore. "It blew my mind." Now both Kesey and Dylan were exploring the road—and where it led to—just as Kerouac had years before.

But Dylan and Kesey weren't the only ones. The success of *On the Road* in 1957 gave a voice to the angst of the younger generation and their nonconformist ideas, which had been roiling beneath the staid surface of the 1950s. Cassady, Kerouac, Ginsberg, and their fellow Beats, like blacklisted filmmakers and political radicals, had never fit into the black-and-white movie that was Eisenhower's America. That America had segued seamlessly into John F. Kennedy's Camelot, where his Ivy League Knights of the Roundtable—the Best and the Brightest—were poised to fix the nation's ills with technocratic and pragmatic solutions, regardless of the problem at hand: the Cold War, civil rights, or Vietnam. Only when Kennedy, after having dragged his feet for two years, delivered the boldest presidential endorsement yet of civil rights legislation was it apparent that America had begun to change course.

Then, in rapid succession, the nation underwent a series of traumas: the Kennedy assassination, the murder of the three civil rights workers by racists in Mississippi, followed a month later by the race riots in New York and other Northern cities during what was supposed to be Freedom Summer. The latter events threatened to overshadow the hopeful passage of the Civil Rights Act in June—a historic change that required all the protean powers of President Johnson, Senator Hubert H. Humphrey, and Robert F. Kennedy, and the all-important cooperation and support of Senator Everett Dirksen, the Republican Minority Leader. Despite this bipartisan cooperation in Washington, DC, the nation as a whole seemed to be digging further into the trenches of their own beliefs.

And now with a presidential election just months away in November, this ideological rift was epitomized by the stark choice being offered to voters: one the one hand, the Left's newly minted liberal hero, President Johnson; and on the other, the far-right conservatism of Senator Barry Goldwater, who would brag in his July nomination acceptance speech that "extremism in the pursuit of liberty was no vice and . . . moderation in the pursuit of justice no virtue." Goldwater frightened people. He refused to rule out using nuclear weapons in Vietnam, where the nation was on its way to another Asian ground war—a fear that President Johnson would soon exploit with his controversial "Daisy" TV ad, which featured a little girl mindlessly picking a flower in a field, as a voiceover begins counting down a missile launch; the whole screen then fades to black as a nuclear mushroom exlodes. The nation's future seemed up for grabs, between wildly opposing forces.

Kesey felt the seismic activity, and it affected his writing. In fact, the novelist began to doubt the impact that books could have. "I began to suspect," Kesey confessed, that his own novels "might not have a lot to do with the world." It was one of the reasons why he wanted to embark on this psychedelic journey to see the country and the World's Fair. "We decided to go drive across the country . . . across the United States, go to the World's Fair and just to experience the American landscape and heartscape." It was in that spirit that Kesey and his friends, dubbed the Merry Pranksters, began their journey. But the group wasn't just going to drive cross-country stone cold sober. They had a large supply of lysergic acid diethylamide, LSD, the psychedelic drug that was, in the summer of 1964, completely legal.

Discovered by the Swiss scientist Dr. Albert Hofmann in 1943, LSD, which induced hallucinations, was snatched up the US military for use as a weapon in the fight against Communism. Military brass hoped to use it as a truth serum to aid in interrogations or to embarrass America's enemies. LSD was also used by psychiatrists to treat patients, including actor Cary Grant, the personification of the dapper Hollywood leading man, who said his acid trip gave him "the peace of mind" that he had been searching for all his life.

As a student at Stanford University, where he was an English major, Kesey agreed to become a human guinea pig at a veterans hospital where LSD and other mind-altering drugs were being tested. (Ginsberg had undergone a similar government-funded research project in 1959.) Kesey's experience inspired *One Flew Over the Cuckoo's Nest* and changed his life. Now it was about to change American history.

As the Merry Pranksters made their way from the West Coast, with pit stops in Houston, Texas, and Louisiana, up the East Coast to New York, few people knew what to make of them. Hippies and psyche-delic trips were still in the future for most Americans, while the Merry Pranksters were all veteran acid-droppers. When their Technicolor dream bus drove down a busy midtown Manhattan side street, music blasting, Pranksters hanging out the windows or sitting on the platform on the roof, it was a shock even to seen-it-all New Yorkers. Children ran after them; pipe-smoking gentlemen snapped photos; Beatles-obsessed teens laughed in excitement; and respectable women gasped in bemused amazement. People weren't afraid; they were intrigued.

In New York, in mid-July, the Pranksters picked up two guests: Ginsberg, who had attended the 1939 World's Fair as a child and who was going to help round up his old friend Kerouac for a party; and the novelist Robert Stone, a pal from Kesey's Stanford days, who was now living in New York with his family. Together they headed to the World's Fair to experience its vision of America. "To Ken, to America in 1964, world's fairs were still a hot number," Stone wrote decades later. "Fairs and carnivals, exhibitional wonders of all sorts, were his very meat."

That much, at least, Kesey and the Fair's creator, Robert Moses, could agree on. But there was one other important link connecting the two: the road. Moses had devoted his life to creating the open roadways and elevated highways that had transformed the American landscape that Kerouac and now Kesey had committed themselves to exploring; the inescapable reality is that there couldn't be any *On the Road*s or Merry Prankster road trips without highways, or men like Moses who built them.

When Kesey and company finally arrived at the World's Fair, they were shocked by what they saw. It had nothing—absolutely nothing—to do with their LSD-fueled dreams. The Merry Pranksters, avatars of what would soon come to be known as the hippie movement, didn't see their vision of America's future at the Fair. It wasn't there among the fountains and rides, the Walt Disney–designed shows, or even the post-modern architecture of Philip Johnson with its trippy pop art murals. And it certainly wasn't to be found among the multitude of corporate America's displays—the giant-size tire Ferris wheel, the life-size dinosaurs of Sinclair Oil, or any of the various offerings of GE, GM, Ford, Chrysler, or DuPont—or even the life-size rockets sent by NASA.

As if hung over from a bad acid trip, Kesey and the Pranksters left Flushing Meadow disappointed. "The Fair was trippy and great when you were high," noted Paula Sundsten, the stunning beauty who was better known by her Prankster moniker Gretchen Fetchin. She had made the journey for the most practical of reasons: She wanted a summer job at the Fair as a synchronized swimmer (none were available). But one of the Pranksters made a diary entry that summed up the group's consensus about their trip succinctly: "The World's Fair is not a kool place."

It seemed that they were at the end of the road, but Ginsberg suggested one last stop before heading back West. He wanted Kesey to meet Dr. Timothy Leary, the onetime professor who had been booted from Harvard along with his colleague Robert Alpert for questionable practices during their experiments with LSD. Since the fall of 1963, the academics had set up their experiments in a sixty-four-room, four-story Gothic mansion that sat upon 2,500 acres of lush, green land in Millbrook, New York, lent to them by Peggy Hitchcock, a rich socialite who was part of their inner circle. Although Leary was still years away from becoming the hippie guru who extolled the youth of America to "turn on, tune in, drop out," he was well on the way. Whatever he and the other hangers-on desired—whether sex, drugs, and rock 'n' roll or tai chi or chanting Hare Krishna—everything could be explored at Millbrook, and all of it in the name of mind expansion.

For now, Leary was taking a trickle-down approach to spreading the gospel of LSD by introducing it to the cultural elites: poets like Ginsberg, publishers like Grove Press's Barney Rosset, socialites like Hitchcock and her family, jazzmen like composer-bassist Charles Mingus, and hip comedians like Lenny Bruce. Soon bastions of the Establishment, like Time Inc. founder Henry Luce (a World's Fair director) and his wife, Clare Boothe Luce, experimented with the drug.

Like Leary at the time, Mrs. Luce thought LSD should be kept from the commoners, claiming, "We wouldn't want everyone doing too much of a good thing." Others argued for a different approach. Michael Hollingshead, Leary's onetime associate, tried in vain to organize a Pavilion of the Mind Exhibit at the World's Fair. He wanted to use "light, sound, color and technical innovations" to create what he called "an exhibit both contemporary and exciting . . . among the many tens of millions who are expected to visit the fair." (World's Fair executives were unimpressed with his idea.)

Ginsberg wanted to organize a summit of the LSD tribes. East Coast meets West Coast. Up in Millbrook, the poet said Kesey could encounter Leary's International Federation for Internal Freedom movement.

"Great," Kesey said. "IS-IS comes to the IF-IF."

What exactly was IS-IS? Ginsberg wanted to know.

"Intrepid Search for Inner Space," replied Kesey.

Ginsberg should have known then that the summit wouldn't go well. Aside from acid, the tribes had little in common. When the Westerners arrived at the Millbrook compound, Leary and Alpert and a group of about twenty others were just coming down from "a very intense and profound trip" according to Alpert, who would later be known by his Zen moniker, Ram Dass. "It was a very deep trip and it went on all night long." After that metaphysical journey, they were all ready for sleep; that's when the rambunctious Pranksters showed up. As the bus rolled up to the house, Chris Lehman-Haupt, one of the younger Pranksters, hurled smoke bombs, some landing through the mansion's open windows, filling the rooms with billows of green smoke. "It was like the Huns coming to visit Camelot," noted another Prankster, Rob Bevirt.

Things deteriorated from there. Alpert was courteous to his guests, but Leary mostly stayed upstairs, trying to recoup from his acid trip and the flu. He did make an appearance, and even talked with Cassady and Ginsberg on the bus. The Pranksters milled about the house. Some explored the ground's waterfall; others relaxed and ate a decent meal. But the Pranksters didn't dig the mystical vibe that surrounded the Millbrook crowd, preoccupied as they were with the metaphysical texts of Eastern spiritualism: the *Tao Te Ching*, the *I Ching*, and *The Tibetan Book of the Dead*. To the Pranksters, they seemed to talk another language. *What's all this nonsense about death?* Kesey and company were about *Life* and *Living*, the *Here-and-the-Now*, not what comes later. They dubbed Leary's scene "The Crypt Trip" for its gloomy outlook. Each group ultimately wanted the same thing—as Leary later said, "to weaken faith and conformity to the 1950s social order"—but each would explore their own ways of changing the culture.

As disappointed by the World's Fair and Leary as Kesey and the Pranksters were, Ginsberg, the poet of the Beat Generation, heir to the Whitmanesque tradition in American poetry, could see what was happening. He spoke both their languages: He understood the Pranksters' penchant for fun, but he was no stranger to mysticism or Eastern philosophy. He understood what Kesey's search for a "kool place" was really about. "The real significance of Kesey's bus trip in the summer of 1964 was as a cultural signal that happened just as the nation was on the precipice of enormous awakening and change," Ginsberg said. "It was like a very colorful flag going up a flagpole, signaling the news that something was about to happen, something was about to shake."

PART THREE

BRINGING IT ALL BACK HOME

26.

New York is frowning, tight-lipped, short-tempered. It is a city without grace. . . . It is a city that cries "Jump" to a would be suicide perched on a window ledge.

—"New York: A City Destroying Itself,"
Fortune, September 1964

By August 1964 the New York media had reached the general consensus that the World's Fair was becoming a financial fiasco. They knew the Fair—which Robert Moses had described that month as "a summer university education, as well as a world tour"—would fall short of the forty million visitors Moses and company had predicted for its first six months. On August 4 the Fair celebrated its twenty millionth visitor; there was now less than eleven weeks left before the Fairgrounds closed for the year. The failure of the three biggest musical revues at the Fair— Radio City Musical Hall producer Leon Leonidoff's *Wonder World,* an "aqua-stage spectacle"; the Texas Pavilion's *To Broadway With Love*; and Dick Button's Ice Capades—didn't help dispel the growing sense that Moses' Fair was in trouble.

A July 22 *Gallagher Report,* a newsletter geared toward the advertising and marketing industries, had been tracking the Fair's attendance numbers and doing the math: There were "few winners" and "many losers" among exhibitors. More specifically, it saw Thomas J. Deegan's advertising campaign as "ineffective" and "inadequate." Despite acknowledging that attendance was affected by New York's image problems—surging violent crime and race riots—the report was blunt in its appraisal of the real dilemma: "Robert Moses is mostly to blame."

While dismissing such criticism out of hand, Moses knew that the Fair had serious obstacles to overcome. He had accurately predicted that business would boom during the summer while school was out and the tourist season was at its busiest; the same had happened with the 1939–40 New York Fair. Likewise, as soon as autumn stripped the trees bare, the kids would go back to school and tourists would return home—and business would, inevitably, drop off. There was no way for him to get to a two-year total of seventy million visitors, and he knew it. The figure had been at worst wholly fictional, at best extremely optimistic. "Everyone knows the seventy-million figure had no real precedent—was a guestimate," admitted one Fair executive in mid-July.

That had never stopped Moses from running with it, however, dropping the number in speeches, Fair literature, and his regularly issued Progress Reports. Politicians from New York to Washington had picked up on it, too: During his December 1962 speech at Flushing Meadow, President Kennedy had upped the figure to seventy-five million. Moses' plan called for forty million visitors in the Fair's first year, thirty million in its second, which would result in an estimated $100 million in profits. Then, after all notes and debts had been paid off, the World's Fair Corporation would have close to $23 million for Moses to transform Flushing Meadow into the world-class park that he had long dreamed about.

The financial health of the Fair had been a hot topic of debate inside the World's Fair Corporation for months. In mid-May the chairman of the Finance Committee, George Spargo, took exception to Fair comptroller Erwin Witt's rather sunny report on the Fair's balance sheets. Moses, however, wouldn't hear of such negative complaints. He insisted the Fair was "in the black" and would pay the remainder of the Fair's notes in October as planned. "I think [the] report is all right and I shall support it," he informed Spargo, and accused the latter of being "consistently pessimistic."

Spargo was considering taking the issue up with the Fair's Executive Committee—essentially going over Moses' head—but the Fair president issued a warning: "If the word were to get around that the Executive Committee has no faith in a balance to finish the park, it would be futile to make plans for this purpose, and a considerable part of my own interest in the Fair would disappear." Moses was not about to blow his chance at creating his long-envisioned post-Fair park because one of his executives wanted to take a conservative approach to bookkeeping.

Three days later, when Spargo handed in his resignation, Moses had already tapped George S. Moore, president of First National City Bank, as his replacement. He admitted to Moore that there were some "tough problems" involving several pavilions and various concessions, but overall the Fair was the picture of financial health. "The Fair as a whole is in no jeopardy whatever," he noted casually, "because of these incidental emergencies which seem to be unavoidable."

Defensive as ever, Moses mistook every article that wasn't lavish praise as a personal attack. When a *New York Herald Tribune* reporter described the Fair as "Pop Art"—connecting the experimental architecture yet commercial nature of many of the pavilions with the experimental yet commercial aspects of the most important art movement of the day—Moses was livid, and lodged a complaint with the paper's editor. He was simply unable to see that, in many ways, his Fair *was* as contemporary and "of-the-moment" as an Andy Warhol silkscreen or a Roy Lichtenstein comic book panel. Moses wasn't interested in the here and the now; he built things—at least in his mind—for the ages, and the Fair was intended to help him build one more.

But even as he battled the press and warded off internal problems, Moses took a strong stance against any politician, regardless of party affiliation, who wanted too much from the Fair. When the Florida Pavilion was hurting for cash and Governor C. Farris Bryant, a segregationist Democrat, wanted a loan of $1 million, Moses balked, complaining to an aide that Bryant was a "fresh red-headed bozo." In August, when the Democratic National Convention wanted free passage to the Fair to entertain its delegates during its Atlantic City convention— where President Lyndon B. Johnson would be nominated—Moses said no, noting that he had turned down the Republicans, too.

Moses did, however, bestow favors as he saw fit and for his own reasons. He had invited a contingent of nuns from Good Samaritan Hospital on Long Island to spread the word about the Fair—and through the auspices of the good sisters, incur a little friendly publicity—but their visit went awry. Afterward, the Mother Superior wrote him personally to complain that she and her group had waited three and a half hours for a horrible lunch at the Ballantine Beer Pavilion's Rathskeller and then were overcharged. Moses went ballistic, complaining that some Fair workers "are expert at making enemies of decent people and getting me into trouble unnecessarily." He had an executive drive out to the Mother Superior's convent, apologize in person, and pick up the tab for the nuns' entire afternoon in Flushing Meadow.

The incident revealed a serious weakness of the Fair: the deterioration of quality among many Fair employees at the lower strata. The Fair was, in many ways, too big, too unwieldy—too much of a top-down bureaucracy with no way of controlling itself. Ultimately, such problems were the result of Moses' management style, which, depending on the issue at hand, alternated between micromanagement (choosing the menu for a meeting of VIPs) and laissez-faire (refusing to be drawn into the Jordan mural controversy).

In early August, Dr. Arthur Lee Kinsolving, president of the Protestant Council of the City of New York, which had organized the Protestant Pavilion, accused Moses of allowing labor unions to overcharge his pavilion and others. Moses insisted that the high prices were for "emergency repair work at all hours and at night," noting that he was only charging what were "going rates for union labor" in New York. Incensed at Kinsolving's complaints, Moses then instructed an aide to draft a reply blasting the Protestant rector. "We can't let this pious breast-beater get away with anything as raw as this," he wrote.

If the Master Builder felt he was always under attack, particularly from the media, it was probably because not a single day went by when one of Gotham's half-dozen daily newspapers didn't run a story critical of either Moses or the Fair or both. Trying to broker a truce between the World's Fair and some of the New York papers, Bernard Gimbel lunched with A. M. Rosenthal of the *New York Times*. The department store tycoon (and Moses confidant) was one of the movers and shakers that Rosenthal thought it was his business to know as the Metro editor for the Paper of Record.

Gimbel delivered Moses' message that the *Times* wasn't helping the Fair, at least as far as Moses saw it. Rosenthal was sympathetic but firm. "We are trying very hard to capture the spirit of the Fair ourselves," the Timesman said, defending his paper's coverage. "Sometimes we have to write articles that do not make very pleasant reading but this is part of our job, as I am sure you will agree. We try to balance by carrying articles almost every day on the stimulation to be found at the Fair." As the man who had brought the ghastly Kitty Genovese murder story to light— he would publish a brief but poignant book on the case, *Thirty-Eight Witnesses*, just months after the murder—Rosenthal knew all about the unpleasant side of New York City.

Fairness, however, didn't factor into Moses' conception of how the media should treat his great exhibition. He wanted good publicity, period, even if the first months of the World's Fair coincided with some of the worst crimes and urban unrest in New York history. Richard J. Whalen, then a rising star at the Henry Luce–owned monthly, captured the scene in his September 1964 *Fortune* magazine cover story, titled "New York: A City Destroying Itself."

Whalen, who also authored a warts-and-all biography of Kennedy patriarch Joseph P. Kennedy Sr. despite protest from the family, wrote about New York as only a native could. Born and raised in Queens, and a graduate of Queens College, Whalen named names, making a case that New York's lackluster political class was an abject failure. None of the mayors who had followed in Fiorello La Guardia's giant footsteps could equal "the Little Flower" he wrote; instead, New Yorkers had elected a parade of "midgets" who had failed its citizens time and again.

Whalen's litany of complaints was long and undeniable: Violent crime was soaring—a 13 percent rise overall, with a 52 percent rise on the subway—water and air pollution was horrific (sneezing in New York could leave one's handkerchief stained with black soot); traffic was paralyzing, overbuilding and bad urban planning out of control. Meanwhile, race relations had sunk to a new low. The growing militancy among some of the city's underclass wasn't to blame for the riots; instead Whalen believed the true cause was the "alienation and hopelessness in the ghettos, and apathy in the city at large." The very existence of ghettos in a city of such material opulence was an indictment of "the indifference of the powerful." New York City, he declared, was on "a death march."

According to the *Fortune* piece, one of the architect's of New York City's self-destructive impulses was the man who had alternately built and demolished so much of the five boroughs: Moses. Although Whalen admired Moses' administrative prowess, he wrote what so many politicians were afraid to say; namely, the Master Builder wielded "too much authority for one man. . . . [Moses] rules as an absolute despot, beyond the reach of public opinion." Since Mayor La Guardia left office in 1946, no one could control Moses; that is, if any of the mayors and governors—ostensibly his bosses—had even bothered to try. "Moses was a law unto himself," said Whalen, who charged Moses with building not because it was in the interest of New Yorkers, but simply because he could. For Whalen, Moses' worst offense was his attempt to erect the Lower Manhattan Expressway, or Lomex, by razing sizable chunks of downtown Manhattan.

Similar to the aborted Mid-Manhattan Expressway—the elevated six-lane highway that would have sliced Manhattan in half from one side of 30th Street to the other, which Robert Kopple had helped derail in 1958—the Lower Manhattan Expressway was a 1.5-mile long, elevated eight-lane highway that was nearly the width of one city street. Lomex would have decimated a half-dozen downtown districts, including parts of Little Italy, Chinatown, SoHo, and Greenwich Village—vibrant, living, diverse neighborhoods filled with working-class families, unique architecture, and small businesses that contributed to the health and diversity of the city's economy. "That road could never have been created by someone who loved New York City," said Whalen. "It would have been a Great Wall of China cutting the city in two."

By 1962 Jane Jacobs and others, like *New York Times* architecture critic Ada Louise Huxtable, were waging a powerful campaign against Moses and Lomex, rounding up a diverse assortment of working-class immigrants and downtown denizens: bohemians, activists, intellectuals, small business owners. However, Moses had his allies, too, including organized labor—who loved the Master Builder for the abundance of jobs he created. When one white New York City union leader was informed that Lomex would damage the city's economy by destroying ten to twelve thousand jobs, mostly held by blacks and Puerto Ricans, he replied, "I can't be worried about them."

It was exactly projects like Lomex—imposed on New Yorkers without their consent by Moses and with the backing of those who would benefit, like the city's building trade unions—that were, in short, killing New York City. "In New York, the voices of special interest are never still, while the voice of common interest is seldom raised," Whalen wrote in *Fortune*.

The public battle over Lomex came to a head at a December 1962 Board of Estimate meeting. Carmine DiSapio, a sharp-tongued, sunglasses-wearing Greenwich Village assemblyman, denounced Moses—a "cantankerous and stubborn old man"—and his Lower Manhattan Expressway in a rousing speech. To the elation of the activists and the New Yorkers whose lives and livelihoods were at risk, the Board of Estimate voted unanimously against the expressway. (As per his style, Mayor Robert F. Wagner Jr. let others take the tough stand, then sided with the majority.) It was an ignominious defeat for Moses; the Lower Manhattan Expressway was one of his most cherished dreams. To the Master Builder, both Lomex and the Mid-Manhattan Expressway were the personification of "the World of Tomorrow" promised by the Futurama exhibit of 1939–40 World's Fair: a city created by and for the automobile.

However, Moses wasn't about to let the issue die. Instead, as he had done many times before, he waited. And waited. And then, when he thought he had outwaited his opposition, he pushed again to get the Lower Manhattan Expressway built in August 1964. By May 1965, thanks to lobbying from Moses, David Rockefeller, and union leaders, Mayor Wagner had reversed himself: The Lower Manhattan Expressway would be built after all. Once again Jacobs led her crusaders against Moses and City Hall, this time finally winning when a dashing blond-haired congressman, John V. Lindsay, won the 1965 mayoral election. Lindsay killed the project—and Moses' dream—once and for all.

What the Master Builder never seemed to realize was that the negative press and criticism he garnered for trying to impose public works such as the Lower Manhattan Expressway on New Yorkers, against their will, couldn't help but overshadow the World's Fair, tar-and-feathering the exhibition in the minds of millions. Whalen's *Fortune* article—expanded into a book in 1965—also planted a question in the minds of Americans from coast to coast: What business did New York City—or Moses, for that matter—have hosting a World's Fair, particularly one devoted to the utopian theme of "Peace Through Understanding"? It was a question with no easy answers.

Asked to respond to the *Fortune* story by the magazine's publisher, Moses didn't bother to hide his contempt. "You ask why should *Fortune* want to do such a story?" he wrote. "Search me. I don't know. It is full of errors and misinformation." Although he wrote a letter to the editor, published in the following issue, Moses refused to let the subject go. He hoped to write a lengthy response in the pages of the *New York Times,* but publisher Punch Sulzberger took a pass.

Moses wrote the essay anyway and printed it at his ever-busy printing press as a pamphlet, circulating his broadside to the media, politicians, bankers, dignitaries, VIPs, friends, associates, and his considerable number of fans. "The Fair, the City, and Its Critics" was Moses' agitprop attack against all the nay-saying New Yorkers who "soil their own nest" and forever badmouth New York as a "hopeless place of vulgarity, wrath and tears." Unfortunately for Moses, that was essentially what New York City was becoming by the end of 1964. And everyone seemed to know it—except for him.

27.

After the publication of Richard Whalen's scathing *Fortune* story, Robert Moses could console himself with the abundance of letters he received each week praising him and his Fair. Whole classes of schoolchildren, organized by their teachers, would write letters in their wondrously childish scrawl, often illustrating their notes with crayoned pictures of the day at the Fair. In response, Moses wrote back to the teacher, thanking the children and including World's Fair literature as a souvenir.

Moses also fielded some complaints, including a few about the "adults only" puppet show, *Les Poupées de Paris,* about which a Staten Island woman complained was "filled with off-color jokes, vulgar remarks about sex, scantily clad puppets (only puppets—it's true—but they can look so real) doing suggestive gyrations." And Moses was being asked to write his autobiography, which he flatly refused, while exchanging letters with former CIA chief Allen Dulles over the latter's article about James Bond scribe Ian Fleming (Moses was a fan).

The Fair even managed to get some good press from the decidedly left-leaning *New York Post,* courtesy of columnist Sylvia Porter Collins. She assured Moses that he could count on more friendly clippings since her source was one of Moses' top men, Martin Stone ("a close and treasured friend . . . that I trust implicitly"). Even the *New York Herald Tribune,* the paper that Moses most consistently railed against for its Fair coverage, wrote a favorable piece on September 1 about the rich variety of global cultures that were on display, including the Sierra Leone National Dance Troupe, dancers and musicians from Indonesia and Zambia, and the Flamenco Theatre of Madrid. *That* was the kind of press Moses wanted to see in the morning papers.

By early September Moses was focused on the Fair's second season, which would begin on April 21, 1965—just seven months away. Topping his list of improvements for next year was luring Brazil and the Soviet Union to invest in pavilions, hopefully by simply taking over one of the failed operations. But Moses suspected that once again, Cold War politics and the State Department's secretive machinations would torpedo his efforts. "I think we are being taken for a ride again," he lamented in a memo to Charles Poletti. "The State Department seems to be playing all sides and all angles as usual."

Also priorities on Moses' to-do list were organizing a health pavilion of some kind with the help of the Mayo Clinic or some other nationally recognized operation, and creating an exhibit devoted to the accomplishments of organized labor. He wrote Walter Reuther, president of the United Auto Workers, CIO-AFL, in mid-September, pledging "space and cooperation" and the willingness to send his top people to meet with the labor leader "anytime, anywhere."

In the meantime, he received praise from dignitaries ranging from Academy Award–winning directors like Frank Capra and Elia Kazan to Supreme Court Justices Hugo Black and John M. Harlan II. He also received notes of thanks from important senators whose careers would be determined by the growing war in Vietnam: Senator Wayne Morse of Oregon, a liberal Republican and one of only two senators to vote against President Lyndon B. Johnson's Gulf of Tonkin resolution, who described Moses as "one of my favorite public servants"; and vice presidential candidate Senator Hubert H. Humphrey, Democrat of Minnesota, whose devotion to Johnson's Vietnam policy would ultimately prove his politically undoing. All of the above thanked Moses for the white-glove treatment they received while at Flushing Meadow, and all considered the World's Fair as yet another feather in the Master Builder's cap. The praise of such elite VIPs insulated Moses further from his numerous critics among the New York newspapers.

As September ended, Moses once again railed against the newspapers, and chastised his own staff for leaks about his attempts at luring the Soviet Union to the Fair for the 1965 season (the *Herald Tribune* quoted a confidential memo regarding the Fair's Soviet plans). On September 23 two stories irked Moses: The first was a page-one story in the *Wall Street Journal,* whose opening line read "Forget the shows—but DON'T miss the commercials . . ." before going on to celebrate the corporate commercialism of the Fair. While Moses was certainly pro-business, he didn't want the cultural impact of his Fair to be slighted. That same day, the *Trib* took a parting shot at Moses, saying the Fair president was late for a celebration at the Illinois Pavilion on Illinois Day. (Moses was outside with Governor Otto Kerner and Ambassador Adlai Stevenson, Kerner's predecessor.)

Then on September 30, the *Herald Tribune* published a piece about the $150,000 loan that Cardinal Richard Cushing of Boston had given to the Vatican Pavilion. The money had come from a fund controlled by the cardinal—a personal friend of President Kennedy (he had presided over the nationally televised funeral). The article, based on leaked information, also revealed that Cushing was lending his personal collection of JFK memorabilia to the Massachusetts exhibit in the New England Pavilion in 1965. Moses ripped into his publicity chief, Thomas J. Deegan, promising that he would find the guilty party. "We may have to employ private detectives," Moses threatened, "which seems almost incredible."

Moses then publicly labeled the New York media as "hyenas" and "jackals," terms that his friends in the press, including Roy S. Howard, whose company owned the *New York World-Telegram,* and William Randolph Hearst Jr. publisher of the *New York Journal-American,* the flagship newspaper of the Hearst media empire, took umbrage with, forcing Moses to backpedal a bit. In early October, perhaps wanting to call a truce or perhaps just defend the way they covered the Fair and New York City, the New York Reporters Association held its annual supper at the Top of the Fair restaurant. While Moses abstained from attending, the association's president, Charles Grutzner of the *New York Times*, told the Fair executives in attendance to "tell Bob Moses that we love him and we love his Fair and we thank him for his hospitality." Moses quickly wrote Grutzner a memo thanking him for his kind words. "Of course, I never said all of these boys or more than a *small*, vicious, articulate *minority* were hyenas. You know *that*. The rest, the great majority, have been fair, friendly, enormously helpful and in fact indispensable."

With the close of the World's Fair first season only weeks away, members of the Exhibitors Council of Public Relations Subcommittee, which included top executives from top-rated corporate pavilions such as GE, Coca-Cola, and Electric Power and Light, issued their report on the Fair's PR campaigns to date and their recommendations for the future. The report found that exhibitors had done little "direct advertising since Opening Day" and that in 1965 such opportunities would naturally diminish. ("I don't agree," scrawled Moses in the margins of his copy of the report.) In their assessment, the Fair wouldn't attract 40 million paying customers in 1965; at maximum they predicted 26.5 million. (Moses: "I disagree completely. This is fundamental.") They warned that if the Fair "goes ahead" and repeats its "patterns of the past, they would miss their two-year attendance goal of 70 million by as much as 20 million— 28 percent below forecast." (Moses: "Nonsense.")

Moses then shot down almost every one of the report's suggestions. The corporate executives wanted a powerful winter and spring promotional program, including films and traveling shows ("doubtful"); advertisements in national magazines and out-of-town newspapers from April to September 1965 ("no"); a sustained ad campaign in New York media for radio, papers, and television ("too expensive"); and more special events in the summer season ("in the works already"). The only suggestion Moses approved was to create a dedicated staff among the Fair's public relations people to develop new plans for the 1965 season ("good idea").

Moses refused to yield to the experts who understood show business and public relations better than he did, just as he refused to listen to critics who second-guessed the need for many of his urban renewal projects or elevated highways. When the Fair's Executive Committee wanted answers as to why the biggest shows, such as the Texas Pavilion's *To Broadway With Love,* had failed so spectacularly, Moses was at a rare loss of words. "We don't know," he wrote the committee. "Nobody does." But even Moses could guess why the Lake Amusement Area flopped. "We must admit that our fixed policy not to invite a conventional midway on the Lakefront, which might have attracted large crowds, as against the conservative principles we adopted, was also a contributing factor," he confessed.

But all that seemed forgotten as the World's Fair closed its gates on October 21. Three days prior, a Westinghouse Time Capsule was buried in a ceremony at the Fairgrounds, just as Fair organizers had done twenty-five years earlier. Inside were objects that epitomized the nation's mindset in 1964: credit cards, a Bible, freeze-dried food, plastic wrap, a ballpoint pen, tranquilizer pills and birth control pills (two relatively new pharmaceuticals that would transform how Americans dealt with their mental health and their sex lives), a piece of the *Mercury Aurora 7* spacecraft, and a copy of the Beatles latest album, *A Hard Day's Night,* which was also the name of their hit movie. The band—or the mass hysteria they provoked among American and British teenagers—was seen as ephemeral, a passing fad, something that upon the opening of the capsule at some point in the distant future, would provoke a chuckle or puzzled amusement. In less than a year's time, however, World's Fair organizers would see and *hear* firsthand just how powerful, loud, and popular Beatlemania remained.

28.

The critics build nothing.
—Robert Moses, December 8, 1964

With the first season of the World's Fair over, Thomas J. Deegan spoke at a mid-November Rotary Club luncheon. The quick-with-a-quip, round-faced Irishman was a consummate schmoozer by nature, and he boldly predicted the Fair would pull in 37.5 million visitors in its second season. "Any attraction that can draw 27 million people in a six-month period has to be considered successful," Deegan told the crowd, while noting that the World's Fair had finished the year with a $12 million surplus.

Originally, the World's Fair Corporation estimated that the Fair would attract 40 million during its first season and 30 million in its second. However, in 1964 the Fair attracted 27 million paying custom-ers (another 5 million had seen the Fair gratis)—13 million less than promised. Now Deegan was predicting that Season Two would bring in 7.5 million *more* customers than originally planned. This wasn't just unjustified optimism; it was pure fantasy. But Deegan was playing a classic shell game: Assuming the Fair would attract 27 million again, he added another 10.5 million customers to arrive at his predicted figure. But what he didn't say was that those 10.5 million customers represented the approximately $10 million advance tickets bought at a discount in 1963 and never used; the money from the sales was long gone, which meant approximately 10.5 million customers could visit the Fair in 1965—for free.

How the year-old Fair was now going to attract additional custom-ers remained a mystery. Moses had already nixed the notion that the Fair would open for an unprecedented third season, noting that most of the structures weren't built according to strict city codes. They were built only to last two years. Furthermore, Moses insisted that no new pavilions would be created in the new year, yet somehow, he told reporters the exhibition would be a "brighter, gayer place."

The same day that Deegan's promise made the papers, Moses was secretly working his network of powerful connections to orchestrate a scheme that, if executed, would make world history: Moses wanted Pope Paul VI to come to the World's Fair. The idea was the height of hubris: No pontiff had ever come to the United States. But Moses knew that his World's Fair was different; through the intercession of his friend Cardinal Francis Spellman, the most powerful clergyman on this side of the Atlantic, Pope Paul's predecessor, the late Pope John XXIII, had given his personal blessing to the creation of the Vatican Pavilion and allowed the Vatican's treasured attraction, Michelangelo's *La Pietà*, to leave St. Peter's Basilica for the first time in history. Now Moses was petitioning Spellman, who was in Rome for the Second Vatican Council, to personally invite the pontiff to Flushing Meadow. "This would be a high point in the Fair and would be enormously appreciated by all the people of the country," Moses wrote.

Although Pope John XXIII had died by the time the Fair opened, Pope Paul VI quickly bestowed his own blessing on the Fair by allowing his gem-encrusted papal tiara to be shown in the Vatican Pavilion. What's more, breaking with tradition, Pope Paul had already been the first pontiff to travel extensively outside of Italy. He was, in fact, the first pope to fly on an airplane, making a historical trip to see the Holy Land, visiting Israel and Jordan, in January 1964—a trip that had captured the world's imagination (and landed him on the cover of *Life* magazine). Just a few weeks after Moses' telegram to Spellman, the pontiff would journey to Lebanon and India. A papal World's Fair visit was nothing more than a pipe dream at this point, but more than anything else, Moses made a habit of thinking big.

Two days before Thanksgiving, Moses sent another letter, this time to Abraham Beame, New York City Comptroller. Forced to come clean about the Fair's finances, Moses informed Beame that that it was unlikely—still possible, but very unlikely—the World's Fair would be able to pay back the "entire $24 million" it owed New York City. With little choice, and already privately expecting this was the case, Mayor Robert F. Wagner Jr. and his staff had adjusted the proposed 1965–66 budget accordingly. "You can only count on something you are sure is going to be there," Wagner complained to reporters.

Beame was more direct than the mayor. An ambitious bean counter with an accounting degree from City College, the five-foot-two Beame wasn't the well-born son of a United States senator, but rather the product of Brooklyn's Democratic Party machine. He had worked his way up from a Lower East Side tenement to the top ranks of City Hall and knew his way around a ledger. He already had one eye on Wagner's job and knew better than most—or was at least willing to say so publicly—that Deegan's and Moses' predictions were meaningless. "If next year's operations are no better than they were this year," Beame told reporters, "it seems hardly likely that we will get any of this money."

By December Moses was drawing up his wish list of improvements for the 1965 season, which included: getting the set for the film *The Agony and the Ecstasy*, Hollywood's biopic of Michelangelo and his struggle to paint the Sistine Chapel, for display in the Vatican Pavilion; pressing state and industrial exhibitors to come up with new exhibits for their pavilions; a new show for the immensely popular Johnson's Wax Pavilion; a new attempt at getting industrialist Joseph H. Hirshhorn's modern art collection to the Fair; a medical exhibit of some kind; and acquiring Pan American Airlines chief Samuel Pryor Jr.'s vast doll collection, which included dolls from all over the world, some priceless works of art as well as toys. In reality, the only new attraction the World's Fair could count on was the Belgian Village—eleven acres of old-world charm, with cobblestone streets, archways, and beer gardens. Beset with financial problems and labor overruns, the attraction had finally opened at the end of the Fair's first season. It would soon introduce Americans to a staple of Belgian cuisine: the Belgian waffle.

Moses also wanted some repairs made to the amphitheater, in the hopes of attracting a new tenant, perhaps the same promoters that booked popular acts—such as Joan Baez and the Beatles—to perform at Forest Hills Tennis Stadium. As far as Moses was concerned, the repairs should come out of the city's budget, since it was the city that would take over the structure when the Fair ended. But Beame thought the Fair should pay for it, especially since the city was already likely on the hook for $24 million. Moses complained to Samuel Rosenman that Beame and others "had joined hands in an effort to force the Fair to pay half or more of the . . . repairs. This is out of the question." He was prepared to shut down the amphitheater for the entire 1965 season.

As 1964 turned to 1965, the outlook for the World's Fair turned dark. Shortly after New Year's, the news broke that the Top of the Fair restaurant, which had been struggling for a while, was now, after trying to work out deals with its creditors for several months, officially bankrupt. This was hardly the kind of headline Moses had envisioned for the Fair as it launched a new advertising campaign aimed at subway riders.

Out-of-towners were unlikely to visit the Fair a second time, the Master Builder realized, especially since he was about to announce a price hike (allegedly because "all Fair costs have risen"). Adult tickets would now cost $2.50, while children's prices would remain at $1 and schoolchildren who came with their classes would still pay 25 cents. Moses and company were banking on attracting New Yorkers—including those millions of commuters from Long Island and the Tri-State area who had not been to Flushing Meadow yet, or who lived close enough that they wouldn't have to pay for a hotel. Moses, who throughout his long career chose to build roads instead of extending public transportation, now requested the New York City Transit Authority add more signs about the Fair on the subway system and add an express line on the Flushing IRT direct from Times Square. And to show their commitment to their pavilions and the Fair, twenty-six large industrial exhibitors like Ford and GE prepared a $75 million publicity campaign to lure customers in the 1965 season.

But by the middle of January 1965, there was no escaping the fact that the World's Fair Corporation's numbers just didn't add up. Fair comptroller George S. Moore, who had replaced Erwin Witt, was dismayed at the inconsistency of the Fair's balance sheets and Moses' failure to provide accurate numbers. As one banker in the know told the *New York Times*, Moses' story kept changing. "First there was a surplus," the banker complained, "and then suddenly there wasn't any."

Moore had had enough, and confronted Moses about it. "Bob, we've found bills of six and seven figures that weren't booked," he said. "We just can't continue without reliable information."

"George, your figures are wrong," Moses responded. "You don't know what you're talking about."

"Bob, I've been in the banking business all my life, and if there's one thing I know, it's a column of figures."

Things went south from there. On January 12, at a meeting of the World's Fair Executive Committee, Moore wanted more information, including audits, for his committee to examine. Moses wouldn't hear of it. He accused the banker of trying to ruin his Fair. This was how things were done at Flushing Meadow, according to Moses, and, "If you don't like it, you can get the hell out."

"Don't *you* question my loyalty, Bob," Moore shot back. "Let me remind the committee, you showed your 'confidence' and 'loyalty' to the Fair by putting your salary in escrow right at the start." It was true: Long before the Fair ever sold a ticket, Moses had put aside six years' worth of his entire salary—more than $600,000—along with enough money to cover his top executives.

"You're a son of a bitch," Moses snarled.

Six days later, Moore and four other top New York bankers, including Moses' close ally David Rockefeller, head of Chase Manhattan bank—and brother of the governor of New York—quit the Fair's Executive Committee. The financial titans of New York, some of the very people who had pushed for Moses over Robert Kopple five years earlier, were now abandoning him. "We have to know the score," Moore told the *New York Times*, "and we do not."

Now the Fair's decisions were under serious scrutiny. Reporters wanted to know why the Fair, during the summer, had made a down payment of $7.5 million toward the $30 million in bonds it owed. At the time, Fair executives were bragging that they had a $50 million surplus and that by October the bonds would be paid in full. Despite his admission that the Fair had considerably less, Moses refused to explain how or why it had happened. "Until we get some solid information on what's going on there and tight budget controls," declared one New York banker, "they're not getting any more money from us."

With local politicians promising to investigate Moses' monetary "shenanigans" and with Beame telling reporters that as city comptroller he had the legal authority to examine the Fair's books, Moses went on the attack, releasing a lengthy statement that took aim squarely at Moore, and backed up his claims with twenty supporting documents. Moses accused the First National City Bank president of missing important meetings, forbidding his bank to lend money to financially troubled pavilions, and for voting "as chairman of the finance committee, to retire, long before they were due" the $7.5 million of notes. "If this money were on hand now," declared Moses, "there would be no immediate financial problems whatsoever."

Now having successfully muddied the waters by turning the Fair's financial woes into a narrative of *he said, he said,* Moses buried more bad news in the statement's last paragraph: The World's Fair would need approximately $3.5 million in operating cash to open the 1965 season. He then softened his tone, assuming a more diplomatic posture. "We need boosters, not knockers," he wrote. "Our lives at the Fair are a challenge, not a truce, and I suppose we should be grateful for the storms and stimulants however motivated. We have survived worse weather."

A week later, there was a hard rain of embarrassment: Of the $71 million plus in expenditures from the 1964 season, the Fair had spent more than $27 million in maintenance and security costs. Keeping a small army of union laborers and the private Pinkerton police force on twenty-four-hour call had added up. At a meeting of Fair directors, Senator Jacob K. Javitz, a close associate of Moses—and a close friend of Moore—wanted to know how many directors were needed to call an emergency board meeting. Javitz, who had supported Moses and the Fair from the beginning, was preparing to go over the Master Builder's head "unless we get answers we need on these financial matters."

Afterward, Moses entertained questions from reporters. Belligerent as ever, he told the gathered members of the media that Moore,

Rockefeller, and the other bankers had based their decisions on bad data. They were simply misinformed, Moses declared.

"Was it you who misinformed them?" a Timesman asked.

"What the hell is the use of asking such a provocative question?" Moses shouted, before telling the reporter to relax and "have a drink."

The Thomas J. Deegan Company—owned and operated by Deegan, the World's Fair executive vice president—was dropped by the Fair after its annual $300,000 compensation was revealed. Moses had hired his right-hand man's company, the public now knew, without taking any other bids. With the Fair bleeding cash, having a top executive pay his own company $1.2 million in retaining costs confirmed in many people's minds that there was something far more odorous in Flushing Meadow than the toxic sludge of the Flushing River.

The parting of ways was originally thought to be Deegan's own doing, but many suspected that Moses had ordered the move after relations between the pair deteriorated. Moses was said to be furious when, while traveling to Japan to see the 1964 Tokyo Olympics, he had learned that Deegan had dismissed ninety-five Fair workers to cut costs without consulting him; thirty-two of the employees worked for a company owned by a close friend of Moses. Dismissing Deegan's company was considered to be payback.

By early February 1965, Moses' feud with city comptroller and mayoral hopeful Beame had spilled over into the courtroom. Beame wanted to subpoena the Fair's books. Meanwhile, Arthur T. Roth of the Long Island–based Franklin National Bank announced that he would lend Moses the $3.5 million necessary to open the exhibition in April. Undeterred by all the negative publicity and court battles, Moses continued with his plans for a post-Fair Flushing Meadow Park. While publicly he admitted that the Fair was unlikely to generate the $23 million in profits he needed, privately he sought alternative funding.

Mayor Wagner made his task easier by insisting that Moses was under no real obligation to pay back any of the $24 million in taxpayer funds the city had lent the Fair; it was all just a "gentleman's agreement." After all, the struggling Fair had still added to civic coffers, including large boosts to New York's hotels and restaurants. Broadway shows, the museums, taxis, the MTA, and airports had all seen spikes in business, too—all facts that Moses reminded his detractors of repeatedly. When asked about the Fair's fiscal priorities during a televised interview, Moses said that after meeting the World's Fair debt obligations, he had every intention of giving the city "a park a great deal better than what we inherited."

After the interview, Moses flew to Spain to meet with Spanish dictator General Francisco Franco in Madrid and give the former Hitler ally a World's Fair medal for his generous support of the universally hailed Spanish Pavilion. At least one newspaper was unable to resist the obvious caption to the photo of the two shaking hands: DICTATOR MEETS DICTATOR. But while Moses was meeting with Franco, back in United States discussions where being held between Mayor Wagner, Governor Nelson A. Rockefeller, and Senator Javitz in New York City and Washington, DC. The topic? Replacing Moses, who at this point, they believed, had damaged the World's Fair's image—and their considerable investment. What good was it to launch a new ad campaign and seek a fresh start for the Fair's second season if Moses was going to be in the papers every day attacking someone and keeping the Fair's finances under a shroud of secrecy?

The idea was to kick the now seventy-six-year-old Moses upstairs, giving him an honorary status, and replace him with a new CEO. Of course, anyone who knew Moses—and Wagner had known him since he was a child—had to understand such a plan was unworkable. Still, they tried, and Wagner sent his good friend John A. Coleman, a former chairman of the New York Stock Exchange, to meet with Moses on his behalf. When asked by a reporter how he thought Moses would react, Coleman was honest. "I don't know," he said. "You know Mr. Moses—he might throw me out of his office. Or he might hit me in the eye and blacken it. All I intend to do is listen to him." While Coleman left the meeting unharmed, Moses refused to listen to his suggestions.

One Manhattan member of the New York City Council insisted that Mayor Wagner simply remove Moses from the World's Fair

Corporation, but the mayor—as per his style—insisted that he had no authority to do so. It was up to the World's Fair's Board of Directors. Before anyone could make a move against him, Moses used his parliamentarian knowledge of the Fair's bylaws and insisted on a vote of confidence. When all was said and done, Moses won: Twelve directors voted in his favor; nine—including Deegan and Moses himself—abstained. Hearing the news, a friend wrote the Master Builder, congratulating him on his unanimous victory. "It was hardly unanimous," Moses wrote back.

Chastised but unbowed, Moses continued to plan for the Fair's second season. He arranged for the Hallmark Company to sponsor an exhibit devoted to Winston Churchill, who had died the month before. And Moses set his sights beyond 1965. He began steering $6.4 million in Triborough Bridge and Tunnel Authority funds to his park. Finance Committee chairman George V. McLaughlin, a Moses loyalist for four decades, quit, refusing to go along with the plan, calling it "a stretch of the law." Indeed, the only connection between the TBTA and the World's Fair was the man who headed both: Moses. According to Moses' law, a park was in the interest of the public and the TBTA was a public authority, and he found an obscure bylaw to back up his case.

No one—not his friends, not his bosses, and certainly not some city councilman—was going to stop Moses from reaching his goal. Creating parks might have been siding with the angels, according to the Master Builder, but he was all too happy to employ decidedly non-angelic means to achieve his ends.

29.

You don't need a weatherman to know which way the winds blows.
—"Subterranean Homesick Blues," Bob Dylan, 1965

When Bob Dylan returned to the recording studio in mid-January 1965, he wanted a new sound for his next record. "The sound of the streets," he called it. "That ethereal twilight light, you now. It's the sound of the street with the sun rays . . . it's an outdoor sound that drifts even into open windows that you can hear. The sound of bells and distant railroad trains and arguments in apartments . . ."

Dylan was in the middle of a major metamorphosis. While his previous album, *Another Side of Bob Dylan,* represented a shift in lyrical direction, musically the LP was still a folk record; the album's only instrumentation were Dylan's poetic rasp, an acoustic guitar, and harmonica. Still, there was something about his new tracks like "All I Really Want to Do" and "It Ain't Me Babe" that seemed ready-made for a band. At his Carnegie Hall concert on Halloween 1964, Dylan played a new song called "If You Gotta Go, Go Now (Or Else You've Got to Stay All Night)." It was pure rock 'n' roll in rhythm and sentiment, but he performed it in his usual acoustic setting.

Since he had first heard the Beatles, Dylan wondered what his own music would sound like in a band context. On January 13, at New York's Columbia Studios, he found out. The sessions began with Dylan recording nearly a dozen songs with his acoustic guitar but accompanied by the Loving Spoonful's John Sebastian on electric bass. Two days later, with a full band backing him up, Dylan recorded a new version of "If You Gotta Go, Go Now" that was truer to the song's intention. With its bluesy beat and roaring electric guitars, the track was the most conventional rock 'n' roll song he had yet written, complete with stripped down, uncomplicated lyrics: "Listen to me, baby / There's something you must see / I want to be with you, gal / If you want to be with me." "Blowin' in the Wind" this was not. It was left off the finished album (the song wouldn't officially be issued in the United States for nearly thirty years), but British pop band Manfred Mann turned the song into a No. 2 hit in the UK nine months later.

After three days, the sessions had yielded more than a dozen master-takes, and Dylan's new album was complete. Two months later the release of *Bringing It All Back Home* formally announced Dylan's new artistic direction. Of the album's eleven songs, seven were recorded with a band—voluminous electric guitars and soaring organ over a rollicking rhythm section—while the four tracks on side two were traditional acoustic Dylan. There wasn't a conventional protest song among them. When Joan Baez first heard the album, she wasn't impressed. "I'm afraid the message that comes through from Dylan in 1965 . . . is, 'Let's all go home and smoke pot, because there's nothing else to do,'" she said. Later she would complain that Dylan "just wanted to rock 'n' roll."

With *Bringing It All Back Home*, Dylan was following the Beatles' direction and taking the music where, he said, it "had to go." But the album's title, intentionally or not, was a reminder to the Beatles and their British brethren that his new music was baptized in the sacred river of the blues, a musical genre that—along with its tributary offspring such as rock 'n' roll, R&B, country, and even folk—was purely American. As Dylan reminded one British heckler on his UK tour in 1966, where he sometimes performed with an American flag as a backdrop: "This is not British music. This is American music." He was reclaiming his country's musical heritage as his own.

While Dylan was making his first foray into rock 'n' roll, the Byrds released their version of "Mr. Tambourine Man"—one of the acoustic tracks from *Bringing It All Back Home*. The Byrds, whose stated mission, according to its founder, guitarist/vocalist Roger McGuinn, was to fill the "gap" between the Beatles and Dylan, translated the song's kaleidoscopic poetry into rock vernacular: all jingle-jangly guitars and three-part harmonies, set to a smooth backbeat. When McGuinn played it for Dylan, the songwriter was astonished. "Wow, you can dance to that!" he told McGuinn.

The Byrds' single of "Mr. Tambourine Man" was released in April 1965 and flew to the top of the charts, becoming a No. 1 hit that June. Meanwhile, Dylan's first-ever single, "Subterranean Homesick Blues," a happy marriage of stream-of-consciousness poetics and Chuck Berry–like boogie, stalled at No. 39 on *Billboard*'s Hot 100 chart. That same month the Byrds released their debut album, also titled *Mr. Tambourine Man*, nearly half of which consisted of Dylan songs transformed by the group into radio-ready rock anthems. As the Byrds and other pop groups like Sonny & Cher cracked the Top 10 with his music, Dylan became inextricably linked to the "folk-rock" trend that was dominating pop radio.

It also had an effect on the songwriter's outlook. "It got me thinking about the *Billboard* charts," he admitted decades later. "I hadn't thought of that before."

30

Well, they'd impeach a president though that would run out, wouldn't they?
> —President Lyndon B. Johnson in conversation with
> Senator Richard B. Russell about removing American
> troops from Vietnam, May 1964

Once on the tiger's back, we cannot be sure of picking the place to dismount.
> —Undersecretary of State George Ball's warning against
> further military action in Vietnam to
> President Johnson, October 1964

Having dispatched—*destroyed* would not be too harsh a term—his Republican opponent, Senator Barry Goldwater, at the polls in November 1964, Lyndon B. Johnson had reason to celebrate. It was, at the time, the most lopsided presidential election in history. As he would later reveal, the Texan had felt ill-suited to follow the Harvard-educated, Boston-bred President John F. Kennedy prior to his landside victory. Before the assassination, there were even rumors among Washington's social set that the Kennedys would drop Johnson from the ticket in 1964. Taking Kennedy's place in those dark weeks after the events of Dallas had left LBJ feeling "illegitimate, a naked man with no presidential covering, a pretender to the throne, an illegal usurper."

But now, that all changed. He had reinvented the moniker "Landslide Lyndon," which Texas newspapermen derisively had called him after his paper-thin victory that marked the ignominious beginning of his senatorial career. President Johnson was now the choice of nearly forty-three million Americans to lead their country and serve as commander in chief, and he had every intention of doing so. The man was on a roll, having taken his slain predecessor's domestic agenda—in particular, his stalled Civil Rights Act of 1964—and made its passage through a belligerent US Senate his number one priority, doing what no president had done before. Few had dreamed that any president would be able to do such a thing, much less a Southerner who had fought civil rights throughout his career. As Johnson told one civil rights leader who asked how and why he had converted to their cause, Johnson replied, "Well, to quote a friend of yours, 'Free at least, free at least, thank God Almighty, I am free at last.'"

No longer having to appease the pro–Jim Crow vote in Texas, Johnson was preparing to put his own stamp on the nation, moving the country along the lines of his own political agenda: the Great Society. He had previewed this vision throughout the spring of 1964, including at the World's Fair, both on opening day, when he was publicly chastised and ridiculed by college-aged activists, and upon his return to the Fair just a few weeks later on May 9 to greet a meeting of union workers. That same month, Johnson had spoken to a throng of University of Michigan students—receiving a far friendlier reaction than from the Queens College students who had gathered at the World's Fair—where the president regaled them with his liberal vision of what America could be: "The Great Society . . . demands an end to poverty and racial injustice," he declared. The America that he envisioned was "a place where every child can find the knowledge to enrich his mind and enlarge his talent . . . where the city of man serves not only the needs of the body and the demands of commerce but the desire for beauty and the hunger for community."

Johnson was in his element pushing his ambitious domestic agenda, wanting to wage a "War on Poverty." His task was made easier by the large Democratic majorities in the Senate and the House of Representatives. So confident was the newly elected President Johnson that, standing with his wife, Lady Bird Johnson, at his side, he proclaimed at the White House tree-lighting festivities a week before Christmas Day 1964 that "these are the most hopeful times since Christ was born in Jerusalem."

There was just one nagging problem that clouded Johnson's bold new vision to transform America into a far more egalitarian land: Vietnam. In fact, just two days before Christmas, two more American "military advisors" had been killed there. By the start of the new year, 267 Americans had been killed in Vietnam since 1959.

Had President Kennedy lived and received a second term, Vietnam would have been his problem to solve; now it had fallen to Johnson. The Asian country quickly became a top priority. As the world watched Kennedy's burial on November 25, 1963, President Johnson issued a secret executive order insisting "all senior officers of the government" support the government's policy—that is, *his* policy—in Vietnam. Johnson would not accept disloyalty or dissent in his administration. The next month, when Secretary of Defense Robert McNamara returned from a fact-finding mission in Vietnam, he told reporters that all was going well, but then gave a completely different story to the commander in chief. It was only the end of 1963, and already McNamara had concluded that current American policy would lead to a stalemate at best; at worst, the Communists would seize control of the country.

More hawkish voices urged the president to step up the military's involvement. "We are swatting flies, when we should be going after the manure pile," declared Air Force Chief of Staff General Curtis LeMay, the same man who had advocated a military showdown with the Soviet Union during the Cuban Missile Crisis and called Kennedy's diplomatic solution to the crisis "the greatest defeat in our nation's history."

By March 1964, when McNamara returned from another trip, he told Johnson that American prospects had "unquestionably been growing worse." Seeking other opinions on the vexing matter, Johnson turned to his old mentor, Senator Richard B. Russell of Georgia, who was as against having American troops in Vietnam as he was giving civil rights to black Americans. Johnson knew that Russell had a history with Vietnam: As anti-Communist as they came, and deeply conservative in foreign policy, Russell pleaded with his friend to get out of Vietnam and get out now. In 1954 both men had gone to President Eisenhower and argued against supporting France's colonial wars in Indochina—"[I] said we'd never get out, be in there fifty years from now," Russell reminded his president.

Then in May 1964, the same month that Johnson was unveiling his Great Society, Russell issued another warning to his old friend. Having just heard testimony from McNamara at a Senate hearing, the senator wondered if the defense secretary, despite his Ivy League education and impressive résumé, knew all the pertinent facts. "He's a can-do fellow," Russell admitted. "But I'm not too sure he understands the history and background of those people out there as fully as he should." As much as he trusted his old friend's instincts, however, Johnson refused to heed his advice.

Instead, his advisers drew up secret plans to increase military operations. But they needed an incident, a trigger to justify their actions. On August 4, 1964, the same day that the bodies of Andrew Goodman, James Chaney, and Mickey Schwerner were dug out of the Mississippi earth, Johnson's team got it. Since July 30, US warships had been in the Gulf of Tonkin, off the coast of Communist-controlled North Vietnam, assisting small boats from the pro-US "South" Vietnam as they attacked military stations. On August 2, North Vietnamese ships sped toward the USS *Maddox,* which opened fire while US planes attacked from above. Such cat-and-mouse operations continued until finally, on August 4, the *Maddox* reported that they were under attack by enemy torpedoes and opened fire. It was exactly the moment the Johnson administration had been waiting for, an attack on a peaceful US vessel, an act of war.

Back in the United States late at night on August 4, President Johnson broke into regularly scheduled television and radio programming to inform the American public that US ships had come under fire by enemy troops. In response, he ordered two bomber planes to attack North Vietnamese targets. Privately, Johnson had his doubts about what had happened. "Hell, those dumb stupid sailors were just shooting at flying fish," he snorted to a staffer.

Within days, President Johnson ushered through Congress the Gulf of Tonkin Resolution—which passed the House of Representatives without a single dissenting vote and the Senate by a margin of ninety-eight to two. The president now had congressional approval to "take all necessary measures to repel an armed attack against the forces of the United States and to prevent further aggression."

With his electoral victory that November, Johnson was now hold-ing all the cards. He might have talked peace—he had said as much at the World's Fair in April and May, and again and again throughout the 1964 campaign when painting his opponent Senator Goldwater as the warmonger—but now, having sold the American public on his peace-ful intentions, it was Johnson who was setting the stage for one of the worst tragedies in the nation's history. And he had plenty of support from the media, Congress, and the American public. His advisers, led by McNamara, were urging him for more decisive action.

After the Gulf of Tonkin Resolution in early August, Johnson's assistant secretary of defense, John McNaughton, suggested ways that such actions could be justified. The American military should create "a series of provocative actions . . . similar to those leading up to the Gulf of Tonkin incident," he wrote Johnson. If North Vietnam responded militarily—as they hoped it would—then the basis for further military action would be solidified and Johnson could escalate if he wished. After all, how could the greatest military power that the world has ever known lose to a ragtag bunch of Communist guerrillas from a Third World country?

After North Vietnamese fighters attacked an American air base in mid-January 1965, killing eight US troops and wounding more than a hundred, Johnson told his National Security Council, "I've had enough of this." A month later, the president approved the beginning of Operation Rolling Thunder, the largest sustained bombing campaign in US history. From February 1965 until the end of the war a decade later, American bomber pilots blasted North Vietnam with three times as many bombs as were dropped in the entirety of the Second World War.

By the end of March 1965, just weeks before the World's Fair opened its second season, McNaughton drafted another secret memo. This one was the most brutally honest answer to the question that millions of Americans would ask in the decades after the war ended: Why were we fighting in Vietnam? According to McNaughton, the answer broke down according to percentages: 70 percent of the reason why we were there was "to avoid a humiliating US defeat"; 20 percent of the reason why was to keep South Vietnam "from Chinese hands"; and the final 10 percent was to help the South Vietnamese "enjoy a freer way of life."

Then, a few weeks later, General William Westmoreland, the top military commander in Vietnam, requested forty thousand American troops. The average age of such soldiers was nineteen years old. Instead of riding the eight-story Ferris wheel at the World's Fair, sampling the waffles at the Belgian Village, being lifted by the "People Wall" in the IBM Pavilion, or enjoying the myriad light shows and fountain displays as dusk settled over the Fairgrounds, strolling the Fair's paved walkways hand-in-hand with their sweethearts, many of these same nineteen-year-olds would draw their last breath in Southeast Asia. And the main reason they—and tens of thousands more like them—died so young, as McNaughton pointed out, was so the president, his cabinet, and his military advisers could save face.

31.

There is an amazing democracy about death.
—Reverend Dr. Martin Luther King Jr.

Since the racial violence of Birmingham in the spring of 1963, Americans had witnessed an astounding amount of brutality perpetuated against their countrymen at the hands of their fellow citizens. The mauling of Birmingham's children by Bull Connor's police force, with their fire hoses and attack dogs, had been followed by the September church bombing that killed four little girls in their Sunday best. Two months later came the fateful bullets ringing out in the Dallas daylight, killing the nation's youthful president, and seven months after that, the cold-blooded murders of Andrew Goodman, James Chaney, and Mickey Schwerner, the trio of civil rights workers left to decompose in the Mississippi mud for six weeks in the summer of 1964, a season that also saw bloody riots—some might say insurrections—in several Northern urban ghettos. Then, of course, there were the young Americans being sent home from Vietnam in body bags.

The early months of 1965 offered no respite. As Robert Moses waged war with his critics, leaving New Yorkers to wonder if the World's Fair would even have a second season, crime in the city continued to rise. Following *Fortune*'s September 1964 cover story on the political and physical demise of New York—reissued and expanded into a 1965 book—the *Herald Tribune* launched a series of articles titled "A City in Crisis" detailing the myriad problems the crumbling metropolis and its citizens faced. With all the talk of civil rights for African Americans and other minorities in both the Southern Jim Crow states and the Northern cities, many non-minority Americans began to feel that they too needed new laws for protection. "We also need a great civil rights march in our city," one New Yorker wrote to the *Herald Tribune*, "to insure to us the civil rights to live in our homes, to ride in our subways, to walk in our streets and parks at any hour without fear of being murdered, robbed and raped."

Moses got a similar letter the same month the *Herald Tribune* launched its soul-searching series. Joseph A. Sweeney, age seventy-three, of Brooklyn wrote to the Master Builder, exhorting him not to feel bad if the World's Fair didn't open in 1965. It wasn't his fault, Sweeney said, it was New York's—"There are reasons for it, and it's the times we are living in now," he explained. Recalling how he and his wife used to attend the 1939–40 World's Fair three or even four times a week, Sweeney said he had enjoyed the latest Flushing Meadow exhibition—finding it "instructively educational and entertaining"—but that they were too afraid to go out frequently. "Now the people are prisoners in their homes," Sweeney wrote Moses. "Very few risk going out after dark with the muggings, rapings, robbery and pocket book snatching going on." His wife was mugged one evening right in front of their Brooklyn apartment building, while Sweeney was robbed one early afternoon on Christmas Eve.

The violence touched everyone. For months, Malcolm X's wife, Betty Shabazz, had been receiving death threats, a campaign of harassing phone calls carried out by her husband's enemies. On Valentine's Day 1965, shortly after their returning to New York from a trip to Detroit, the house where the couple lived with their five daughters was firebombed. Although the frightened family escaped unscathed, Malcolm had to know that the members of the Nation of Islam, who for months had been threatening to kill him, now meant what they said.

A week later, at one of his regular Sunday talks at the Audubon Ballroom in Harlem, just as Malcolm X began speaking, a ruckus erupted in the audience. A young black man stood up and shouted, "Nigger, get your hand out of my pockets!" As Malcolm's bodyguards tried to restore order, three other young black men rushed the stage and shot the fiery orator to death in full view of four hundred people, including his wife, who rushed onstage to cradle her husband's bullet-ridden body. In one bloody instant, one of the most powerful voices in the struggle for black freedom was silenced.

Despite the passage of the historic Civil Rights Act the year before and the overwhelming victory by Lyndon Johnson's Democratic

Party, there was plenty of work to be done to further the cause of freedom for America's twenty-two million African Americans. The newest battleground was Selma, Alabama, a poor, rural area of the state whose leading politician had challenged President Johnson for the Democratic nomination.

Governor George C. Wallace might have talked like a folksy, country-bred good ol' boy, but he was nobody's fool. He was already preparing to ride the anti–civil rights resentment of the South all the way to the White House. And to achieve his goal, he would only have to tweak his message to capture the Northern "white backlash" vote—all those white, ethnic, working-class rank-and-file Democrats—in America's crime-ridden big cities, the same ones who were now afraid to leave their homes or felt left out of Johnson's "Great Society." Wallace was every bit the Democrat that Johnson was; it was his party, too, and he planned on stealing it right from under Johnson's bulbous Texan nose. But that would have to wait until the next presidential cycle in 1968; for now, Wallace was just biding his time.

Five days after Malcolm X's murder, a peaceful civil rights protest in Marion, Alabama, turned deadly. On February 26, Jimmie Lee Walker, his mother, his eighty-two-year-old grandfather, and others marched to a local jail where a civil rights protester was being held. As they sang and prayed, they were set upon by a group of Alabama state troopers, who dispersed the crowd, swinging nightsticks and brandishing guns. Walker and his family ran inside a local restaurant and were followed by the police, who clubbed the elderly grandfather until he collapsed on the floor. When Walker's mother tried to help, the state troopers turned on her. When Walker tried to shield his mother with his body, they pulled him away and shot him twice at point-blank range. He died shortly thereafter.*

In response, on March 7 Martin Luther King Jr. and John Lewis organized six hundred activists from their two organizations, the Southern Christian Leadership Conference (SCLC) and the Student

---

* A grand jury refused to bring charges against his murderer, State Trooper James Bonard Fowler. Finally, in 2010—forty-five years after killing Jackson—a seventy-seven-year-old Fowler was sentenced to six months in jail.

Nonviolent Coordinating Committee (SNCC), at the Brown Chapel African Methodist-Episcopal Church in Selma, Alabama. Their plan was to march peacefully, walking the entire fifty miles from Selma to Montgomery, the state capital, to protest Walker's death as well as the months of beatings and violence directed against local blacks who attempted to register to vote in Alabama.

As the marchers left Selma and walked across the steel arches of the Edmund Pettus Bridge—named for a Confederate general—and over the muddy banks of the Alabama River, they were confronted by state troopers. Also on hand was the sheriff of Dallas County, Jim Clark, who stood ready on horseback to use any means necessary to stop the protest. Sheriff Clark was every bit as unhinged and hate-filled as Connor, and known for his links to Ku Klux Klan groups.

Just one minute after instructing the protesters—men, women, children, and the elderly—to go home, the troopers rushed the crowd, tossing tear gas and swinging cattle prods, nightsticks, or makeshift weapons like a hose laced with barbed wire, attacking old and young alike. Some protesters ran, only to be chased down by one of Clark's mounted henchman; others were attacked as they kneeled silently and prayed for God's help.

"Get those god-damned niggers!" Clark shouted as he waded into the crowd, striking anyone in his path. It was a bloodbath. Dozens were sent to the hospital. The SNCC's Lewis was clubbed in the head; he thought he had finally reached the end. "People are going to die here," the twenty-five-year-old civil rights leader recalled thinking as he was attacked. "I'm going to die here." The events of "Bloody Sunday," as it quickly became known, were captured by print and television journalists—some of whom were also attacked—and was broadcast across the country that night. More televised bloodshed for the living rooms of America.

Two days later there was another march, this time led by King. He stopped after crossing the bridge—as directed by a federal court order. Still, that march claimed another life: A Boston minister, the Reverend James Reeb, a married man with four children, was attacked by Klansmen that night, dying from his wounds a few days later.

On March 15 President Johnson addressed the nation and promised complete solidarity with the civil rights movement. He was now going to send an unprecedented *second* civil rights bill up to Capitol Hill to guarantee the right of all Americans to vote. Then, in a moment that shocked many, Johnson closed his speech by looking into the cameras and co-opting the words of the movement, sung and shouted by tens of thousands over the years, pausing momentarily between each word to allow the full weight of the moment to sink in: "And we shall overcome," intoned the president.

Watching television at a friend's house that night, King later recalled, he wept tears of joys. On March 21 King led some three thousand protesters on a third march from Selma across the Edmund Pettus Bridge to Montgomery, protected the entire way by the Alabama National Guard, now under the direction and orders of the US government. Governor Wallace could do nothing but peek out at the victorious protesters, hiding his shameful face behind the curtains of the state capitol.

Exactly a month later, on April 21, the World's Fair opened for its second and final season, still proclaiming, despite the bloody events of the previous four months, a utopian standard of "Peace Through Understanding." The message, by now, either seemed utterly meaningless or desperately needed to be said again and again. For this opening day, President Johnson sent Vice President Hubert H. Humphrey to address the thousands of VIPs—including Governor Nelson A. Rockefeller, Mayor Robert F. Wagner Jr., and West Berlin's Mayor Willy Brandt, who also addressed the crowd—in the Fair's Singer Bowl. Afterward, the smiling Humphrey walked among the Fair faithful next to Chief Justice Earl Warren, taking in the sights and being followed everywhere he went. HUMPHREY STARS AS SHOW REOPENS, the *New York Times* exclaimed the next day.

If only the vice president had been that popular at the White House. Just two months before attending the Fair, Humphrey wrote a plaintive memo to Johnson, pleading with him to get out of Vietnam lest it rip apart the Democratic Party and damage support for his extensive domestic agenda. There would be no better time than the present: "1965 is the year of minimum political risk," he argued; if they acted now, they cold repel any "political repercussions from the Republican Right."

For his political honesty, the VP was shunned by the president, who did not seek his opinion on the matter for more than a year. Instead, Johnson heeded the voices of his generals and Secretary McNamara. On March 8, Johnson approved the use of US Marines in Vietnam. By April, Operation Rolling Thunder was carpet bombing North Vietnam, the precise targets picked by President Johnson himself, now convinced that such air warfare would bring a quick end to the conflict.

However, even as American troops were busy fighting in Vietnam—or occasionally being sent to Alabama to protect American citizens from the KKK—the World's Fair managed to hold a celebratory second season opening. There was another parade with Disney characters and dancers, Miss America, and special guest Olympic runner Abebe Bikila of Ethiopia, who carried with him a message from Ethiopian Emperor Haile Selassie as he ran from Manhattan to Flushing Meadow—a publicity stunt dreamed up by Moses personally to draw attention to the Fair's African republics and highlight the Fair's international attractions.

The second opening day also benefited from far sunnier weather than the year before, resulting in more than 150,000 visitors—60,000 more than the Fair's opening day a year earlier. Happily for Moses, another planned protest from a local CORE chapter failed to materialize on opening day. But four days later, a hundred peaceful protesters marched with signs denouncing Mayor Wagner, accusing him of doing nothing to fix the slums or schools or address police brutality in the ghettos. The protest, held in front of the New York City Pavilion, was quiet and peaceful and didn't interfere with Fairgoers—only 110,614 of whom showed up that day, a disappointing turnout for a weekend date and probably due to the chilly weather (and news of yet another protest march).

Real trouble began when a much smaller group of white teenagers from Brooklyn's East New York neighborhood, claiming to be part of a organization called SPONGE—or the Society for the Prevention of Negroes Getting Everything—led a counterprotest against CORE. Although some carried signs proclaiming their support for Governor Wallace, it wasn't so much a protest as it was an opportunity for them to harass the civil rights activists.

George Schiffer, a lawyer for CORE, complained to the Fair's security chief, Stephen P. Kennedy, the former New York City police commissioner. He asked that the East New York group stage their protest in another area of the Fairgrounds. "I don't see any pickets," Kennedy deadpanned. "I don't see any disorder. I just see people enjoying the fresh air and seeking peace through understanding."

"I wouldn't be surprised if you sent them over here," Schiffer shot back.

Not long after, a fight broke out between the groups, and a CORE picketer was punched in the face; only then did Kennedy's guards get involved. Although the melee was over shortly after it began, the incident was further proof that racism and ignorance were not confined to the states of the Old Confederacy; there was plenty of such sentiment to go around in New York City, even a melting pot like Queens.

Soon after the NAACP got wind of a song that was featured in the Chrysler Pavilion's new show and quickly lodged a complaint. The song, "Dem Bolts," was a play on the old minstrel show tune "Dem Bones." Although at first the carmaker changed some of the offending words—dropping the *Amos 'n' Andy*–like "dem" in favor of "them"—the Detroit automaker eventually scrapped the song rather than risk a national boycott of their cars, which the civil rights group threatened. Similarly, an employment agency placed a newspaper advertisement—"WANTED: Blue-Eyed Blondes"—for jobs at the World's Fair. The NAACP immediately raised a red flag. Just as quickly, Moses wrote a letter to the group and other civil rights organizations explaining the Fair had nothing to do with the offending ad, nor did it endorse racial hiring policies. The agency quickly withdrew the ad and apologized.

In the first weeks of the '65 Fair, more trouble brewed between the American-Israel Pavilion and the Jordan Pavilion. The American Jewish

Congress had successfully sued for the right to hand out flyers in front of the Jordan Pavilion denouncing the offending mural; in retaliation, the Action Committee on American-Arab Relations handed out flyers in front of the American-Israel Pavilion telling Americans not to purchase "Israeli War Bonds." (That provoked the pro-Israeli group to set up a free lunch of kosher bologna and beer, taunting the pro-Palestinian group to partake in the free food.)

As the opposing groups continued to distribute their flyers day after day, tempers flared. On May 1 a group of Israelis taunted a group handing out the anti-Israel flyers. Soon the Pinkerton police were separating two men. The entire episode was hardly the World's Fair's finest moment: Over the course of the Fair's two seasons, the opposing groups made sure the seemingly intractable problems of the Middle East extended to Flushing Meadow.

By the spring of 1965, among the Fair's other problems was the stewing violence that was enveloping New York City. On May 22 an elderly woman was standing at a Queens subway station awaiting her train, when a twelve-year-old girl approached her. Without saying a word, the girl plunged a knife into the woman until she bleed to death. That very same night, at Flushing Meadow, a group of young people snuck into the Fair by riding in the back of a delivery truck for a small fee. Karnick Yeterian, a twenty-year-old dental technician from the Bronx, and his friends decided to jump off the truck early, figuring they wouldn't have to pay the driver. When the driver's friends demanded Yeterian pay his nickel for being snuck inside, he just ignored them and set out to see the Fair. That's when Henry Roman, age fourteen, jumped the dental technician and threw him to the ground; then Raphael Villa, fifteen, plunged a hunting knife into his chest. Another murder, this time over a nickel.

The crimes were unrelated, but to the citizens of New York—particularly Queens, where both murders took place—they illustrated one fact: In Birmingham, innocent children were killed for the color of their skin; in New York City, children killed over nickels, or for no reason all.

By June the burgeoning anti–Vietnam War movement had also crept into the Fairgrounds, when the Student Peace Union passed out flyers in front of the US Federal Pavilion, even though they had been denied the right to do so by Moses, who was still dealing with the political migraine from the American-Israel/Jordan Pavilion mess. The quartet of students were largely ignored by Fairgoers before being removed. One young Fair worker, Michael Cohen, age nineteen, reported to work at the Wisconsin Pavilion with a placard that read ALL HANDS OFF VIETNAM, or at least tried to: He was stopped at the gate by the Pinkerton police, had his Fair pass revoked, and had to pay $2.50 for a ticket to go to work.

For whatever reason, Moses granted permission for an August rally by an organization called Women Strike for Peace, which wanted to commemorate the dropping of the atomic bomb in Japan as well as call for the end of hostilities in Vietnam. On August 6 four hundred women dressed in black, under the careful watch of the Pinkerton guard, marched silently—they were allowed to picket as long as they did not disturb Fairgoers' fun—around the Unisphere. At other times of the day, they marched to the Japanese Pavilion and handed out flyers asking Fairgoers to remember the tens of thousands who had died in the flash of a mushroom cloud.

In Washington, DC, on that same August day, President Johnson signed the Voting Rights Act of 1965, which had been passed by over-whelming majorities in the House of Representatives and the US Senate. It was the second historic legislative victory for the Johnson administration and the postwar civil rights movement, which had fought for more than ten years to achieve equality under the law. While no one should have thought that the struggle for black freedom was over, the stated goals of groups headed by King, Lewis, and James L. Farmer Jr. had now been achieved. There would be plenty more to do, but one era of the movement was over—at least to those millions of Americans who mis-takenly thought that eradicating inequality could be accomplished with the stroke of a pen. In reality, the struggle to redeem America's racist soul was just beginning.

For those African Americans who could already vote—in places like New York, Chicago, Boston, and Los Angeles—freedom and equality meant something else entirely; the Voting Rights Act of 1965 wasn't going to radically alter their lives. The de facto desegregation that they had been living with was not going to change. For them, the legislative changes delivered over the last year were far too little and far too late. Their anger was about to boil over, just like it had the previous summer in Harlem and Bedford-Stuyvesant, only this time it would be the Watts section of Los Angeles that would light a fire that the nation could not ignore.

32

"Beatles Say—Dylan Shows the Way"
—Melody Maker, January 9, 1965

As the World's Fair entered its final weeks, the Beatles arrived in New York on August 13 to kick-start their 1965 North American tour. The *New York Times* issued a friendly warning to the band: Since their last US concert, at the Forest Hills Tennis Stadium eleven months earlier, the musical landscape had shifted dramatically. For the first time since their stateside debut the previous February, the Beatles had competition.

Under a blaring six-column headline—THE BEATLES WILL MAKE THE SCENE HERE AGAIN, BUT THE SCENE HAS CHANGED—the *Times'* pop music critic, Robert Shelton, argued that although the group had inspired a seismic "upheaval in pop music, mores, fashion, hair styles and manners," the Liverpool quartet no longer had a monopoly over the charts. In 1965, pop radio had become a free-for-all.

From January to August, a dizzying array of groups had snared No. 1 hits on the *Billboard* charts, including the Supremes, the Four Tops, the Temptations, and the Beach Boys. There was also a steady onslaught of mop-topped British Invasion groups attempting to cash in on the Beatles' popularity, like Herman's Hermits, Wayne Fontana and the Mindbenders, and Freddie and the Dreamers. There were even home-grown Beatles imitators like Gary (son of Jerry) Lewis and the Playboys, who began a string of hits starting with "This Diamond Ring." Also scoring their first No. 1 hit on this side of the Atlantic were the Beatles' friendly rivals, the Rolling Stones, with "(I Can't Get No) Satisfaction," an instant classic that stayed atop the charts for a full month. With Keith Richards's full-throttle, fuzzed-out guitar and Mick Jagger's snarling vocals, "(I Can't Get No) Satisfaction" was edgy, dark, and dangerous. It made the Beatles sound like bumble-gum pop.

Although the Beatles were an indisputable global phenomenon—having already sold some one hundred million singles and twenty-five million albums worldwide—from January to August 1965, they had occupied the top spot on the US charts for only five weeks with three different singles. An amazing feat, no doubt, but it paled in comparison to the band's chart domination in 1964: six No. 1 singles (at one point they held the top spot for fourteen consecutive weeks); five Top 10 hits; two Top 20 songs; plus another that reached the Top 40. So dominant were the Beatles in 1964 that, during a week that April, just as the World's Fair was about to open, they had twelve singles on *Billboard*'s Hot 100 chart, including the top five spots. By August 1965, the *Times* could legitimately claim the Beatles had suffered "a slight popularity decline."

Not that the Beatles had any reason to worry. Still in their early twenties, John Lennon and Paul McCartney were arguably the most popular songwriting duo in pop music. Bands began to follow the Beatles' lead, and even occasionally surpass them. The Animals, who like the Beatles hailed from England's gritty, industrial north, played a particular brand of hard-edged R&B-inflected pop, and scored a major hit in September 1964 with their rendition of "House of the Rising Sun," an old folk standard. Woody Guthrie and Lead Belly had both recorded the song, as did Joan Baez and Bob Dylan. The Animals' version, however, would become the definitive one.

Instead of strumming the song's simple chord progression like a folkie would, guitarist Hilton Valentine turned the old standard into an instantly catchy riff, while Alan Price added haunting blasts of electric organ as vocalist Eric Burdon sang in a blues-drenched, soul-weary voice. By September 1964 the song was lodged atop the charts—the first British Invasion band after the Beatles to hit No. 1—and stayed there for three weeks. This prompted *The New Yorker* to compare the two bands in whimsical political terms: The Animals were new and exciting, like Bobby Kennedy; meanwhile the Beatles were passé, a la Hubert H. Humphrey.

The track was unlike any previous pop recording: The Animals weren't pining for a girl or craving some innocent romance; they were singing about spiritual ruination. By the summer of 1965, songs with mature lyrics were state-of-the-art for rock 'n' roll, and it was a trend, as the *Times* pointed out, "not reflected on Beatles records."

The Beatles knew it, too. As Lennon would confess years later, in those early Beatlemania days, he and McCartney didn't worry much about lyrics. "The words were almost irrelevant," Lennon said, while McCartney admitted, "We weren't that fussy about [the words], because it's only a rock 'n' roll song. I mean, it's not literature." However, others didn't feel that way. When asked at a 1965 press conference about the significance of lyrics, Dylan declared, "The words are just as important as the music. There would be no music without the words." Actual poets like Allen Ginsberg and Michael McClure couldn't have agreed more: They hailed Dylan as one of their own, a literary adherent to their Beat Generation.

But lyrically speaking, the most interesting song in 1965 was "Eve of Destruction"—an anthem of anxiety penned by a nineteen-year-old West Coast songwriter named P. F. Sloan. Recorded by gravel-voiced ex-folkie Barry McGuire, it became a No. 1 hit in September 1965, going on to sell more than one million copies. And unlike any Beatles song, "Eve of Destruction" referenced Red China, Vietnam, and the plight of the young American draftee: "You're old enough to kill, but not for voting." For the first time, young Americans—millions of whom Robert Moses was still hoping to attract to his World's Fair—could listen to the music flowing from their radios and hear about the anxieties of their generation: the Vietnam War, civil rights, the Cold War, and the threat of a nuclear holocaust—and all of that in just over three and a half minutes. Pop music was no longer *just* entertainment.

The music industry soon labeled this trend "folk-rock"—the marriage of the meaningful lyrics of folk music to the sounds of a rock band. The prevailing conventional wisdom of the time regarded rock 'n' roll as ephemeral pop made for teenyboppers, vacuous fluff played by musical neophytes on electric instruments, whereas folk music was authentic American music, passed down from generation to generation and performed on acoustic instruments by serious musicians like Baez, Pete Seeger, and, of course, Dylan. Folk didn't follow trends. The topical "protest songs" folksingers wrote—or interpreted—were concerned with politics and social justice. They didn't shout "yeah, yeah, yeah" or wear mop-tops. Nor did they trouble themselves with vulgar commercial concerns such as hit records (at least not publicly). The union of these two disparate musical genres was the next step in the evolution of rock 'n' roll, and the Beatles—the originators of the rock renaissance—were in danger of being left behind.

However, if the Beatles were feeling any pressure after landing at JFK International Airport in mid-August, they didn't show it. Unlike on previous tours, the Fab Four didn't wave to the crowd waiting hours for their arrival. Instead, they shuffled into a limo and headed via police escort to the Warwick Hotel in midtown Manhattan, where they eluded 1,500 fans stationed outside the hotel by sneaking in a side door. The band still met reporters in a de rigueur press conference, and were as quick-witted as ever, but the buoyancy of that magical first meeting with the American media was gone. It was clear the Beatles were weary of the endless interviews—"farcical affairs," Lennon called them—touring, and Beatlemania in general.

It only took one glance at the cover of the band's fourth UK album, *Beatles for Sale,* released in late December 1964, to see the transformation. In the photo the foursome, set against an out-of-focus autumnal background, look dour and dog-tired. They're wearing heavy overcoats with the collars pulled up and thick scarves, as if a storm were heading their way.* The cracks in the band's public facade were beginning to show.

Inspired by the limitless parameters of Dylan's poetic musings, Lennon began exploring more sophisticated themes in his lyrics. With songs like "I'm a Loser," which despite its ironically upbeat tempo, featured oddly confessional lyrics—"Although I laugh and I act like a clown/beneath this mask I am wearing a frown." "That's me in my Dylan period," Lennon later said of the song.

This new mood carried over to the band's latest album, *Help!* whose title track and first single was a desperate plea—literally—for help. But

---

* Not that US fans ever saw it: The band's American record company routinely repackaged their albums, changing photos and songs as they saw fit. Instead, in America the album was morphed into *Beatles '65,* with different tracks and a series of cheeky photographs of the Fab Four looking like mod versions of eccentric English gentlemen, sitting in their tailored suits and holding umbrellas indoors.

once again the song's message was obscured by the track's upbeat tempo; it topped the *Billboard* charts in late August, sounding as optimistic as anything the Beatles had ever recorded. "I was fat and depressed and I *was* crying out for 'Help,'" Lennon said in one of his last interviews.

Regardless of the band's studio accomplishments, onstage their musical and lyrical innovations were lost amidst the howling, hysterical teenage fans. And on their ten-city, two-week North American tour—for which each Beatle was reportedly insured for $5.5 million by Lloyd's of London—the screams would only get louder as the Beatles made history again. The band alternated between enormous outdoor sports arenas such as Atlanta County Stadium (like Shea, it was one of the new multipurpose civic stadiums being built around the country) and Chicago's venerable Comiskey Park, and indoor venues such as San Francisco's Cow Palace and Memorial Coliseum in Portland, Oregon, the latter show immortalized in verse by Ginsberg, who attended the gig, much to the band's delight. ("We hear that Allen Ginsberg is in the audience," announced Lennon in between songs from the stage. "We send him our regards.")

No pop band or performer—including Elvis—ever played to audiences this size. And the tour's opening show, at Shea Stadium in Flushing, Queens, would be, in the words of the *New York Times*, the biggest gathering of Beatles fans "ever seen and heard in one place."

The show at Shea was the idea of New York promoter Sid Bernstein. A showbiz veteran, Bernstein had booked the Beatles' two concerts at Carnegie Hall in February 1964, but found the venue was too small to meet ticket demand. "We had turned away thousands of fans," Bernstein said. The hunt began for a larger New York venue. At first Madison Square Garden was considered, but ultimately was deemed too small. This was a first: No pop group had even been too big for such a large-scale arena. Then it struck Bernstein: Shea Stadium, home of the New York Mets (who were conveniently out of town in mid-August).

Shea was a brand-new facility, having opened on April 17, 1964—just four days before the World's Fair. It was easily accessible by subway, the Long Island Rail Road, and a battery of highways, newly refurbished by Robert Moses. In fact, it would be as if the Beatles were actually playing the World's Fair itself. Thousands of teenagers—Moses' target audience—could, ostensibly, attend the Fair during the day and see the Beatles at Shea that night. In addition, Shea was nearly four times the size of the fifteen-thousand-seat Forest Hills Tennis Stadium, where they had played the previous August.

"I suggested Shea Stadium . . . to the Beatles' manager, Brian Epstein," recalled Bernstein. "He asked, 'Do you think we could sell it out?' and I told him 'I'll give you $10 for every unsold seat.'" He wouldn't have to pay a single dollar: The Beatles sold out all 55,600 seats—an unprecedented audience in the annals of popular music.

On the evening of August 15, the band flew from Manhattan to Queens via a Boeing Vertol 107-II helicopter. Although R&B saxophonist King Curtis, one of the many opening acts on the bill, was in the middle of his set as the Beatles' helicopter passed over the stadium, a deejay broke into the PA system to alert the crowds of their arrival. "You hear that up there? Listen . . . *it's the Beatles!*" The stadium exploded with the light of thousands of flashbulbs as fans aimed their cameras skyward, snapping photos as the Beatles flew past. The band peered through the helicopter's windows at the ocean of fans below. "It was terrifying at first when we saw the crowds," recalled George Harrison, "but I don't think I ever felt so exhilarated in all my life."

The helicopter landed on the heliport on top of the Port Authority Building at the World's Fair. As they exited their helicopter, they waved to the two hundred or so local Queens kids, who only had to walk down the street and wait by the metal fence just on the other side of the Grand Central Parkway. Immediately, the Beatles were corralled into the Port Authority Building, ushered into a Wells Fargo armored truck, and driven the short distance across the Fairgrounds to Shea. Thousands of Fairgoers probably didn't take notice of the armored truck carrying four of the most famous people in the world as they wandered Flushing Meadow that night.

After arriving at Shea, the truck drove straight into the bowels of the stadium, and the band found Ed Sullivan waiting for them in the visiting team's dugout. Sullivan's production company had thirteen cameras stationed throughout the stadium to document the concert (it would air as a television special in 1967). As the Beatles stood in the dugout looking at the frenzied fans, they couldn't help but laugh; the scene was absurd, Fellini-esque. "It seemed like millions of people," McCartney recalled. "But we were ready for it." They were probably the only ones. Jagger and Richards were watching from the front row behind the Mets' dugout. The Rolling Stones frontman seemed shaken by the spectacle of mass hysteria. "It's frightening," Jagger told a friend.

At 9:17 p.m. after Sullivan introduced them, the band emerged from the dugout in matching black pants, boots, and tan jackets, holding onto their guitars and waving to the throngs of fans as they made their way to the makeshift stage near second base. Immediately the 55,600-strong crowd exploded. Once onstage the Beatles tore into "Twist and Shout," the first of their twelve-song, thirty-minute set, which included their most recent hits like "I Feel Fine," "Ticket to Ride," "Help!" and "Can't Buy Me Love." The *New York Times* declared that the noise generated by the screeching masses was true to "the classic Greek meaning of the word pandemonium—the region of all demons."

Twin rows of fifty 100-watt amplifiers—specially made for the occasion by Vox—ran along the baselines, but barely a note was heard by anyone, not the band, the fans, or even Bernstein, who stood directly underneath the stage with Epstein. Scores of fans fainted, while dozens of others stormed the field and hopped over barricades while desperately trying to elude police. The fans were so excited to see their idols, to be *this close* to four live Beatles, they couldn't be bothered to actually listen to the music. "It was ridiculous!" Lennon later complained. "We couldn't hear ourselves sing.... You can see it in the film, George and I aren't even bothering playing half the chords, and we were just messing about." Lennon even admitted to a British reporter a few days after the concert that he wasn't always sure what key the band was in. The music had become almost meaningless compared to the spectacle of the Beatles themselves.

When their thirty minutes were up—per their manager's instructions, they were not to play "a minute more or a minute less"—they waved good-bye then hurried into a nearby car and sped off. Several young female fans had to be carried from their seats to a makeshift first-aid station. A group of girls in the first row begged the police along the baselines for a souvenir from the field. "Please, please," they cried. "Give us some blades of the grass. They walked on the grass."

While the Beatles were disenchanted with the musical quality of the concert, their promoter, at least, was ecstatic over the box office receipts. "Over 55,000 people saw the Beatles at Shea Stadium," bragged Bernstein. "We took $304,000, the greatest gross ever [at that time] in the history of show business." According to *Variety*, the sum "shattered all existing . . . box office records." And, as promised, Bernstein handed over $160,000 to the Beatles, but not before he made Epstein another offer: He would guarantee the Beatles $250,000 if the band returned to Shea Stadium the following summer, this time for two shows.

The Beatles' Shea Stadium concert had shown—for anyone who still needed proof—that the Fab Four were no passing fad; the sight of 55,600 frenzied teenagers proved the Beatles were a commercial entity unlike anything the entertainment industry had ever seen. A year after resurrecting the rock 'n' roll industry, the Beatles' Shea Stadium concert redefined the economic reality of touring; by the end of the 1960s, such concerts would become a huge windfall for record companies and a massive source of revenue for rock bands.

Earlier that summer, in June, while the Beatles were maturing, thanks to his influence, Dylan entered Columbia Records' recording studio on Seventh Avenue in Manhattan to begin the sessions that became his next album, *Highway 61 Revisited*. On June 16, backed by an ad-hoc rock band that included guitarist Michael Bloomfield of the Paul Butterfield Blues Band and an improvised organ riff by Al Kooper, who was now working as a session musician, he recorded "Like a Rolling Stone." This incendiary electric vamp was a musical revolution in six minutes and thirteen seconds. Before recording the song, Dylan had been pursuing literary ambitions, working on a novel and a number of plays. But after culling the lyrics from an angry letter he wrote—which he described as "a long piece of vomit"—while flying back from the UK, he had found his true voice. "I'd never written anything like that before and it suddenly came to me that was what I should do," he told a journalist. "After writing that, I wasn't interested in writing a novel or a play . . . I want to write songs."

Although a number of tracks on Dylan's previous album, *Bringing It All Back Home*, had featured a rollicking backup band, he had never recorded anything like this. Dylan took an acetate recording of the finished track to the Woodstock, New York, home of his manager, Albert Grossman, who invited friends to an impromptu listening party. For Paul Rothschild, who would later gain fame as the producer of the Doors, the song was a revelation. "I had them play the fucking thing five times straight before I could say anything," he said. "What I realized while I was sitting there was that one of US—one of the so-called Village hipsters—was making music that could compete with THEM—the Beatles and the Stones and the Dave Clark Five—without sacrificing any of the integrity of folk music or the power of rock 'n' roll. . . . I knew the song was a smash, and yet I was consumed with envy because it was the best thing I'd heard any of our crowd do and I knew it was going to turn the tables on our nice, comfortable lives."

Four days after the song was released as a single, Dylan played the Newport Folk Festival. His first appearance that July 1965 weekend was at an afternoon songwriting workshop, where he played acoustic versions of "All I Really Want to Do" and "Mr. Tambourine Man." He was set to play the following night, as the weekend's headliner. On Sunday, July 24, while the crowd applauded his arrival, Dylan, in a black leather jacket and with a Fender Stratocaster strapped around his shoulder, took to a darkened stage with a rock band that including Bloomfield and Kooper. When the lights went on, there was Dylan with an electric blues band ripping through a roaring version of "Maggie's Farm."

When the song was over, there was confusion. Mixed in with the tepid applause was what sounded like boos and catcalls. Someone shouted "Bring back Cousin Emmy!" referring to the old-time Appalachian country singer who had performed earlier in the day. Undaunted, the band forged ahead, playing a limp version of "Like a Rolling Stone," then currently climbing up the charts. There were more angry shouts: "Play folk music! . . . Sellout! . . . Put away that electric guitar!" The band struggled through "It Takes a Lot to Laugh, It Takes a Train to Cry" before cutting the song short amid an unruly chorus of boos. Kooper, however, later said that's not what happened at all: "Those weren't boos, they were cries of 'More! More!'" Whatever the crowd was yelling, Dylan apparently had had enough. "That's it!" he shouted and walked off. As Kooper noted, that really wasn't strange either: The band, which had only begun rehearsals the day before, only knew three songs.

Ultimately, Dylan was coaxed back onstage to pacify the crowd. Whatever they thought of his music, they had reasonably expected a longer set. He ran through "Mr. Tambourine Man" and "It's All Over Now, Baby Blue," a fitting end to his career as the spokesman of his generation. In film footage of the performance, what looks like a single tear can be seen streaking down Dylan's left cheek.

While others debated the meaning of Dylan's appearance at Newport, the man himself laid low. "Like a Rolling Stone" was moving up the charts; by late August it would land at the No. 2 spot on *Billboard*'s Hot 100 (kept out of the top spot by the Beatles' "Help!"). Dylan was now a pop star with a Top 10 single.

When he reemerged, it was to play the first show of his upcoming American tour at Forest Hills Tennis Stadium on August 28. Just two weeks after the Beatles had proven their staying power at Shea Stadium in nearby Flushing, Dylan would defiantly confront his angry audience at Forest Hills, a fifteen-thousand-seat, open-air stadium where the US Open was traditionally held. It was the second history-making rock concert in Queens in as many weeks, while within the confines of the World's Fair, Guy Lombardo and his Royal Canadians were holding court six nights a week—just as Robert Moses insisted they should.

Unlike Newport, the sold-out crowd at Forest Hills knew exactly what to expect. Dylan gave them fair warning in the *New York Times*. "It's all music: no more, no less," he said a few days before the concert. "I know in my own mind what I'm doing. If anyone has imagination he'll know what I'm doing. If they can't understand my songs they're missing something." He went on to distance himself from his early albums. "I get very bored with my old songs," he complained. "I can't sing 'With God on My Side' for fifteen years." Dylan admitted he didn't have all the details worked out yet, but there was one thing fans should expect: The concert would be loud. "I'll have some electricity," he warned.

To many of Dylan's fans, the sight of electric guitars and amplifiers was a sign that their hero had betrayed them and their cause. So was the black leather jacket (one journalist even referred to it as a "sell-out jacket"), the Cuban heels and black shades that he began to wear, were just more proof. But the final insult was the presence of New York's cheesy Top 40 deejay, Murray the K—aka "the Fifth Beatle"—who walked onto the Forest Hills stage and introduced Dylan in his patented, faux-hipster lingo. "It's something new," he told the crowd. "It's not rock. It's not folk. It's this new thing called Dylan."

The crowd unleashed a howl of boos. Dylan, who had once stood on the same stage as Martin Luther King Jr. is now cavorting with Murray the K? That was more than his New Left–leaning college fans could take. Soon Dylan appeared onstage armed with an acoustic guitar and harmonica. If the crowd was angry, they didn't show it. As he played recent material like "She Belongs to Me," "Gates of Eden," and "Love Minus Zero/No Limit," they listened intently and applauded in all the right spots. It seemed like the battle was over.

But after intermission Dylan returned with his Fender Stratocaster and a band that included guitarist Robbie Robertson and drummer Levon Helm (both of whom would later form The Band), and once again Kooper on organ, and the latter's childhood friend from Queens and musical partner, Harvey Brooks, on bass. Dylan issued a warning to the band before taking the stage. "I don't know what it will be like out there," he told them. "It's going to be some kind of a carnival, and I want you all to know that up front. So just go out there and keep playing no matter how weird it gets."

Once onstage they kicked off with "Tombstone Blues" from *Highway 61 Revisited*, which would be released the following week. If the Beatles' Shea Stadium concert was an example of hysterical idol worship, then

Dylan's Forest Hills concert was a revolt against their hero. The Queens crowd began to boo violently. At the end of each song, they shouted cat-calls that made Newport seem like an old-time religious revival. "Traitor!" someone shouted. "Where's Ringo?" mocked another. Undeterred, the band kept playing, including a totally revamped "I Don't Believe You" from the acoustic *Another Side* LP and newer songs like "From a Buick 6" and "Maggie's Farm." Dylan was confronting his unruly audience head-on, offering no quarter.

The atmosphere was violent, chaotic. Fruit flew through the air, pelting the musicians. Shouts of "We want the old Dylan!" ceded to organized chants of "SCUMBAG!" More than a dozen kids blew past police, rushed onto the stage, and ran around between the baffled musicians. One fan knocked Kooper off his seat. "I think the audience at Forest Hills reacted like they did because they read about Newport," Kooper recalled, "and in their minds, they thought booing was the right thing to do." Dylan instructed his band to draw out the haunting intro to "Ballad of a Thin Man" for five minutes to cool the crowd down. The ploy worked. As Dylan sang the song's soon-to-be famous line—"Something's going on here, but you don't know what it is, do ya, Mr. Jones?"—he had come face-to-face with fifteen thousand angry Mr. Joneses.

Then, during the finale, the tide changed again. As the band roared their way through Dylan's hit single "Like a Rolling Stone," the audience shifted gears. Now they were singing along—they even knew the words!—and their chorus filled the breezy, late summer air. This was only the second time Dylan had played it live, but the fans were ecstatic throughout the six-minute-plus song.

Dylan had won, and on his terms. DYLAN CONQUERS UNRULY CROWD reported the *New York Times*. Later at the after-party, the musicians were still spooked, but Dylan was ecstatic. He went around hugging his band. "That was fabulous! It was great!" he exclaimed. "It was like a carnival." Several days later, while flying to Los Angeles to play the Hollywood Bowl, Dylan was asked for his reaction to the Queens crowd. "I thought it was great," he said. "I really did. If I said anything else I'd be a liar."

After the respective concerts at Shea Stadium and the Forest Hills Tennis Stadium—neither rock 'n' roll nor the Beatles or Dylan would ever be the same. For the Beatles, the powerful screams of their fans threatened to drown out everything the band had achieved: their innovative music, their joy of live performance, and nearly their sanity. "They gave their screams and their money," Harrison said in the mid-1990s of the band's Beatlemania years, "but the Beatles gave their nervous systems." The band, disillusioned with being worshipped, ended their touring career a year later. On August 29, 1966, just one year after their triumph in Flushing, they played their last official concert at San Francisco's Candlestick Park. Although they would reinvent themselves again and again over the next three years, each time expanding the scope of pop music, by the end of 1969 the band would exist in name only.

For Dylan, his historic concert at Forest Hills was the culmination of his journey from the North Country of Minnesota. Having achieved the critical success that other entertainers could only dream of, he turned his back on the expectations and political rhetoric of his fans. He refused the musical and lyrical limitations of folk music and in the process reinvented rock 'n' roll to fit his own poetic standards. Dylan openly declared his artistic freedom from his audience, who wanted him to be the poet laureate of their generation. But he wasn't interested in the job. "Don't follow leaders, watch your parking meters," as he sang in "Subterranean Homesick Blues," wasn't just a clever line; he meant it.

By 1966, when he continued his tour in Europe, during one show in England, as fans serenaded him with boos and catcalls, a dispirited Dylan deadpanned, "Aw, come on. These are *all* protest songs." The message—and the joke—was lost on the crowd. During one widely bootlegged concert in Manchester, England, a fan famously shouted "Judas!" in response to his new rock 'n' roll outlook. A half-century later, Dylan is still carrying the scars of those years. "[These people] tried to pin the name Judas on me. Judas, the most hated name in human history!" he told *Rolling Stone* in 2012. "And for what? For playing an electric guitar?"

It's only fitting that the historic Shea and Forest Hills concerts took place against the backdrop of the World's Fair. While the Fair promised a new world of peace, understanding, and fraternity among nations, millions of young Americans who had already enjoyed Moses' exhibition saw through the illusion. Many more of them, the more politically savvy, felt that the Tomorrow-Land world of the Fair, no matter how noble its intentions, was a technological chimera bought and paid for by the political and corporate elites who had waged the Cold War, had their finger on the A-bomb, had resisted civil rights for millions of Americans, and had launched a new war in Vietnam. In August 1965, right outside the gates of the Moses' fabricated Eden, American youths were turning to new, more liberating forms of entertainment—even if they took umbrage with some of their heroes' ideas. Soon this new music—embraced and celebrated by millons who recognized the beauty and power of rock 'n' roll—would spur on a cultural revolution that would upend the nation itself.

By December 1965, even Andy Warhol was trying to ride the rock 'n' roll wave. After getting a tip from a friend, he found an unconventional rock outfit dubbed the Velvet Underground at Café Bizarre; by April 1966, he was the band's manager and helped land them a recording contract (and designed their classic 1967 self-titled debut). An entirely new and different youth culture was taking shape, and in the summer of 1965, it made Moses' World's Fair seem old and woefully out of date.

Gone were the expectations that the Fair would break even ... what was not gone, however, was the patently evident fact that a great many people were, in the semi-dazed manner of Fairgoers, having a magical experience.
—"Goodbye to World's Fairs," *Harper's*, October 1965

It was an inescapable fact that the World's Fair was not going to reach 37.5 million visitors in its second season. Thomas J. Deegan had so blithely predicted the figure the previous November, but Robert Moses conceded failure with six black-and-white signs he posted over the Grand Central Parkway and other expressways leading to the Fair in September 1965. The signs claimed that more than 50 million people would have attended the Fair by the time it ended, 20 million less than Moses and New York politicos had originally promised.

There was another problem with the signs: They were illegal. Moses, who had opposed advertising along his highways for decades, never sought permission from New York City Traffic Commissioner Henry A. Barnes to place the signage. He simply put them up, and at thirty-five words long, they were considered a traffic-jam-inducing road hazard. Barnes gave Moses forty-eight hours to take them down or, he told reporters, "I'll have my men remove them." Twenty-five years earlier during the 1939-40 World's Fair, Moses had given a similar order to Billy Rose, the show business promoter, who had placed an advertisement for his Aquacade exhibit about three hundred feet from where one of Moses' new signs hung. The Fair president now wrote Barnes—whom he regularly badmouthed—telling him to "keep his hairshirt on" and to "do his homework," claiming he was within his rights. The matter devolved into yet another public spat between Moses and a city official. Moses would win this battle. Like so many who had fought the Master Builder before him, Barnes backed down.

As the Fair neared the end of its run, the politicians were piling it on. City Councilman Paul O'Dwyer, who wanted to follow in his brother

William O'Dwyer's footsteps and become mayor of New York, suggested that the city assume control of the World's Fair—through "condemnation proceedings if necessary." O'Dwyer told the *Times*: "Going to the Fair has been a fine educational experience for the well-heeled. But there are three million people in the city who could not afford to go. I want them to be able to see the Fair." O'Dwyer's real motivation was likely to prevent City Comptroller Abraham Beame, also seeking the Democratic nomination for mayor, from stealing all the headlines. A Fair spokesman called the idea "politically motivated and silly." Moses refused to dignify it with a comment.

But Beame could not be laughed off or ignored. By now the city comptroller had issued an interim report on the Fair's financial management. Beame found that Moses had refused to hear competitive bids for big-ticket expenses like security (awarding the contract to the Pinkertons) and labor (hiring Allied Maintenance Company for around-the-clock service)—two expenses that left a lot of red on the Fair's balance sheets. Beame also claimed that Moses had spent millions on loans to certain pavilions—"improper payments," according to the comptroller—that could not be recouped, and that some items had been overpaid. An expensive air-conditioning unit had even been lost, the report said.

Moses refuted the charges immediately. Calling competitive bids "a waste of time," he found the weakest link in his opponent's case and attacked it: dust mops. In a statement to the press, he insisted the Fair hadn't paid three times for the same items—$58.25 worth of dust mops. Instead, he noted, the bills were lost, and auditors mistook the carbon copies for three bills for the same item. A simple enough mistake, but exactly the kind of minor detail that Moses could use to muddy the waters and claim Beame's report was "made on the basis of wholly irresponsible assumptions clearly refuted by the facts which the auditors had." Moses asserted that such an error "reflects upon their ability as auditors and the value of any of their judgments."

He also questioned the timing of Beame's report, as did others. "I deplore the timing of Beame's public attack on the Fair as so obviously a despicable campaign stunt," Dr. Ralph J. Bunche, the United Nations undersecretary and Fair director, wrote Moses. In the middle of all this negative news, Fair attendance was on an upswing: August had been the busiest month in Fair history, while on Sunday, September 5, the Fairgrounds were jam-packed with a record 317,310 customers.

Three days after his public statement against Beame's report, Moses issued a confidential memo to top Fair executives, noting that rumors of "a very large sum" to be set aside for cleaning up the Fairgrounds, demolition, and restoration of the park were "sheer rubbish." He explained, "There is a relatively small sum ticketed for these purposes, all of it legitimately, properly and necessarily set aside." It was still his intention, he claimed, to make "the largest possible payments to note holders." Despite what any politician said, or what kinds of accounting reports were released to the press, Moses was planning, just as he always had, for his post–World's Fair park.

After Beame secured the Democratic nomination for mayor on September 15, Moses wrote him a private letter, with a markedly different tone; if Beame did win, Moses would have to coexist with him. Not that such an occurrence was likely: Beame was already the underdog. His competitor, Representative John V. Lindsay, the blond Upper East Side congressman, whose movie star good looks and liberal political viewpoint were the Republican Party's answer to the Kennedys, was already highly favored. But Moses wasn't taking any chances.

It was in this private context that Moses chose to remind Beame that as "a director and member of the Fair Corporation," the city comptroller had voted to ratify the Pinkerton and Allied Maintenance contracts, over which his auditors were now chastising the World's Fair. Having revealed the ace up his sleeve, Moses extended an olive branch. "I have no desire to keep the pot boiling," he wrote. "I hope there will be no more reports with correctable errors and unsubstantiated innuendoes." Moses then offered Beame his assistance. "The city of New York has plenty of real problems. The World's Fair is not one of them. It will soon be history. If you are elected Mayor, I am prepared to lend my full cooperation and that of organizations with which I am associated. Cooperation, however, is a two-way street."

Meanwhile, Moses was engaged in confidential negotiations to pull off the public relations coup of a lifetime: getting the Holy Pontiff of the Roman Catholic Church, Pope Paul VI, to come to the World's Fair—and, in the process, creating an unbelievable amount of publicity for his exhibition. Moses had first planted the seeds in a November 1964 telegram to Cardinal Francis Spellman, who was staying at Rome's Grand Hotel during a session of the Second Vatican Council. A month later, thanks to Cardinal Spellman's intercession, Deegan had a private meeting with the pope in late December 1964 while in Rome on a family holiday. Moses had pressed him to personally invite the pontiff to the World's Fair. Deegan assured him he would try, but that Moses shouldn't get his hopes up. "It is a long, long shot," Deegan telegrammed the Master Builder from Rome on Christmas Eve 1964. "Please don't be disappointed if I don't score. Up to now in history, no one else has."

The ploy—the most unlikely of ideas—actually seemed to be working; at least a papal visit hadn't been ruled out yet. As of September 11, the pope was tentatively scheduled to come to New York for just one day and address the United Nations, a historic first on many levels: Such a visit would be the first time a pope set foot in the United States; it would mark the first time that millions of Catholic New Yorkers could see their pope in the flesh, or that a pontiff would address the General Assembly of the United Nations. His every word and deed would be followed by the world's media. While his trip would only last a day—fourteen hours to be exact—Pope Paul VI would, naturally, celebrate mass to a large outdoor crowd. The only question was: Where? Yankee Stadium was held out as an option, which, of course, Moses bitterly opposed.

Instead, Moses convinced his friend Cardinal Spellman—who as the Archbishop of New York was acting as the pope's official host—to use his own pull within the Vatican bureaucracy to lure the pontiff to either the Fair's Singer Bowl or nearby Shea Stadium. Having the pope at the same nearby venue that the Beatles had just sold out would lure more people to the Fair. And if the pope was that close to the exhibition, wouldn't it make sense for the Vicar of Christ to stop by the Vatican Pavilion, bestowing his blessing on the exhibit—and Moses' Fair?

The Master Builder, who never stopped dreaming big, was certainly going to try, and by the end of September, he had reason to hope: He had received a "for your eyes only" memo directly from Rome. At the end of his 14-hour trip to New York, the pope was to arrive at the Fair via bubble-top car at 10:30 p.m. on October 4, the note read, and would head directly to the Vatican Pavilion before returning to JFK Airport that night to fly home. Things could still change but, for now, that was the plan.

What Moses likely didn't know was that Cardinal Spellman and Pope Paul VI did not care for one another. As one of the most conservative and powerful Princes of the Church, Spellman was at ideological odds with the liberal pontiff, who continued the Vatican II reforms begun by his predecessor, the patron saint of liberal Catholics, Pope John XXIII (whom Spellman also disdained). Spellman wanted no part of reforming the church, and he swore before attending Vatican II, as the council was called, that "no change will get past the Statue of Liberty."

Spellman was also a vehement anti-Communist and one of the most vocal supporters of President Lyndon B. Johnson's Vietnam policy, publicly saying that anything "less than victory [in Vietnam] was inconceivable." The New York papers would soon be calling Vietnam "Spelly's War." Such pro-war sentiments were viewed as an embarrassment by the Vatican, putting America's most powerful bishop at odds with the peaceful decrees of Pope Paul VI and his predecessor, both of whom struggled to bring their church into the modern age. As Italians, the popes had seen firsthand the causes and effects of world war. Now Pope Paul was continuing his predecessor's attempts to make the Vatican a tool of peaceful diplomacy, opening up channels—official and unofficial—to the Soviet Union, China, and Vietnam. For Spellman, such a soft stance toward Communism was nothing less than heresy.

Spellman's antagonism, nevertheless, was well closeted. When it came to fulfilling his obligations, the cardinal fulfilled his duty. The pope's plane touched down at John F. Kennedy International Airport at 9:30 a.m. on October 4, on a brisk autumn morning, and Spellman was there to greet him.

"Welcome to America," he said to the pontiff with a warm smile.

"God bless you," said the pope, embracing him warmly.

The two huddled in the rear of a bubble-top open-air limousine—a necessary precaution since officials had been warned of a possible attempt on the pontiff's life—driving past crowds of New Yorkers who waved excitedly to the pope. Arriving at St. Patrick's Cathedral on Fifth Avenue, the seat of the cardinal's holy office, the men feasted at a private lunch in the walnut-paneled dining room in Spellman's luxurious private quarters.

Pope Paul didn't stay too long; he soon left to see President Johnson at the Waldorf Astoria—the first meeting between a pope and a US president on American soil. The cardinal thought he would be accompanying the pope, having acted as a liaison between the men, but he was informed that the pontiff had his own papal translators. Although a soft-spoken man and not prone to confrontation, Pope Paul was here on a mission and that mission—speaking directly with President Johnson about poverty, Vietnam, and India (where the pope had recently traveled) and addressing the United Nations—did not include Cardinal Spellman. No stranger to power, or how it was wielded, the cardinal knew he was being sidelined. For this pope, "Peace Through Understanding" was not just a slogan; it was the very reason he had come to New York.

After talking with President Johnson, the pope addressed the United Nations. The General Assembly was packed with representatives from all its member states (except Albania, which boycotted in protest) and VIPs like former First Lady Jacqueline Kennedy, accompanied by her brother-in-laws, Senator Robert F. Kennedy and Senator Edward Kennedy. Pope Paul, a frail-looking man with deep-set, even sad eyes, dressed in white vestments, received a standing ovation as he strode to the podium and addressed the General Assembly. The pontiff drew a line in the sand and let the entire world know what he thought of the Cold War and the Vietnam policies that the Johnson administration had embraced and that Cardinal Spellman had so eagerly supported.

Jamais plus la guerre!" the pope intoned in French, just one of the languages that he would speak that day. "No more war, never again war! Peace.

It is peace which must guide the destinies of peoples and all mankind." While allowing that defensive weapons were a foreseeable fact of life, he pleaded with the world's leaders to "drop your weapons; one cannot love while holding offensive weapons." Calling the United Nations "the world's greatest hope," the pope said that within its walls, all nations must be equal. He then warned his audience against the sin of pride that was at the root of the "struggles for prestige, for predominance, colonialism, egoism."

To anyone who was *really* listening, Pope Paul's words were a public admonishment to his errant cardinal and President Johnson and the foreign policy of the United States of America. For their part, Spellman and Johnson could do nothing but sit back, smile, and along with the other 2,200 dignitaries, applaud the pontiff. And just in case neither man got the message, that evening at an outdoor mass held at Yankee Stadium (against Moses' wishes), the pope was even more blunt: "Politics do not suffice to sustain a durable peace."

Pope Paul's pleas fell on deaf ears, none more deaf than those of Cardinal Spellman, who the following year would further embarrass the Vatican and the pope with yet more verbal warmongering. During a Christmas trip to visit American soldiers in Vietnam, Spellman reminded troops that they were "holy crusaders" waging "Christ's war against the Vietcong and the people of North Vietnam."

After the Yankee Stadium mass, just as Moses had wished, it was off to the World's Fair. The pope arrived late in the evening, and after having viewed Michelangelo's masterpiece and the other treasures of the Vatican Pavilion with President Johnson at his side, he stood on an outdoor balcony overlooking the Fair faithful and blessed them. Imagining the "religious convictions" that Michelangelo must have felt as he created his statue, the pontiff said, "We feel that these same religious convictions can move men in a similar way to seek peace and harmony among the peoples of the world." It was a historic public relations coup: A World's Fair devoted to "Peace Through Understanding," and Moses had pulled the necessary strings to get the Vicar of Christ to make time during his historic fourteen-hour trip for the Fair and bestow his papal blessings on the exhibition.

The papal visit wasn't the only history-making event that week in New York. The day before the pope's arrival, President Johnson had flown in for a symbolically resplendent ceremony that would take place on Liberty Island, home of the Statue of Liberty. On a clear blue morning, surrounded by both Senator Kennedys, Johnson sat at a desk with the presidential seal and signed the 1965 Immigration Act, a piece of his late predecessor's domestic agenda that his brothers now championed. The law changed decades of discriminatory—and inherently racist— quotas that greatly limited the number of immigrants from southern and eastern Europe; Asia, Africa, and the Middle East; and South and Central America, all the while allowing far larger numbers of immigrants from the "whiter" northern Europeans nations. "From this day forth those wishing to immigrate to America shall be admitted on the basis of their skills and their close relationship to those already here," Johnson said. "This is a simple test, and it is a fair test."

The bill was close to the president's heart, as it had been to his predecessor. At the time of his death, President Kennedy had been working on a book, *A Nation of Immigrants*—released posthumously in 1964—to curry public opinion for the bill, which in multiple polls, the American public were either against or indifferent to. President Johnson considered it one of the most important pieces of his Great Society legislative agenda, saying the law amends "a very deep and painful flaw in the fabric of American justice."

Although he believed the signing was a historic event, Johnson also predicted that the law "will not affect the lives of millions. It will not reshape the structure of our daily lives, or really add importantly to either our wealth or our power." While that might have been the president's intention, the new law would throw open the doors of America to the very same nations that had come to the World's Fair, and had softened the blow of the BIE's boycott. Just as the postcolonial world came to Flushing Meadow in 1964 and 1965, it would come to Queens, and America, to stay in the decades after the Fair.

For two days in early October 1965, as the World's Fair entered its final weeks, thanks to President Johnson and Pope Paul VI, the exhibition's utopian themes—multiculturalism and peace—took center stage while the world watched.

With barely two weeks to go, the World's Fair was busier than ever. New Yorkers who had ignored the Fair or taken the exhibit—"this wondrous World of Oz that had existed in our own backyard," as one Queens resident put it—for granted for so long, now rushed to see what everyone had been talking, and arguing, about. Even after its record Labor Day weekend, the Fair had been booming—still not enough to dig the Fair out of its financial hole, but gratifying nonetheless.

Then during the very last week, as the crowds lined up for their first (or last) glimpse of Walt Disney's talking Abraham Lincoln or another peek at Michelangelo's *La Pietà*, or leisurely enjoyed a Belgian waffle in the Belgian Village or watched the dancers from around the world perform their routines for the last time, attendance passed the fifty-one million mark, making Moses' Fair the most attended international exhibition: nearly seven million more than the 1939–40 World's Fair, and ten million more than the Belgian Expo in 1958. There was even some truth to Moses' declaration that "the Fair had done more for New York than any comparable event in history anywhere." Indeed the Fair had been a boon to the city's economy: Hotels, merchants, restaurants, Broadway shows, and cultural institutions all saw increases in business.

As the Fair's closing day approached, there was even an attempted thaw in relations between Moses and some of his most vociferous critics in the media. "I think you might agree that the over-all balance of what we have printed about the Fair, especially lately, has been decidedly favorable," Jock Whitney, the multimillionaire publisher of the *New York Herald Tribune*—and one of Moses' personal bêtes noires—wrote to the Master Builder in early October. Moses wasn't convinced, but he did reach out to those who he felt had helped, like *Daily News* columnist Jimmy Jemail. "We count you among those who have stood by the Fair from start to finish."

Then on October 17, the World's Fair's last day, a record 446,953 people passed through its gates. At midnight, the turnstiles closed as the color-shrouded fountains of the Unisphere and the Pavilion of Light glowed brightly one last time. Families took it all in and the thousands of workers—from security and maintenance men to ticket collectors, performers, waiters, and cooks—left the Fairgrounds for good.

The fantasy, at long last, was finally over.

EPILOGUE
TOMORROW NEVER KNOWS

On a warm and sunny day in early June 1967, Robert Moses and other city luminaries gathered once again at the former site of the World's Fair in Queens, New York, while the Sanitation Department Band played. This ceremony, held eighteen months after the Fair closed its gates forever, was a farewell and a grand opening. The official mandate of the World's Fair Corporation had ended; the oddly shaped pavilions and overcrowded restaurants that had serviced fifty-one million Fairgoers over the course of 1964 and 1965 had been torn down and disposed of. With its mission complete, the Fair Corporation was relinquishing control of the newly manicured 1,258 acres of green space to New York City. Now rechristened Flushing Meadows–Corona Park, it was the second-largest park in the five boroughs.

Uncharacteristically, Moses did not deliver a speech, although as the man of the hour, he introduced the various speakers to the crowd. In a moment rife with symbolism, the seventy-eight-year-old Master Builder, who had spent four decades dreaming of converting the "the ash dump" of Flushing Meadow into the "the finest park in the City," ceremoniously lowered the World's Fair flag that had marked the territory as his own since he began organizing the exhibition in 1960. After Moses did so, August Heckscher, now his successor as parks commissioner, lifted the official flag of New York City to flap in the wind underneath the blue June sky. The imaginary promised land of Moses was now rejoined to the city he had built. "Guard it well, Mr. Mayor, and Mr. Parks Commissioner," he said. "It has echoed to the sounds of many footsteps and voices. The world has beaten a path to its doors. Now we return it to the natives."

As he toured the festivities in the new park that day, attending a swimming race, cutting the ribbon at the new pitch-and-putt golf course, or, along with Cardinal Francis Spellman, dedicating a commemorative bench marking the former site of the Vatican Pavilion, Moses was mobbed by autograph-seekers. Everywhere he went, young and old sought him out. Still, despite the adulation of the crowds, who were making the most of their new park by picnicking and sunbathing, Moses reverted to form at the unveiling of Donald De Lue's statue of George Washington.

The critics had savaged De Lue's bronze sculpture, *The Rocket Thrower*, which Moses had commissioned for the World's Fair and kept for the post-Fair park; the *Times'* John Canaday called it "the most lamentable monster, making Walt Disney look like Leonardo Da Vinci." It was one of the many slights that Moses had not forgotten. "We have been told by sour, unhappy critics and avant-garde planners that our fair lacked fun in the modern vernacular," he intoned. "It all depends on your definition. The fair had inspiration which will long outlast the cheap, strident ballyhoo and sensationalism which we refused to exploit and accommodate."

And to a degree he was right. Although Moses' Fair was a financial disaster—investors only earned 62.4 cents on the dollar, while New York City recovered only $1.5 million of its $24 million loan to the Fair Corporation (and city accountants wouldn't see that money until 1972)—it had been immensely popular. The most popular World's Fair to date, in fact. The 1964–65 New York World's Fair would attract 1.3 million more customers then the 1967 Montreal Expo, then currently under way in the northern Canadian city.* While Moses' technological Eden might have been a simulacrum, and due to his financial mismanagement, Flushing Meadows–Corona Park did not resemble the grandiose park he had long envisioned, by the summer of 1967, the bygone days of the World's Fair must have seemed, to many, like an idyllic respite in the life of the nation.

Since the Fair shut its gates, the Vietnam War had raged uncontrollably in that faraway land. The sustained aerial bombardment of North

---

* The Montreal Expo, officially sanctioned by the BIE, would attract sixty nations and 50.3 million customers in just one six-month period.

Vietnam, code-named Operation Rolling Thunder, that had begun in February 1965 was followed by American ground troops, which began arriving the following month. The war was so divisive; a second battlefront had opened stateside as the antiwar movement grew into something akin to open rebellion. On April 15, 1967, more than one hundred thousand people, including the Reverend Martin Luther King Jr. and Dr. Benjamin Spock, marched from Central Park to the United Nations; nearly another hundred thousand marched that same day in San Francisco. The war's American architects—President Lyndon B. Johnson and the "best and brightest" minds he had inherited from the Kennedy administration, New Frontiersmen like Secretary of Defense Robert McNamara and National Security Advisor McGeorge Bundy— had perpetuated the lie that the United States was winning in Vietnam, that the proverbial light at the end of the tunnel was coming into focus.

None of it was true.

And each month the proof of their lies—young dead Americans in US government body bags—was shipped home to their families. Johnson's popularity was plummeting. After his historical victory in 1964, the American people began to turn on him during the 1966 midterm elections. By June 1967, with the upcoming presidential election only months away, he feared defeat at the polls, or worse, that the junior Democratic senator from New York, Robert F. Kennedy, would rally the antiwar vote, uniting the campus radicals with the Northern liberals that Johnson was convinced had never accepted him, and reclaim the White House in the name of his martyred brother.

Despite his historic passage of the civil rights laws of 1964 and 1965, the forgotten ghettos of urban America burned, as riot after riot took its toll on the national psyche. What had begun in Harlem in August 1964 would spread to Philadelphia, Newark, Chicago, Boston, and in July 1967, Detroit. Nonviolent civil disobedience had seemingly run its course. The break between the young activists—like the Brooklyn chapter of CORE, with its World's Fair stall-in—and the national civil rights organizations had metastasized into a complete rupture. "Black Power" was the *cri de guerre* of the day, not "We Shall

Overcome." Two years after Malcolm X's assassination, young radicals, both black and white, had decided that "the ballot" approach was inadequate; there was, after all, only so much that civil rights legislation could achieve. Now many, like the Black Panther Party in Oakland, California, were choosing "the bullet."

New York's urban nightmares—crime, pollution, poverty, racial hostility—continued to mount. Crime rates rose each year since 1964; the details of such horrendous murders like that of Kitty Genovese on a quiet tree-lined street in Queens would continue to shock Americans. Their occurrence, however, was to be expected. There was violence in the streets, and thanks to the nightly news broadcasts of the Vietnam War, in living rooms throughout the nation; it was inescapable. And if someone refused to fight in Vietnam and to say no to violence, as Muhammad Ali did in April 1967, there would be serious repercussions. "I ain't got no quarrel with the Viet Cong," Ali exclaimed. "No Viet Cong ever called me a nigger." For his civil disobedience, Ali was stripped of his heavyweight championship title and banned from boxing. (The US Supreme Court would overturn the ruling in 1970.)

The social upheaval that had begun to boil over during the World's Fair had coalesced into a cultural revolution. On January 14, six months before Moses lowered the World's Fair flag, thirty thousand people congregated in San Francisco's Golden Gate Park for "A Gathering of Tribes for the Human Be-In." The event wasn't a "sit-in" or a stall-in but a new kind of happening; it united the various elements of the burgeoning youth culture: hippies, hipsters, acidheads, rock fans, antiwar college radicals, tree-huggers, and Zen apostles.

Ostensibly there to protest a recent law banning LSD, the event was really the psychedelic generation's coming-out party; and serving as guides for this new Aquarian Age were three members of the Beat Generation, poets Allen Ginsberg, Gary Snyder, and Lawrence Ferlinghetti, all of whom had been pushing the cultural envelope and protesting America's Cold War mentality in one form or another since the 1950s. Timothy Leary, the godfather of the acid movement, was there, too, telling the crowd they should "turn on, tune in, drop out." In many ways, the Human Be-In was an epochal World's Fair of the mind, and an inner exhibition for a new generation.

While Ken Kesey wasn't there, he had helped make it possible. After returning to the West Coast from the World's Fair sojourn in July 1964, Kesey and his Merry Pranksters went about holding a series of "Acid Tests" in California. Throughout 1965 the free rock concerts, where an early iteration of the Grateful Dead held court, along with psychedelic light shows and free LSD, helped Kesey spread the Gospel of Acid.

Always one to recognize the commercial implications of a popular trend, Andy Warhol saw the Day-Glo writing on the wall and began backing a nascent rock group called the Velvet Underground in late 1965. They became the house band for his touring multimedia show, the Plastic Exploding Inevitable. Throughout 1966 the part-happenings, part-concerts featured Warhol's experimental films beamed onto the venues' walls, while the Velvet Underground played and bright pop art colors flashed everywhere. The band's classic debut, *The Velvet Underground & Nico,* complete with a Warhol-designed cover—an electric yellow banana and the words PEEL SLOWLY AND SEE—debuted in May 1967 and would go on to become one of the most influential rock albums of all time.

By June the summer of 1967 would be proclaimed the Summer of Love, as thousands of teens and young Americans converged on the Haight-Ashbury district of San Francisco, seeking to immerse themselves in a new lifestyle of free love and drugs. Just two weeks after the lowering of the World's Fair flag in Flushing Meadows–Corona Park, the first rock festival of its kind was held south of San Francisco. The event was called the Monterey International Pop Festival, and it was there that the world at large was introduced to Janis Joplin, the Jimi Hendrix Experience, and the Who. Rock music had come a long way since that cold February day in 1964 when the Beatles' Pan Am flight touched down at JFK International Airport in Queens.

The Beatles themselves had undergone a musical and physical transformation. On June 1, 1967, just two days before the Flushing Meadow ceremony, the band released what many considered their masterpiece:

Sgt. Pepper's Lonely Hearts Club Band. "Any of these songs is more genu-
inely creative than anything currently to be heard on pop radio stations,"
opined William Mann, classical music critic for *The Times* (London). It
certainly was an entirely *new* kind of rock album, conceptual in nature,
with a psychedelic and pop art–influenced album cover, and fueled by
the band's ongoing experimentation with drugs, particularly LSD. By
expanding the parameters of what rock music was—or could be—and
using the recording studio as a "fifth" member of the band, the Beatles
provided the Summer of Love with a new psychedelic soundtrack.

Even as the Beatles were exploring the limits of pop music and
new ways of recording it, Bob Dylan was headed in an entirely different direction. After the chaotic concert in Forest Hills, he launched an
American tour, where belligerent fans taunted him at every stop, pausing briefly during the winter of 1966 to record the double LP *Blonde on
Blonde.* Believed by many to be *his* masterpiece, Dylan's album was the
culmination of the blues-based electric sound that he had been experi-
menting with since *Bringing It All Back Home.* He soon launched a world
tour, where he and his backup band endured more hostile audiences in
Australia and Europe.

Dylan was quickly burning out: too much success, too many drugs,
too much of everything. While on hiatus in Woodstock, New York, on
July 29, 1966, he crashed his motorcycle and retreated from the public
eye. Convalescing in both body and spirit, he turned his back on the
political movements he inspired and eschewed the transfigured electric
sound of his last three records, returning to a stripped-bare, simple folk
and country style, which resulted in the album *John Wesley Harding.* "I
asked Columbia [his record company] to release it with no hype," Dylan
said, "because this was the season of hype." The psychedelic revolution
would go on without him.

That wasn't the only music Dylan was making in 1967. During
the Summer of Love, he was holed up in the basement of a house near
Woodstock, New York, where he and his touring band—the five members of which would soon be known to the world as the Band—recorded
a plethora of new songs that sounded like old, arcane standards straight

out of the Americana songbook, which would eventually be released years later as *The Basement Tapes*. In the midst of what many thought of as the dawning of a new age, Dylan and the Band were turning back the clock—at least musically—to a simpler, seemingly less complex era.

If by 1967 the World's Fair seemed to represent an earlier, less complicated time for many who didn't like the direction the country was taking or the youth movement, with its lax attitude toward sex and drugs and its refusal to accept America's Cold War ideology, which had made the Vietnam War a reality, then they were fooling themselves. It was an illusion, no more real than the Pepsi-Cola Pavilion's "It's a Small World" boat ride created by the late Walt Disney (who, like Lenny Bruce, died in 1966). In fact, the years 1964 and 1965 were far from peaceful, and there was little, if any, understanding in New York City or the country at large.

Instead, Moses unwittingly had created a World's Fair that was emblematic of its times and displayed all the contradictions of postwar America: It espoused noble ideals, yet failed to live up to them; it purportedly sought peace, but often sowed conflict; despite the critics, it did celebrate art, but all the while preached the Gospel of Commerce and Industry. Although he converted the Fairgrounds into the second-largest park in the city, Moses' new park fell far short of his vision. Failure was not something that the Master Builder took well; and having endured a lifetime of Moses venting his volcanic temper at them, the New York press couldn't help but bask in his defeat. (That is, what was left of the New York press after a disastrous newspaper strike put the last nail in the collective coffins of the *Herald Tribune*, the *World-Telegram*, and the *Journal-American*.)

Still, Moses' World's Fair would prove prescient in ways even its creator couldn't envision. The 1964–65 New York World's Fair with its symbol, the Unisphere—literally a sculptural global village— showed its millions of visitors what a multicultural world actually *looked* like. The media, so intent on ridiculing Moses for his mishandling of the BIE fiasco—which was certainly accurate—missed the larger story: Smaller, developing nations, the new republics of the Third World, had populated Moses' Fair.

And thanks to the 1965 Immigration Act, signed in the shadow of the Statue of Liberty weeks before the Fair ended, which finally rid America of its racist immigrant quotas, people from those same nations—Mexico, India, Pakistan, Korea, and many more—were allowed to come to America in search of a better life, just as their European counterparts had been doing for centuries. The seeds of America's twenty-first-century political, social, and demographic transformation were sown during the years of the World's Fair.

Americans now live in a global village reminiscent of the 1964–65 World's Fair, even if peace through understanding continues to elude us.

ACKNOWLEDGMENTS

This book began with a conversation with my friend Amber Canavan in the fall of 2007. We were both freelance editors at American Express Custom Publishing at the time. One day, Amber casually mentioned that her husband was an agent, in case I had a book idea that I wanted to pitch. A few months later, over lunch at the Oyster Bar in Grand Central Station, I told her husband, Jud Laghi, who became both an agent and friend, the rough idea I had. With his help and patience, the idea of this book was born. A heartfelt thanks to them both.

I would like to give special thanks to my editor, Keith Wallman, whose deft editing helped turn a manuscript into a book. I also thank Lyons Press and its staff that has helped with this project, particularly Meredith Dias and Lauren Brancato.

A number of people read this book while it was a manuscript in progress, lending their expertise. I would like to thank Emily Raboteau, whose advice during those early days helped me focus my vision for the book and gave me the confidence to plow ahead. Thanks also to Lindsey Abrams for her editorial suggestions and her encouragement, and Michael Polizzi for taking the time to read these pages and offer his valuable insights.

I first began thinking about Queens, New York, as a subject after I wrote a number of pieces about ordinary New Yorkers from my home borough while working as a freelance contributor to the much-missed City section of the *New York Times*. I would especially like to thank Frank Flaherty, my former editor at the City Section, for taking a chance on a random pitch from a freelance writer he had never met, and for helping me start a journey that has culminated in this book.

During my years in magazine publishing, I worked with some amazingly talented people, far too many to recount here, but I would like to give special thanks to those who encouraged me along the way, particularly during the early days of my career: Jonathan Van Meter, Diane Cardwell, Linda Rath, Gilbert Rogin, Bruce Frankel, Steve Dougherty, Jamie Katz, Jim Kunen, William Plummer, and Joe Dolce.

Thanks goes to my excellent editors and friends who kept me busy and working when I was a freelancer: Rachel Elson, Josh Moss, Sara Clemence, Laura Rich, Dan Jewel, Sue Rozdeba, Steve Marsh, Jon Auerbach, and Jared Shapiro. I would also like to thank my friends and colleagues at the late *Fortune Small Business,* especially Adriana Gardella, Richard Murphy, Jessica Bruder, Jeff Wise, Julie Lazarus, and James Lochart. During my years in the pressure cooker of weekly magazines, I learned many of the skills that served me well in the writing of this book. I had the good fortune to make many friends who made the tough times fun. A special thanks goes to Deborah Moss, Lydia Paniccia, Greg Emmanuel, Alec Foege, Orville Clarke, Matt Coppa, Antoinette Campana, Chris Kensler, Sydney Applegate, Bob Meadows, and Nadia Cohen. Thanks to my friends and professors at CCNY, particularly Jane Marcus and Mark Mirsky; and to colleagues at Lehman College: Ann Worth, Terrence Cheng, Evelyn Ackerman, Nika Lunn, Brendan McGibney, Maria-Cristina Necula, Sol Marguiles, Norma Strauss, and Nancy Novick.

I would like to single out Al Kooper, George Lois, Richard J. Whalen, Gay Talese, Brian Purnell, Peter Eisenstadt, Bill Cotter (for his fair-priced photos), and Marta Gutman for taking the time to share their expertise and memories with me. And once again I would like to acknowledge the staff of the Manuscripts and Archives Division of the New York Public Library for their help and support of this project, as well as archivists at the Brooklyn Historical Society and the Columbia Center for Oral History.

A special thanks to my parents, family, and friends for their enduring support. Thanks to Justin Rizzo for all his helpful suggestions. And finally, my most sincere gratitude goes to my wife, Kelly, and my wonderful children, Leo and Zoë. I have been working on this book, in one form or another, for most of my children's lives, missing many events and gatherings along the way. I would not have been able to finish this project without the love, support, and patience of my wife. And for that, she has my enduring thanks and love.

330

NOTES

To tell the story of the 1964–65 New York World's Fair is to tell the story of Robert Moses. And any serious inquiry into the complex nature and legacy of Moses begins with Robert A. Caro's celebrated work, *The Power Broker: Robert Moses and the Fall of New York* (Vintage, 1975). Since Caro's book first appeared forty years ago, other works have contributed to the understanding of New York's enigmatic Master Builder. Perhaps the most important of these is the magisterial *Robert Moses and the Modern City: The Transformation of New York*, edited by Hilary Ballon and Kenneth T. Jackson (W. W. Norton, 2008).

Another important, and entertaining, book is *Wrestling With Moses: How Jane Jacobs Took on New York's Master Builder and Transformed the American City* by Anthony Flint (Random House, 2009), which details the epic battles between Jacobs and Moses. Peter Eisenstadt's *Rochdale Village: Robert Moses, 6,000 Families, and New York City's Great Experiment in Integrated Housing* (Cornell University Press, 2010) is another valuable work that examines a forgotten episode in the sordid history of public housing in New York City.

There is also Moses' own attempt at autobiography—or something like it: *Public Works: A Dangerous Trade* (McGraw-Hill, 1970), a 952-page attempt to preempt *The Power Broker*'s critical assessment of his legacy. Another absolutely indispensible study of Moses can be found in Marshall Berman's *All That Is Sold Melts Into Air* (Penguin, 1988); Berman's musings about Moses are an epiphany. I am indebted to all of these works; all have helped shaped my thinking of Moses, his legacy, and the World's Fair.

While there are a few books on the 1964–65 World's Fair, among the best of these are the pair of photo books by Bill Cotter and Bill Young, *The 1964–65 New York World's Fair* and *The 1964–65 New York World's Fair: Creation and Legacy* (both published by Arcadia Publishing). These books, as well as my conversations with Bill Cotter and the excellent website that both authors maintain, which functions as an online archive of World's Fair photos, articles, and memorabilia, helped make the Fair come alive for me.

Another all-important text was *Remembering the Future: The New York World's Fair From 1939 to 1964* (Rizzoli, 1989), a collection of invaluable essays by the likes of Morris Dickstein and Helen A. Harrison; the same is true of Lawrence R. Samuel's *The End of the Innocence* (Syracuse University Press, 2007). All of the above were excellent guidebooks to the 1964–65 World's Fair. Another key book for understanding America in the early 1960s was *The Last Innocent Year: America in 1964, the Beginning of the "Sixties"* by John Margolis (Harpers, 1999), a brilliant and concise work of narrative nonfiction.

During his lifetime, especially, during his years with the World's Fair, there was little, if anything, that Robert Moses said or did that didn't end up in the New York papers. While I have primarily relied on the *New York Times*—which assigned some of its very best reporters to the Fair, including Gay Talese, McCandlish Phillips, and Robert C. Doty, among others—I also perused hundreds of articles from the metropolitan papers, primarily from the years 1959 to 1967, including the *New York Post*, the *New York Daily News*, the *Journal-American*, the *New York Herald Tribune*, the *New York World-Telegram*, and the *Wall Street Journal*. Often these articles—and Moses' belligerent response—became part of the story, as I note in the text. I have also read articles from the most important magazines at the time, including *Time, Life, Fortune, Sports Illustrated, The New Yorker, The Saturday Evening Post, Esquire, Reader's Digest*, and *Harper's*, among others.

But by far the most important aspect of my research—and the most important influence on this book—is the time I spent examining the archives of the Robert Moses Papers and the 1964–65 World's Fair Archives housed in the Manuscripts and Archive Division at the New York Public Library (NYPL) on 42nd Street. I spent months poring over the fourteen boxes of the Moses collection pertaining to the Fair and several boxes of his correspondence, as well as eleven more boxes of the Fair archives. Together these collections—thousands of pages of memos, letters, clippings, photos, speeches, progress reports, etc.—formed a meticulous diary of Moses' actions, thoughts, words, feelings, and intentions over the course of his seven years as head of the World's Fair Corporation, and all the people, including presidents, business leaders, and ordinary folks, with whom he corresponded. At every turn, the unfailingly professional and knowledgeable staff of the Manuscripts and Archive Division assisted me in my work. I offer a most gracious thanks for their help.

PART ONE: THE GREATEST SINGLE EVENT IN HISTORY

I.

My depiction of the ground-breaking ceremony in December 1962 is based on newspaper articles of the day, largely from the *New York Times*, which ran the full text of President Kennedy's speech. I also based my narrative on photographs of his visit and a short newsreel of his arrival found online. Much of the behind-the-scenes drama of Kennedy's visit to Queens, the administration's battles to secure congressional funding, the Cold War–era intrigue surrounding the Fair, and Moses' public battles with congressional leaders was detailed in the *New York Times* and other papers. Important documents were also found in the Robert Moses Papers, the World's Fair Archives at the NYPL, and accessed online at the John F. Kennedy Library (jfklibrary.org), where, thankfully, pertinent presidential papers have been digitized.

Bruce K. Nicholson's memoir *Hi Ho, Come to the Fair: Tales of the New York World's Fair* (Pelagian Press, 1989) provided an eyewitness account of Kennedy's visit to the Fairgrounds— thanks to my friend Suzanne Rozdeba for helping me track it down. Footage of Kennedy's April 1963 call to the World's Fair from the White House can be found online. Rick Perlstein's magnificent *Nixonland* (Scribner, 2008) provided details on Senator Paul Douglas—as well as inspiration. The Illinois senator's opinion of Robert Moses can be found in *The Power Broker*.

For the history of World's Fairs, I turned to *World of Fairs: The Century of Progress Expositions* by Robert W. Rydell and *Fair America: World's Fairs in the United States* by Robert W. Rydell, John E. Findling, and Kimberly D. Pelle, as well as *World's Fairs* by Erik Mattie. Moses' role in the 1939–40 New York World's Fair is detailed in *The Power Broker* and Moses' own *Public Works*, as well as referenced time and again throughout Moses' own papers.

My understanding of the events and legacy of the Cuban Missile Crisis was formed primarily by *A Thousand Days: John F. Kennedy in the White House* by Arthur M. Schlesinger Jr. (Mariner Books, 2002), the celebrated historian's account of his years in the Kennedy White House; *President Kennedy: Profile of Power* by Richard Reeves (Simon & Schuster, 1993), which gives you a front-row ticket to Kennedy's Oval Office; *The Icarus Syndrome: A History of American Hubris* by Peter Beinart (Harper, 2010); and *Robert Kennedy: His Life* by Evan Thomas (Simon & Shuster, 2000). Other books that were consulted for information about this terrifying episode in American history were *Postwar: A History of Europe Since 1945* by Tony Judt (Penguin, 2006); *The Liberal Hour: Washington and the Politics of Change in the 1960s* by G. Calvin Mackenzie and Robert Weisbrot (Penguin Press, 2008); *Brothers: The Hidden History of the Kennedy Years* by David Talbot (Free Press, 2007); *An Unfinished Life: John F. Kennedy, 1917–1963* by Robert Dallek (Little, Brown, 2003); and Michael Dobb's *One Minute to Midnight* (Knopf, 2008).

2.

Robert Kopple's quotations about the origins of the World's Fair were taken from an interview he gave to the *New York Times* ("Blending of Ideas in 2 Opposing Minds Went Into Creation of the Exposition," April 22, 1964). Details about Kopple, as well as the Mutual Admiration Society, were gleaned from Charles Poletti's recollections found in Columbia University's Oral History Project. Kopple is also featured prominently in "Hi Ho, Come to the Fair," Martin Mayer's article from the October 1963 issue of *Esquire*.

The *New York Times* and other papers provided details of Moses' visit to the nation's capital, which the Master Builder also recalls in *Public Works*. The World's Fair difficulties with the BIE are detailed in the aforementioned *Esquire* article, the *New York Times*, and Bruce Nicholson's *Hi Ho, Come to the Fair*, as well as "Diplomacy at Flushing Meadow," by John Brooks, which appeared in the June 1, 1963, issue of *The New Yorker*, the most detailed account of the international difficulties that plagued the Fair from the start.

3.

This biographical chapter on Moses was influenced by my readings of Caro's *The Power Broker*, Flint's *Wrestling With Moses*, and the essays in *Robert Moses and the Modern City*, such as Martha Biondi's "Robert Moses, Race, and the Limits of an Activist State" and Hilary Ballon's "Robert Moses and Urban Renewal." I also consulted *To Stand and Fight: The Struggle for Civil Rights in Postwar New York City* by Martha Biondi (Harvard University Press, 2003).

Also helpful in researching this chapter was Moses' lengthy *New York Times* obituary ("Robert Moses, Master Builder, is Dead at 92" by Paul Goldberger, July 30, 1981), as well as Al Smith's *Times* obit ("Alfred E. Smith Dies Here at 70; 4 times Governor," October 4, 1944); I also found "Unhappy Warrior" by Elizabeth Kolbert from the March 5, 2001, issue of *The New Yorker* informative. Numerous newspaper articles were also useful, particularly "A Few Rich Golfers Accused of Blocking Plan for State Park," *New York Times*, January 8, 1925. The Wagner quotations were found in the Reminiscences of Robert F. Wagner, Jr., at the Columbia Center for Oral History (June 23, 1976, p. 97–100; Jan. 14, 1977, p. 349–351; March 15, 1978, p. 747). Many thanks to Columbia's staff, particularly Kristen La Follette, Breanne LaCamera, and Hana Sutphin Crawford, for their help.

For information on Lewis Mumford, I turned to *Sidewalk Critic: Lewis Mumford's Writings on New York*, edited by Robert Wojtowicz (Princeton Architectural Press, 2000), a collection of his brilliant *New Yorker* writing. I also consulted *The Lewis Mumford Reader* (Pantheon, 1986), edited by Donald L. Miller, who also penned *Lewis Mumford: A Life* (Grove, 1989).

4.

Among the Reminiscences of Charles Poletti at the CCOHC was his quote about Robert Kopple (May 23, 1978, p. 551–552). In writing this chapter, I also read Caro's *The Power Broker* and Ballon and Jackson's *Robert Moses and the Modern City*. Martin Mayer's *Esquire* story was integral to understanding how Kopple started the World's Fair. Once again the online archive of the *New York Times* and its articles detailing Moses' takeover of the World's Fair, particularly "Originator of Fair Dropped by Moses," April 9, 1960, were wonderful sources.

5.

Hi Ho, Come to the Fair discussed Moses' trip to Paris. Once again John Brooks's June 1963 *New Yorker* piece and Martin Mayer's October 1963 *Esquire* piece were essential to understanding the behind-the-scenes power struggles and international problems of Moses' Fair, as was Lawrence R. Samuel's *The End of the Innocence*. Many articles in the *New York Times* and other papers detail Moses' handling of the BIE and feature his commentary on the Paris-based organization. I found details about this episode, as well as the Master Builder's battles with the short-lived Design Committee, in the Robert Moses Papers and the World's Fair Archives at the New York Public Library.

Helen A. Harrison's "Art for the Million, or Art for the Market?" is the best single source on Moses, the Fair, and art, and is found in *Remembering the Future*. Poletti's comments about the US State Department sabotaging the Fair's relationship with the Soviet Union are in his oral history at Columbia University. The *New York Times* detailed the Soviet Union saga at the World's Fair, as did Moses himself in *Dangerous Trade*. Deegan's quotation about the Fair being "the greatest single event in history" appeared in *The New Yorker*'s June 1963 issue.

6.

The two biographies I relied on for this chapter were Neal Gabler's authoritative *Walt Disney: The Triumph of the American Imagination* (Vintage, 2006) and Bob Thomas's *Walt Disney: A Biography* (Star, 1981). Also helpful were letters and memos corresponding to Disney's involvement with the World's Fair from Robert Moses' papers at NYPL. I also consulted "Disneyland, 1955: Just take the Santa Ana freeway to the American Dream" by Karal Ann Marling from the Smithsonian American Art Museum (found through jstor.org). Also useful were the aforementioned Cotter and Young books; *Remembering the Future*, and *The End of the Innocence*.

7.

The saga of Robert Moses and race is a complicated one that, particularly where it concerns the World's Fair, was played out in the New York papers. A number of stories from the *New York Times* are mentioned by name in the text, as well as *New York Post* columnist James A. Wechsler, who bravely called out both Moses and New York's powerful building trades for their stances. My narrative drew from such newspaper accounts and all the relevant memos, letters, and correspondences about the Fair's racial controversies found in the Robert Moses Papers and World's Fair Archives at the New York Public Library.

The controversy that surrounded Moses' building of public pools in the late 1930s has been brilliantly analyzed by Professor Marta Gutman of the City College of New York, including her essay "Equipping the Public Realm" from *Robert Moses and the Modern City* and her essay "Race, Place, and Play" from *Journal of the Society of Architectural Historians* (December 2008). I would also like to thank Professor Gutman for taking the time to speak with me on this subject. The information about Moses and Rochdale Village was gleaned from Peter Eisenstadt's *Rochdale Village: Robert Moses, 6,000 Families, and New York City's Great Experiment in Integrated Housing* and Moses' unlikely relationship with Abraham Kazan; I would also like to thank Peter Eisenstadt for taking the time to speak with me about his work. Also key was the lengthy *New York Times Magazine* piece "When Blacks and Whites Live Together" by Harvey Swados (November 13, 1966).

Moses wrote, often brilliantly, on many topics; his *New York Times Magazine* piece "What's Wrong with New York?" from August 1, 1943, is just one example. Bruce K. Nicholson discusses his colleague Dr. George H. Bennett joining the Fair's International Division in *Hi Ho, Come to the Fair*.

8.

The Kennedys' stance on civil rights is treated with fairness and clarity in Richard Reeves's *President Kennedy*; insights were also drawn from Schlesinger's *A Thousand Days*. The most elegant works on the civil rights movement I came across were *Pillar of Fire: America in the King Years, 1963–65* by Taylor Branch (Simon & Schuster, 1998) and *Better Day Coming: Blacks and Equality, 1890–2000* by Adam Fairclough (Penguin, 2001). A wonderfully enlightening book on the topic is *Sweet Land of Liberty: The Forgotten Struggle for Civil Rights in the North* by Thomas J. Sugrue (Random House, 2008). Also important was Louis E. Lomax's *The Negro Revolt* (Signet, 1963). Another necessary text for understanding this crucial moment in American history is *America Divided: The Civil War of the 1960s*, third edition, by Maurice Isserman and Michael Kazin (Oxford University Press, 2008).

As ever, periodicals from the time, such as *Time*, the *New York Times*, *Harper's*, and *The New Yorker*, proved to be full of vital information. My former colleague Hilton Al's essay on James Baldwin, "The Making and Unmaking of James Baldwin," from the February 16, 1998, issue of *The New Yorker* was especially useful (and insightful).

9.

For this chapter, I relied primarily on the relevant articles in the *New York Times* and other New York papers that dealt with the explosive summer of 1963 in the Big Apple. Moses' decision not to pursue a pavilion devoted to "the progress and problems" of African Americans was found among the Robert Moses Papers. For my understanding of the civil rights "Big Four," I turned to the aforementioned Kennedy books, particularly *President Kennedy* and *A Thousand Days*; *Pillar of Fire: America in the King Years, 1963–65*; *Better Day Coming: Blacks and Equality, 1890–2000*; and *Sweet Land of Liberty: The Forgotten Struggle for Civil Rights in the North*. Also helpful were *The Autobiography of Martin Luther King Jr.* edited by Clayborn Carson (Grand Central Publishing, 1998); and James Farmer's autobiography *Lay Bare the Heart* (Arbor House, 1985). Also consulted were *Kennedy, Johnson, and the Quest for Justice: The Civil Rights Tapes* by Jonathan Rosenberg and Zachary Karabell (W. W. Norton, 2003); *America Divided*; and *The Last Innocent Year*. I found some of Louis E. Lomax's writings in *Harper's* as well as in his book *The Negro Revolt*.

The stall-in saga of Brooklyn CORE is, in my opinion, one of the great forgotten moments of the civil rights movement. It was first covered in the New York papers. (Please see my notes for Chapter 20 for more.) My description of the March on Washington drew from the above books and newspaper accounts. Bob Dylan's and Joan Baez's participation in the March on Washington is detailed in *Positively Fourth Street* by David Hadju (North Point Press, 2002); *America Divided*; and elsewhere. Dylan's quotation at the end of the chapter is from *Dylan: An Intimate Biography* by Anthony Scaduto (Signet, 1971).

10.

The Angela Davis quotation in this chapter is from the documentary film *The Black Power Mixtape: 1967–1975* by Göran Hugo Olsson, an amazing historical document itself. American Experience's *Freedom Riders* is also an all-important film about the early 1960s. I based my narrative of the four young children murdered in the Birmingham bombing on newspaper accounts, the aforementioned Kennedy and civil rights book, and Spike Lee's documentary *Four Little Girls*.

11.

As often was the case, the *New York Times* became part of the World's Fair narrative when it published its front-page story "World's Fair Gains Impetus Despite Snubs" by Robert C. Doty on September 9, 1963. This happened again and again thanks to Moses' belligerent attitude toward the media. The Gay Talese quotations on Moses and his relationship to the media are detailed in *The Kingdom and the Power* (New American Library, 1969). A very special thanks to Gay Talese—the greatest nonfiction writer of them all—for taking the time to answer my questions and share his memories of covering the Fair.

Moses' handling of the H. L. Hunt episode was detailed in the daily newspapers, and his commentary could be found among his papers at the New York Public Library. Moses also addressed this episode in his book *Public Works*. The same was true of the Fair's ensuing art controversy—in this case the *New York Herald Tribune* took the lead in its criticism of the Fair. My understanding of the *Herald Tribune*, and its place in both American politics and the New York media world, is based on *The Paper: The Life and Death of the New York Herald Tribune* by Richard Kluger. Also helpful was Emily Genauer's *New York Times* obituary. Helen A. Harrison's essay in *Remembering the Future* deals with the whole episode brilliantly. I found Moses' reaction, rebuttal, and commentary among his papers, including his surprising defense of Philip Johnson's postmodern New York State Pavilion. I found Ada Louise Huxtable's pieces on the Fair and Johnson both in the *New York Times* and in her wonderful collection *On Architecture: Collected Reflections on a Century of Change* (Walker, 2008).

12.

Moses' reaction to the Kennedy assassination was found among his papers at the New York Public Library. While I was researching and writing this book, *Magic Trip*, the never-seen decades-old film that Ken Kesey and the Merry Pranksters shot of that first fateful cross-country trip to the World's Fair, was released. In the film Kesey discusses his desire to visit the World's Fair and his reaction to the JFK assassination.

The early references to the Beatles in the *New York Times* ("Britons Succumb To 'Beatlemania'" by Frederick Lewis, *The New York Times Magazine*, December 1, 1963) were particularly helpful—and quite amusing to read from this distance. While there are many, many books on the Beatles, there are, in reality, few good ones. Among the best are *Read the Beatles: Classic and New Writings on the Beatles, Their Legacy and Why They Still Matter*, edited by June Skiller Sawyers (Penguin, 2006), which was key to trying to understanding the Fab Four and the impact they had in both Britain and the United States in 1963–64. There is also the authoritative Bob Spitz biography, *The Beatles* (Little, Brown, 2005), and my personal favorite, *Can't Buy Me Love: The Beatles, Britain, and America* by Jonathan Gould (Three Rivers Press, 2007), which successfully puts the band in its appropriate social, historical, and cultural context.

13.

For America's shocked reaction to the death of President Kennedy, I turned to *The Last Innocent Year* as well as Robert A. Caro's fourth volume of his biography of Lyndon B. Johnson, *The Passage of Power* (Knopf, 2012). I also drew from the *New York Times* coverage, particularly Gay Talese's articles quoting people on the street. Moses' desire to pay homage to the slain president is detailed in various memos and letters to Edward Durrell Stone in the Moses Papers at the New York Public Library.

My account of New York City's crackdown on the downtown art scene was drawn from a wide range of sources (see my notes for Chapter 19). Information for this chapter came from Ed Sanders's memoir *Fug You* (Da Capo, 2011) and *I Celebrate Myself: The Somewhat Private Life of Allen Ginsberg* by Bill Morgan (Viking, 2006). Louis Menand's *New Yorker* essay on Andy Warhol ("Top of the Pops," January 11, 2010) was also an important revelation on the subject. References to the *New York Times*' infamous article "Growth of Overt Homosexuality in City Provokes Wide Concern" on December 17, 1963, can be found in various books, including *City Poet: The Life and Times of Frank O'Hara* by Brad Gooch (Knopf, 1993) and Arthur Gelb's often brilliant memoir of his time at the *Times, City Room* (Berkeley, 2003). I found the article itself in the *New York Times* archive. I based my account of Dylan's infamous reaction to receiving the Tom Paine Award from various Dylan biographies, including *No Direction Home: The Life and Music of Bob Dylan* (Da Capo, 1986) by Robert Shelton, the former music critic for the *New York Times*.

PART TWO: SOMETHING NEW

14.

Moses' complaints regarding the US Pavilion and his steadfast refusal to have the Beatles play any part in the World's Fair are detailed in memos from his papers. My description of the Beatles' arrival in New York is based on *The Last Innocent Year*, as well as *The Beatles Come to America* by Martin Goldsmith (J. Wiley, 2004); Bob Spitz's *The Beatles*; and Jonathan Gould's *Can't Buy Me Love*.

Once again, newspaper accounts of the band's arrival were, perhaps, the most enlightening sources and—no surprise—the *New York Times*' coverage of Beatlemania was second to none: "The Beatles Invade, Complete With Long Hair and Screaming Fans," February 8, 1964, and Theodore Strongin's musical critique of the band helped illustrate how the Beatles were viewed by critics in 1964. The same is true of *Time*'s February 21, 1964, dispatch on the band, "Singers: The Unbarbershopped Quartet." The *New Yorker* ran a series of Talk of the Town pieces about the Fab Four in early 1964 that were also useful.

Helpful too was the band's own *Anthology* (Chronicle Books, 1997). John Lennon's memories of that fateful first trip to America are from his 1970 interview with Jann S. Wenner, which is collected in *Lennon Remembers* (Verso, 2000). I also consulted *Shout! The Beatles in Their Generation* by Philip Norman (Fireside, 1981) and *Read the Beatles*. Dylan's reaction to the band is drawn from David Hadju's *Positively 4th Street*. Louis Menand's essay "Why They Were Fab" (*The New Yorker*, October 16, 2000) was also immensely helpful.

I would be remiss if I didn't mention the multiple Beatles documentaries I watched in an attempt to place myself in the middle of the mass hysteria known as Beatlemania, including *Anthology* and *The Beatles: The First U.S. Visit* by Albert Maysles.

15.

The Fab Four's meeting with Cassius Clay is recounted in many places, but the most informative is David Remnick's masterful biography on Muhammad Ali, *King of the World* (Random House, 1998). Clay/Ali's connection to Malcolm X is also discussed in Manning Marable's brilliant *Malcolm X: A Life of Reinvention* (Viking, 2011). I also consulted Nick Tosches's *The Devil and Sonny Liston* (Little, Brown, 2000). But most fun of all was my afternoon with the effervescent George Lois, the brilliant mind who produced all those *Esquire* covers in the 1960s. My thanks to him for his hospitality and taking the time to meet with me.

The various works of art, books, plays, and films that broke taboos in 1964 were detailed in various papers from the time and *The Last Innocent Year*. I also consulted *The End of Obscenity* by Charles Rembar (Harper & Row, 1968). Also important was Louisa Thomas's 2008 profile of Barney Rosset in *Newsweek* ("The Most Dangerous Man in Publishing"); his obituary in the *New York Times* from February 22, 2012; and the 2007 documentary on Rosset, *Obscene*. The long-forgotten *New Statesman* article by Paul Johnson is among the pieces collected in *Read the Beatles*.

16.

My trusty old copy of *Malcolm X Speaks* (Grove, 1966), acquired years ago from a used bookstore, was my guide to the powerful commentary on American life that is Malcolm X's "The Ballot or the Bullet" speech. Audio files of the speech are readily available online. *Malcolm X: A Life of Reinvention* was key to understanding the speech and Malcolm's evolution as a civil rights fighter. I also consulted Martin Luther King Jr.'s autobiography for this chapter and various newspaper accounts that referenced Malcolm X during this period in his life.

17.

A. M. Rosenthal's short book, *Thirty-Eight Witnesses: The Kitty Genovese Case* (Melville House, 2008), is a sad testimony to this unforgettable episode in New York City history. I also consulted the original *New York Times* stories. Arthur Gelb recounts the sordid affair in his *City Room* memoir. A 1964 Talk of the Town piece about Rosenthal's book from *The New Yorker* was also helpful. I found the letters regarding crime in New York City that Moses began receiving shortly after the Genovese murder among his papers at the New York Public Library. One of the best stories I came across on the subject was a piece titled "Kitty, 40 Years Later" by Jim Rasenberger in the late great City Section of the *New York Times* (February 8, 2004).

18.

My narrative about Andy Warhol, pop art, and the World's Fair drew from many sources. For starters there is the aforementioned Helen A. Harrison essay from *Remembering the Future*. Key to understanding Warhol and his work *Thirteen Most Wanted Men* is Richard Meyer's chapter on the subject from his brilliant 2002 book, *Outlaw Representation: Censorship and Homosexuality in Twentieth-Century American Art* (Beacon) as well as "Andy Warhol Remembered" by Mark Lancaster from the *Burlington Magazine* (March 1989), which recounts Lancaster's trip to Flushing Meadow with Warhol. Also invaluable was Calvin Tompkins wonderful profile on Warhol, "Raggedy Andy," which I found in *The Sixties: The Art, Attitudes, Politics, and Media of Our Most Explosive Decade*, edited by Gerald Howard (Washington Square Press, 1982).

Also helpful—and amusing—were Warhol's own *The Philosophy of Andy Warhol* (Harcourt, 1975) and *Popism: The Warhol Sixties*, cowritten with Pat Hackett (Harcourt, 1980). The best biography on Warhol that I came across was *Pop: The Genius of Andy Warhol* by Tony Scherman and David Dalton (Harper, 2009). I also consulted *Philip Johnson* by Franz Schulze (Knopf, 1994). Louis Menad's aforementioned "Top of the Pops" *New Yorker* essay on Warhol was also helpful for this chapter. Roy Lichtenstein's homage to Jack Kirby was found in *Marvel Comics: The Untold Story* by Sean Howe (Harper, 2013).

For general background knowledge about the postwar New York art scene and the pop art movement, I turned to *New Art City* by Jed Perl (Knopf, 2005) and *City Poet*, Brad Gooch's biography of poet Frank O'Hara, an important player in the New York art world. Tompkins' *New Yorker* profiles of Robert Rauschenberg ("Moving Out," February 29, 1964) and Philip Johnson ("Forms Under Light," May 23, 1977) were also invaluable. Ada Louis Huxtable's *New York Times Magazine* piece on Philip Johnson's work ("He Adds Elegance to Modern Architecture," May 24, 1964) was both useful and enlightening.

Reading the work of *Times* art critic John Canaday was an experience I will not soon forget; it's no wonder that his rapierlike wit and precise prose irked Robert Moses so much. His pieces, such as "Pop Art Sells On and On—Why?" (*The New York Times*, May 31, 1964), were intrinsic to understanding the pop art revolution. And his pieces about art and the World's Fair, as the text shows, became part of the Fair story.

Other works I consulted on Warhol and pop art were: *Andy Warhol* by Carter Ratcliff (Abbeville Press, 1983); *Andy Warhol: A Retrospective*, edited by Kynaston McShine (Bullfinch Press/Little, Brown, 1991), especially Robert Rosenblum's essay "Warhol As Art History"; *Warhol* by David Bourdon (Harry N. Abrams, 1995); and *Andy Warhol and the Can That Sold the World* by Gary Indiana (Basic Books, 2010). Among the illuminating essays to be found in the late Robert Hughes's collection, *Nothing If Not Critical* (Penguin, 1992), is a wonderful piece on Warhol.

19.

My chapter on the New York City crackdown on the downtown bohemian art scene drew from stories in the New York papers, mostly the *Times*, about the Wagner administration's efforts and Operation: Yorkville. Information about how these events actually affected artists like Frank O'Hara and Allen Ginsberg was found in the aforementioned biographies such as *City Poet*, *I Celebrate Myself*, and Ed Sanders's memoir *Fug You*. O'Hara's World's Fair poem can be found in *The Collected Poems of Frank O'Hara*, edited by Donald Allen (California University Press, 1995).

It is always a pleasure to reread the work of Allen Ginsberg; I kept my City Lights volumes of his work on my desk while writing this chapter and frequently turned to *Allen Ginsberg: Collected Poems 1947–1980* (Harper & Row, 1984). I drew on information from *The American Pope: The Life and Times of Francis Cardinal Spellman* by John Cooney (Times Books, 1984) and *The Trials of Lenny Bruce: The Fall and Rise of an American Icon* by Ronald K. L. Collins and David M. Skover (Sourcebooks, 2002). Arthur Gelb's *City Room* has wonderful scenes about Lenny Bruce. Steve Allen was the subject of a November 10, 1962, Talk of the Town piece in which he mentions Bruce; the April 20, 1966, issue of *The New Yorker* ran a Notes and Comment piece upfront that served as an obituary of the famed comedian.

The story of Ralph Ginzburg's and Robert F. Kennedy's roles are recounted in *The Last Innocent Year*. Rick Perlstein's *Nixonland* discusses the Abraham Fortas fiasco. I also consulted the works of my former professor at Queens College, John Tytell. His book *Living Theatre: Art, Exile and Outrage* (Grove, 1995) was very helpful in understanding the downtown scene in the early 1960s.

The information about filmmaker, poet, and archivist Jonas Mekas was gleaned from all the above-mentioned books about the downtown art scene plus several Talk of the Town pieces in *The New Yorker* from 1962 to 1965, as well as a lengthy profile from the January 6, 1973, issue by Calvin Tomkins.

20.

As I have noted, the stall-in saga of Brooklyn CORE and the World's Fair is a forgotten chapter in the history of the civil rights movement. The story played out in the New York papers, beginning with the *Journal-American*'s original story, and quickly became national news. Besides the *Times'* authoritative coverage, I found numerous articles in the Arnold Goldwag/Brooklyn CORE Collection at the Brooklyn Historical Society, plus flyers, pamphlets, and telegrams from Arnold Goldwag to the Kennedys and others. Much thanks to the helpful staff there for their assistance.

Elements of the story were found in *The Last Innocent Year* (which includes Martin Luther King's response); *The Making of the President: 1964* by T. H. White (Atheneum, 1965); and *Before the Storm: Barry Goldwater and the Unmaking of the American Consensus* by Rick Perlstein (Nation Books, 2001). Tamar Jacoby is one of the few writers to devote time to the subject, as she does in her book *Someone Else's House: America's Unfinished Struggle for Integration* (Basic Books, 1998).

Most helpful of all was Professor Brian Purnell, whose work I first encountered when I found his PhD thesis online. He later turned the thesis into a book chapter, "'Drive Awhile for Freedom': Brooklyn CORE's 1964 Stall-In and Public Discourses on Protest Violence," in *Groundworks: Local Black Freedom Movements in America*, edited by Jeanne Theoharis and Komozi Woodward (NYU Press, 2005). I am also grateful to Professor Purnell for answering my questions about the stall-in and its significance in the history of the civil rights movement in the North. Moses' comments and reactions to the episode were found in the files of his papers in the New York Public Library. James Farmer wrote about the episode in his autobiography, *Lay Bare the Heart*.

21.

The opening day events at the World's Fair were culled from newspapers and magazines covering the day's festivities, as well as *The End of the Innocence* and Bill Cotter and Bill Young's two Fair books. The *New York Times* covered the clashes on the 7 Train and the events inside the World's Fair, especially the booing of President Johnson, whose speech was found online at the LBJ Presidential Library (lbjlibrary.org). The many memos, letters, etc. found in the Robert Moses Papers and World's Fair Archives helped illuminate the picture. The material about the planned stall-in came from the sources listed in the previous chapter.

22.

The June 5, 1964, *Time* cover story was found in the magazine's online archives. The May 23, 1964, *Saturday Evening Post*'s story on Moses, "The Old S.O.B. Does It Again," was found among the Robert Moses Papers; both are invaluable documents on Moses and the Fair. The information about the actual Fair was drawn from Bill Cotter and Bill Young's photo books; *The End of the Innocence*; the Walt Disney biography; *The 1964 World's Fair Guidebook* (published by Time-Life Books); and newspaper clippings about those first days at the Fair. Also important were Ada Louise Huxtable's assessment of the World's Fair, found in her collection, *On Architecture*, and Professor Vincent J. Scully Jr.'s "If This Is Architecture, God Help Us" from the July 13, 1964, issue of *Life* magazine. Once again, John Canaday's take on the World's Fair in the *New York Times* was both unique and amusing.

The details regarding the film *Parable* were gleaned from the many memos and letters Moses exchanged with his officials on the subject. "The Jordan Mural Affair"—as Moses referred to it in his book, *Public Works*—received major coverage in the New York papers. Documents about this episode were found in the Robert Moses Papers and World's Fair Archives at the New York Public Library. As usual with Moses, the whole affair was played out in the press, and in this case, the courts. The details of the Board of Directors' meeting were found at the library.

23.

To recount the tale of Andrew Goodman, Mickey Schwerner, and James Chaney, I relied primarily on *The Last Innocent Year* by Jon Margolis. I also relied on *Three Lives for Mississippi* (University of Mississippi Press, 2000) by William Bradford Huie, a Southerner who understood the region's history and codes, a journalist who had written about the Klan and Jim Crow for national magazines, and a novelist. He originally reported on the Goodman, Schwerner, and Chaney case for the *New*

York Herald Tribune. Also invaluable in my research was *Freedom Summer: The Savage Season of 1964 That Made Mississippi Burn and Made America a Democracy* by Bruce Watson (Penguin, 2010) and *We Are Not Afraid* by Seth Cagin and Philip Dray (Bantam, 1989). I found Lewis E. Lomax's dispatch "Road to Mississippi" in a 1964 issue of *Ramparts* at the Brooklyn Historical Society.

My account of the Harlem riots depended largely on the reporting of the *New York Times,* Arthur Gelb's *City Room,* and James Farmer's *Lay Bare the Heart.* The riots are also touched upon in other books, including *Freedom Summer, Sweet Land of Liberty, America Divided,* and *The Last Innocent Year.* I found the great Ralph Ellison's *Harper's* piece on Harlem in their digital archive. Richard J. Whalen's September 1964 cover story for *Fortune,* "New York Is a City Destroying Itself," touches on the riots and Robert Wagner's time as mayor.

24.

Among the documents of the Robert Moses Papers and the World's Fair Archives at the New York Public Library, I found the letters from would-be Fairgoers who wrote Moses asking for his assurance that they would be safe if they came to New York in the summer of 1964; others wrote to tell him they were not coming. Also in the Moses Papers were the memos detailing his thoughts and plans for Season Two of the Fair. Moses' problems with the Lake Amusement Area made it into various periodicals, including the *New York Times, The New Yorker,* and the *New York World-Telegram,* among others.

Sally Rand's history performing at various World's Fairs, as well as the role of burlesque shows and stripteases at various Fairs, was found in Robert Rydell's *World of Fairs.* Edward Ball wrote a great piece about sex in the utopian visions of World's Fairs in "Degraded Utopias," *The Village Voice,* Fall Art Special 1989. Thanks to Heidi B. Coleman of the Isamu Noguchi Archives for helping me find it. This chapter also benefited from my interviews with Bill Cotter and the great Al Kooper, who shared his memories about growing up in Queens, playing the World's Fair, and playing with Dylan at both the Newport Festival and the Forest Hills concert in 1965. A special thanks to him.

A special *mille grazie* also goes to Justin Rizzo—*il mio fratello da un'altra madre*—for cluing me in about Dave Brubeck's World's Fair–themed songs on *Time Changes,* as well as *The Death of the Grown-Up: How America's Arrested Development Is Bringing Down Western Civilization* by Diana West (St. Martin's; 2008), which recounts Benny Goodman's meeting with the Beatles and references his daughter Rachel Goodman's *Esquire* piece about that surreal moment. I based my account of Bob Dylan's recording and activities in the summer of 1964 on Robert Shelton's *No Direction Home,* Dylan's own *Chronicles Volume 1* (Simon & Schuster, 2004); and the pieces in *The Essential Interviews: Dylan on Dylan,* edited by Jonathan Cott (Hodder & Stoughton, 2006), particularly Nat Hentoff's piece from the October 24, 1964, issue of *The New Yorker,* "The Crackin', Shakin', Breakin', Sounds." *Like a Rolling Stone: Bob Dylan at the Crossroads* by Greil Marcus (PublicAffairs, 2005) is essential reading for anyone trying to understand Dylan, his music, or its place in American culture, as is, of course, David Hadju's *Positively 4th Street.* For Dylan's meeting with the Beatles, I also consulted Bob Spitz's *The Beatles* and the above-mentioned books.

25.

I based my narrative on Ken Kesey from a number of sources: Tom Wolfe's *The Electric Kool-Aid Acid Test* (Signet, 1969); *Can't Find My Way Home: America in the Great Stoned Age, 1945–2000* by Martin Torgoff (Simon & Schuster, 2004); *On the Bus: The Complete Guide to the Legendary Trip of Ken Kesey and the Merry Pranksters and the Birth of the Counterculture* by Ken Babbs and Paul Perry (Thunder's Mouth Press, 1990); and *Prime Green: Remembering the Sixties* by Robert Stone (Harper, 2007). I also consulted *The Holy Goof* (Thunder's Mouth Press, 2004), a biography of Neal Cassady by the late William Plummer, a gentleman and a scholar, whom I had the pleasure of knowing. Kesey is also mentioned in Margolis's *The Last Innocent Year.*

Magic Trip was key to understanding the cross-country trip undertaken by Kesey and the Pranksters. Several quotes were drawn from that wonderful documentary. Also useful were *I Celebrate Myself,* Bill Morgan's Allen Ginsberg biography. John Tytell's incomparable *Naked Angels,* his literary biography of the Beat Generation, was as inspiring today as when I first read it more than twenty years ago as a young college student. I also consulted T. H. White's *The Making of the President 1964* and Rick Perlstein's *Before the Storm*.

PART THREE: BRINGING IT ALL BACK HOME

26.

This chapter is largely based on the relevant documents found in the Robert Moses Papers and World's Fair Archives about the end of the Fair's first season. It is also based on Richard J. Whalen's September 1964 cover story for *Fortune*, "New York: A City Destroying Itself"; his book of the same name released the following year; and Moses' reaction not only to Whalen's piece but to all the stories then appearing in the New York papers about crime and the city's other ailments at the time. I also had the pleasure of speaking to Richard Whalen. A very special thanks to him.

Critical to understanding the saga of the Lower Manhattan Expressway was Anthony Flint's *Wrestling With Moses* and *Robert Moses and the Modern City*, as well as Ric Burns's amazing documentary *New York*, particularly Episode Seven: The City and The World.

27.

All the relevant newspaper articles noted in the text were found in the Robert Moses Papers at the New York Public Library, as were Moses' memos and letters about those articles and his exchange with Charles Grutzner of the *New York Times*. The report by top executives of the Fair's biggest industrial pavilions and Moses' pointed reactions were also found in the archives.

28.

The Fair's post–Season One problems were detailed among the files in the Robert Moses Papers and World's Fair Archives. The whole affair played out in the New York daily papers, particularly the *New York Times* and the *New York Herald Tribune*, which by then had become the paper most likely to irritate Moses on a daily basis. Details of Moses' showdown with George Spargo appeared in *Life*. Bruce Nicholson recounts his trip to Madrid with Moses to meet General Franco in his book, *Hi Ho, Come to the Fair*.

29.

Bob Dylan's experiments in the recording studio in early 1965 are recounted in Robert Shelton's *No Direction Home*; Greil Marcus's *Like a Rolling Stone: Bob Dylan at the Crossroads*; and David Hadju's *Positively 4th Street*, among other Dylan books. Al Kooper's memoir, *Backstage Passes & Backstabbing Bastards* (Backbeat Books, 2008), was also helpful. Dylan's albums from this time, *Another Side of Bob Dylan, Bringing It All Back Home, Highway 61 Revisited*, and *The Bootleg Series, Vols. 1–3: 1961–1991* and *The Bootleg Series, Vol. 6: Bob Dylan Live 1964*, were all essential.

30.

I based the events of the early days of the Johnson administration on Jon Margolis's *The Last Innocent Year*. Also useful was Robert Caro's *Pathway to Power*. James Farmer's *Lay Bare the Heart* provided insights and details about meeting President Johnson. Rick Perlstein's *Nixonland* also gives a wonderful account of the Gulf of Tonkin incident.

31.

In the wake of the Kitty Genovese murder and race riots, the media took a long, hard look at New York City. Following Richard J. Whalen's lead, the *Herald Tribune* began a series titled "City in

Crisis" (later compiled into a book of the same name). Malcolm X's life and death are recounted in *Malcolm: A Life of Reinvention*. The story of Selma is recounted in *America Divided* and *The Autobiography of Martin Luther King*, among other places, including newspaper reports.

Details about the World's Fair's second season were found in the New York Public Library's archives, *The End of the Innocence*, and the New York newspapers. Details about the murders in Queens were found in *New York: A City Destroying Itself* (Morrow, 1965) and in newspaper accounts. The passage of the Voting Rights Act of 1965 was detailed in the aforementioned civil rights books.

32.

The details for this chapter about the Beatles and Bob Dylan in the summer of 1965 were pulled from more than a dozen sources, such as newspaper accounts, mostly from the *New York Times*, particularly Robert Shelton's report "The Beatles Will Make the Scene Here Again, but the Scene Has Changed" (August 11, 1965), an early serious attempt to rate the band's effect on pop culture and the culture at large; and "The Sky Glows Over Queens as the Beatles Take Over Shea Stadium" (August 16, 1965). Essential to my narrative were *Read the Beatles*, Jonathan Gould's *Can't Buy Me Love*, and *Anthology* by the Beatles. My account of Bob Dylan's Forest Hills concert is based on David Hadju's *Positively 4th Street*, Robert Shelton's *No Direction Home*, Al Kooper's *Backstage Passes & Backstabbing Bastards*, and newspaper reports.

Joe Mannarino told me about the Beatles' arrival at the World's Fair, and Al Kooper told me about the Forest Hills experience from the stage. Robert Shelton filed many excellent stories on Dylan for the Paper of Record, while a December 12, 1965, *New York Times Magazine* piece, "Public Writer No. 1?" by Thomas Meehan examined the literary creditability that college students bestowed on Dylan. Critical to my assessment of Dylan at this time were D. A. Pennebaker's *Don't Look Back* and *'65 Revisited*, as was *The Other Side of the Mirror: Bob Dylan Live at the Newport Folk Festival 1963–65*, directed by Murray Lerner. *Dylan Speaks: The Legendary 1965 Press Conference in San Francisco* was also helpful. Martin Scorsese's *No Direction Home* is a brilliant and informative documentary by any barometer.

33.

Robert Moses' battles with Abraham Beame and other city officials were documented in the New York metropolitan papers of the day and in World's Fair documents found in both his papers and the Fair Archives at the New York Public Library. I based my narrative of Pope Paul VI's arrival in New York, his visit to the World's Fair, his trip to the United Nations, and his interactions with Cardinal Francis Spellman on a number of sources, including *The American Pope* by John Cooney; *The Pope's Journey to the United States*, written by staff members of the *New York Times* and edited by A. M. Rosenthal and Arthur Gelb (who produced the quickie paperback since the Paper of Record was on strike); and the *New York Times'* lengthy account, "Pope Paul's Visit to New York and Peace Appeal to U.N." by A. M. Rosenthal (October 11, 1965). The historic trip was covered by all the major media. The accounts of the pope's trip in both *Life* and *Time* were also helpful. Moses had been angling to have the pope visit the World's Fair long before there was even a glimmer of hope. The relevant documents on the subject were found among his papers at the New York Public Library.

EPILOGUE: TOMORROW NEVER KNOWS

The June 3, 1967, ceremony in Flushing Meadows–Corona Park was covered in the *New York Times*. I also found an amusing Talk of the Town piece about it in *The New Yorker*. I got the figures on the Montreal Expo from *World's Fairs* by Erik Mattie. Information about the Human Be-In was gleaned from the Ginsberg biography *Song of Myself*; Martin Torgoff's *Can't Find My Way Home* and Charles Perry's wonderful *Haight-Ashbury: A History* (Wenner Books, 2005). The William Mann quote was found in *Read the Beatles*.

SOURCES

ARCHIVES & COLLECTIONS
Arnold Goldwag/Brooklyn CORE Collection, Brooklyn Historical Society
Charles Poletti interview, Columbia Center for Oral History
Charles Poletti Papers, Series 1, Box 7, Columbia University
Gilmore Clarke Papers, Box 2, Columbia University
Jane Jacobs, An Oral History Interview with the Greenwich Village Society for Historic
    Preservation, 1997.
John F. Kennedy Presidential Library (www.jfklibrary.org)
Lyndon B. Johnson Presidential Library (www.lbjlibrary.org)
Robert F. Wagner Jr. interviews, Columbia Center for Oral History
Robert Moses Papers, Boxes 47–52, 119–132, Manuscript and Archive Division, New York Public
    Library
World's Fair Archive, Boxes 49; 141; 185; 262; 267; 281–282; 321–322; 337–338; Manuscript and
    Archive Division, New York Public Library

NEWSPAPERS & MAGAZINES (SELECTED)
Amsterdam News
Long Island Star Journal
New York Daily News
New York Herald Tribune
New York Journal-American
New York Post
New York Times
New York World-Telegram
Village Voice
Wall Street Journal
Washington Post

Billboard
The Economist
Fortune
Harper's
Life
Newsweek
The New Yorker
Popular Mechanics
Reader's Digest
Rolling Stone
The Saturday Evening Post
Sports Illustrated
Time

OTHER WORKS CONSULTED
Acocella, Joan. "Perfectly Frank," *New Yorker*, July 1993.

Alterman, Erc. "Expletive Included," *New York Times*, August 9, 1998.

"Avant-Garde Art Going to the Fair," *New York Times*, October 5, 1963.

Baldwin, James. "A Report from Occupied Territory." *The Nation*, July 11, 1966.

Barrow, Tony. *John, Paul, George, Ringo & Me: The Real Beatles Story*. New York: Thunder's Mouth Press, 2005.

Baumann, Edward. "Al Carter, First or Last at Big Events," *The Chicago Tribune*, July 12, 1987.

Berman, Marshall. *All That is Solid Melts into Air*. New York: Penguin Books, 1988.

Bigart, Homer. "'64 Fair Seeking Global Flavor," *New York Times*, December 2, 1962.

Bloom, Jack M. *Class, Race, and the Civil Rights Movement*. Bloomington: Indiana University Press, 1987.

Brawley, Arthur. "The Fire on New York's Famous Little Island," *Sports Illustrated*, July 23, 1962.

Cannato, Vincent J. *The Ungovernable City: John Lindsay and His Struggle to Save New York*. New York: Basic Books, 2002.

Carlin, Peter Ames. *Paul McCartney: A Life*. New York: Touchstone Books, 2010.

Caro, Robert A. "The City-Shaper." *The New Yorker*, January 5, 1998.

Chiasson, Dan. "Fast Company." *The New Yorker*, April 7, 2008.

Coleman, Ray. *Lennon: The Definite Biography*. London: Pan Books, 2000.

D'Antonio, Michael. *Forever Blue: The True Story of Walter O'Malley, Baseball's Most Controversial Owner, and the Dodgers of Brooklyn and Los Angeles*. New York: Riverhead Books, 2009.

Dalrymple, Theodore. "The Architect as Totalitarian," *City Journal*, Autumn 2009.

Dickstein, Morris. *Gates of Eden: American Culture in the Sixties*. New York: Penguin Books, 1989.

Dunlap, David W. "Scrutinizing the Legacy of Robert Moses," *New York Times*, May 11, 1987.

Dunn, Gary, and Harvey Pekar. *Students for a Democratic Society: A Graphic History*. New York: Hill & Wang, 2008.

Dylan, Bob. *Chronicles: Volume One*. New York: Simon &and Schuster, 2004.

Ellison, Ralph. "Harlem Is Nowhere," *Harper's*, August 1964.

Epperson, Bruce. "Eminence Domain: Reassessing the Life and Public Works of Robert Moses," *Technology and Culture*, Volume 48, Number no. 4, (October 2007).

Freeman, Henry Ira. "Originator of Fair Dropped by Moses," *New York Times*, April 9, 1960.

Fortune, the Editors of. *The Exploding Metropolis: A Study of the Assault on Urbanism and How Our Cities Can Resist It*. Garden City, NY: Doubleday Anchor, 1958.

Gaddis, John Lewis. *The Cold War: A New History*. New York: Penguin Books, 2007.

Ganz, James, and Eric Lipton. *City in the Sky: The Rise and Fall of the World Trade Center*. New York: Times Books, 2003.

Gelb, Arthur, and A. M. Rosenthal. *The Pope's Journey to the United States*. Written by Staff Members of the *New York Times*. New York: Bantam, 1965.

Genauer, Emily. "Showplace for Artists: An Old Story Becomes New," *New York Herald Tribune*, August 18, 1963.

Giedion, Sigfried. *Space, Time and Architecture: The Growth of a New Tradition*. Fifth Edition. Cambridge, MA: Harvard University Press, 1976.

Gitlin, Todd. *The Sixties: Years of Hope, Days of Rage*. New York: Bantam, 1993.

Goldberger, Paul. "Robert Moses, Master Builder, is Dead at 92," *The New York Times*, July 30, 1981.

———. "Eminent Dominion," *The New Yorker*, February 5, 2007.

Gottehrer, Barry. *New York: City in Crisis*. New York: David McKay Company, 1965.

Gratz, Roberta Brandes. *The Battle for Gotham: New York in the Shadow of Robert Moses and Jane Jacobs*. New York: Nation Books, 2011.

Gutman, David, and Elizabeth Thomason (editors). *The Dylan Companion*. Boston: Da Capo Press, 2001.

Haley, Alex. *The Autobiography of Malcolm X*. New York: Ballatine Books, 1992.

Hayes, Harold (editor). *Smiling Through the Apocalypse: Esquire's History of the Sixties*. New York: Delta Books, 1971.

Hunt, Richard P. "Moses Quits 5 State Posts, Charging Governor Asked One of Them For Brother," *New York Times*, December 1, 1962.

"Indignant Rabbi," *New York Times*, February 15, 1967.

Jackson, Sharyn Elise. "International Participation of the 1964–65 New York World's Fair," (B.A. thesis, New York University, 2004).

Judt, Tony. *Postwar: A History of Europe Since 1945*. New York: Penguin Books, 2006.

Kaplan, Fred. *1959: The Year Everything Changed*. New York: J. Wiley & Sons, 2009.

Kennedy, John F. *A Nation of Immigrants*. New York: Popular Library, 1964.

Koestenbaum, Wayne. *Andy Warhol*. New York: Penguin Books, 2001.

Kramer, Jane. *Allen Ginsberg in America*. New York: Fromm, 1997.

Larrivee, Shaina D. "Playscapes: Isamu Noguchi's Designs for Play," *Public Art Dialogue*, Vol. 1, Issue no. 1, (March 2011).

Lattin, Don. *The Harvard Psychedelic Club*. New York: Harper One, 2010.

Leary, Timothy. *High Priest*. Classic Reprint Series (www.forgottenbooks.com).

Lehman, David. *The Last Avant-Garde: The Making of the New York School of Poets*. New York: Anchor Books, 1999.

Leland, John. *Hip: The History*. New York: Ecco, 2004.

Lopate, Phillip. "A Town Revived, a Villain Redeemed." *New York Times*, February 11, 2007.

Lowe, Jeanne R. *Cities in a Race with Time*. New York: Vintage Books, 1968.

Lysaght, Alan, and David Pritchard. *The Beatles: Oral History*. New York: Hyperion, 1998.

Marquese, Mike. *Wicked Messenger: Bob Dylan and the 1960s*. New York: Seven Stories Press, 2005.

Matusow, Allen J. *The Unraveling of America: A History of Liberalism in the 1960s*. New York: Harper & Row, 1984.

Meehan, Thomas. "Public Writer No.1?" *The New York Times Magazine*, December 12, 1965.

Menand, Louis. "Why They Were Fab." *The New Yorker*, October 16 and 23, 2000.

———. "Acid Redux," *The New Yorker*, June 26, 2006.

———. "Drive, He Wrote," *The New Yorker*, October 1, 2007.

———. "Top of the Pops," *The New Yorker*, January 11, 2010.

Morgan, Bill (editor). *The Letters of Allen Ginsberg*. Boston: Da Capo Press, 2008.

Moses, Robert. "What's the Matter with New York?" *The New York Times Magazine*, August 1, 1943.

———. "Mr. Moses Dissects the 'Long-Haired Planners,'" *The New York Times Magazine*, June 25, 1944.

———. "A Report by Mr. Moses on New York Traffic," *The New York Times Magazine*, November 4, 1945.

———. "Slums and City Planning," *The Atlantic Monthly*, January 1945.

———. "Build and Be Damned," *The Atlantic Monthly*, December 1950.

———. "The Traffic Menace, in Both Peace and War," *The New York Times Magazine*, April 29, 1951.

———. "Problems: Many—And a Program," *The New York Times Magazine*, February 1, 1953.

———. "Are Cities Dead?" *The Atlantic Monthly*, January 1962.

———. "Moses Meets the Press—Head On," *The New York Times Magazine*, August 15, 1962.

Mumford, Lewis. "Mother Jacobs' Home Remedies," *The New Yorker*, December 1, 1962.

———. *The City in History*. New York: Harcourt, Brace and World, 1962.

Norman, Philip. *John Lennon: The Life*. New York: Ecco, 2008.

Ouroussoff, Nicolai. "Complex, Contradictory Robert Moses," *New York Times*, February 2, 2007.

Perry, Charles. *Haight-Ashbury: A History*. New York: Wenner Books, 2005.

Pogrebin, Robin. "Rehabilitating Robert Moses," *New York Times*, January 23, 2007.

Powell, Michael. "A Tale of Two Cities," *New York Times*, May 6, 2007.

Randolph, Eleanor. "Robert Moses, Builder, Left Behind His Power Tool," *New York Times*, February 14, 2007.

Remnick, David. *King of the World*. New York: Random House, 1998.

Rogers, Cleveland. "Robert Moses: An Atlantic Portrait," *The Atlantic Monthly*, February 1939.

Ross, Alex. "The Wanderer," *The New Yorker*, May 10, 1999.

Rotolo, Suze. *A Freewheelin' Time: A Memoir of Greenwich Village in the Sixties*. New York: Broadway Books, 2009.

Rybczynski, Witold. *The Look of Architecture*. New York: Oxford University Press, 2001.

———. *Makeshift Metropolis*. New York: Scribner, 2001.

Schonberg, Harold C. "What Attracts More People Than the Beatles? Beethoven!" *New York Times*, August 22, 1965

Schwartz, Joel. *The New York Approach: Robert Moses, Urban Liberals, and Redevelopment of the Inner City*. Columbus: Ohio State University Press, 1993.

Sheff, David. *All We Are Saying: The Last Major Interview with John Lennon and Yoko Ono*. New York: St. Martin's Press, 2000.

Smith, Michael L. "Representations of Technology at the 1964 World's Fair." In *The Power of Culture: Critical Essays in American History*, edited by Richard Wightman Fox and T. J. Jackson Lears. Chicago: The University of Chicago Press, 1993.

Sounes, Howard. *Down the Highway: The Life of Bob Dylan*. New York: Grove Press, 2001.

Stevens, Mark, and Annalyn Swan. *De Kooning: An American Master*. New York: Knopf, 2001.

Swados, Harvey. "When Black and White Live Together," *The New York Times Magazine*, November 13, 1966.

Talbot, David. *Brothers: The Hidden History of the Kennedy Years*. New York: Free Press, 2008.

Talese, Gay. *The Bridge*. New York: Walker & Co. 2003.

Tolchin, Martin. "Fair a Showcase for Civil Rights," *The New York Times*, June 9, 1964.

Tosches, Nick. *The Devil and Sonny Liston*. Boston: Little, Brown, 2000.

Trow, George W. S. *The Context of No Context*. New York: Atlantic Monthly Press, 1997.

Turnbull, Craig. "Please Make No Demonstrations Tomorrow: The Brooklyn Congress of Racial Equality and Symbolic Protest at the 1964–65 World's Fair," *Australasian Journal of American Studies*, Vol. 17, No. 1, (July 1998).

Tyson, Timothy B. "Robert F. Williams, 'Black Power,' and the Roots of African American Freedom Struggle," *Journal of American History* 2, no. 85 (September 1998).

Ultimate Music Guide Issue 13: The Beatles. *Uncut* magazine, 2013.

Von Hoffman, Nicholas. "Beware of the Robert Moses Revisionists," *The New York Observer*, May 27, 2007.

Wechsler, James A. "Fair World," *New York Post*, February 8, 1962.

Wenner, Jann S. *Lennon Remembers*. London: Verso, 2000.

Whitman, Alden. "Francis J. Spellman: New York Archbishop and Dean of American Cardinals," *New York Times*, December 3, 1967.

Wilentz, Sean. *Bob Dylan in America*. New York: Anchor Books, 2011.

"World's Fair Bias Probed by Bunche," *New York Amsterdam News*, February 17, 1962.

The WPA Guide to New York City: The Federal Writers Project Guide to 1930s New York. New York: The New Press, 1993.

WEBSITES

The King Center, www.thekingcenter.org

The Martin Luther King, Jr. Research and Education Institute, www.stanford.edu/group/King/ liberation_curriculum/resources

The Malcolm X Project at Columbia University, www.columbia.edu/cu/ccbh/mxp

Warholsuperstars.org, www.warholstars.org

INDEX

ABOUT THE AUTHOR

Joseph Tirella is a writer and editor whose work has appeared in the *New York Times*, *Vibe*, *Rolling Stone*, *Esquire*, *People*, the *Daily News*, Portfolio. com, and *Reader's Digest*, among other publications. A former senior editor at *Fortune Small Business*, he is currently the Associate Director of Media Relations at Herbert H. Lehman College of the City University of New York. He lives in New York City with his family.